would support nevertheless refuse to se[...]
way some women's organizations of the r[...]
sues" such as education, sanitation, and o..... ...... or social welfare while avoiding
official support for suffrage.

Further Reading

Alvarez, S. E. (1980). *Engendering democracy in Brazil: Women's movements in transition politics*. Princeton, NJ: Princeton University Press.

Badran, M. (1995). *Feminists, Islam, and nation: Gender and the making of modern Egypt*. Princeton, NJ: Princeton University Press.

Blackburn, S. (2004). *Women and the state in modern Indonesia*. Cambridge, UK: Cambridge University Press.

Croll, E. (1980). *Feminism and socialism in China*. New York: Schocken Books.

Fernea, E. W. (1998). *In search of Islamic feminism: One woman's global journey*. New York: Anchor Books/Doubleday.

Forbes, G. H. (1996). *Women in modern India*. Cambridge, UK: Cambridge University Press.

Giele, J. (1995). *Two paths to women's equality: Temperance, suffrage, and the origins modern feminism*. New York: Twayne Publishers.

Hahner, J. E. (1990). *Emancipating the female sex: The struggle for women's rights in Brazil, 1850–1940*. Durham, NC: Duke University Press.

Kumar, R. (1993). *The history of doing: An illustrated account of movements for women's rights and feminism in India, 1800–1990*. London: Verso.

Lerner, G. (1993). *The creation of feminist consciousness from the middle ages to 1870*. New York: Oxford University Press.

McVay, P. (2009). *Envisioning women in world history: 1500 to the present*. Boston: McGraw-Hill.

McVay, P. (2009). Family law as metaphor in colonial politics: A helpful tool in world historical analysis. *World History Bulletin, 25*(1) 18–21.

Macías, A. (1982) *Against all odds: The feminist movement in Mexico to 1940*. Westport, CT: Greenwood Press.

Ping-Chun Hsiung; Jaschok, M; & Milwertz, C. N. (Eds.). (2001). *Chinese women organizing: Cadres, feminists, Muslims, queers*. Oxford: Berg.

Sievers, S. L. (1983) *Flowers in salt: The beginnings of feminist consciousness in modern Japan*. Stanford, CA: Stanford University Press.

Stites, Richard. (1991) *The women's liberation movement in Russia: Feminism, nihilism, and Bolshevism, 1860–1930*, revised ed. Princeton, NJ: Princeton University Press.

West, R. (14 November 1913). Mr. Chesterton in hysterics. *The Clarion*.

Patriarchy in History and Practice

Laurien ALEXANDRE and Carol B. DUNCAN
Antioch University and Wilfrid Laurier University

Patriarchy as a historical concept and as a social system that affects leaders today has been hotly debated by social science researchers, feminist theorists, and even anthropologists. From the glass ceiling in corporate bureaucracies, to leadership styles, to the very structures of the workplace and social settings, the effects and practices of patriarchy need to be examined more closely in order to achieve gender equality.

The word *patriarchy* means, literally, "rule of the father." In this narrowest definition patriarchy means a social system controlled by men, in which lineage is traced through males (patrilineal descent), inheritance is passed through father to sons, and family members are dependent and subservient to the male head of household. In its most precise meaning, patriarchy refers to the system, historically derived from Greek and Roman law, in which the male head of household had absolute legal and economic power over his dependent female and male family members.

The word patriarchy acquired a more general usage, especially in some feminist theories, where it came to mean "male domination in general." This concept was systematically set out in broader feminist terms in the early 1970s by such writers as Kate Millett in her groundbreaking *Sexual Politics,* which posited that patriarchal power is all-encompassing and ubiquitous, and by others, such as Shulamith Firestone, in her landmark *The Dialectic of Sex,* which grounded the universal oppression of *women* and the control of women's reproduction itself in the sexual dichotomy.

In this wider definition of the concept, patriarchy is a system in which men dominate, oppress, and exploit women and in which male dominance over women and children in the family extends to male dominance over women in society in general. From this perspective, males control the economy and occupy positions of power and status. Women are denied access to power and deprived of rights, influence, and resources. And patriarchy as the status quo is used to explain and justify male dominance in major cultural institutions, such as religion, education, and the media.

Dominance and control are perceived to be at the heart of patriarchy. The German sociologist Max Weber spoke of patriarchal power's structures of domination enforced by virtue of authority, that is, the power to command and the duty to obey. Continuing the themes of patriarchal dominance, contemporary writer Alan

G. Johnson argues in *The Gender Knot* that patriarchy is based on control as a core principle and that, as a system, it is driven by a relationship between control and fear. Patriarchy thus depends upon dominance of men over women (and over other men, it might be added) and by definition involves a hierarchy of tiers of power with women on the bottom. This hierarchy means that lower, less-valued tiers will always be dominated by those on top.

Today, many people use the word patriarchy as shorthand for "male-dominated society" with deep social structures that are male-dominated, male-identified, and male-centered. Understanding these characteristics holds important implications for the study of leadership. In that structures are male-dominated, positions of authority and power, such as formal leadership in political, economic, religious, and military institutions, are generally reserved for men. In that they are male-identified, core cultural ideas about what is considered desirable, preferable, or normal are likened to what a culture thinks about men and masculinity, such as the accepted notion of a good leader as being one who is decisive and in control. To the degree that structures and practices are male-centered, the focus of attention is on the actions and thoughts of men, and that male experience comes to represent the human experience, such as the nineteenth-century "great man" approach to history, in which the impact of a few influential men was thought to be of primary importance.

Patriarchy's Story

People have debated the roots of patriarchy for decades. A common response to the question "Where did patriarchy come from?" is simply, "That's the way it's always been. Men are stronger and, therefore, in power." The assumption behind this response is that patriarchy is some sort of biological destiny, a natural order. However, in the 1970s, with the explosion of the second wave of feminism, which broadened the concerns of the movement into the realms of the workplace, the family, and reproductive rights, its vibrant scholarship took issue with the "natural order" approach. Archeological research, for example, began to point out the male-biased interpretations of Old World relics and revealed pre-patriarchal societies based on female gods and matrilineal (inheritance through the female line) social organizations and kinship structures. In *The Chalice and the Blade*, published in 1987, the cultural historian Riane Eisler argues that these societies were not just mirror images of patriarchal society, with women oppressing men, but were less hierarchically designed and that power was equated more with responsibility and love than with fear, control, and privilege. Although such arguments are difficult to make definitively, the fact that such interpretations found public airing in the final decades of the last century demonstrates challenges to patriarchal biases in history, anthropology, and many other fields and disciplines. Instead of seeing patriarchy as a "natural order," these studies and interpretations of matriarchal societies showed that patriarchy was a choice.

In her landmark *The Creation of Patriarchy* (1986), the historian Gerda Lerner offers a theoretical framework for understanding patriarchy's historical creation in the ancient Near East and Greece in the period 3100–400 BCE. These were essentially patriarchal cultures, asserts Lerner, and the control of women's sexuality (reproduction) was an essential element of the patriarchal order. She argues that the subordination of women and their reproductive services preceded the development of private property and served as a model for the ongoing subordination of other humans by the ruling classes.

Through the years, scholars have debated the history of patriarchy. Some have argued that patriarchy is transhistorical and that the oppression of women is a constant through time and place. Critics caution that overgeneralizations that suggest that all women through all time experienced the same oppression and victimization and that all men through all time experienced the same role as oppressor need to be tempered. Such overgeneralizations simply aren't true. This does not mean that patriarchy is not real and ongoing, but rather that we must take care to account for race, class, educational level, ethnicity, religion, a nation's stage of economic development, and the like.

Recent discussions of the concept of patriarchy stress the importance of using the word in ways that recognize difference and complexity in the world. Using the word patriarchy does not require that it be seen as making claims for primacy above all dominant relationships, be they class or race, nor as equivalent to all other forms of inequality. Using the word does, however, offer a way to understand certain dimensions of social structures and gender relations and to discern the co-existences of progress and backlash in different spheres.

As one example, in *Theorizing Patriarchy* (1990), author Sylvia Walby suggests six patriarchal structures or sites that are in process at any one time—sexuality, the household, employment, culture, the state, and male violence. In each of these sites, different sets of practices are relatively autonomous yet interconnected in complex ways. The degree and form of male dominance in each of these sites change over time and place, and the relationships between them are what form patriarchy's character in a particular culture.

Such an approach has implications for understanding the relationship of patriarchy and leadership. Forms of patriarchal practices in the paid labor world, for example, limit women's access to leadership positions, exclude women from more desirable forms of work, segregate women into jobs with less pay and status, and create obstacles to women's fullest realization in the workplace. State structures may legislate equal pay while opposing family leave legislation that would increase women's ability to achieve fullest employment opportunities. While all of that is going on, patriarchal orientations in the media lead to images of sexual objectification while presenting images of the "new" superwoman leader. As these examples show, the interplay of structures is complex and diverse and sometimes contradictory. To understand the degree and form of patriarchy at any one historical time and place, one needs to look at these structures and the interplay within and between them. This multitiered approach allows for an understanding of change, of improvements in one site, for example, while keeping in mind the intensification of patriarchy in another, and other factors, such as age and ethnicity.

Matriarchy and Myth

While the use of the concept of patriarchy to explain women's oppression gained currency in contemporary feminist theorizing, its opposite—matriarchy (literally, from the Greek, "rule of the mothers," but understood more commonly as rule by women)—has never been as widely accepted, and some have even doubted the past that it describes. A debate emerged within feminist religious studies circles concerning the reality of pre-patriarchal cultures in which women's lives and interests were celebrated. The work of scholars such as Carol P. Christ, Merlin Stone, and Marija Gimbutas recast and reinterpreted the historical record. Christ, for example, challenged the historian Mircea Eliade's account of religious development as androcentric or male-centered and recast the role of women in the foraging and Neolithic eras as vitally important. She used the notion of "woman the gatherer" to challenge the assertion that "man the hunter" was central to the social reproduction of human societies. But these reinterpretations have largely been dismissed as unfounded and wishful, based more on a desire to create a sacred history than on sound archaeological interpretations. In fact, the use of archaeological evidence to further contemporary feminist views of prehistory has been seriously questioned. From this vantage point, the complexities of hunter/gatherer societies are largely erased in favor of speculations about the role of women in these early societies.

Even the assumption of a matriarchy based on the existence of matrilocality and matrilineality has been questioned. (Matrilocality refers to situations in which a husband lives with the wife's family on the wife's family's land. Matrilineal descent traces lineage through the mother's line.) Matrilocality and matrilineality, however, are distinct from matriarchy because their existence is not based on women's having political and social power over men. Finally, the overwhelming focus on the goddess, especially through the female body, life cycle, and reproduction potentiality, may produce a kind of essentialism about women's experiences that could, ironically, reinforce patriarchal notions of femininity.

Another aspect of the matriarchy/patriarchy debate is the importance of female power and claims of matriarchal social order among many first peoples. Whether some of these societies were or are matriarchal, the claim that women had much more power and authority in them, and the claim by some that they are now and then were matriarchal, are important aspects of their ethnic identity. Matriarchal or at least non-patriarchal social organization functions to distinguish these societies from the patriarchal societies that took over their territory.

These debates and attempts to challenge male-dominant accounts of religious history point to the use of matriarchy and patriarchy as concepts that speak as much about how we view historical relations between men and women as they do about contemporary gender relations. These concepts are clearly not neutral, and their use to address the development of gender relations in human societies continues to be contested.

Patriarchy and Leadership

Leadership is embedded in deeply ingrained patriarchal systems and structures, for example, in women's access to and distribution of resources, in genderized perceptions of effective leadership traits and qualities, and in expectations of who can lead, where leadership takes place, and for what purposes. Certainly those in the United States are not subjected to the absolute "rule of the father" in all spheres of public and private life. Even the term *head of household* is more gender neutral, given the radical shifts in modern family arrangements.

The last quarter of a century has brought expanding research on leadership and gender and on the relationship between the two. Researchers have emphasized issues of opportunities and excluding practices, such as the glass ceiling and unequal access, practices that keep women from leadership positions. Factors such as the actual exercise of leadership and gender differences in style, effectiveness, priorities, and expectations have gained ground. A new or redefined notion of leadership itself, one that is empowering rather than overpowering, and found in informal and relational ways, has also emerged.

During most of recorded history women have been largely excluded from formal leadership positions. We may understand this exclusion in many ways, provide statistical portraits and describe the consequences. Even in just one of the patriarchal structures identified earlier—employment—the practices are complex and varied. Women typically earn less than men, engage in more unpaid work than men, and hold different and usually lower-status jobs. Although the percentage of women joining the paid work force has risen steadily since World War II, men and women typically do not work in the same occupations, and that occupational segregation is an international phenomenon. Even in the upper echelons of work, patriarchal practices frame the ways in which professions themselves are sex-segregated and gender-coded, with those professions that were mostly male-segregated—such as the practice of medicine—having more status, wealth, and power and those professions that were more women-identified—such as nursing and social work—having less status.

The invisibility of women as leaders and their exclusion from formal leadership positions—whether in industry or in the state—have much to do with the practices of patriarchy. The glass ceiling is not the entire story. Patriarchy sinks deep into cultural values and concepts, and the expectations of leaders/leadership are perfect examples. Leadership studies actually started off with the great man theory, a phrase whose male biases couldn't be more self-evident. The next stage of leadership studies identified traits, and we should not be surprised that the predominant cultural expectation of leaders asserts that they are decisive, in control, and heroic, typically characteristics associated with males in power. More female-associated characteristics, such as being relational and compassionate, and demonstrating a willingness to negotiate, are often viewed as weaknesses in leaders. Feminist organizational scholar Amanda Sinclair proposes "a close but obscured connection between constructs of leadership, traditional assumptions of masculinity, and a particular expression of male heterosexual identity" (Sinclair 1998, 1).

Rethinking patriarchy and its practices has implications for rethinking what leadership is and what it could be. Take, for example, notions of leaders' exercise of power and control—the heart of patriarchy. In his landmark book, *Leadership*, the political scientist James MacGregor Burns defines power "not as property or entity or possession but *as a relationship*" (Burns 1978, 15). Although not articulating his position in order to dethrone patriarchy, Burns believes that those who hold power over others are not leaders; rather, they are simply power wielders. Leaders, on the other hand, hold power differently. They share power, and they empower their followers. If this definition were to become truly accepted and practiced, women might be far more likely to be recognized as leaders and to feel more comfortable leading.

We could argue that the "power as control" approach to leadership is rooted in a decidedly male hierarchal distribution of resources, influences, and position. Instead of simply seeing the exercise of power over employees, for example, as an archaic style that is no longer useful in contemporary workplaces, the dominance and hierarchal model could be seen as patriarchal structures and practices.

Is Patriarchy Over?

We might be tempted to imagine, given all the progress in women's lives and rights in the United States today, that patriarchy is over. We must recognize, however, that the degrees and forms evolve through time and in various ways in the spheres of modern life. Women, for example, remain dramatically underrepresented in formal leadership positions in the major institutions of the United States. Although more women are now elected officials holding public office, the percentages are nowhere representative of the population as a whole and are far below those of many other highly industrialized democracies in the world. Although few women lead corporations, more women have reached the ranks of senior management, although women still hold less than 5 percent of the upper-management and executive positions. Although the absolute exclusion of women from paid work is diminishing, their segregation into low-paying industries and occupations and part-time work has declined only a little. Women are gaining access to the public sphere of paid employment but are subordinated to men within it.

As feminist scholar Cynthia Cockburn states:

> "Patriarchy" is not merely a colourful term used by feminists to rebuke men. It is not a thing of bygone days, nor a rhetorical flourish. It is an important dimension of the structures of modern societies, whether capitalist or state socialist. It is a living reality, a system that quite observably shapes the lives and differentiates the chances of women and of men. The struggle for sex equality . . . is an attempt to contradict, to undo, patriarchy. (as cited in Bryson 1999, 322)

Similarly, the efforts to rethink and redefine who is a leader, and what leadership is, challenge patriarchal practices and, in that way, move society that much closer to gender equality.

Further Reading

Anonymous. (1995). Patriarchy is such a drag: The strategic possibilities of a postmodern account of gender. *Harvard Business Review, 108*(8), 1973–2008.

Burns, J. M. (1978). *Leadership*. New York: Harper Torchbook.

Bryson, V. (1999). Patriarchy: A concept too useful to lose. *Contemporary Politics, 5*(4), 311–324.

Carli, L. & Eagly, A. (1999). Gender effects on social influence and emergent leadership. In G. Powell (Ed.), *Gender & work* (pp. 203–222). Thousand Oaks, CA: Sage.

Eisenstein, Z. (Ed.). (1979). *Capitalist patriarchy and the case for socialist feminism*. New York: Monthly Review Press.

Eisler, R. (1987). *The chalice and the blade*. San Francisco: HarperCollins.

Feldman, S. (2001). Exploring theories of patriarchy: A perspective from contemporary Bangladesh. *Signs: Journal of Women in Culture & Society, 26*(4), 1097–2038.

Firestone, S. (1970). *The dialectic of sex: The case for feminist revolution*. New York: Farrar Straus and Giroux.

Johnson, A. G. (1997). *The gender knot: Unraveling our patriarchal legacy*. Philadelphia: Temple University Press.

Lerner, G. (1986). *The creation of patriarchy*. New York: Oxford University Press.

Lewis, M. (1990). Interrupting patriarchy: Politics, resistance, and transformation in the feminist classroom. *Harvard Educational Review, 60*(4), 467–488.

Marshall, G. (Ed.). (1998). Patriarchy. In *A dictionary of sociology*. New York: Oxford University Press.

Mies, M. (1986). *Patriarchy & accumulation on a world scale: Women in the international division of labor*. London: Zed Books.

Millett, K. (1977). *Sexual politics*. London: Virago.

Rhode, D. (Ed.). (2003). *The difference "difference" makes: Women and leadership*. Palo Alto, CA: Stanford University Press.

Sinclair, A. (1998). *Doing leadership differently: Gender, power and sexuality*. Victoria, Australia: Melbourne University Press.

Townsend, J.; Zapata, E.; Rowlands, J.; Alberti, P.; & Mercado, M. (1999). *Women & power: Fighting patriarchies and poverty*. London: Zed Books.

Walby, S. (1990). *Theorizing patriarchy*. Oxford, UK: Blackwell Press.

Gender Stereotypes and Women Leaders

Roya AYMAN and Mark C. FRAME
Illinois Institute of Technology and
Middle Tennessee State University

Stereotypes effect everyone, but can hinder women leaders significantly in the workplace. Studies reveal that women are subjected to preconceived notions both in terms of whether they should lead and how they should lead. Yet the emergence of more women leaders is slowly changing notions of the most effective forms of leadership, and this will influence the development of future leaders.

Preconceived notions regarding who a leader is and how to be an effective leader often determines who actually becomes a leader, how leaders are perceived, and how they are evaluated. The low number of women in leadership and decision-making positions, as compared to figures for men, have been associated with traditional thinking (United Nations, 1999) and the presence of gender stereotypes (Heilman 2001, Ibarra & Hansen 2009). With the influx of diversity in the work force, people in positions of leadership now come from a variety of social and cultural groups. Those who interact with them tend to view these leaders through the filters of their own stereotypes, expectations, and implicit theories (Ayman 1993).

Implicit Theories and Stereotypes

An implicit theory is an unspoken assumption regarding the world and others (Ashmore and del Boca, 1979). An individual's implicit theories affect their expectations and their interpretations of the world around them. Stereotypes, usually overgeneralized attributes that describe groups of people, are a subset of implicit theories that come into play in our expectations of others (Wegner and Vallacher 1977). Although stereotypes often have negative connotations, stereotypes can be positive or negative and they may be partially accurate or inaccurate (Aries 1996; Glick and Fiske 1999).

Stereotypes affect both an individual's perceptions and their subsequent reactions toward others. For example, when an individual first meets another person, an assessment occurs—as a means of self-protection—to determine whether this person should be considered a friend or a foe (Fiske and Ruscher 1993; Henley 1975). Stereotypes allow people to infer quickly, if not always accurately, another person's attributes and whether they should be considered trustworthy (Glick and Fiske 1999). Individuals who respond automatically to stereotypes are not always aware of it or its cause.

As implicit theories and stereotypes are developed within social and cultural milieus, individuals will vary in terms of their stereotypes and how they use them (Aries 1996). Research demonstrates, however, that there is some agreement regarding gender stereotypes and the characteristics and expectations associated with them, especially in the realm of leadership.

Gender Roles, Norms, and Stereotypes

Women have traditionally been stereotyped as more socially sensitive and interpersonally capable than men (Korabik 1999). In various studies, the traditional stereotypes of women included attributes such as being less competent in tasks that are required for jobs outside the home. Bem (1974) identified many characteristics which were associated with stereotypes of women such as being nurturing, compassionate, considerate, weak, subservient, emotional, subjective, tactful, aware of other's feelings, and having feelings that are easily hurt. Stereotypes associated with men, on the other hand, typically included traits such as leadership, and being dominant, aggressive, independent, objective, and competitive.

Some theorists have posited that stereotypes can be prescriptive or descriptive (Glick and Fiske 1999). Prescriptive stereotypes describe what group members *ought* to be like. Descriptive stereotypes merely *suggest* what group members are like. These distinctions are important when discussing gender stereotypes in leadership because women in leadership roles tend to deviate from the prescriptive stereotypes that have historically affected women, yet they are often viewed negatively based on descriptive stereotypes (Heilman 2001).

Implicit Leadership Theory and Women

Implicit leadership theory (Schyns and Meindl 2005, Junker and van Dick 2014)) contends that individuals have expectations of leaders. The extent to which one individual perceives another as a leader depends upon such expectations about the characteristics and behaviors of leaders, and the degree to which the person being observed has these characteristics.

Research has demonstrated that these implicit leadership theories can impact the perception of a leader's behavior. A series of studies in the 1980s showed that when observers have expectations of a person's behavior, they tend to report behaviors that match their expectations. For example, if they are told a leader is effective, they describe that leader as acting the way they expect an effective leader to act, even if these descriptions do not match the way the leader is behaving (for more detail see Rule, in press).

To establish a presence of implicit leadership theories, several studies have explored the similarity between expectations for different categories of leaders (Lord, Foti, and DeVader 1984) and traits that were associated with leaders versus non-leaders (Lord, DeVader, and Alliger 1986). Although different leaders activate different expectations in the mind of the respondents, across studies the traits that had the highest association with leaders were intelligence, masculinity, and dominance. These traits seem to fit the traditional stereotypes of a man more than that of a woman.

Furthermore, research in the area of implicit leadership theories and leadership categorization has shown that expectations of managers within the United States has predominantly resulted in descriptive terms such as aggressiveness, rationality, self-confidence, independence, and competitiveness. Studies with adults (Koenig, et al. 2011; Duehr and Bono 2006) and with children (Ayman-Nolley and Ayman 2005), found that across ages, although observers associate a male image with leaders, women and girls tend to be more open toward woman leaders. Therefore, women in leadership positions are likely to find they do not fit the implicit leadership theories of most men.

Gender Stereotypes and Leadership Emergence

Eagly and Karau (1991) demonstrated that overall, men were perceived as being more competent and were more readily accepted as leaders when they acted in a confident and assertive manner. Although the nature of the task moderated this relationship, men were more likely than women to be thought of as leaders and emerge as leaders (Eagly and Karau 1991). For women, the same qualifications of assertiveness and confidence could be detrimental when they are faced with traditional gender stereotypes. Carli and Eagly (1999) in their summary of the research on influence and leadership emergence highlighted this double bind women face in leadership. Studies conducted in the United States have demonstrated that self-efficacy and self-promotion are advantageous in hiring and promotion practices for men. Both men and women, however, consider women who engaged in these behaviors as undesirable (e.g., Rudman 1998). It seems that the only time it is socially appropriate for a woman to boast without repercussion is when the task is seen as traditionally feminine.

In task groups, Mullen, Salas, and Driskell (1989) summarized their meta-analysis findings by stating that the frequency of participation in groups is strongly related to leadership emergence. Carli and Eagly (1999) further clarified this by stating that when an individual's contributions are related to the group's task, the previous findings are supported, but when a person's contributions are related to social issues, the relationship between the amount of contribution and leadership emergence is weaker. Research has also demonstrated that, in general, women's task contributions are more likely to be ignored and potentially lead to negative reactions. Butler and Geis (1990) demonstrated that team members provided more negative and unsupportive responses to women solo leaders, than men who were solo leaders or women who co-led. Therefore, gender stereotypes play a critical role in limiting the opportunities for women to emerge as leaders—decreasing women's access to leadership roles and increasing the obstacles they must overcome in order to become leaders (Eagly and Karau 2002).

Gender and Leadership Style and Effectiveness

Once in leadership positions, women leaders face both the question of similarity of their style with men in the same situation and how effective they are as leaders. The distinctions between these two questions have not always been clear in leadership research. Leadership style refers to the leader's behavior. Observers' implicit leadership theories affect what they see or remember when they evaluate a leader's leadership style. Leadership effectiveness is concerned with the outcomes of this behavior against an expected standard. A critical distinction between these two different approaches is that in studying the style, researchers ask about the frequency and occurrence of leadership behaviors. In measuring leadership effectiveness, investigators ask how well the leader performed leadership behaviors.

Gender Stereotypes and Leadership Style

The literature and research on leadership behavior and style is quite extensive. Three main paradigms of leadership behavior that have received attention are the Ohio State two-factor model of leadership behavior (Bass 1990), the decision-making model (Vroom and Yetton 1973), and transactional and transformational leadership model (Avolio, Waldman, and Yammarino 1991; Bass 1998). The two-factor approach focuses on two categories of behaviors: (1) task-related behaviors and (2) behaviors that maintain the relationship between the leader and other team members. The decision-making model focuses on a leader's choice of decision-making strategies and whether they are autocratic ones or participative ones (Ayman 2004). Finally, the more recent paradigm in the study of leadership styles is the transactional and transformational model of leadership behaviors. The transactional model focuses more on a give-and-take relationship between leaders and team members, and the transformational model centers on developing a relationship between the leader and team members.

Eagly and Johnson's (1990) meta-analysis included studies conducted with the first two models mentioned above. The findings demonstrated that no difference was found in the perception of men and women leaders engaging in considerate behaviors or initiating task-oriented behaviors. They did, however, report that women leaders were perceived as being more participative than their men counterparts. Yet the date and the setting of these studies may have affected the results. In more traditional settings, where the male stereotype was more dominant, gender differences were more pronounced. Studies that were conducted earlier showed more differences between men and women leaders. Also, in studies conducted in the field, where the women participants were handpicked or self-selected, the differences were noticed less.

More recently, Eagly and colleagues have added to this classic work and reported results regarding the role of a leader's gender in transactional and transformational leadership styles (Eagly et al. 2003). These studies found that women leaders, when compared to their male counterparts, were perceived as slightly (but significantly) more likely to engage in transformational behaviors and contingent reward behaviors (in which a leader uses rewards or encouragement to guide team members). They also found that men leaders, when compared to women leaders, were perceived as more transactional leaders, meaning, for example, that they may avoid giving direction when performance goals are being met.

Therefore, one could conclude that men and women are perceived somewhat differently due to the presence of traditional gender stereotypes. To find out if this has any bearing on women's professional lives or their success as leaders, a critical question remains, "Are men and women equally successful?" Logic would dictate that if transformational leadership is an effective style of leadership (Lowe, Kroeck, and Sivasubramaniam 1996), then women should be considered more effective than man, since this is the style they seem to favor. Yet is this the conclusion of leadership studies?

When reviewing the research findings on leadership effectiveness, one should keep the following in mind. The majority of these studies describe the behaviors of leaders through the eyes of their subordinates. Thus, if the observers are more traditional in their stereotypes of women, or if the conditions are those where traditional male roles are dominant, this could cause them to perceive men and women behaving dissimilarly. For example, Becker, Ayman, and Korabik (2002) compared women and men leaders in a managerial environment to those in a school administration environment. In the managerial environment, women who tried to act according to the norms of management faced more disagreement with their subordinates on how they behaved than women in the school administration environment. So, the answer to the question, "Are men and women leaders behaving similarly or differently?" may be contingent upon the eyes of the perceiver, who is influenced by his or her stereotypes, expectations, and the social norms around them. The perceivers of these women leaders are faced with challenges of their mixed expectations regarding gender stereotypes and implicit leadership theories (Ayman, 1993; Eagly and Karau 2002), which could affect their memory.

Gender Stereotypes and Leadership Effectiveness

Leadership effectiveness is an evaluation process. The scope of the question can be general such as, "How effective is the manager?" or very specific such as, "How well does he or she do in specific activities and show specific competencies?" The results of two meta-analyses have addressed these questions and demonstrated that women are rated slightly less favorably as leaders than their men counterparts in situations that are more traditionally dominated by men (Eagly, Makhijani, and Klonsky 1992; Eagly, Karau, and Makhijani 1995).

One meta-analysis included studies where the respondents observed the leader in action and studies that used paper-people, where respondents rated leaders described in a vignette. They found gender differences in evaluations of leaders when the task of the group was more masculine, when the majority of raters were men, and when the leaders were perceived as acting with agentic qualities (e.g., decisive, resilient, proactive, strategic) rather than engaging in interpersonal and communal behaviors (Eagly & Karau 2002). Specifically, they found only a small tendency for subjects to evaluate women leaders less favorably than men leaders This tendency, however, was more pronounced in situations when men evaluators rated women occupying male-dominated roles, such as in college athletics, business, and manufacturing. In another study, Ayman, Korabik, Morris (2009) demonstrated that women who were transformational leaders were evaluated more harshly by the male subordinates than by the female subordinates.

In measuring leaders' effectiveness, particularly when dependent on subjective measure, the gender stereotypes held by the rater and the traditional nature of the setting are concerns. In one study, women leaders in business and manufacturing organizations showed less agreement between how they rated themselves and how their subordinates rated them compared to women leaders and their subordinates in traditionally gender-balanced organizations and men leaders and their workers regardless of the organization (Speron, Ayman, and Korabik 2000). It appears that women are out of touch with the expectations of their raters when the setting has masculine factors.

Many scholars have acknowledged that 360-degree feedback, in which colleagues both above and below provide anonymous feedback and critique, is a great source of information that allows leaders to improve their skills and abilities. Women leaders can benefit from this method to become more aware of the expectations of those around them.

Reflections on the Study of Leadership

The ability to effectively lead people has traditionally been a highly prized skill. Leadership ability is typically rewarded with higher pay and additional benefits. Historically there have been women leaders who have been both effective and popular (Leon 1995, 1997). Until the 1970s, leadership had been the province of men, and even now men dominate the highest positions of leadership in US organizations. Much has been written about the "glass ceiling" that holds women back from leadership positions, the career progression of women, and role of gender stereotypes in leadership, yet de facto conclusions have not been reached. More recent work of Eagly has argued that the metaphor has now changed to "the labyrinth" instead of the glass ceiling (Eagly and Carli 2007), which demonstrates the complexity of the path to be a leader as a woman.

We notice two issues about gender stereotypes and leadership. One: subordinates perceive women leaders as acting in a more participative and transformational manner than male leaders. Second: women leaders are rated as being less effective than male leaders when these women are rated by men, when the women are leaders in masculine settings, and when they are engaged in agentic behaviors (those displayed by an agent). The presence of traditional gender stereotypes affects our society's perception and evaluation of women leaders. Stereotypes of women and their effect on the perceptions of subordinates and leaders on female leadership roles, will affect women's access to leadership positions, particularly in nontraditional fields.

Expectations, however, are changing for leaders. In the past, leadership was perceived as masculine, with emphasis on dominance as an attribute. The number of self-help books for women exhorting them to become more assertive and to learn men's ways of leadership and management are numerous. The result of this movement, coupled with equal employment policies and affirmative action in selection, may have increased the number of women in leadership positions and created a norm that dictated that women leaders had to be tougher than their men colleagues.

Beginning in the late twentieth century, research showed a backlash for women who are perceived as agentic (Rudman and Glick 2001, 1999; Rudman 1998). One explanation for this backlash could be gender-role spillover (Guteck, Morasch, and Cohen 1982). Gender-role spillover occurs when women act like men and are perceived as being out-of-role. These out-of-role behaviors could be an impetus for an unfavorable rating (Eagly and Karau 2002). Another explanation of this backlash could be that the world of work has endorsed transformational leadership as an effective leadership style. This leadership style gives credence to and emphasizes interpersonal sensitivity and mentoring in leadership. This could be the beginning of a significant change in the image of effective leadership. Therefore, the image of a decisive, domineering leader is being replaced with the image of a leader who balances decisiveness with relationship building and caring for his or her team members.

It appears that the role of leader is becoming more acceptable for women and friendlier toward some of the feminine values held by the women's culture (Yonder 2001). This is a state of transition—new sets of expectations are evolving with new norms. Gradually the old norms and expectations are being challenged, and women and men leaders, and their observers, will benefit from reexamining their reactions and automatic responses.

Researchers and theorists conclude that while gender stereotypes have an impact on leadership, that relationship is more complex than first thought. Gender stereotypes are still prevalent partly due to the diverse roles women fulfill within organizations and society as a whole. From the traditional generic stereotype of women, relatively new subtypes of stereotypes have developed. The obvious barriers for women leaders are diminishing, yet the subtle effect of stereotypes and implicit theories still remain and affect how leaders are chosen and evaluated.

Further Reading

Aries, E. (1996). *Men and women in interaction: Reconsidering the differences*. New York, NY: Oxford University Press.

Ashmore, R. D. & del Boca, F. K. (1979). Sex stereotypes and implicit personality theory: Toward a cognitive-social psychological conceptualization. *Sex Roles. 5*(2), 219–248.

Atwater, L. E.; Waldman, D. A.; & Brett, J. F. (2002). Understanding and optimizing multi-source feedback. *Human Resource Management Journal. 41*, 193–208.

Avolio, B. J.; Waldman, D. A.; & Yammarino, F. J. (1991). Leading in the 1990s: the four I's of transformational leadership. *Journal of European Industrial training, 15*, 9–16.

Ayman, R. (2004). Situational and contingency approaches to leadership. In R. J. Sternberg, J. Antonakis, & A. T. Cianciolo, (Eds.), *The nature of leadership*. Thousand Oaks: Sage.

Ayman, R. (1993). Leadership perception: The role of gender and culture. In M. Chemers, & R. Ayman (Eds.), *Leadership theory and research: Perspectives and Directions* (pp. 137–166). NY: Academic Press.

Ayman, R.; Korabik, K.; & Morris, S. (2009). Is transformational leadership always perceived as effective? Male subordinates' devaluation of female transformational leaders. *Journal of Applied Social Psychology, 39*(4), 852–879.

Ayman-Nolley, S. & Ayman, R. (2005). Children's implicit theory and leadership. In B. Schyns and J. R. Meindl (Eds.), *Implicit Leadership Theories: Essays and Explorations* (pp. 227–274). Greenwich, CT: Information Age Publishing.

Bass, B. M. (1998). *Transformational leadership: Industrial, military, and educational impact.* New Jersey: Lawrence Erlbaum Associates.

Bass, B. M. (1990). *Bass & Stogdill's handbook of leadership: Theory, research, and managerial applications,* 3rd edition. New York: Free Press.

Becker, J.; Ayman, R.; & Korabik, K. (2002). Discrepant perceptions of leadership behavior: Gender, self-monitoring, and leadership context. *Group and Organization Management: An International Journal, 27*(2), 226–245.

Bem, S. L. (1974). The measurement of psychological androgyny. *Journal of Consulting and Clinical Psychology, 42,* 155–162.

Butler, D. & Geis, F. L. (1990). Nonverbal affect responses to leaders: Implications for leadership evaluations. *Journal of Personality and Social Psychology, 58,* 48–59.

Carli, L. L. & Eagly, A. (1999). Gender effects on social influence and emergence of leadership. In G. Powell (Ed.), *Handbook of gender and work* (pp. 203–223). Thousand Oaks, CA: Sage Publications.

Eagly, A. H. & Johannesen-Schmidt, M. C. (2001). The leadership styles of women and men. *Journal of Social Issues, 57,* 781–797.

Eagly, A.; Johannesen-Schmidt, M.; van Engen, M. L.; & Vinkenburg, C. (2002). Transformational, transactional, and laissez-faire styles: A meta-analysis comparing men and women. *Psychological Bulletin, 129,* 569–591.

Eagly, A. & Johnson, B. (1990). Gender and leadership style: A meta-analysis. *Psychological Bulletin, 108*(2), 233–256.

Eagly, A. & Karau, S. (2002). Role Congruity Theory of prejudice toward female leaders. *Psychological Review, 109,* 573–598.

Eagly, A. & Karau, S. (1991). Gender and the emergence of leaders: A meta-analysis. *Journal of Personality and Social Psychology, 60,* 685–710.

Eagly, A.; Karau, S.; & Makhijani, M. (1995). Gender and the effectiveness of leaders: A meta-analysis. *Psychological Bulletin, 117,* 125–145.

Eagly, A., Makhijani, M., & Klonsky, B. (1992). Gender and the evaluation of leaders: A meta-analysis. *Psychological Bulletin, 111,* 3–22.

Elsser, K. M. & Lever, J. (2011). Does gender bias against female leaders persist? Quantitative and qualitative data from a large-scale survey. *Human Relations, 64* (12), 1555–1578. doi:10.1177/0018726711424323

Embry, A.; Padgett, M. Y.; & Caldwell, C. B. (2008). Can Leaders step outside of the gender box? An examination of leadership and gender role stereotypes. *Journal of Leadership and Organizational Studies, 15*(1), 30-45. doi:10.1177/1548051808318412

Fiske, S. T. & Ruscher, J. B. (1993). Negative interdependence and prejudice: Whence the affect? In D. M. Mackie & D. L. Hamilton (Eds.), *Affect, cognition, and stereotyping: Interactive processes in group perception* (pp. 239–268). New York, NY: Academic Press.

Frame, M.; Ayman, R.; Raju, N.; & Goff, M. (1999). *Executive level multi-rater performance ratings: Measurement equivalence across source and gender.* Paper presented at 14th annual meeting of the Society for Industrial & Organizational Psychology, Atlanta, Georgia.

Glick, P. & Fiske, S. T. (1999). Sexism and other "isms": Interdependence, status, and the ambivalent content of stereotypes. In W. B. Swann Jr.; J. H. Langlois; & L. A. Gilbert (Eds.), *Sexism and stereotypes in modern society: The gender science of Janet Taylor Spence* (pp. 193–221). Washington DC; American Psychological Association.

Guteck, B. A.; Morasch, B.; & Cohen, A. G. (1982). Interpreting social sexual behaviors in a work setting. *Journal of Vocational Behaviors, 22,* 30–48.

Heilman, M.E. (2001). Description and prescription: How gender stereotype prevent women access up the organizational ladder. *Journal of Social Issues, 57,* 657–674.

Henley, N. (1975). Power, sex, and nonverbal communication. In B. Thorne & N. Henley (Eds.), *Language and sex: Difference and dominance* (pp. 184–203). Rowley, MA: Newbury.

Junker, N.M. & van Dick, R. (2014). Implicit theories in organizational settings: A systematic review and research agenda of implicit leadership and followership theories. *The Leadership Quarterly, 25,* 1154–1173.

Korabik, K. (1999). Sex and gender in the new millennium. In G. Powell (Ed.), *Handbook of gender and work* (pp. 3–16). CA Sage Publications.

Leon, V. (1997). *Uppity women of Medieval times.* New York, NY: MJF Books.

Leon, V. (1995). *Uppity women of ancient times.* New York, NY: MJF Books.

London, M. (2002). *Leadership development: Paths to self-insight and professional growth.* Mahwah, NJ: Lawrence Erlbaum Associates.

Lord, R.G.; DeVader, C. L.; & Alliger, G.M. (1986). A meta-analysis of the relation between personality traits and leadership perceptions: An application of validity generalization. Procedure. *Journal of Applied Psychology, 71*, 402–410.

Lord, R. G.; Foti, R. J; & De Vader, C. L. (1984). A test of leadership categorization theory: Internal structure, information processing, and leadership perceptions. *Organizational Behavior and Human Performance, 34*, 343–378.

Lowe, K.B.; Kroeck, K.G.; & Sivasubramaniam, N. (1996). Effectiveness correlates of transformational and transactional leadership: A meta-analytic review of the MLQ literature. *Leadership Quarterly, 7*, 385–425.

Mullen, B.; Salas, E.; & Driskell, J. E. (1989). Salience, motivation, and artifact as contributors to the relation between participation rate and leadership. *Journal of Experimental Social Psychology, 25*, 545–559.

Rudman, L.A. (1998). Self-promotion as a risk factor for women: The costs and benefits of counterstereotypical impression management. *Journal of Personality and Social Psychology, 74*, 629–645.

Rudman, L.A. & Glick, P. (2001). Perspective gender stereotypes and backlash toward agentic women. *Journal of Social Issues, 57*, 743–762.

Rule, N. (in press) Social cognition and leadership. In John Antonakis and David V, Day (Eds). *The Nature of Leadership 3rd* Edition.

Schein, V. (2001) A global look at psychological barriers to women's progress in management. *Journal of Social Issues, 57*, 675–688.

Schyns, B. & Meindl, J. R. (2005). *Implicit Leadership Theories: Essays and Explorations.* Greenwich, CT: Information Age Publishing.

Speron, E., Ayman, R., & Korabik, K. (2000). *Multi-rater agreement on leader's performance: Gender, self-monitoring, and organization's type.* 15th annual meeting of the Society for Industrial & Organizational Psychology. New Orleans, Louisiana.

United Nations. (16 November, 2000). *Resolution adopted by the general assembly: Further actions and initiatives to implement the Beijing declaration and platform for action.* Retrieved September 22, 2003, from the U.N. division of advancement of women: http://www.un.org/womenwatch/daw/followup/ress233e.pdf

Vroom, V. H. & Yetton, P. W. (1973). *Leadership and decision-making.* Pittsburgh: University of Pittsburgh Press.

Wegner, D. M. & Vallacher, R. R. (1977). *Implicit Psychology.* New York: Oxford University Press.

Yonder, J.D. (2001). Making leadership work more effectively for women. *Journal of Social Issues, 57*, 815–828.

Childhood Socialization and Leadership Development

Saba AYMAN-NOLLEY
Northeastern Illinois University

The socialization of leaders in our society is an important field of study
and has particular interest for those interested in how woman leaders differ from their male counterparts in terms of childhood leadership styles,
development, and influences. More research needs to be done in order to
understand the various ways in which the socialization of girls affects their
success as leaders in the realms of business, politics, and the social fields.

All societies, organizations, and institutions depend for their success and progress largely on their leaders, both male and female. The study of children and
their socialization conveys valuable insight into how societies prepare and
nurture individual boys and girls to become leaders. Studies of the development of
children as leaders throughout their childhood years would be most valuable if they
identified characteristics and environments most conducive to producing leaders.
This, however, would require longitudinal or systematic retrospective studies. Any
cursory look at the literature of developmental psychology reveals no such study of
the socialization of leadership in children. Over the last century however, there have
been many studies of child leaders, their characteristics, styles of leadership, and to
a much smaller degree environmental antecedents of their leadership. It is possible,
therefore, to talk about what we know about leadership in children and its development, and in particular about gender differences and particular issues related to the
development of leadership skills in girls and young women.

At the outset, it is important to mention that the body of literature on leadership in children is disparate and noncohesive, spread as it is over almost a century.
Although the study of leadership has been a popular topic, the majority of research
has focused on adults.

Childhood Leadership and Its Relation to Popularity and Dominance

Childhood leadership has often been studied as a construct imbedded in other concepts, such as dominance and popularity. When relating popularity to leadership,

it has been shown that not all popular children are identified as leaders, although child leaders are among the most popular. Most child leaders who are popular are found to be elected and appointed leaders. Regardless of their sociometric status, emerging child leaders are more likely to be effective leaders (for example, in managing the group's task well and attending to the group's emotions and needs) than the popular children who are not leaders. Based on these results, we can safely say that although childhood leadership and popularity are connected, they should initially be studied as separate constructs.

Studies of dominance have primarily concentrated on characteristics such as toughness and the ability to get one's way. Ethological studies (studies examining how human character forms) conducted in nursery schools have kept the notions of leadership and dominance closely related. In adults, some aspects of dominance, such as directing and organizing, are related to a leadership style that is a controlling and structuring rather than supportive and considerate. In a study published in 2001, Ryoko Yamaguchi found that the task conditions that promote more dominance in children are different than those that promote leadership, with performance-based tasks bringing about dominance and mastery tasks, in which the children work at their own pace to achieve a set goal, increasing leadership and positive behavior. Mastery conditions promoted both group cohesion and focus on the study's math task, whereas performance conditions led to the emergence of one child who overpowered the group process. Dominance, like popularity, is related to but not synonymous with leadership, and should be considered a separate construct.

Trends in the Study of Leadership in Children

Studies focusing specifically on leadership in children, although small in number and disparate in focus, are similar to those focusing on adults. Paralleling a similar trend in studies of adult leaders, studies of leadership in children from the 1930s through the 1950s tried to tease out specific personality characteristics of the child leaders. These characteristics included high intelligence and a desire for achievement, as well as confidence, popularity, and sociability. Child leaders were found to have a greater sense of humor, versatility, and strong social skills in general. Many studies found that student leaders were often boys who were active in sports; these boys were healthier and had more vitality than their non-leader peers.

The 1960s through the early 1980s saw a move away from the examination of personality traits and toward studies of children's leadership behaviors and styles. Some of the earliest work of this type resembled trait studies, specifically those contrasting a task orientation with a people orientation. In the 1970s, R. C. Hardy, continuing in the tradition of the contingency model of leadership effectiveness, found that children who were task-oriented leaders were more effective in highly favorable and unfavorable situations, whereas relationship-oriented leaders were most effective in moderately favorable situations.

Observational studies of leadership behavior in preschool-aged children in the context of their peer interactions in nursery classrooms have found different styles of leadership. As early as 1933, for example, Mildred Parten found two distinctive directive leadership behaviors: "artful" (tactful), and "forceful" (aggressive). Research by A. P. Hare published in the 1950s revealed similar patterns among thirteen-year-olds. Hare found that leaders were either self- or group-oriented, participatory or supervisory. He also found that these different types of leaders worked differently with their groups and developed different kinds of relationships with the other group members. In a study published in 1963, Dexter Dunphy identified two types of leaders in Australian adolescent groups. The first were crowd leaders who were the group representative to the outside, and the second were clique leaders who were the coordinators within the group. In 1959, Cassel and Haddox reported that gifted children who were in positions of leadership tended to use parliamentary patterns of leadership rather than authoritative or laissez-faire styles. Most studies, including those with preschoolers, have found that leadership positions and dominance ranks gained by children remain relatively stable over time.

From the early 1980s and to the present, there have been very few studies of leadership in children from any perspective. Studies of this period can be categorized in three broad areas: There are studies inspired by Piaget's cognitive theory, showing the relation between children's developmental level and their descriptions of leaders; there are studies interested in training and application of leadership in children; and there are studies on the socialization of leadership and parental influences on leadership in children. In none of these areas can one find large numbers of studies or a systematic approach that yields conclusive results. There are a handful of very valuable studies in each area, however, that are important to review and bring to mind.

Piaget-Inspired Studies: Leader Schemata

In the 1980s the study of leadership in children was influenced by Piaget's theory and an increased interest in cognitive psychology in general. Tina Daniels-Beirness (1986), Matthews, Lord, and Walker (1988), and Robert Selman (who focused on interpersonal awareness in children in works published in 1979 and 1980 and with Jaquette in 1978) described a structuralist view of the development of leadership concepts in children. This body of research suggests that children define their understanding and expectations of leaders differently at different ages, with the differences paralleling Piaget's stages of development. When comparing children from kindergarten to sixth grade, it was shown that younger children used more physical characteristics in defining leaders while older children used more affective and motivational characteristics.

Concerned about theoretically imposed approaches to studying children's perceptions of leadership, Saba Ayman-Nolley, Roya Ayman, and Jeffrey Becker conducted research in 1993 that examined children's implicit theory of leadership through children's own drawings of leaders. While they found that children in kindergarten through eighth grade mostly had a schema of a leader that was a white male, this was not uniformly true; there were grade, gender, and ethnicity effects. About half the girls drew female leaders, and their drawn leaders were more likely to be smiling. The older children's leaders were more autocratic with fewer smiles and distinctly larger bodies. Roya Ayman and Saba Ayman-Nolley conducted a second study in 1995 that looked at children's verbal descriptions of their schema of a leader and found results very similar to the drawing data. A small number of parents in this study returned a parent questionnaire about their schema of a leader; analyzing these revealed that more sixth-grade responses agreed with those of their parents than did third-grade responses (50 percent as opposed to 30 percent). Girls' responses agreed more with their parents than did boys' (63 percent as opposed to 33 percent). The African-American children's responses were more likely to agree with their parents' responses than were the white children's (70 percent as opposed to 35 percent). Data have recently been collected for a ten-year replication of the drawing studies that should shed light on the effects of sociocultural changes on children's schema of the leader.

Socialization and Familial Influence

Although the question of the antecedents of leadership and its development in children is a very important and valuable one, the body of work devoted to this topic is very small. In 1983 Bruce Klonsky published results of the most comprehensive work in this area—his study of sport leaders in a New York high school. One of his many findings was that the socialization process that yielded male leaders was different from the one that produced female leaders. Males seemed to benefit from intense socialization such as high parental achievement demands, maternal principled discipline, and parental authority discipline. For female leaders the family factors that seemed to play influential roles were having a major voice in the familial decision-making processes, low-intensity socialization, and low to moderate parental warmth.

Almost ten years later, James Whorton and Frances Karnes examined the relationship between parent and child leadership styles and their perceptions. They concluded that those parents who desire their children to assume positions of leadership should engage in a parenting style that they called "delegating." Of course the children would have to be able and willing to do things on their own. In a 1992 article, Hartman and Harris reported that parents had a greater influence on boys' leadership than girls' leadership; interestingly, the boys' perception of their parents' leadership seemed to have had more of an influence than parents' actual behavior (as reported by the parents). In a study published in 1995, Frances Karnes, Suzanne Bean, and J. C. McGinnis found that female students in a leadership program saw their immediate family as the greatest influence on their leadership potential. This overwhelming ranking of familiar antecedents was followed by influences from their teachers and their opportunities for involvement in student government.

There is a reasonable body of literature that has shown that there are more political leaders among first-born males than any other birth-order ranking. Joan Newman, Jill Pettinger, and J. B. Even have hypothesized that "Perhaps family practices provide girls with the skills required for face-to-face interpersonal leadership and conciliation rather than training in competition and aggressive assertion which may be required for the confrontations of many political offices" (Newman, Pettinger, and Even 1995, 126).

Another area of work on children and leadership in the last two decades has been in developing leadership training programs. There is, however, very little conclusive data and systematic inquiry on the effectiveness of these programs.

Gender Differences

Although almost every study reports significant differences between boys and girls, gender differences in children's leadership, as in other areas, are inconclusive.

The differences across all studies and factors seem to equal out, with boys and girls possessing different strengths. Among early studies, Madaline K. Remmlein (1938) showed boy leaders to be endowed with scholarship, intelligence, and socioeconomic status; Caldwell and Wellman (1926) obtained somewhat similar results for girl leaders who rated high in scholarship, citizenship, and I.Q.

When dominance and leadership are viewed together, more striking differences appear. Overall, dominance in boys tended to be identified more in the domains of athletics and intelligence; dominance in girls, on the other hand, was related to domains of being fashionable, well-groomed, and attractive.

In looking at gender differences in leader behavior, a 1978 study by Hynes, Richardson, and Asher showed social sensitivity to be a predictor of self-reported leadership for boys and not girls. This was further supported the following year by Victoria Fu, who demonstrated that both boys and girls were more likely to be identified as successful leaders if they acted in gender-appropriate ways. Klonsky, Phillips, Piato, and Blanchet reported in 1991 that girls more frequently assumed leadership roles in social and classroom activities in contrast to boys' interest in more instrumental leadership roles. In 1976 Lockheed presented evidence that even in children's groups, when males are present there is suppression of female verbal expression and less possibility of leadership behavior from female group members. In 1990 Singer suggested that overall girls "attached a greater value or significance to being in leadership positions" (Singer 1990, 152). Along those lines, Morris (1991) found that adolescent school leaders tended to be girls.

In a study published in 1996, Ganz reported that male adolescents indicated that they were drawn to positions of leadership mostly because of a sense of competence or a desire to have control over an activity, whereas the girls were more likely than boys to choose leadership positions out of a sense of duty. ("Somebody has to do it.") Ganz also found that female students in decision-making positions were more likely than boys to engage in the ethic of care and response. Not too different from these results are those of Moore (1988), who found that overall, teachers were more likely to perceive girls as having more leadership skills than boys. These researchers also found that high-equity environments in desegregated schools are better environments for nurturing leadership in females and minorities than their low-equity segregated counterparts.

It is interesting to note that Karnes, Bean, and McGinnis found that females who were attending a leadership training program believed that in the future there would be more female and minority leaders in our society. These same girls strongly disagreed with the generalized statement: "Males make better leaders than females." When looking at children's image of a leader, Ayman-Nolley and colleagues found that girls were just as likely to draw male leaders as female leaders, whereas boys drew solely male leaders. Other research supports that pattern in boys' and girls' choices of heroes.

Outlook for the Future

As a result of the discontinuity and nature of methodology used to examine leadership in children over the last half of the twentieth century, major questions remain unanswered. The use of adult categories and measures has made it difficult to arrive at conclusive findings about many aspects of leadership in children. It is clear that there is a need for more studies of leadership in children in almost every area, especially in leadership styles, leadership concepts, leadership development, and socialization. It is important that the field moves toward a multi-method, multi-theory approach. Furthermore, it is crucial that those interested in this field support a steady and systematic approach to unraveling the mysteries of how some people become great leaders and some do not. Understanding children's concepts of leadership and how they construct associated schemata will help us develop strategies to cultivate in them the skills to be great future leaders. It must be remembered in all these attempts, however, that it is essential to keep cultural and gender variations in mind. To date we know very little about cultural differences in children's concepts and styles of leadership. This is probably one of the least-studied areas of childhood leadership. The coming century is ripe with numerous possibilities for important scholarly research into the development and socialization of leaders.

Further Reading

Ayman-Nolley, S. & Ayman, R (1995, April). *Development and socialization of children's schemas of leaders and leadership.* Paper presented at the biennial meeting of the Society for Research in Child Development, Indianapolis, IN.

Ayman-Nolley, S.; Ayman, R.; & Becker, J. (1993, March). *Children's concepts of leadership through their drawings.* Poster session presented at the biennial meeting of the Society for Research in Child Development, New Orleans, LA.

Freedman (Eds.), *Dominance Relations* (pp. 177–191). New York: Garland STMP Press.

Caldwell, O. W. & Wellman, B. (1926). Characteristics of school leaders. *Journal of Educational Research, 14,* 1–15.

Cassel, R. N. & Haddox, A. (1959). Comparative study of leadership test scores for gifted and typical high school students. *Psychological Reports, 5,* 713–717.

Daniels-Beirness, T. (1986). *Children's understanding of leadership: Conceptual differences with age.* Unpublished doctoral dissertation, University of Waterloo, Canada.

Dunphy, D. C. (1963). The social structure of urban adolescent peer groups. *Sociometry, 26,* 230–246.

Fiedler, F. E. (1978). The contingency model and the dynamics of the leadership process. In L. Berkowitz (Ed.), *Advances in experimental and social psychology* (pp. 59–111). New York: Academic Press.

Fleishman, E. A. (1957). A leader behavior description for industry. In R. M. Stogdill & A. E. Coons (Eds.), *Leader Behavior: Its description and measurement.* Columbus: Bureau of Business Research, Ohio State University.

Fleming, E. G. (1935). A factor analysis of the personality of high school leaders. *Journal of Applied Psychology, 67,* 326–333.

Fu, V. (1979). Preschool leadership-followership behavior. *Child Study Journal, 9,* 133–140.

Ganz, C. (1996). Gender and leadership in adolescence: Perspectives and aspirations of eighth graders. Unpublished doctoral dissertation, Seattle University, Seattle, WA.

Garrison. K. C. (1933). A study of some factors related to leadership in high school. *Peabody Journal of Education, 11,* 11–17.

Gash, H. & Conway, P. (1997). Images of heroes and heroines: How stable? *Journal of Applied Developmental Psychology, 18,* 349–372.

Gellert, E. (1961). Stability and fluctuation in the power relationships of young children. *Journal of Abnormal and Social Psychology, 62,* 8–15.

Gellert, E. (1962). The effect of changes in group composition on the dominant behavior of young children. *British Journal of Social and Clinical Psychology, 1,* 168–181.

Gowen, J. C. (1955). Relationship between leadership and personality measures. *Journal of Educational Research, 48,* 624–627.

Greenwood, J. C. (1993). Racial and gender differences in hero selection: Similarity still dominates identification patterns. Paper presented at the meeting of the American Psychological Society, Chicago, IL.

Hardy, R. C. (1975). A test of the poor leader-member relation cells of the contingency model on small classroom groups. *Child Development, 46,* 958–964.

Hardy, R. C.; Sack, S.; Stanley, J.; & Harpine, F. (1973). An experimental test of the contingency model on small classroom groups. *Journal of Psychology, 85*, 3–16.

Hare, A. P. (1953). Small group discussions with participatory and supervisory leadership. *Journal of Abnormal Social Psychology, 48*, 273–275.

Hare, A. P. (1957). Situational differences in leader behavior. *Journal of Abnormal Social Psychology, 55*, 132–135.

Harrison, C. W.; Rawls, J. R.; & Rawls, D. J. (1971). Differences between leaders and non-leaders in six-to-eleven-year-old children. *Journal of Social Psychology, 84*, 269–272.

Hartman, S. J. & Harris, O. J.. (1992). The role of parental influence in leadership. *Journal of Social Psychology, 132*(2), 153–167.

Hensel, N. (1983). Developing emergent leadership skills in elementary and junior high school students. *Roeper Review, 5*(4), 33–35.

Hynes, K.; Richardson, W. B.; & Asher, W. (1978). Project talent revisited: Cross validity self-report of leadership. *Journal of Experimental Education, 47*, 106–211.

Karnes, F.; Bean, S.; & McGinnis J. C. (1995). Perceptions of leadership held by young females. *Journal of Secondary Gifted Education, 6*(2),113–119.

Karnes, F. & Chauvin, J. (1985). The leadership skills. *G/C/T, 9*(3), 22–23.

Klonsky, B. (1983). The socialization and development of leadership ability. *Genetics Psychology Monographs, 108*, 97–135.

Klonsky, B.; Phillips, R.; Piato, R.; & Blanchet, P. (1991). *Grade and sex differences in children's leadership expression.* Poster session presented at Society for Research in Child Development, Seattle, WA.

Liu, L.; Ayman, R.; & Ayman-Nolley, S. (2014). Children's image of leadership in China. In S. Turnbull et al. (Eds.), *Worldly Leadership: Alternative Wisdoms for a Complex World* (pp. 105–134). London: Palgrave Macmillan.

Lockheed, M. E. (1976). *The modification of female leadership behavior in the presence of males.* Princeton, NJ: Educational Testing Service.

Lord. R. G.; DeVader, C. L.; & Alliger, G. M. (1986). A meta-analysis of the relation between personality traits and leadership perception: An application of validity generalization procedures. *Journal of Applied Psychology, 71*, 402–410.

Matthews, A. M.; Lord, R. G.; & Walker, J. B. (1988). *The development of leadership perceptions in children.* Unpublished manuscript, University of Akron, OH.

Moore, H. A., (1988). Effects of gender, ethnicity, and school equity on students' leadership behaviors in a group game. *Elementary School Journal, 88*(5), 514–527.

Morris, B. (1991). Perceptions of leadership traits: comparison of adolescent and adult school leaders. *Psychological Reports, 69*, 723–727.

Newman, J.; Pettinger, J.; & Even, J. B. (1995). "My big sister the town supervisor": Family leadership training is not just for boys. *Sex Roles, 33*, 121–127.

Parten, M. B. (1933). Leadership among preschool children. *Journal of Abnormal and Social Psychology, 27*(4), 430–440.

Remmlein, M. K. (1938). Analysis of leaders among high school seniors. *Journal of Experimental Education, 6*, 413–422.

Richardson, W. & Feldhusen, J. (1986). Leadership education: Developing skills for youth. New York: Trillium Press.

Selman, R. L. (1979). *Assessing interpersonal understanding: An interview and scoring manual.* Cambridge, MA: Harvard-Judge Baker Social Reasoning Project.

Selman, R. L. (1980). *The growth of interpersonal understanding.* New York: Academic Press.

Selman, R. L. & Jacquette, D. (1978). *Stability and oscillation in interpersonal awareness: A clinical developmental approach.* In C. B. Kearsy (Ed.), Twenty-fifth Nebraska symposium on motivation (pp. 261–304). Lincoln: University of Nebraska Press.

Singer, M. (1990). Cognitive correlates of adolescents' aspirations to leadership: A developmental study. *Journal of Adolescence, 13*, 143–155.

Sluckin, A. (1983). Dominance relationships in preschool children. In D. R. O'Mark, F. F. Strayer, & D. G. Freedman (Eds.), *Dominance Relations* (pp. 159–177). New York: Garland STMP Press.

Whorton, J. E. & Karnes, F. (1992). Comparison of parents' leadership styles: Perceptions of parents and student leaders. *Perceptual and Motor Skills, 74*, 1227–1230.

Yamaguchi, R. (2001). Children's learning groups: A study of emergent leadership, dominance, and group effectiveness. *Small Group Research, 32*, 671–697.

PART II

Women and Social Change

Women's Emancipation Movements

Cynthia CURRAN

Saint John's University / College of Saint Benedict

Gender discrimination occurs everywhere, and while women's emancipation movements occur worldwide, the struggles experienced and the potential solutions vary widely. Because of this, answers to gender inequities are best addressed by women working together within a culture to advocate for change that is acceptable to all. Across the globe, women have found different ways of confronting or negotiating these issues that reflect the variety of their histories and societal customs.

During the nineteenth and twentieth centuries, women's emancipation movements, whether they were called the "woman question," "women's rights," or "feminism," challenged the Western family economy in which the primary role of women is that of wife and mother, with waged work being a secondary role. Because people saw the domestic sphere as primary, women's work outside the home was undervalued and undercompensated. This distinction caused male domination of the political system with little hope of a reorientation of women's position in society. During the past two centuries women (and a number of men) worked to change this system politically, economically, and socially with varying degrees of success. They rarely took race and class into account, and people usually had an unacknowledged view of universalism toward women in other parts of the world. That is, the position of many Euro-American feminists was that all women have the same oppression to overthrow and that common tactics will be useful in all circumstances.

Today, students of women's lives recognize that geography and culture are important factors. Although many feminists claim a universal theory of injustice and advocate a universal platform of change, their experience tends to be limited to industrialized and democratic nations. Areas of the world that have experienced long histories of colonization or that have operated under forms of socialist, collective political systems present radically different challenges to women and call for varying approaches to change. For these reasons the term *women's movements* (plural) is more appropriate for the twenty-first century. The plural (*movements*) acknowledges the validity of dissimilar approaches, and the plural (*women's*) rather than *woman* recognizes that not all women face the same issues in widely divergent geographical areas. The elimination of the word *rights* is a nod to those cultures that do not see adversarial positions as desirable in finding solutions. Women's movements reflect the different histories, cultures, and political systems of people who have a gender in common but perhaps little else.

Britain and the United States

During the nineteenth century, suffrage (the right to vote) received the most emphasis among women's rights groups, but many middle-class women also saw social reform as their defining characteristic. With the rapid urbanization caused by industrial changes, the middle class grew in influence; women asserted their participation by addressing the miseries caused by the new orientations of society and wished to influence legal reforms by exercising the vote.

In addition to working for suffrage and engaging in good works, women during the nineteenth century on both sides of the Atlantic Ocean were interested in the very nature of womanhood. They debated fiercely what makes women different than men, and they discussed what all women desire. They may not have assumed that women of all classes and races were the same, but agreed that gender alone is the overriding difference in social constructions.

Women's concerns were much the same in both countries with minor exceptions. Women in the United States tended to claim some moral superiority because the United States was seemingly more democratic and equitable than Britain, but British reformers tartly pointed to the existence of slavery in many US states.

By 1924, both groups had achieved suffrage (although women under age thirty did not gain the vote in Britain until 1928), opened employment for many women, and amended the most oppressive marriage laws. At this point many feminist groups turned to public health issues, especially birth control, and expanded legal rights for women. No single issue, however, emerged to unite all women as suffrage had. Women seemed to be somewhat disappointed with the goals achieved and confused about future goals.

The major discouragements to women seemed to stem from the absence of change after women were granted the vote. The majority of women in both countries seemingly were not won over to reformist or radical platforms in women's issues. Despite changes in the law, men did not accept women as political and economic equals. The biggest disappointments for women were in the inability of feminist groups to redress the inequalities in marriage.

The drawbacks inherent in legal changes were clear when the Equal Rights Amendment failed to pass in the United States in 1923 and again during the last quarter of the twentieth century. The unlimited optimism of the Victorian era was squelched by the inability to achieve equal rights in the legal arena.

Political Variations: Latin America

Although Latin America is close to the United States in geographical terms, the differences in political, racial, and economic structures have influenced the development of different sorts of feminist concerns. In Latin America, women's movements cannot be separated from the context of military authoritarianism and the struggle toward political freedom movements in the past, and often those who study Latin

American politics discount the interaction of women with politics, although it was historically important.

Feminist newspapers played an important role in disseminating ideas as long ago as the nineteenth century in Brazil. Since the mid-twentieth century, urban life has provided a backdrop for networks of neighborhood women agitating for better services and lower consumer prices. Women participated in strikes and joined political parties even before they had the right to vote, which came much later than in the United States or in Britain. Ecuador was the first Latin American nation to grant women's suffrage in 1929, although it did not possess a liberal democratic tradition, and Colombia was the last Latin American nation to grant women's suffrage in 1957. The suffrage movement in Latin America produced uninspiring results. As in the United States and Britain, it was led mainly by middle-class women, and it aimed to produce reform rather than radical social changes. Women's suffrage did not cause a significant change in Latin American societies in part because women who did vote supported the status quo and were subservient to the politically conservative Catholic Church. No large-scale shift in attitudes occurred in part because no concerted effort took place to join economic and educational change for women with the right to vote.

Because suffrage came so late and because it failed to institute real change in women's lives in Latin America, few people would have predicted the emergence during the 1970s of women's movements that were important in destabilizing military regimes. In addition to agitating politically, women's human rights groups, feminist groups, and organizations of poor urban women began to cooperate.

In Argentina, for example, women who previously had never involved themselves in politics and did not define themselves as feminists stepped onto the political stage to protest the loss of their husbands and family members, known as "the Disappeared"— people whom military regimes regarded as enemies. The attention that the women's testimony received from the press around the world affected military rule.

Other feminist groups were formed by women from leftist parties who were frustrated by the failure of the left to take women's issues seriously. They agitated for women's issues as well as for the end of military dictatorships. By the late 1980s, the most striking aspects of the women's movements in Latin America were the contributions the movements made in overthrowing military dictatorships and in reconstructing civil society. By the end of the twentieth century, this experience in cooperation led many people to concentrate on issues of class and race; poor women developed the organizational skills to combat sharp cutbacks in state spending, and women's demonstrations forced political leaders to change course.

Postcolonialism and Culture: South Asia

The example of South Asia shows that social justice and equality in family life cannot be separated from culture. Unlike women's movements in Euro-America, women's movements in India and surrounding countries have to negotiate ardent nationalism, divergent religious practices, secularism, and polarized political views to present an agenda directed toward change in women's lives.

In addition to confronting a multilingual and multi-caste society, reformers can appear to oppose ancient practices. The complexity of a postcolonial society includes the danger that a platform that advocates modernization can be construed as conflicting with tradition. Reform that advocates the equal rights of women can be manipulated into appearing to be linked with the views held by the former colonial power.

In addition to confronting suspicion of reform, advocates of women's rights in South Asia must confront the tensions among major religions that have sharply conflicting positions. For example, some Hindu traditionalists have supported sati (immolation of widows on their husbands' funeral pyres) in the face of feminist opposition and its outlawing since 1829. In the same vein, Sikh extremists have continued to deny inheritance rights to women, and Muslims have resisted the granting of maintenance to divorced wives. In general, efforts by women to initiate reform have been hindered by those who oppose reform as an erosion of religious tradition and power.

South Asian feminists face many complexities beyond simple changes in policy. Before independence, many feminists believed that an independent nation would naturally bring with it equal opportunities for women. The decades after independence have demonstrated that the situation is far more complex, not least because women do not always share the same goals. Another issue is that South Asian feminists must maintain a clear distinction between themselves and Western feminists, in order to deflect accusations of sympathies with a colonial past.

Stereotypes and Diversity: Africa

The colonial past also influences aspects of the present in many Africa countries, including the perceptions of African women. People in the West have often perceived African women as victims of oppression rather than as agents of change. Yet women in many African countries are frequently the primary economic providers for their households, working as farmers and traders. This complicated power structure challenges Western understandings of marriage and households as partnerships in which men are the main providers, and household funds are pooled. When women challenge the web of social relationships, as in South Asia, opponents appeal to custom and tradition as against "colonial" influences.

The education of girls is often an issue between advocates of gender equality and the resident power structure in many African nations. Schools both strengthen social values about femininity and reinforce domesticity in girls. For example, nutrition education programs focus on how meager resources can be used to greatest effect, but if girls were encouraged to understand the causes of food scarcity, they might challenge policy. African governments frequently point to great improvements in education for girls and women by publishing statistics reflecting a strong commitment in education. Interpreting data published by governments is problematic, however, because statistics are notoriously unreliable in the developing world. Statistics often create the illusion of precision and certainty, but that illusion serves political ends by projecting a positive image while obscuring political indifference.

Even those girls in African countries who are well educated often are not able to translate schooling into self-determination. Professional women sometimes find that because of social influences, their husbands make most of the decisions that affect their lives. More education might mean less control over one's life. No single generalization is possible.

African women are usually portrayed as a powerless group subject to poverty and ignorance, in contrast to Western women, who are portrayed as educated, modern, and free to make their own choices. These portrayals often lead to programs that reinforce patriarchal ideology and inequalities. Women in African countries may have access to programs that stress women's health and reproductive issues, and while these programs are useful, emphasis on such issues recognizes unequal power relations in the family but does not address ways to remove gender stereotypes.

Reformers in African countries should address women's problems in a multi-faceted way. Local women need support from grassroots movements as well as recognition from international groups. African women are rarely asked to help design programs and strategies because standards for evaluation are frequently projections of Western analyses and models. Women in Africa must be asked to project their own goals for their own futures; they should be allowed to trust their own insights as the basis for resolving issues of gender equality.

Socialism and State Power

International politics as well as historical events often affect attitudes toward women today. Countries that have undergone radical political change demonstrate the interaction of the personal and the political. The rapid disintegration of a socialist or Communist political system does not mirror a parallel change in gender relations.

In socialist societies, the view of women reflects that of the German political philosopher Karl Marx and the German socialist Friedrich Engels: that the subordination of women is just another aspect of class oppression. Engels believed that with the abolition of private property and the integration of women into work, women would gain economic independence and equality. The flaw in this construction is that male control of female sexuality and inheritance predates the existence of the bourgeois family and industrialization. In reality, in socialist societies the male political leadership often had much the same view of the role of women as did their bourgeois counterparts.

The notion of a large socialist family was quickly established as a desirable goal, and so abortion was abolished in the Soviet Union in 1936. The state encouraged women to remain primarily responsible for child care as well as to accept employment in the public arena. This Soviet model of women's dual role was quickly adopted as the basis of state policy in Eastern Europe, and the needs of the state took precedence over those of women. Because women were primarily responsible for activities in the private sphere, they frequently received blame for social problems such as juvenile crime and alcoholism, which were not addressed by the state.

Under the socialist system, radical measures were implemented on maternity leave and child care, but they were not progressive enough because parenthood was seen as the exclusive purview of women. Because of their heavy domestic duties, women were increasingly displaced in labor and political arenas. When we see this from a gendered perspective, this is not true reform.

These gender stereotypes and inequalities remained in effect during the post-revolutionary period, but little attention is given to this area because the focus is on economic reforms. Just as the socialist system influenced by Marx and Engels did not bring true equality for women, we have no reason to suppose that a free market economy and democratic elections will change male dominance and female subordination. No single women's movement has emerged in Eastern Europe or in the nations of the former Soviet Union. The millions of ethnically and regionally disparate women would be unlikely to identify with a single movement, and little assistance is offered by the rest of the world, which is focused on political and economic issues.

Culture and Change: China

China presents an interesting amalgam of the gendered views of the socialist state, but with distinctive regional and social differences. Traditionally, people in China viewed women as having a passive role in society, and this view was further complicated by the term *feminist*. People viewed feminism as a Western concept, hence a bourgeois concept to be avoided. The first women's emancipation movement in China came about as a result of state-initiated policy. In 1949, with the establishment of the People's Republic of China, the new socialist Chinese government decided to prohibit such oppressive customs as the binding of women's feet and prostitution. The official policy was to advocate full women's employment. Women were given the rights to education, the vote, and full employment. Because jobs were assigned, however, women were frequently channeled into inferior or powerless positions. This fact was not recognized because women's rights were seen as having been achieved through the efforts of the state, with no input or effort from the women themselves.

As was the case in the former Soviet Union, the People's Republic of China shaped gender relationships to suit the interests of central policy. Although massive changes were introduced during the 1950s, during the Cultural Revolution (1966–1976) the use of oppositional terms such as *right–wrong, correct thought–incorrect thought*, and *socialist–bourgeois* served to outline what was acceptable. No organization of women working for change could exist because under the rule of the Cultural Revolution, women already had equality.

Despite legislation, a large gap remained between women's legal status and their social status. Gender issues affected power relations between women and men in that, as in the former Soviet nations, the idea that women are mainly responsible for standards of morality and family order was presented as "scientific fact." This idea that nature subjects women to lives dominated by reproductive concerns permeates Chinese approaches to education and employment. At the same time, the state is not a gender-neutral domain of power. More than any other Chinese state activity, the imposition of family planning that allowed only one child per family has been represented in the United States, especially during the Reagan-Bush era, as the quintessence of Communist oppression.

Recent movements toward privatization and a market economy have brought no improvement in women's autonomy in China. When privatization began in 1977, the idea that emancipation came not from individual efforts but rather from the state remained firmly in place. Further difficulties were introduced with the dissolution of the planned economy; now women have more difficulty in getting jobs because competition favors men, and women often must resign when they have a child.

The experiences of 1995's Fourth World Conference on Women held in Beijing provide a lesson in the cultural differences in women's movements. The Chinese women's movement that emerged from the Fourth World Conference is characterized by groups who are interested in promoting social change rather than depending on the Chinese state to improve the conditions of women. The groups and their tactics, however, are interesting reflections of the Chinese approach. No mass membership groups with demonstrations and organized displays exist as in the West, but rather the Chinese movement focuses more on service and voluntary work. Many people concentrate on scholarly work in women's studies centers at universities. Such groups are careful not to impinge upon state authority but instead to provide assistance to women or to increase knowledge. They concentrate on issues that are not addressed by the state. In this way, the state recognizes that certain types of social movements are not a threat to its power. The women's groups present issues of particular interest such as reproductive health, domestic violence, and sexual harassment as being global in nature. This presentation removes any critical tone that could be applied to the Chinese power structure, and so the power structure is more willing to tolerate steps to improve conditions in these areas. Work by women on reforms may be beneficial even to the state because the state is unwilling to pursue certain activities.

These particularly Chinese facets of a women's movement provides a counter-example to the stereotype of a rigid, inflexible Chinese Communist regime. Chinese women are able to work toward reform and still appear cooperative rather than confrontational. The use of negotiation shows that gender attitudes and methods of reform are deeply rooted in culture and cannot be viewed as universal in nature.

Gender Past and Future

Women around the globe are divided by their histories, by their class or income levels, by the political basis of their nation, by their religious beliefs, and by their social expectations. The one fundamental similarity, however, in each culture is that gender provides a basis for discrimination and deprivation. We cannot prescribe one plan of action to improve the lot of women everywhere, but the recognition that gender is a crucial aspect in the consideration of political and economic reform is an essential beginning. Solutions to gender inequities are best constructed by women working together within a culture to negotiate change that is acceptable to the dominant power structure rather than presenting a universal program that may cause unintended results. Women's emancipation movements are global in scope because gender disparities occur everywhere, but the problems suffered and solutions undertaken vary widely. Gender may be universal, but no universal solution to gender inequities exists.

Further Reading

Bloch, M.; Beoku-Betts, J. A.; & Tabachnick, B. R. (Eds.). (1998). *Women and education in sub-Saharan Africa: Power, opportunities, and constraints.* Boulder, CO: Lynne Rienner.

Bolt, C. (1995). *Feminist ferment: "The woman question" in the USA and England.* London: UCL Press.

Bryceson, D. F. (Ed.). (1995). *Women wielding the hoe: Lessons from rural Africa for feminist theory and development practice.* Oxford, U.K.: Berg.

Chaudhuri, M. (1993). *Indian women's movement: Reform and revival*. London: Sangam Books.

Connolly, L. (2002). *The Irish women's movement: From revolution to devolution*. New York: Palgrave.

Evans, H. (1997). *Women and sexuality in China: Dominant discourses of female sexuality and gender since 1949*. Cambridge, U.K.: Polity Press.

Gilmartin, C. K.; Hershatter, G.; Rofel, L.; & White, T. (Eds.). (1994). *Engendering China: Women, culture, and the state*. Cambridge, MA: Harvard University Press.

Hahner, J. E. (1990). *Emancipating the female sex: The struggle for women's rights in Brazil, 1850–1940*. Durham, NC: Duke University Press.

Hodgson, D. L. & McCurdy, S. A. (Eds.). (2001). *"Wicked" women and the reconfiguration of gender in Africa*. Portsmouth, NH: Heinemann.

Jaquette, J. S. (Ed.). (1989). *The women's movement in Latin America: Feminism and the transition to democracy*. Boston: Unwin Hyman.

Jaquette, J. S. (Ed.). (1994). *The women's movement in Latin America: Participation and democracy*. Boulder, CO: Westview Press.

Kumar, R. (1993). *The history of doing: An illustrated account of movements for women's rights and feminism in India 1800–1990*. London: Verso.

Major, A. (2010). *Sovereignty and social reform in India: British colonialism and the campaign against sati, 1830–1860*. Abingdon: Routledge.

Rai, S.; Pilkington, H.; & Phizacklea, A. (Eds.). (1992). *Women in the face of change: The Soviet Union, Eastern Europe and China*. London: Routledge.

Wesoky, S. (2002). *Chinese feminism faces globalization*. New York: Routledge.

Women's Suffrage in the United States

Denise R. JOHNSON, PhD
Independent Historian

The nineteenth century was witness to numerous social reform movements, with women's suffrage among the most prominent. The suffrage movement began in 1848 and was led by Susan B. Anthony and Elizabeth Cady Stanton. The fight for women's rights expanded after the passage of the Nineteenth Amendment, granting women the right to the vote. During the following decades, women continued to agitate for change, leading to the women's movement, which permanently altered the American social landscape.

Women in the United States, beginning in 1848, fought for three-quarters of a century to gain the right to vote. Women's suffrage, along with abolition of slavery and reformations of labor, was one of the three greatest reforms in US society. The suffrage movement was born from female activism led by women such as Elizabeth Cady Stanton (1815–1902) and Susan B. Anthony (1820–1906), who brought women across the nation into the movement and helped pave the road to equality for future generations of women. The outstanding leadership of early suffragists like Anthony and Stanton sparked the interest of future generations of suffragists, who joined the national crusade as leaders and participants in the women's suffrage movement.

Women historically have engaged themselves in a wide array of reform movements. As it turns out, many of the reform movements of the nineteenth century occurred simultaneously and were led by women who counted among their primary goals the vote for women. The women's suffrage movement was not an isolated event; rather, it stemmed from the abolition movement and other reform movements that came about through the moral reforms proposed by evangelical Protestantism during the 1830s. Acting on moral principles and church dogma, men and women alike sought to reform an ailing society riddled with social injustices that included slavery and intemperance. Some women participated in the public sphere as abolition agents and as public speakers for the emancipation of slaves. Others worked for a temperate society under the leadership of moral reform groups such as the Women's Christian Temperance Union. Temperance societies believed that curtailing alcohol consumption would help alleviate violence in society, control domestic strife, and eradicate child abuse and neglect. Women often worked harmoniously among male reformers, and many women accepted their gendered space within the hierarchy of a male-dominated society. As more women became exposed to public activism and public speaking, however, many began to reject the restrictions placed on them by church leaders, male officials, and dominating spouses and fathers. Conflicting views regarding women's roles in public activism led to heated debates and splits within various churches.

Women's Suffrage during the Pre-Civil War Era

Churches in the United States during the eighteenth and nineteenth centuries promoted clearly defined roles for men and women in society. Most of the United States exercised a system of separate spheres in which women were expected to be keepers of the home and of morality. As a result, women had relatively little activity in the public sphere, thus making the private sphere of motherhood and housewifery their lot in life. Women were to be of pure heart, chaste, pious, and, above all else, submissive to their husbands and God. Men, on the other hand, were allowed to exercise their authority in both the home and in public. Masculine privilege from the colonial period until the late nineteenth century included controlling property in marriage, having sole custody of children if divorce occurred, and having the right to serve in public office and the right to vote. Religious ideology brought from England and other countries kept the notion of separate spheres in place. Church rhetoric was occasionally redefined by progressive religions, however, in a way that afforded women the opportunity for greater autonomy and equality in the United States. For example, religious sects such as the Quakers held strong egalitarian principles, and because of conflicts over slavery and other issues that denied basic human morality, splits in the sect occurred. One progressive Quaker group, the Hicksites, believed that slavery was morally wrong on all levels. Likewise, the Hicksites allowed women a fuller range of activism, including public speaking. It is no coincidence that many of the most outspoken leaders for women's suffrage were Quaker women such as Lucretia Mott (1793–1880) and Susan B. Anthony. Other churches did not allow female leadership in church or public life, however. Many churches supported slavery and restricted the lives of women. These churches exercised a hierarchy based on traditional patriarchy and embellishments or misinterpretations of the Bible in order to support gender oppression and racial superiority.

In spite of restrictions on their lives, many women refused to be silent and passive in a male-dominated society. By the 1840s, many reform movements outgrew their religious origins and became increasingly secularized. The secularization of reform movements created conflict between church leaders and women of the movements. Women such as the sisters Angelina and Sarah Grimke took to task clergymen who sought to contain the outspoken leadership of women. Men such as William Lloyd Garrison (1805–1879) added to the anticlerical agitation with their secularized views, which gained a stronghold during the 1840s. Garrison proposed the immediate release of slaves in bondage and argued for the common humanity of both blacks and whites. Paramount to Garrison's rhetoric was the belief that a revolution in people's ideas must precede and underlie institutional and legal reform. Garrison put many clergy in an uproar over his notions of equality. Prior to Garrison's declarations, the clergy controlled women's moral energy, thus containing the public activism of zealous female leaders. The abolition movement during the 1840s was the catalyst for women leaders such as the Grimke sisters, Lucretia Mott, Elizabeth Cady Stanton, Lucy Stone, and later Susan B. Anthony in advocating a society that supported equal rights for women. Societies emerging from the Northeast to Indiana and Ohio all had a common goal—equal rights for women, with suffrage as the main goal.

Seneca Falls and the Women Question

As reform movements became secularized, women such as Susan B. Anthony and Elizabeth Cady Stanton emerged as some of the most tenacious leaders. Garrisonian rhetoric of immediatism, which proposed the complete emancipation of slaves, was utilized within the suffrage movement and called for the swift and complete enfranchisement of women; thus the demand for total equality became fundamental to the women's rights movement. Initially women leaders sought to reform property laws for married women, divorce laws, and child custody laws. Some historians have suggested that women's suffrage stemmed from Garrison's abolition rhetoric; given the overall upheaval in US society, however, advocating suffrage may have been a natural inclination for disgruntled and disenfranchised women. In 1848, Elizabeth Cady Stanton and Lucretia Mott organized the first women's rights convention, which was held in Seneca Falls, New York, with more than five hundred women attending. Stanton modeled the convention's Declaration of Sentiments after the preamble of the Declaration of Independence, and at the top of the list of grievances was the lack of the vote for women. Stanton, Mott, and other participants realized that the vote would give women access to the public arena and help them fight inequalities protected by unfair laws. Although the Seneca Falls convention captured national attention, and women swelled the ranks of suffragists, equal voting rights for women would not be gained until 1920. Nonetheless, the seeds of discontent had been sown.

Early Leaders

The women's suffrage movement did not emerge as a monolithic event during the nineteenth century. As education for women improved and religious mores became less restrictive, women emerged as determined advocates of suffrage. Elizabeth Cady Stanton and Susan B. Anthony deserve their accolades; however, the women's suffrage movement was led by many women. Like Stanton and Anthony, these women found their motivation for suffrage activism in other arenas of social reform. The early feminists, beginning before the Civil War, gradually moved into the public sphere of activism. The notion of separate spheres for men and women continued to exist in the United States in the mid-nineteenth century, and misogynistic rhetoric continued through social and family customs, church teachings, and restrictive genders laws.

Among the early suffrage leaders were Angelina (1805–1879) and Sarah Grimke (1792–1873). At first glance the Grimke sisters would not have appeared to be likely social reformers. They were born in South Carolina, the daughters of a prominent slaveholder. Their emergence, as Southern women, into the public sphere of social reform during the 1830s was unusual. Both sisters, after experiencing the horrors of slavery firsthand, worked for the abolition of slavery. Their personal convictions came at great personal cost: They were cut off from family wealth and severed their Southern ties permanently. By 1836 the Grimke sisters had become outspoken members of Garrison's American Anti-Slavery Society, speaking out against slavery and for women's rights. Although their public speaking earned them much scorn, they refused to be cowed by ministers who spoke out against women's public activism and advocated slavery. Women such as the Grimke sisters began to absorb the anticlerical message of Garrison and emerged as leaders for women's rights and suffrage. Sarah argued that men and women were created equal in God's eyes and that virtue is not a particular attribute of one gender over the other. Some male abolitionists sought to contain the outspoken sisters, but their message had already been heard and their leadership established. As a result, the Grimke sisters were followed by other women who took an anticlerical stance and applied those principles to their lives and used them in the fight for equality.

Susan B. Anthony

Of all the prewar activists, Susan B. Anthony was likely the most committed in her leadership. Anthony simply would not settle for less than the complete dedication of her peers to enfranchisement of women. Between the years of 1854 and 1860 Anthony canvassed New York, seeking new members for the women's suffrage movement. Her efforts for "the cause" led many small-town suffragettes to lead small groups of feminists to fight for the vote. Likewise, Lucy Stone (1818–1893) and many others, including men, continued to encourage disgruntled women to take a stance against the inequalities of their male-dominated society. Elizabeth Cady Stanton, fully enmeshed in a life of domesticity and motherhood, continued to contribute to the movement when she could. The suffrage movement grew slowly, however, and was stifled by the Civil War. Many feminists put their energies into the war effort—making bandages and clothing, caring for the sick and wounded, alleviating the suffering of runaway slaves, and continuing to fight for abolition. Not until after the war and passage of the Fourteenth and Fifteenth Amendments, granting African Americans citizenship and black males voting rights, did women reemerge as determined suffragists. After the war in 1865, enfranchisement moved to the forefront of the women's rights movement, creating schisms within the movement regarding enfranchisement of black men and the continuing disenfranchisement of all women.

Postwar Suffrage Strategies and Strife

By 1869, two women's suffrage organizations emerged from the American Equal Rights Association that had formerly been led by Elizabeth Cady Stanton and Susan B. Anthony. The two groups had conflicting views over voting rights for black males that resulted from the passing of the Fifteenth Amendment. The women of the National Woman Suffrage Association (NWSA) believed that women should have been awarded the franchise before black men. The NWSA was led exclusively by women and sought legal recourse through federal legislation. The organization became more radical, resulting in a large array of feminist agendas. The NWSA attracted numerous charismatic members such as Fanny Wright (1795–1852) and Victoria Woodhull (1838–1927), both of whom supported women's suffrage but also had personal agendas under the umbrella of women's rights. Numerous utopian movements and radical reform movements became a part of the rapidly changing landscape of the postwar United States. The free love movement proposed by Victoria Woodhull, Fanny Wright, and others proved shocking to conservative citizens and was rejected in many circles. Radical reforms such as vegetarianism and spiritualism were short-lived or rejected by mainstream society. Overall, the alternative cultures that emerged during the latter half of the nineteenth century demonstrate that the nation was progressing toward modernity and that the fight for women's enfranchisement would not be stifled. Nineteenth-century women would continue to fight for the vote along with the most radical reformers who held personal liberty as the truest form of freedom. Members of the NWSA held to the anticlerical views adopted early in the movement and refused to use exclusionary tactics.

As a result of the conflict over the Fifteenth Amendment, a second organization—a conservative branch of the women's suffrage movement—emerged and became known as the American Women's Suffrage Association (AWSA). AWSA was led by Lucy Stone and her husband, Henry Blackwell, and unlike NWSA, had both male and female members and leaders. A longtime comrade of Anthony and Stanton, Stone broke away from NWSA over the Fifteenth Amendment. Stone was responsible for the 1869 schism that set feminists at odds with each other. AWSA rejected the radical position of the NWSA and rejected inclusion of members such as Woodhull. The strategies Stone, Blackwell, and other members used included appealing to state legislatures to gradually gain women enfranchisement over time. As time passed the two organizations realized that their strength would be greater united, and the two groups merged in 1890 as the National American Woman Suffrage Association (NAWSA).

A New Generation of Suffragettes

Elizabeth Cady Stanton, Susan B. Anthony, and Lucy Stone led the newly emerged NAWSA. Anthony was elected president and retained the leadership until 1900. After Stanton published *The Women's Bible* (a critical look at the Bible) in 1895, NAWSA considered her too radical, and the organization distanced itself from her. Leaders of NAWSA continued to demand a constitutional amendment but also realized that the support of individual states was vital to the success of the movement and put more emphasis on state victories.

The NAWSA felt the support of Southern women was crucial, and the organization tolerated segregation in its state affiliates. This practice came to a head at a historic Washington, DC, suffrage march in 1913, when activist NAWSA officials told antilynching crusader and journalist Ida B. Wells-Barnett (1862–1931) that she and other African American women would not be allowed to march with their state affiliates, and instead would have to stay together as a group at the back of the parade. In reaction to racism within the women's suffrage movement and to focus on educating African American women on the need for all women to obtain the vote,

69

a number of black women's suffrage organizations emerged, led by Barnett; Mary Church Terrell (1863–1954), one of the first African American women to earn a college degree; and others.

Progressivism and the Vote

Around 1900, progressive reforms swept the nation in response to wide-scale poverty, vice, and overall social upheaval brought about by the Industrial Revolution, unfair economic and regulatory practices, and an increasingly corrupt political system. Labor organizers and social reformers fought for relief, and the Progressive Era ushered in corresponding legislation to alleviate political and social problems. Unlike in early reform movements, all classes of society became part of the progressive reform movement, and as a result suffragists gained a wider audience. Leaders such as Alice Paul (1885–1997) created the National Women's Party, and Carrie Chapman Catt (1859–1947) created a "winning plan." During World War I Catt encouraged state suffrage leaders to appeal to national representatives and to drop suffrage work in support of the war. Catt's goal was for the movement to appear patriotic to President Wilson, who could send suffrage legislation through Congress. Catt's plan worked, and Wilson submitted to Congress the Women's Suffrage Amendment, which was passed on to the states in 1919. In spite of the political resistance of the antisuffragists, on 26 August 26 1920, three-fourths of the state legislatures ratified the Nineteenth Amendment, giving women full voting rights. By the summer of 1920, women had gained the right to vote in a special session arranged by President Wilson in Nashville, Tennessee. Through the hard work and leadership of several generations of women, the moment of victory had finally arrived.

Further Reading

Anthony, K. (1954). *Susan B. Anthony: Her personal history and her era.* New York: New York University Press.

Archer, J. (1991). *Breaking barriers.* New York: Viking Penguin.

Auster, A. (1984). *Actresses and suffragists: Women in the American theatre, 1890–1920.* New York: Praeger.

Barry, K. (1988). *Susan B. Anthony: A biography of a singular feminist.* New York: New York University Press.

Buechler, S. (1990). *Women's movements in the United States: Women suffrage, equal rights, and beyond.* New Brunswick, NJ: Rutgers University Press.

Burns, K. & Ward, G. C. (1999). *Not for ourselves alone.* New York: Alfred A. Knopf.

Daley, C. & Nolan, M. (Eds.). (1995). *Suffrage and beyond: International feminist perspectives.* New York: New York University Press.

Davis, P. (1970). *A history of the national women's rights movement.* New York: Source Book Press.

DuBois, E. (1978). *Feminism and suffrage.* Ithaca, NY: Cornell University Press.

DuBois, E. (1992). *Elizabeth Cady Stanton/Susan B. Anthony correspondence, writings, speeches* (Rev. ed.). Boston: Northeastern University Press.

DuBois, E. (1998). *Women's suffrage and women's rights.* New York: New York University Press.

Edwards, T. (1990). *Sowing good seeds: The Northwest suffrage campaigns of Susan B. Anthony.* Portland: Oregon Historical Society Press.

Flexner, E. (1975). *Century of struggle: The women's rights movement in the United States.* Cambridge, MA: Harvard University Press.

Ford, L. (1991). *Iron jawed angels: The suffrage militancy of the national women's party, 1912–1920.* Lanham, MD: University Press of America.

Frost, E. & Cullen-DuPont, K. (1992). *Women's suffrage in America: An eyewitness history.* New York: Facts on File.

Garner, L. (1984). *Stepping stones to women's liberty: Feminist ideas in the women's suffrage movement, 1900–1918.* Madison, NJ: Fairleigh Dickinson University Press.

Ginzberg, L. (1990). *Women and the work of benevolence: Morality, politics, and class in the nineteenth century United States*. New Haven, CT: Yale University Press.

Graham, S. (1996). *Woman suffrage and the new democracy*. New Haven, CT: Yale University Press.

Kerber, L. & DeHart J. (1995). *Women's America: Refocusing the past*. New York: Oxford University Press.

Kraditor, A. (1981). *Ideas of the woman suffrage movement, 1890–1920*. New York: Columbia University Press.

Lutz, A. (1976). *Susan B. Anthony: Rebel, crusader, humanitarian*. Boston: Beacon.

Melder, K. (1977). *Beginnings of sisterhood: The American woman's rights movement, 1900–1850*. New York: Schocken Books.

Rawkow, L. & Kramarae, C. (1990). *The revolution in words: Righting women, 1868–1871*. New York: Routledge.

Sherr, L. (1995). *Failure is impossible: Susan B. Anthony in her own words*. New York: Times Books.

Solomon, M. (1991). *A voice of their own: The woman suffrage press, 1840–1910*. Tuscaloosa: University of Alabama Press.

Leadership in the Women's Movement

Diane M. RODGERS
Northern Illinois University

The women's movement is a world-wide phenomenon with three waves of different leadership objectives and priorities. The first wave of suffragist leaders strategized around voting rights; the second wave built on this victory, challenging other institutional gender inequalities and embracing a nonhierarchical leadership style. Third wave leaders emerged from a generation who benefitted from these social changes and who utilize more formal or individualized leadership approaches and online technology to organize the ongoing fight for equality.

The women's movement has strongly influenced ideas about leadership throughout its history. The first wave of the women's movement began in the 1800s and tapered off during the 1940s as industrialized countries granted women the vote, which was one of the early goals of the movement. A revival of the women's movement termed the "second wave" began during the mid- to late-1960s, focusing on the status of women in society. As this struggle continued and positive changes occurred, a younger generation of women emerged during the 1990s with a different perspective and their generation is considered the "third wave" of the women's movement. This wave coexists with the organizations and goals of second wave feminists. During the first wave, the fact that women took leadership roles to fight for women's suffrage and other rights was significant, as it meant that women became leaders in the public sphere. And while this continued to be true to some extent during the second wave, it is also true that during the second wave women challenged traditional notions of leadership. Currently, in the third wave, some organizations within the women's movement are offering feminist leadership training, and online organizing is predominant.

The First Wave: Women's Suffrage

Women first became leaders in the women's movement during the battle for women's suffrage. New Zealand was the first country to grant women suffrage, doing so in 1893. Meri Te Tai Mangakahia (1868–1920) successfully fought for the inclusion of Maori women. (The Maori are New Zealand's indigenous population.) New

Zealand women's early victory in gaining the vote inspired leaders of the women's suffrage movement all over the world.

The fight for suffrage and other women's rights was international. The International Council of Women (ICW) was founded in 1887, with Ishbel Hamilton-Gordan, or Lady Aberdeen (1857–1939), from the United Kingdom, as its first president. The International Woman Suffrage Alliance (IWSA) was formed in 1904, with Carrie Chapman Catt (1859–1947), from the United States, as its president. Many women were influential in their own countries as well as in the international struggle for suffrage. In Japan, Ichikawa Fusae (1893–1981) was one of the founders of Fusen Kaku-toku Domei (Women's Suffrage League). She led the women's suffrage movement in Japan, which granted the franchise for women, the right to be a candidate, and to attend political meetings in 1945. Subsequent to these victories, Fusae was elected to the parliament five separate times between the years of 1953–1980. Huda Shaarawi, (1879–1947), founded the Egyptian Feminist Union in 1923 and was its president for twenty-four years. The EFU fought for women's suffrage, advances in education, and legal reforms for women. Shaarawi was the vice president of the International Alliance of Women for Suffrage and Equal Citizenship in 1935.

Connections with Other Movements

The women's movement in the first wave was not only international but also addressed issues of race and class oppression. Feminist leaders were strengthened by their ties to other movements, even when controversy and disagreement arose between leaders of these movements. Many women were involved in the struggle for women's rights and the right of labor to organize and were leaders in both of these areas. Kate Mullany (1845–1906) is an example of a woman who was both a feminist and a labor leader. She worked with Susan B. Anthony and others suffragists on the needs of women workers, and in 1864 formed the Collar Laundry Union, the first female union in the United States.

Leadership Differences and Shifting Priorities

Splits in leadership during the first wave of feminism occurred over whether to embrace a liberal, single-issue agenda or a more far-reaching, multi-issue agenda. Leadership styles differed not only over philosophical ideas but also over whether to use moderate or militant tactics. For instance, although not all women and men in the suffrage movement in Britain embraced militancy, British suffragettes were known for their militant leadership. While the president of Britain's National Union of Women's Suffrage Societies (NUWSS), Millicent Garrett Fawcett (1847–1929), favored a means of change through legal reform within the existing political system, Emmeline and Christabel Pankhurst (1858–1928; 1880–1958), mother and daughter suffragists who were prominent leaders of the more militant branch of suffragettes, favored direct action by way of lawful and unlawful protests. Their organization, the Women's Social and Political Union (WSPU) began utilizing destruction of property as a more militant tactic beginning in 1908, including breaking windows of government buildings and forcing entrance into the House of Commons. Once arrested for these tactics, the women initiated hunger strikes in further protest. Some members left the WSPU when leaders decided on arson as a tactic; more arrests ensued as some buildings were destroyed. The same split between moderates and militants emerged in the US women's suffrage movement as well, when Alice Paul (1885–1977), a young radical American woman influenced by the British suffragettes, left the NWSA and founded the Congressional Union for Woman Suffrage in 1914. The latter utilized such direct action tactics as strikes, demonstrations, and parades. Alice Paul later founded the National Woman's Party in 1916 and is credited with helping pass the Nineteenth Amendment (granting women the vote) to the US Constitution in 1920. She subsequently turned her leadership skills towards passage of the Equal Rights Amendment, which was introduced to Congress in 1923.

The Second Wave

As in the first wave of the women's movement, the second wave was divided between those with a reform orientation and those favoring more radical approaches. Reform organizations tended to be more bureaucratically structured, with designated leaders holding appointed offices. The goals of these organizations were usually various political reforms. The leaders were generally expected to be spokespersons and to oversee the direction of the organization. The more radical branches of the movement utilized collective leadership, rotated leadership, or rejected the idea of leadership altogether. The goals of the radical branches included the creation of an alternative women's culture through the development of independent women's presses, recording companies, bookstores, music festivals and coffeehouses. Women involved in forming a viable alternative women's culture tended to use terms such as *organizer* or *cultural worker* rather than *leader*. Many of the organizations, both moderate and radical, created during the second wave still exist, and some aspects of the women's alternative culture have even been adopted by the mainstream culture.

The Development of Nonhierarchical Leadership

One distinct form of leadership that emerged from the second wave of the women's movement was nonhierarchical leadership, which was embraced to varying extents by both moderate and radical groups. At least ideologically, this leadership style existed in the leftist organizations of the 1960s, which many women had been involved in before becoming involved in the women's movement. Nonhierarchical leadership runs counter to many common ideas and theories concerning leaders: The usual definition being that a leader persuades others to become followers based on the leader's personal characteristics, such as a charismatic personality. The followers agree to give the leader authority and adopt the leader's vision.

The women's movement redefined leadership because of the feminist conception of power. For women fighting male domination, the concept of having power over another person was unacceptable. Therefore, rather than seeking power over others, the leaders of the women's movement wanted to empower one another to share leadership. Consciousness-raising (CR) groups of the 1960s and 1970s fostered this type of collective sharing of leadership. Because the purpose of CR groups was to share personal feelings, no woman was felt to be able to speak for another woman. The CR groups became a model of shared leadership. The absence of formal leadership was not without its detractors, however, who argued that the lack of structure made it possible for women who were more outgoing or more opinionated to dominate, despite the ideal of power sharing.

The nonhierarchical, shared leadership style of the women's movement has influenced other organizations, including those in the business world, which have begun to move away from the idea of a single, charismatic leader who issues top-down directives and toward a less hierarchical model, as exemplified by concepts such as team leadership.

Media Representation of the Second Wave

Few women would claim to be leaders of a group within the women's movement, let alone the entire women's movement. But this lack of a single leader has been hard for those outside the women's movement to accept. The mainstream media in particular has pressured organizations within the movement to produce a leader; when they don't, the media will designate someone as the leader. In the United States, several women have been dubbed the leaders of the women's movement by the media, and the media has relied on them to speak for the movement. This was useful for furthering the movement's causes, but it also distorted the idea of leadership in the movement.

Gloria Steinem (b. 1934) was one the most prominent media spokespersons for the women's movement in the United States. She was the co-founder and first editor of *Ms.*, a mainstream feminist magazine that began publication in 1972. Throughout the 1970s, Steinem joined the lawyer Florynce (Flo) Kennedy (1916–2000) on the lecture circuit. Flo Kennedy was a feminist and civil rights activist known for her outspoken style and coalition building. In 1971, she founded the Feminist Party, which nominated the first African-American congresswoman, Shirley Chisholm (1924–2005), for president. In 1973, Kennedy co-founded the National Black Feminist Organization. Other visible spokespersons for the women's movement include Betty Friedan (1921–2006), who wrote *The Feminine Mystique* (1963), a book that described the dilemma of the middle-class housewife. Friedan was one of the founders and the first president of the National Organization for Women (NOW), an organization of feminist activists founded in1966. Bella Abzug (1920–1998) was a feminist congresswoman who co-founded the Women's Environment and Development Organization (WEDO) in 1990. Eleanor Smeal (b. 1939) became president of NOW during the second-wave fight for the slightly re-worded Equal Rights Amendment of 1923; Smeal remains a spokesperson and lobbyist for NOW and co-founded the Feminist Majority Foundation in 1987.

Challenges and Divisions within the US Women's Movement

The development of "media stars" created a rift in viewpoints about feminist leadership. Prominent feminists were highly criticized by others in the movement for taking on such leadership roles, which were seen as self-serving "power trips." That strong criticism led some women to withhold their skills and abilities and to downplay any charismatic tendencies so as not to appear to be taking on leadership roles. It also resulted in a counter critique, as some designated leaders felt that "trashing"—the slang term used for criticizing women for taking leadership roles—was creating weakness within the movement.

The fact that most of the well-known feminists in the United States were white and middle class led to a sometimes divisive and misinformed view of the leadership, goals, and demography of the women's movement. Actual racism and classism encountered within the women's movement was also problematic. Women of color such as Gloria Anzaldúa (1942–2004) and Cherríe Moraga (b. 1952), both Chicana feminists, and Barbara Smith (b. 1946), an African-American feminist, challenged the women's movement to expand its awareness to include the intersection of race, class, and gender. Because of the ongoing work of these and other women of color, a more diverse theory and practices arose within the women's movement.

Another divisive leadership issue that occurred early in the second wave was reaction to the increasing visibility of lesbians as leaders within the women's movement. Afraid that the visible presence of lesbians would discredit the movement, during the early 1970s, the National Organization for Women disavowed lesbians within the organization and the movement, labeling them "The Lavender Menace." This in turn mobilized lesbian feminist leaders to organize for lesbian rights within the women's movement and the larger culture. This challenge in the long run encouraged the leaders of NOW to become more inclusive of women regardless of their sexual orientation.

Expanding towards an International Scope

During the second wave, the women's movement grew internationally. Several important forums and organizations served as a way for feminists to create worldwide coalitions. Perhaps the most visible forums for women worldwide have been the official UN world conferences and the parallel conferences for nongovernmental organizations (www.unwomen.org). The first UN conference for women was the World Conference of the International Women's Year, held in Mexico City in 1975. Following this in 1980, the World Conference of the UN Decade for Women was held in Copenhagen, Denmark. The World Conference to Review and Appraise the Achievements of the UN Decade of Women was held in Nairobi, Kenya, in 1985. Some of the early international issues concerning women were: equal rights, property gains, gains in political and economic power, violence against women, recognition of the importance of unpaid work, and improvements in paid work for women. The Fourth World Conference on Women was held in Beijing, China in 1995. Nearly 17,000 women from more than 180 countries took part in the Beijing conference, and women leaders developed the Platform for Action, arrived at by consensus over twelve days of negotiations, that addressed concerns of women worldwide. Women leaders from nongovernmental organizations (NGOs) organized an independent forum near Beijing to be held simultaneously with 30,000 in attendance. The NGO forums were important because they were more inclusive than the delegations sent by nations to the official UN conference. The Beijing conference was the largest gathering of women in history thus far.

At present, women from around the world who are fighting for human rights, environmental concerns, land use, and sovereignty rights have become influential leaders in the international women's movement and in their own nations. These women are pressing the international women's movement to adopt priorities that go beyond individual rights and the agendas of developed countries. In much of the world, women are involved in agriculture or are low-paid factory workers and therefore directly affected by development efforts and globalization. At Beijing, Vandana Shiva, scientist, author, eco-feminist, and founder of the Research Foundation for Science, Technology and Ecology, spoke on gender justice and development issues. Winona LaDuke, co-chair and one of the founders of the Indigenous Women's Network, presented concerns over land stewardship and sovereignty rights. Human rights, land, and the environment have become important issues for the women's movement.

The Third Wave and the Future of Feminism

As the second wave continued to organize, the daughters of second-wave feminists and a generation of younger women emerged to form a new perspective of feminism that they describe as the "third wave" of the women's movement. In Western industrialized countries, most third-wave feminist leaders have grown up with the gains achieved by members of the second wave and have been exposed to feminist ideas, organizations, and culture while young. The establishment of women's studies departments on university campuses during the second wave has meant that there is now a cohort of young women and men who have been taught the theories of the women's movement in the classroom. Curricula at the primary and secondary level have changed as well, with today's young students being exposed to information about women leaders throughout history.

Within the third wave of feminism there was a shift in attitude about leadership that is evident in the development of formal leadership training. The Feminist Majority Foundation began offering a feminist leader campus program in 1994. Currently the Feminist Majority Leadership Alliances are student-run campus groups that focus on issues such as sexual assault, reproductive rights and international feminism. They receive guidance from campus organizers, information online regarding starting and maintaining a group, and specific leadership skills such as public speaking and dealing with the press. In turn, one of their programs of outreach to the community is to mentor high school girls. The Third Wave Foundation, founded in 1997, is an organization run by girls and women ages fifteen to thirty, and offers support in leadership training and grants for young women organizers. The foundation emphasizes coalition building, as evidenced in their program Reaching Out Across Movements (ROAM), in which young women travel to and meet with other progressive organizations (www.thirdwavefund.org). Third wave feminists use the idea of the intersectionality of identity, setting aside any homogenous notions of women and "women's issues" and thereby broadening the notion of leadership or membership in the feminist movement as well (Crenshaw 1989).

Besides the benefit of formal training in leadership and early exposure to feminist ideas, third-wave feminists have access to new forms of communication, such as social media, which they can use for organizing. Third-wave feminists also distribute their messages through music, events, and publications including independent magazines online referred to as "zines" (www.feministezine). The increasing use of online technologies may also foster a more individual style of leadership that has developed among third wave feminists (Iannello 2010). Some have even begun to claim that online feminism actually constitutes a fourth wave (Cochrane 2013). While they forge a twenty-first-century vision of feminism, with new theories and methods of action, these later waves of feminism are also involved in protecting some of the rights that they grew up with, such as reproductive freedom. The leaders of the third wave and the emerging fourth wave of the women's movement are currently shaping the future through their words and actions and continuing the fight for women's rights.

Further Reading

Ashby, R. & Gore Ohrn, D. (Eds.). (1995). *Herstory: Women who changed the world*. New York: Viking.

Baumgardner, J. & Richards, A. (2000). *Manifesta: Young women, feminism, and the future*. New York: Farrar, Straus and Giroux.

Baumgardner J. (2011). *F'em: Goo Goo, Gaga and some thoughts on balls*. Berkeley, CA: Seal Press.

Bunch, C. (1987). *Passionate politics: Feminist theory in action*. New York: St. Martin's Press.

Crenshaw, Kimberlé. (1989). Demarginalizing the intersection of race and sex: A Black feminist critique of antidiscrimination doctrine, feminist theory and antiracist politics. *University of Chicago Legal Forum*, 139–167

Cochrane, Kira.(2013). *All the rebel women: The rise of the fourth wave of feminism*. Guardianshorts ebook.

Daley, C. & Nolan, M. (1994). *Suffrage and beyond: International feminist perspectives*. New York: New York University Press.

D'Itri, P. W. (1999). *Cross currents in the international women's movement, 1848–1948*. Bowling Green, OH: Bowling Green State University Popular Press.

Ferguson, K. (1984). *The feminist case against bureaucracy*. Philadelphia: Temple University Press.

Ferree, M. M. & Martin, P. Y. (Eds.). (1995). *Feminist organizations: Harvest of the new women's movement*. Philadelphia: Temple University Press.

Hanlon, G. (1997). *Voicing power: Conversations with visionary women*. Boulder, CO: Westview Press.

hooks, b. (2007). *Ain't I a Woman: Black Women and Feminism*. Boston, MA: South End Press.

Iannelo, Kathleen. (2010). Women's Leadership and Third-Wave Feminism. *Gender and women's leadership: A reference handbook*. Ed. Karen O'Connor. Sage Publishing, 70–77.

Kennedy, F. (1976). *Color me Flo: My hard life and good times*. Englewood Cliffs, NJ: Prentice-Hall.

Kirk, G. & Okazawa-Rey, M. (1998). *Women's lives: Multicultural perspectives*. Mountain View, CA: Mayfield Publishing Company.

Koedt, A.; Levine, E.; & Rapone, A. (Eds.). (1973). *Radical feminism*. New York: Quadrangle Books.

Moraga, C. & Anzaldúa, G. [1981] (2015). *This bridge called my back*. 4th ed. NY: SUNY Press.

Radford-Hill, S. (2000). *Further to fly: Black women and the politics of empowerment*. Minneapolis, MN: University of Minneapolis Press..

Scanlon, J. (Ed.). (1999). *Significant contemporary American feminists: A biographical sourcebook*. Westport, CT: Greenwood Press.

Shaarawi, H. (1986). *Harem years: The memoirs of an Egyptian feminist* (M. Badran, Ed. & Trans.). New York: Feminist Press of the City University of New York.

Shiva, V. (Ed.). (1994). *Close to home: Women reconnect ecology, health and development worldwide*. Philadelphia: New Society Publishers.

Smith, B. (Ed.). (1983). *Home girls: A black feminist anthology*. New York: Kitchen Table Press.

Walker, R. (Ed.). (1995). *To be real: Telling the truth and changing the face of feminism*. New York: Anchor Books.

International Reproductive Rights Movement

Chandrika PAUL
Shippensburg University

Women's control of contraception and pregnancy is closely aligned to their position in society. Until the twentieth century, male-dominated governments controlled these rights. Feminists and reproductive-rights advocates called for women to be able to access health information, contraception, and abortion. These rights are not universally guaranteed, however, and abortion remains a contentious issue in many contemporary societies.

The issue of women's reproductive rights came to the fore of society in the twentieth century. Early feminists demanded access to gynecological and contraceptive information; the movement later sought to give women the ability to control their own bodies and make decisions about contraceptives and pregnancy. Feminists and activists argue such rights will give women full participation, power, and status in society.

In 1968, the United Nations International Human Rights Conference overwhelmingly declared that reproductive rights should be acknowledged as basic human rights. This conclusion was based on the rationale that a woman's right to control her own body is an expression of free will. The reality is that for women in many countries, reproductive choice is in the hands of husbands or governments. What should be a woman's most private experience is in fact controlled and shaped by economic, political, and social institutions. Therefore, feminists around the world, irrespective of their ideological and political differences, are united in their desire to see women granted reproductive rights. It is an essential precondition for women's full participation in society.

What Are Reproductive Rights?

Reproductive rights comprise the right to decide timing and spacing of children, the right to access to gynecological and contraceptive information, the freedom to choose from different birth control methods, and the right to terminate a pregnancy if desired. It is an important feminist agenda because these rights are irrevocably entwined with women's political, economic, and social status in society. In the United

States and western Europe, where women are able to control their own fertility, they enjoy, relatively speaking, a higher status in society, whereas in some countries in the developing world, such as Bangladesh, Nepal, or the Central African Republic, where women are denied access to basic information, they are in a disadvantageous state economically, socially, and politically. Lack of information results in uninformed wives and mothers, increased instances of reproductive illnesses, and high maternal and infant mortality rates. Therefore, feminists are united in the view that women around the world should be able to control their own bodies and be granted the right to choose contraceptives and make informed choices about terminating a pregnancy.

Choice before the Twentieth Century

For centuries women across the globe have used vaginal pessaries, herbal douches, the rhythm method, extended breastfeeding, and herbal concoctions to control their fertility and limit births. In strictly patriarchal countries, where boys were preferred to girls, female infanticide was practiced to limit the female population or maintain a desired sex ratio. Trying to restrict fertility is not new; what is new is the concerted effort by feminists to grant women the right to control the decision of whether or not to have children as well as the frequency and number of children, as this has a great impact on their bodies and lives. Reproductive choice, feminists argue, should be in the hands of women and not husbands or governments.

It was in the midst of the momentous changes fostered by the Industrial Revolution of 1760s that the idea of granting women reproductive rights first surfaced. As increased numbers of women were employed in factories, where pregnancy and childbirth would have an adverse effect on their employability, they turned to unreliable birth control and unsafe abortion methods in an effort to control their fertility. In the United States and Great Britain, the common perception was that abortion was not a crime until "quickening" (when the fetus begins moving). The Catholic Church at this time did not have a strong stand on the question of abortion.

In the 1870s, however, as the use of birth control and abortions grew, three groups—male medical practitioners, industrialists, and eugenicists—coalesced and called for outlawing abortion and establishing considerable male control over women's fertility. Male physicians wanted to monopolize women's health by encouraging the rapid medicalization of childbirth. This resulted in marginalizing female midwives. Industrialists wanted to increase their productivity and profits by employing more women and children. Eugenicists argued for the rapid demographic growth of peoples of European descent at the expense of "others." The US government responded with the Comstock Act of 1873, which restricted distribution of any material considered obscene; information on abortion and birth control came under the purview of this restrictive law. As a consequence, women were denied gynecological and contraceptive information.

From 1900 to the 1950s

The beginnings of the twentieth century coincided with the first battle for reproductive rights in the form of demands for access to gynecological and contraceptive information. US activists such as Margaret Sanger (1879–1966) and the socialist Emma Goldman (1869–1940) and British activists such as Marie Stopes (1880–1938) held public forums to advocate that reproductive rights were crucial to improving women's status in society. They argued that working-class and poor women be allowed access to information. Despite being publicly ridiculed, harassed, and arrested under the Comstock Act, Sanger and Goldman successfully overturned it. Sanger founded the American Birth Control League, the forerunner of today's Planned Parenthood. In Great Britain, Marie Stopes continued to campaign for more government funding to open clinics that would provide women with information that would help them to make informed choices.

But efforts to open birth control clinics both in the United States and Europe met with considerable resistance from the government as well as the church, especially during the post–World War I years. A drastic decline in birthrates prompted the United States and most European governments to attempt to control women's fertility by encouraging births. Women were rewarded for producing many children, and indeed, during the decades following World War I, women's fertility was linked to national vitality and prestige. Most European governments introduced comprehensive welfare programs to aid and encourage parenthood. At the same time, eugenicists lobbied hard to influence Western governments to control fertility by restricting the birthrate among groups deemed "socially inappropriate." Abortions and involuntary sterilizations were performed clandestinely, often in unsanitary conditions, on women belonging to these groups.

Abortion Rights

The 1960s were a major watershed in the reproductive rights movement. Women on both sides of the Atlantic discovered feminist theories linking reproductive and sexual freedom to improving the quality of their lives. They began to question their traditional roles as wives and mothers and articulated their need to control their own bodies in order to be liberated. The invention of the birth control pill (approved by the US Food and Drug Administration in 1960) was a major step in that direction, because it allowed women the freedom to be sexually active without the fear of becoming pregnant, if they so chose.

In the United States, the women's movement of the 1960s linked reproductive rights to political, social, and economic power for women in society. Feminists demanded easy access to contraceptive and gynecological information. They also exposed the hazardous conditions under which illegal abortions were performed, primarily on the poor and women of color. They stated that abortions were conducted without anesthesia and frequently in unsanitary conditions that seriously jeopardized the health of the mother.

Therefore, by 1970, the abortion issue emerged as a central issue in the women's reproductive rights movement in the United States. While moderate and liberal feminists argued for reforms in outdated abortion laws, the radicals wanted nothing less than repeal of all abortion laws and the lifting of the government's and the medical establishment's control over abortion. Their slogan was "the personal is political," and they vehemently argued that all women, irrespective of race, ethnicity, and class, should have the right to control their bodies and to choose to have an abortion.

The increased politicization of the abortion issue affected public opinion. By 1970 more and more Americans believed that abortion was a private matter and that a woman should have the right to decide what was best for her. In 1973, the US Supreme Court's *Roe v. Wade* decision granted a woman and her doctor the right to choose an abortion within the first three months of pregnancy. This was an important step toward legalizing abortion, although the right to abortion continues to be contested in the United States to this day.

Following the example of the United States, women activists across the globe are lobbying to legalize abortion. According to the United Nations, around 46 percent of women live in countries such as Germany, India, Argentina, and Saudi Arabia, where abortion is available only under certain circumstances, such as when the pregnancy was caused by incest or rape or when either the mother's health or fetal health is impaired. Around 38 percent of women live in countries such as South Africa, Norway, Holland, or the former Eastern European countries, where abortion is available upon request. In other countries, such as Chile, Malta, and Andorra, abortion is strictly forbidden.

Common Birth Control Methods

Women's ability to make informed choices about birth control is another crucial focus of the reproductive rights movement. Activists for women's reproductive rights argue that because it is the woman whose health is affected by pregnancy, a woman should be the one to make the decision regarding which birth control method to adopt. In many countries women's birth control options are not only limited, but governments, pharmaceutical companies, and husbands often impose their views. Generally speaking, there are four birth control methods: barrier methods, hormonal methods, mechanical methods, and sterilization. The first method comprises diaphragms, condoms, and the cervical cap. These contraceptives provide effective means of preventing pregnancy, and the condom has the added benefit of protecting against sexually transmitted diseases. Hormonal methods consist of birth control pills, Norplant, and Depo-Provera. The intrauterine device (IUD) is a mechanical method of birth control that is believed to work by preventing an egg from implanting in the uterine wall. There are also interuterine systems, which are essentially IUDs that dispense the hormones that prevent pregnancy. Sterilization involves a procedure called tubal ligation, in which the fallopian tubes are tied, thereby preventing eggs and sperm from meeting, and, consequently, pregnancy. Many governments use tubal ligations to forcibly restrict population growth among certain groups.

Population Control Programs

Since the mid-1990s, the reproductive rights movement has focused on population control programs. Despite the existence of the UN Convention on the Elimination of All Forms of Discrimination Against Women (CEDAW), which admonishes governments against implementing aggressive population control programs to promote national interests, most countries in the developing world have such programs, often at the expense of women's health. Governments may be either pro-natalist or anti-natalist. Feminists are critical of both groups, because both restrict women's choices, although with opposite goals.

Pro-natalist governments want to increase their nation's population; they typically outlaw abortion and contraception and seek to gain complete control over women's fertility. Prolonged warfare, loss in productivity, or even, in some instances, increasing numbers of people of racial, ethnic, or religious groups that the government considers undesirable have all been known to provoke a pro-natalist reaction. For example, in 1966 the former Romanian dictator Nicolae Ceauşescu banned abortion and encouraged women to produce as many children as possible because he wanted to increase the national productivity.

Women activists also criticize anti-natalist governments that implement coercive and selective policies. Communist China's one-child policy to restrict population growth is an example of coercive anti-natalism. In such cases the government's desire to control population growth often comes at the expense of women's health. The United States was guilty of anti-natalism in the early 1950s and 1960s, when federal funds were used to perform forced sterilization on Chicano, black, Native American, and Puerto Rican women.

It is paradoxical that while women are responsible for producing the future generations, their right to control their own bodies is limited by public and private forces. Reproductive rights, with all their ramifications, are a reflection and determinant of women's equality in society.

Further Reading

Dixon-Mueller, R. (1993). *Population policy and women's rights: Transforming reproductive choice.* Westport, CT: Praeger.

Hartmann, B. (1987). *Reproductive rights and reproductive wrongs.* New York: Harper & Row.

Hartmann, B. (1995). *Reproductive rights and wrongs: The global politics of population control.* Boston: South End Press.

Jacobson, J. L. (1992). Women's reproductive health: The silent emergency. *New Frontiers in Education, 22,* 1–54.

Birth Control Laws and Advocacy in the United States

Denise R. JOHNSON, PhD
Independent historian

For centuries, women have sought the means to control personal reproduction. While they quietly practiced birth control, often by unsafe means,
Victorian notions of morality in the nineteenth century led to the passing of the Comstock Laws, which sought to suppress birth control as well
as literature promoting it. By the 1930s, the birth control movement had
gained steam, and the pill was introduced in 1960. Abortion and family
planning continue to be hotly contested issues in some states.

Throughout history, women have actively sought safe and effective methods of
birth control. Using folk medicine to prevent unwanted pregnancies, women
often suffered real physical and psychological illnesses. Desperate women
who wished to end an unwanted pregnancy often turned to abortifacients or sought
to abort the fetus themselves. Strange concoctions could proof lethal or cause
permanent damage. Such remedies used to "alleviate menstrual blockage" often
contained ingredients such as lye, mercury, or other potentially lethal substances.
Self-induced or assisted abortions could also prove lethal or permanently debilitat-
ing. Therefore, by the nineteenth-century it became a criminal act to perform an
abortion with any type of object such as a knitting needle during the pre-quickening
stage. The Victorian mindset simply did not allow for any type of behavior deemed
as unprotective of the sanctity of life.

The desire for effective, mass-produced contraceptives fueled the birth control movement, and it gathered strength from the efforts of women like Margaret
Sanger. Commercialized by the mid-nineteenth century, contraceptives were readily available; their effectiveness, however, was often dubious. Nonetheless, early attempts to control births prevailed with some success, and by the 1870s the overall
birthrate dropped significantly. In contrast, by the 1890s the US Catholic population dramatically increased because of Eastern European Catholic immigration and
strict mandates from the pope that made using birth control a sin.

Typically, historians note socioeconomic concerns and health-related issues as
guiding factors in the emergence of the US birth control movement: the health
hazards brought about through multiple pregnancies, and the hardship of rearing
numerous children on meager resources. As immigration swelled the US urban

population during the nineteenth century, poverty became part of the national landscape. Overcrowded tenements were commonplace, and underemployment and unemployment plagued the poor. Maternal and children's health and the need for effective and affordable contraceptives emerged as a prominent issue for many US citizens, although not for the prosperous industrialists and business owners who benefited from the massive immigrant labor pools.

The working poor individuals could barely afford daily subsistence, let alone proper medical treatment. At best, poor women could obtain minimal medical treatment through charitable agencies, such as the public health departments, which some of the larger city governments sponsored. Public health entities, however, often failed to provide substantial health care or offer advice on birth control. And abortions concerned nineteenth-century conservatives, with some state legislatures seeking to restrict or outlaw the procedures.

For poor women, multiple pregnancies, poor health care during gestation, and overwork from childrearing left them in precarious health. To complicate matters, mothers were often forced by necessity to hold jobs outside the home, a situation that further eroded their health and led to child neglect. As a result, desperate women who found themselves pregnant resorted to harmful self-induced abortions or abortions performed by the unskilled, which often resulted in severe bodily trauma or death. Women who could afford them used purgatives, plant abstracts, salts, salves, douches, and other agents designed either to prevent pregnancy or to induce menses, thus aborting unwanted children.

Abortion practitioners were often arrested and jailed as restrictive laws became more pervasive by midcentury. Some physicians who merely gave out birth control advice or devices were shut down and sometimes jailed. Not only were doctors who attended to the working class unwilling to recommend contraceptives, but poor women could not afford available contraceptives like vulcanized rubber condoms, which were readily available by the 1830s. Bound by social mores and religious restrictions, especially those for Catholics, men remained reluctant to take charge of birth control.

Restrictive federal laws were in place by 1873 that forbade the public distribution of contraceptive literature and materials, a situation that resulted in political control of women's bodies under the guise of controlling vice in society. Yet, many upper- and middle-class women had fewer children and managed to control the number of their births, which suggests that certain classes of Americans were able to obtain the most effective contraceptives throughout the nineteenth century.

Opposition Leadership: Andrew Comstock

Dedicated and determined leaders led both sides of the nineteenth-century birth control controversy. At one end of the spectrum were moralists who sought to suppress all forms of birth control, which they labeled as the companion of vice. At the other end were the reformists who sought to liberate women from the hardships of overwork and multiple pregnancies. Both reformers hoped to create a better society where families could grow and create future generations of successful citizens.

Moral reformers did little to alleviate the suffering of poor women and instead punished them for seeking birth control alternatives. One ardent moralist and self-righteous spokesperson for the anti–birth control movement was Anthony Comstock, a devout Christian who emerged as a conservative social leader during the 1860s, continuing his anti-birth control crusade well into the twentieth century. Unfortunately for poor women needing birth control, Comstock's early campaigns were very effective in controlling the distribution of contraceptive devices and birth control literature. Prior to the passing of the federally mandated Comstock Laws in 1873, vice control was a matter left up to various city and precincts. For example, during Comstock's reign in New York, the local Young Men's Christian Association (YMCA) created the Committee for the Suppression of Vice. The group regularly purchased and destroyed birth control goods, shut down book dealers of supposed erotica-based literature, and took over clinics that supplied contraceptives. Eventually the YMCA became an independent operation, and Comstock went on to become the head vice investigator for the New York Society for the Suppression of Vice. By gaining the support of New York's elite citizens, Comstock effectively created an institutional base whose notions of Victorian morality were imposed on society writ large.

The Age of Comstockery and the Leadership of Margaret Sanger

During the 1870s, President Ulysses S. Grant, appointed several men as vice agents for the United States Postal Service. The job of the agents was to screen mail for pornography, literature suspected of encouraging vice, and contraceptives. Andrew Comstock became instrumental in getting legislation passed dubbed the Comstock Laws, which effectively gave the postal service the ultimate authority to suppress vice and to investigate and arrest individuals using the federal mail services to distribute items such as birth control literature and contraceptive devices. Once the restrictive legislation was in place, Comstock arrested numerous individuals, ordered the destruction of thousands of books and pamphlets deemed to be erotica, and confiscated thousands of contraceptive devices. Comstock had little sympathy for the plight of the poor, blaming them for the presence of vice in society because he believed that they lacked proper self-control.

Comstock and his supporters did not meet their goals without resistance. In the late-nineteenth century, women actively sought effective contraceptives, helping to pave the way for a full-scale birth control movement in America. Among the handful of physicians, nurses, and laypersons involved in the movement was Margaret Higgins Sanger, who fought for legal and publicly available birth control.

Sanger was born Margaret Higgins in Corning, New York, in 1879. She was one of eleven children born to first-generation Irish Americans, Michael and Anne Purcell Higgins. Her mother was a dedicated Catholic and her father was a free-thinking, atheist stonecutter prone to drinking. Interestingly enough, religious differences did not destroy the Higgins marriage, which lasted until Mrs. Higgins's death at age fifty in 1899. Margaret Sanger believed that her mother's early death occurred because of the hardships she suffered from eighteen pregnancies and that her parents' ignorance of birth control contributed to her family's poverty and social estrangement. By the time Sanger had finished her public school education, she had concluded that poor women desperately needed birth control in order to preserve their health and to adequately provide for their children.

A natural leader who defied convention, Sanger went on to attend Claverack College and the Hudson Institution, where she received a liberal arts education for three years. She relished relationships she developed with upper-class women at Claverack and made many important social connections that would aid her future leadership role. After a brief stint at teaching, Sanger entered nursing school in White Plains, New York, which helped solidify her determination to promote birth control. As a young nurse working the night shift, she saw poverty and destitution at its worst. She witnessed women suffering from puerperal infections, uterine disorders, and other illnesses brought about by exhaustion from overwork and childbearing. During her early years of nursing she assisted doctors who attended births and practiced midwifery herself in the immigrant tenements. Sanger wrote in her autobiography about the desperate women who begged her for birth control advice.

Although Margaret vowed never to marry, by the time she neared the end of her nursing training at the age of twenty-two, she had married architect William Sanger, with whom she had three children. Yet she did not abandon her nursing career or her mission of promoting birth control. In July 1912, Sanger nursed Sadie Sach back to health. A Russian immigrant who had given herself an abortion and nearly died, she chose abortion because she already had several children she and her husband could barely afford. The physician attending Sach offered the suffering woman no advice about birth control, and about a year later, Sanger witnessed Sachs's death after a second self-induced abortion. At that point, Sanger vowed that she would work to put an end to the unnecessary suffering and poverty brought about from unwanted pregnancies and poor family planning.

Early Beginnings of the Birth Control Movement

In spite of legalities and fear of prosecution, by 1916 Margaret Sanger, along with her sister Ethel and friend Fania Mindell, opened a birth control clinic in one of the poorest neighborhoods in Brooklyn, New York. All three women were arrested and taken to jail, Mindell was released, but sisters Margaret and Ethel served prison sentences for breaking the Comstock Laws.

Sanger fought for legalized birth control for more than fifty years. By 1921, Sanger had founded the *Birth Control Review* and in the same year, Sanger and her friend Mary Windsor were arrested during the first American Birth Control Conference. In spite of legal repercussions, Sanger went on to found the American Birth Control League. Emerging clinics and birth control meetings were routinely shut down during the 1920s and numerous birth control reformers were arrested.

By the 1930s birth control regulations began to ease and male-dominated hospitals and other health institutions began openly supporting birth control and formed alliances with the Birth Control League. A key factor in this support was a 1936 decision in *United States v. One Package* by the Second Circuit Court of Appeals in New York, allowing physicians to legally import contraceptive devices for medical purposes. In 1937, after years of urging by progressive physicians Dr. William J Robinson and former AMA president Dr. Abraham Jacobi, the American Medical Association endorsed birth control in 1937 as an effective means of family planning and protecting women and children's health.

Through the league, Sanger reached thousands who supported family planning. Outreach clinics sprang up across the nation. In 1939, the American Birth Control League and the Clinical Research Bureau merged and became the Birth Control Federation of America (BCFA). By the end of the 1930s, the federation successfully reached the nation's poorest in the rural South, with sociologist and early civil rights advocate W. E. B. Du Bois (1868–1963) serving on an advisory board that led to county health departments supporting family planning.

The 1940s ushered in a host of progressive developments in birth control with leaders such as Kenneth Rose and Dr. Gregory Pincus emerging as prominent supporters. Rose became the national director of the federation, and in 1942 BCFA changed its name to Planned Parenthood Federation of America. Pincus spent several years conducting steroid research in order to create an effective injection or birth control pill that completely modernized contraceptives. His diligent research led to the manufacturing of birth control pills by 1960. The pill went on to become the leading form of contraceptive of all time and proved to be a highly successful method of birth control in the United States. Physicians practicing in Catholic hospitals, however, were routinely fired for not adhering to contraceptive bans and at this point in history federally mandated legislation made it virtually impossible to obtain a legal abortion.

During the 1950s and 1960s, the organization previously led by Margaret Sanger became the International Planned Parenthood Federation. By 1970, Congress had repealed most of the Comstock laws, and birth control gained the acceptance of most Americans. This acceptance was echoed by President Richard Nixon, who in 1970 signed into law Title X of the Public Health Act, which provided funding for national family planning and established the Center for Population Research. The bill had been cosponsored by George H. W. Bush, then a member of Congress, who noted at the time, "We need to make family planning a household word. We need to take the sensationalism out of the topic so it can no longer be used by militants who have no knowledge of the voluntary nature of the program, but rather are using it as a political steppingstone. If family planning is anything, it is a public health matter" (Planned Parenthood Federation of America History—1960s, http://member .plannedparenthood.org).

The topic of abortion has remained hotly contested among clerical leaders and became a subject of partisan politics. Despite the 1973 *Roe v. Wade* decision that paved the way for legalized abortion, opposition continued against family planning and abortion. Following Sanger's example, leaders like industrialist and philanthropist John D. Rockefeller (1839–1937) began funding and organizing worldwide conferences on population control, which continue to be funded to promote family planning globally. The United Nations World Population Conference gained support from most countries for population policies and programs that would positively enhance social and economic growth. Only the Vatican continued to reject family planning, the use of contraceptives, and any type of abortion regardless of circumstances.

Increasingly during the last decades of the twentieth century, birth control information and products became readily available to Americans; at the same time, however, pro-life supporters continued to stymie family planning organizations' activities and to fight for antiabortion laws. The leadership of Ronald Reagan and George H. W. Bush aided opponents of birth control and effectively decreased funding for national family planning organizations, thus encouraging the activities of pro-life supporters. Both presidents actively curtailed funding for family planning. Reagan's executive orders included cutting funds to Third World organizations that performed abortions. The most prominent measure was dubbed the Mexico City Policy (1984), which successfully limited funding for family planning clinics and made it illegal for these organizations to perform abortions or fight politically for legalized abortions—a policy continued by Bush, who had once been a strong supporter of family planning.

As a result, many abortion and family planning clinics were attacked. Doctors, nurses, and supporters were verbally harassed and assaulted, and several were murdered. The conservative leadership during the 1980s created a negative backlash that effectively discouraged legalized abortion.

Although conflicting views continue to exist in the twenty-first century, without the strong leadership of women like Margaret Sanger, the freedom to choose birth control over maternity might not exist in modern America. In spite of inroads made by women in securing birth control and the right to control their own bodies, the topics are continually debated by conservative opponents in both the social and political arenas who continually seek to overturn *Roe v. Wade* and the work of Planned Parenthood. Opponents seemingly become particularly vocal during political campaigns. Moreover, conservative leaders in the House and Senate continually seek to curtail funding for Planned Parenthood and other social programs needed by women. One can almost be assured that turning on the evening news will yield some type of political or social group endorsing an anti-abortion stance or seeking to eradicate government-funded family planning. Seemingly, birth-control-related topics have become more of a concern of the politically ambitious who answer to conservative financers of political campaigns. Also, many of these same political leaders answer to religious leaders such as the Moral Majority, thus revealing a similar mindset that was prevalent during the nineteenth century. Arguments against reproductive rights posed by some political leaders are undoubtedly more about power and gaining reelection than any genuine concern for the health and well-being of the most vulnerable citizens who need effective contraceptives, thus alleviating further problems associated with socioeconomic concerns related to poverty. And so the debate continues to keep existing reproductive rights in place, which effectively protects the rights of all citizens. Regardless of extremist views on family planning and abortion, the gains made by Sanger and her followers have made permanent marks on history that have benefited women and men worldwide.

Further Reading

Archer, J. (1991). *Breaking barriers.* New York: Viking Penguin Press.

Beisel, N. (1997). *Imperiled innocents: Anthony Comstock and family reproduction in Victorian America.* Princeton, NJ: Princeton University Press.

Buhle, M. (1981). *Women and American socialism, 1870–1920.* Urbana: University of Illinois Press.

Brodie, J. (1994). *Contraceptive and abortion in 19th century America.* Ithaca, NY: Cornell University Press.

Chesler, E. (1992). *Woman of valor: Margaret Sanger and the birth control movement in America.* New York: Simon and Schuster.

Dash, J. (1973). *A life of one's own: Three gifted women and the men they married.* New York: Paragon House.

Douglas, E. (1970). *Margaret Sanger: Pioneer of the future.* New York: Holt, Rinehart & Winston.

Forester, M. (1985). *Significant sisters: The grassroots of American feminism 1839–1939.* New York: Alfred Knopf.

Gordon, L. (2003). *The moral property of women: A history of birth control politics in America.* Urbana: University of Illinois Press.

Gordon, L. (2002). *The moral responsibility of women.* Urbana: University of Illinois Press.

Gordon, L. (1976). *Woman's body, woman's right: A social history of birth control in America.* New York: Penguin Books.

Gray, M. (1985). *Margaret Sanger: A biography of the champion of birth control.* New York: Richard Marek Publishers.

Katz, E. (Ed.). (2003). *The selected papers of Margaret Sanger, volume 1: The woman rebel, 1900–1928.* Urbana: University of Illinois Press.

Kennedy, D. (1970). *Birth control in America: The career of Margaret Sanger.* New Haven, CT: Yale University Press.

Knowles, J. & Ringel, M. (1998). *Planned parenthood: All about birth control.* New York: Three Rivers Press.

Lader, L. (1973). *The Margaret Sanger story and the fight for birth control.* New York: Doubleday & Company.

Marshall, R. & Donovan, C. (1991). *Blessed are the barren: The social policy of planned parenthood.* San Francisco: Ignatius Press.

McCann, C. (1994). *Birth control politics in the United States, 1916–1945.* Ithaca, NY: Cornell University Press.

McLaren, A. (1990). *A history of contraception: From antiquity to the present day.* Oxford, UK: Basil Blackwell.

Preston, W. (1994). *Aliens and dissenters: Federal suppression of radicals, 1903–1933.* Urbana: University of Illinois Press.

Reed, J. (1978). *The birth control movement and American society: From private vice to public virtue.* Princeton, NJ: Princeton University Press.

Sanger, M. (1938). *An autobiography.* New York: W.W. Norton & Company.

Sanger, M. (1969). *My fight for birth control.* New York: Maxwell Reprint Company.

Tone, A. (1997). *Controlling reproduction: An American history.* Wilmington, DE: Scholarly Resources.

Vicinus, M. (1973). *Suffer and be still: Women in the Victorian age.* Bloomington: Indiana Press.

Women in the Gay and Lesbian Rights Movement

Donna L. HALPER
Lesley University

Gays and Lesbians have existed throughout history, but homosexuality has often been considered criminal or a mental illness. Starting in the twentieth century, lesbians and gays began to reject those labels and to organize worldwide against punitive laws and attitudes. Important issues in the twenty-first century include the rights of lesbians and gays to marry, become parents, and serve in the military.

Gay men and lesbians have existed throughout history, although attitudes toward them have varied in different eras. In ancient Greece, people tolerated homosexual liaisons under certain circumstances whereas certain verses of the Hebrew, Christian, and Islamic scriptures speak of homosexual behavior as a grave sin. Negative attitudes toward same-sex relationships evolved from interpretations of these scriptures and were written into the civil law in numerous countries. Most of the sexual sins that were listed in the early laws were aimed at men, however. In general, if women were close with each other, they could often simply pass as platonic friends.

Although there have been rumors that certain famous people from the past were gay or lesbian, finding concrete evidence has been difficult for modern historians. Even when there were personal journals or letters, they often did not reveal very much, since the customs of the times mitigated against discussing one's private sexual conduct. This meant reading between the lines was often essential. The so-called "Boston marriage" of Victorian times is a good example of this. Strong and independent women, such as poet Sarah Orne Jewett and author Annie Adams Fields, established loving friendships and lived together as companions; but few documents conclusively show whether these relationships included sex and romance, or were mainly platonic.

Throughout the nineteenth century, people were imprisoned in Europe and in the United States for homosexual acts. While women may have been less conspicuous to outsiders and able to live in relative peace, they too suffered ostracism. In 1928, when the British novelist Radclyffe Hall (1880–1943) published *The Well of Loneliness*, a book that was sympathetic toward its lesbian characters, the British government immediately judged it to be obscene, and all copies were seized. In the

United States, the book, which was described by the *New York Times* as being about "abnormal women," was championed by a number of famous writers and it was able to find a publisher. But the book remained controversial and there were periodic efforts to censor it. It also received a number of negative reviews from book editors who found the subject matter too shocking.

The first gay rights organizations in the United States concerned themselves mostly with the welfare of gay men, such as the Society for Human Rights, founded in Chicago by postal clerk Henry Gerber in 1924 (although by 1925 police had shut it down); and the Mattachine Society, founded by a group of gay men in southern California. In 1955, Phyllis Lyon and Dorothy (Del) Martin, San Francisco-based activists, founded the Daughters of Bilitis (DOB) as an advocacy group especially for lesbians. They also founded *The Ladder*, a publication that was distributed nationally. One of the few magazines aimed at the lesbian audience, it contained news, poetry, short fiction, and information about the activities of DOB chapters.

Although these organizations sought more respect and tolerance, they also advised members to assimilate as much as possible and to avoid dressing or behaving in ways that would call attention to their lifestyle. Later, some militant members of the emerging gay liberation movement would regard them as too willing to remain in the closet and too afraid to stand up for greater acceptance. Yet in a society dominated by the conservative politics of US senator Joseph McCarthy, when homosexuals and lesbians were often arrested for "lewd conduct," or fired from their jobs as potential security risks, the 1950s were not a good time to be vocal about one's sexual orientation.

Although no single event created the US lesbian and gay civil rights movement, most historians agree that the Stonewall Riots were a defining moment. In June 1969 in New York City, police raided a gay bar called the Stonewall Inn. Such raids were common and usually resulted in numerous arrests, yet this time the bar's patrons decided to fight back, leading to three days of civil unrest. In the United States, this was the era of the civil rights and women's rights movements, and that environment may have encouraged gays and lesbians to actively oppose the prejudice they often encountered. The Stonewall Riots mobilized the community and led to an increasing unwillingness to assimilate or accommodate. They also became a defining moment for a number of the men and women who were there, including a young nun named Virginia (Ginny) Apuzzo (b. 1941), who decided to leave the convent and become an activist in the gay rights movement. She fought for the inclusion of a gay rights plank in the 1976 Democratic Party's platform; founded a political action group from Brooklyn, New York called the Lambda Independent Democrats; and became known as a tireless advocate for greater support for people with AIDS. She even got arrested in front of the White House in 1987 while protesting what she saw as President Reagan's inadequate response to the AIDS crisis. In 1997, she was named an advisor to President Bill Clinton, making her the highest-ranking openly gay or lesbian government official at that time.

What happened at Stonewall would happen in many other countries. In India, a country where gay and lesbian acts are still criminal offenses, a defining event occurred in December 1998. Screenwriter and director Deepa Mehta (b. 1950) released *Fire*, a movie featuring a subplot in which two women fall in love. Outraged religious conservatives attacked the theater in Mumbai where the movie was being shown, breaking windows, beating up patrons, and vandalizing the building. Similar events occurred in other Indian cities. This time, however, a coalition of civil libertarians, human rights activists, and free speech advocates joined with members of the lesbian community to march and protest both the attacks and the government's efforts to censor the movie. This protest march marked one of the first times that lesbians had been visible in India; most lived hidden lives, afraid to call attention to themselves. The protest led to the founding of the Campaign for Lesbian Rights. In June 2003, a rally and march were held in Kolkata to protest laws that make homosexuality punishable by ten years in prison; several hundred people marched peacefully in one of the few public demonstrations held by India's gay community.

A number of groups emerged in the United States during the 1970s and 1980s to fight for the rights of gay men and lesbian women. The lesbian feminist movement became active in the United States and Western Europe in the 1970s and 1980s, growing out of what many perceived as feminists' rejection of lesbians and the mostly male gay movement's marginalization of women. Further offshoots of the movement included black and Latina groups, who felt their concerns had not been adequately addressed in previous iterations of feminism.

The National Gay Task Force (NGTF) organized in 1973 (in 1985, it changed its name to the more inclusive National Gay and Lesbian Task Force [NGLTF]), is one of the best-known groups fighting for lesbian and gay civil rights. The organization not only advocates for changes in discriminatory laws in the United States, but also conducts sociological studies about society's changing attitudes, works with the government to develop strategies to combat violence against lesbians and gays, monitors the media for antigay content, and conducts international conferences about gay issues.

When AIDS first appeared in the United States during the 1980s, during which time Virginia Apuzzo served as executive director (from 1982 to 1986), NGLTF was at the forefront in combating myths and prejudices and educating the public about HIV. The more vocal and sometimes controversial organization ACT UP (AIDS Coalition to Unleash Power) also arose at this time. Founded in 1987, it is known for its slogan "Silence = Death" and its commitment to speaking out against discrimination in a demonstrative manner, using tactics of civil disobedience called "direct actions." Although remembered as comprised mostly of middle-class white gays, lesbians and other women participated in ACT UP and were responsible for drawing attention to how women were being affected by AIDS. Another advocacy group, GLAAD (Gay and Lesbian Alliance against Defamation), founded in 1985, monitored the media and advocated for an end to antigay stereotypes in print, broadcasting, and film.

The Lesbian Avengers, a national advocacy group founded in New York in 1992 by six lesbian activists who had been active in ACT UP and other organizations, are committed to fighting discrimination against lesbians as well as to building a grassroots movement that promotes lesbian issues.

British and Australian Activist Groups and Lesbian Leaders

In England, one of the best-known activist groups, OutRage, founded in 1990, also uses civil disobedience methods, staging unique and often provocative direct actions to call attention to discrimination. The largest gay and lesbian rights group in the United Kingdom, Stonewall, founded in 1989, lobbies and works with government officials and members of Parliament to improve the legal rights of gay men and lesbians.

In the political realm, Maureen Colquhoun (b. 1928) became the first lesbian to serve openly in Parliament when she came out in 1976 (she had been elected in 1974). She was subjected to scorn from her male colleagues, who also criticized her for being too much of an outspoken feminist. Such negative publicity led to her losing her seat in Parliament several years later. The next open lesbian to serve in Parliament, Angela Eagle (b. 1961), who was elected in 1992 and came out in 1997, has not been impeded in her career as a Labour Party politician.

In Australia, the first gay rights advocacy organization formed as a chapter of Daughters of Bilitis. Founded in 1970, it was later renamed the Australasian Lesbian Movement, and ceased to operate in 1973. Other organizations took its place and currently, Australia has a number of activist groups, such as the Tasmanian Gay and Lesbian Rights Group, which have fought for the decriminalization of homosexual behavior. Economic advocacy groups, such as the Australian Gay and Lesbian Tourism Association (AGLTA), also work to find gay-friendly and gay-tolerant hotels and places for visitors to shop.

Legislation and Criminality Across the World

Even in countries where homosexuality is still regarded as a sin or a crime, advocacy groups exist, but they run the risk of being shut down by the government. For example, in Nepal in June 2004, the Supreme Court imposed a ban on the Blue Diamond Society, which advocates on behalf of gay men and lesbian women and conducts HIV/AIDS education. Advocacy groups exist in a handful of Muslim countries (most notably Turkey), but in more theocratic cultures gay men and lesbian women have turned to the Internet to discuss issues while avoiding government crackdowns.

In India and South Africa, acts of persecution often single out lesbians, subjecting them to "curative" or "corrective" rape, in the false belief that such actions will "cure" them of their lesbianism. In Russia, since the early 2010s, there has been a steady crackdown on gay rights, with new laws criminalizing "homosexual propaganda." In Uganda, where according to a 2013 report by the Pew Research Center, 96 percent of Ugandans expressed disapproval of homosexuality, the government passed the Anti-Homosexuality Act (AHA) in 2014. After the passage of the AHA, violence against gays and lesbians increased. Ultimately, the Constitutional Court of Uganda invalidated the law, but anti-gay attitudes in Uganda remained unchanged. Perhaps the first country to add to its constitution a provision that outlawed discrimination against gays was South Africa, which did so when its new constitution was written in 1994. But public attitudes have been slow to change, and persecution of gay men and lesbians persists.

Same-sex marriage and civil unions have become an important issue for gay men and lesbian women, and activist groups fight to expand benefits and rights to gay couples. Nearly two dozen countries in the world recognize the rights of same sex couples to marry, mostly in Europe and North America. The United States had previously denied marriage rights to gay couples under the 1996 Defense of Marriage Act (DOMA), but that changed first in 2004, after a Massachusetts lesbian couple, Hillary and Julie Goodridge, sued the state and won the right to marry. Massachusetts thus became the first state to grant marriage equality to same-sex couples. In subsequent years, a few other states also gave gay and lesbian couples the right to marry, but the federal government still did not recognize their relationships. In 2013, the government finally repealed DOMA after a flurry of lawsuits, including that of Edie Windsor (b. 1929) who sued the government after she was taxed on inheritance from her wife as if they had been unrelated.

Then, in April 2015, the US Supreme Court heard oral arguments in *Obergefell v. Hodges* over whether or not gay marriage is a right guaranteed by the Constitution. By a 5-4 vote, the Supreme Court ruled on 26 June 2015 that limiting marriage only to heterosexual couples violates the Constitution's guarantee of equal protection under the law. Mary L. Bonauto (born c. 1961), civil rights project director at GLBTQ Legal Advocates & Defenders (GLAD) and long-time activist, argued for the plaintiffs in both the Massachusetts case and Supreme Court case.

In addition to same-sex marriage, many gays and lesbians are seeking to become parents, either through traditional relationships, assisted fertility, or adoption. For many years, gay couples were forbidden to adopt, but as the public became more accepting of same-sex relationships, attitudes also changed about gay adoption in the United States. Internationally, however impediments remain: only nineteen countries permitted same-sex adoption as of 2015.

Another twenty-first-century issue is the right of gays and lesbians to serve in the military. Thousands of gays and lesbians in the military in many countries, including the United States, have been removed over the years. In September 2011, the US policy known as "Don't Ask, Don't Tell" (DADT), in effect since 1993, was repealed, which meant gay service members no longer needed to fear being discovered and dismissed. In June 2015, the Pentagon began to treat discrimination based on sexual orientation the same as it considers race, religion, color, sex, age and national origin when investigating complaints. In about thirty countries in the world, including most NATO countries, gays and lesbians can serve openly in the military.

Worldwide, many people now see lesbian and gay rights as a human rights issue, and certainly more acceptance exists than when the Stonewall Riots occurred. Politicians who are gay now openly run for office: in Houston, Texas, Annise Parker (b. 1956) was elected mayor in 2009, becoming one of the first openly gay mayors of a major US city; and in Canada, Kathleen O'Day Wynne (b. 1953) became the twenty-fifth premier of Ontario in 2013—the first openly gay head of government in Canada. And being gay is no longer considered a career killer in many occupations. This has been helped by some high profile media stars who came out to their public rather than continuing to live a closeted life. Among the first lesbians to openly acknowledge her sexuality was comedian Ellen DeGeneres, who did so as part of an episode of her ABC-TV show "Ellen" in 1997. At that time, her actions were unique, but today, there are many prime-time television dramas and comedies in which gay characters and gay relationships are central to the plot. Other fields like professional sports are far less accepting, however, and homophobic taunts are still part of locker room culture. In the WNBA, a women's professional basketball league, male executives expressed concern about stereotypic perceptions that female athletes were unfeminine, as well as rumors that star players were lesbians. Worried about alienating fans in conservative cities, league officials offered their players instruction on how to apply makeup and dress fashionably (Abraham 2013).

While gay men and lesbians in most Western countries enjoy far more acceptance than they did even a decade ago, the battle for equality continues. As long as conservative religious views predominate, and as long as stereotypes persist, members of the gay and lesbian rights movement will continue their work.

Further Reading

Abraham, L. (2013, November 4). How slam-dunking, gender-bending WNBA rookie Brittney Griner is changing the world of sports. *ELLE*. Retrieved June 13, 2016, from http://www.elle.com/culture/career -politics/interviews/a12606/brittney-griner-profile

Aengus, C. & Itaborahy, L. P. (2005, May). State sponsored homophobia 2015: A world survey of laws: criminalisation, protection and recognition of same-sex love. Geneva: ILGA.

Anderson, E. (2010). *In the game: Gay athletes and the cult of masculinity*. Stony Brook, NY: SUNY Press.

Cenziper, D. & Obergefell, J. (2016). *Love wins: The lovers and lawyers who fought the landmark case for marriage equality*. New York: William Morrow.

Faderman, L. (2015). *The gay revolution: The story of the struggle*. New York: Simon & Schuster.

Gage, S., Richards, L., & Wilmot, H. (2002). *Queer*. New York: Avalon Press.

Jagose, A. (1996). *Queer theory: An introduction*. New York: New York University Press.

Marcus, E. (2002). *Making gay history*. New York: Perennial.

Pew Research Center. (2016). Changing attitudes on gay marriage. Retrieved June 13, 2016, from http://www.pewforum.org/2016/05/12/changing-attitudes-on-gay-marriage

Pew Research Center. (2013). The global divide on homosexuality. Retrieved June 13, 2016, from http://www.pewglobal.org/2013/06/04/the-global-divide-on-homosexuality

Rimmerman, C. (2002). *From identity to politics: The lesbian and gay movements in the United States*. Philadelphia: Temple University Press.

Smith, R. & Haider-Markel, D. (2002). *Gay and lesbian Americans and political participation: A reference handbook*. Santa Barbara CA: ABC-CLIO.

Snyder, R. C. (2006). *Gay marriage and democracy: Equality for all*. Lanham, MD: Rowman & Littlefield.

An Overview of Conservation and Environmental Movements

Polly Welts KAUFMAN
Adapted from "Women and Conservation" in the Encyclopedia of World Environmental History *with contributions from J. Donald Hughes and Heather Eaton.*

In the United States, women began organizing for environmental conservation as early as the turn of the twentieth century. Later, in the developing world, women took on environmental destruction as a phenomenon that would directly harm their communities. The idea of sustainable development was introduced in the 1980s by a commission led by a Norwegian woman, and in the years since, women have worked across the globe and on many fronts to protect the environment.

Concern for the environment began early for women in the United States, and their initial concerns were for conservation. The General Federation of Women's Clubs (GFWC) organized its forestry division in 1902, and for a time reported to the male-dominated American Forestry Association (AFA) and Conservation Congress about women's work in conserving forests and protecting watersheds. The GFWC supported the Minnesota Federation of Women's Clubs in saving the state's Chippewa Forest Reserve, the California Federation in establishing Big Basin State Park to protect a grove of redwoods, and the passage of the federal Weeks Act in 1911 to establish national forests in the East. The Louisiana Federation led in the development of the Waterways Committee that spawned water conservation projects in thirty-nine states with goals of protecting pure drinking water and clean waterfronts.

Inspired by the California Federation, members of the GFWC—by then numbering 800,000 women—broke with the AFA over the issue of the preservation of Hetch Hetchy Valley in Yosemite National Park. The women joined naturalist John Muir in unsuccessfully opposing a plan to create a reservoir for the city of San Francisco in that valley. GFWC members responded to the loss by putting their efforts behind what they called "the conservation of natural scenery" and the development of national parks. Under the direction of GFWC president Mary Belle King Sherman (1862–1935), they lobbied Congress to pass the bill that established the National Park Service in 1916.

National Parks and the Preservation of Species

American women of the early twentieth century also led in the preservation of bird and plant species. Women of the Audubon societies faced an issue with women's fashionable hats. The use of bird feathers as decoration, in particular the "aigrette" feathers from snowy egrets and great white herons, threatened those birds with extinction. Mabel Osgood Wright (1859–1934), president of the Connecticut Audubon Society and editor of *Bird Lore*, organized the secretaries of the initial nineteen state Audubon societies, all of whom were women but one, to campaign against the practice and to support protective legislation.

In the 1930s and 1940s, Rosalie Edge broke with the National Audubon Society to form the Emergency Conservation Committee (ECC) to publish pamphlets condemning actions that threatened conservation. She believed that the National Audubon Society's alliance with hunters made the Society oppose a federal bag limit on migratory birds and accept the practice of baiting ducks. The ECC's efforts stopped park rangers from controlling the white pelican population in Yellowstone National Park, protected a grove of sugar pines in Yosemite National Park, and rescued old-growth forests by helping to develop a constituency to create Olympic National Park.

The women-run Garden Club of America, organized nationally in 1913, supported the work of state and local garden clubs to protect native plants and birds. Minerva Hamilton Hoyt, conservation chair of the California Garden Club, protected desert plants by her drive to establish Joshua Tree National Monument in 1936. In the 1940s, the Garden Club of America organized its eight thousand members to oppose mining in Organ Pipe Cactus National Monument in Arizona and the lumbering of virgin timber in Olympic National Park. Later they joined the successful protest against building Echo Park Dam in Dinosaur National Monument in Utah and Colorado.

By midcentury, one of the ways by which US women preserved species and landscapes was to seek federal and state protection of public lands in addition to monitoring existing public lands. Marjory Stoneman Douglas became a spokesperson for the importance of the Florida Everglades as a habitat for vanishing species. Bettie Willard and Estella Leopold helped establish Florissant fossil beds in Colorado to save a deposit of fossils that are 38 million years old. Among women who organized to protect the shorelines of the Great Lakes by working to establish state and national parks were Genevieve Gillette in Michigan and Dorothy Buell, president of the Save the Dunes Council in Indiana. Biologist Liane Russell organized the Tennessee Citizens for Wilderness Planning to keep dams out of wild rivers in Tennessee. Members of the Ohio League of Women Voters, shocked by the fires that erupted from the oil and debris in the Cuyahoga River, put their membership behind establishing a national park in the Cuyahoga Valley. Hundreds of women worked to protect the Alaskan wilderness by lobbying for the Alaska Lands Bill passed in 1980. They included long-time environmentalist Margaret E. Murie and Alaskan Celia Hunter, the first woman president of the Wilderness Society.

Developing Countries

By the late twentieth century, the conservation ethic was also well established in developing countries. Women's concerns stemmed from their need to provide food, fuel, and water for their families and communities in a sustainable way. In Kenya, Wangari Maathai (1940–2011) founded the greenbelt movement in 1977 to transform women from "tree killers" into "tree planters" (Vollers 1988, 11). Within ten years more than five hundred communities had developed tree nurseries, and twenty-five thousand households had established wood lots. Women in Ghana in Africa conserved wood by developing a device for smoking fish that uses one-tenth as much wood as in the past.

One of the most famous environmental protests was the Chipko movement, which began near Himalayan villages in north India in March 1973 when peasants stopped loggers from cutting down trees by threatening to hug (*chipko*) the trees and place their bodies in the path of the axes—civil disobedience inspired by the nonviolent methods of Indian nationalist Mohandas Gandhi. The trees were valuable to villagers for fuel, fodder, small timber, and protection against flooding. Many demonstrators were women, who are the wood gatherers there. The movement mushroomed from there and in the 1980s included protests of limestone mining, in which a successful suit was launched to shut down the mines.

Women who have demonstrated concern for the relationship of humans to nature have often suffered for that concern, in the developing world and elsewhere. Wangari Maathai, who received the 2004 Nobel Peace Prize, was beaten and imprisoned for her environmental work. Judi Bari, a leader of the 1990 Redwood Summer protests against the logging of giant redwood trees in California, was maimed by a bomb placed under her car seat in an attempt to kill her. The American Catholic nun, Sister Dorothy Mae Stang, a naturalized Brazilian citizen who had worked for thirty years on behalf of the rural poor and the environment of the Amazon basin, was shot to death at the order of landowners in 2005. Appropriately, she often wore a T-shirt with the motto: "The death of the forest is the end of our life."

New Efforts and Concerns

Beginning in 1970s, another set of voices and views on feminism and sustainability were bringing forth a new set of concerns with the term *ecofeminism*. First used in 1974 by the French feminist Francoise d'Eaubonne (1920–2005), ecofeminism sees connections between the domination of nature and the exploitation of women. Ecofeminism has activist and academic roots with women working in everything from urban ecology to antiwar movements to conservation. At the time, some hailed the movement as a new wave of feminism.

In the late 1980s, Gro Brundtland (b. 1939), a Norwegian politician who had served three terms as prime minister, rose to the forefront of leadership on environmental issues. She is best known in this regard for her role as chair of the UN World Commission on Environment and Development. In 1987, the commission issued *Our Common Future*, also known as the Brundtland Report, which addressed the alarming ecological effects of development, and coined the phrase and the idea of "sustainable development."

In 2001, the World Wildlife Fund (WWF) instituted its Women and Conservation Initiative to offer grants, training, and technical assistance to women in conservation in addition to giving annual awards for accomplishments. For the first awards, WWF selected Meidi Kasmidi from Sulawesi, Indonesia, who worked to establish

Bunaken Marine Park and introduce concepts of marine conservation to those fishing outside the park; and Mauricia Gonzalez Garcia from Chiapas, Mexico, whose organization, Linea Biosfera, has trained a network of advocates in agro-ecology, human rights, and health in ten Central American communities.

Further Reading

Englehardt, N. (2001) *World Wildlife Fund acknowledges women's contribution to conservation*. Retrieved June 20, 2001, from www.worldwildlife.org

Kaufman, P. W. (1996). *National parks and the woman's voice: A history*. Albuquerque: University of New Mexico Press.

Maathai, W. (1988). *The green belt movement: Sharing the approach and the experience*. Nairobi, Kenya: Environment Liaison Centre International.

Merchant, C. (1996). *Earthcare: Women and the environment*. New York: Routledge.

Norwood, V. (1993). *Made from this Earth: American women and nature*. Chapel Hill: University of North Carolina Press.

Shiva, V. (1988). *Staying alive: Women, ecology, and development*. London: Zed Books.

Vollers, M. (1988). Healing the ravaged land. *International Wildlife, 18*(1), 4–9.

Women in Sustainable Development and Ecofeminism

Heather EATON
Saint Paul University

In the early 1980s, environmentalism emerged as a particular concern of feminists. Organizations, conferences, and studies around the world have since declared that sustainability is not possible without equity, justice, and economic and political growth for women. The result is a global awareness of various connections between women and development, and women and ecology. While groups and activists differ in approach and emphasis, all share the desire for a sustainable future.

Feminist views on sustainability are broad and deep, covering hundreds of topics from thousands of women and organizations, which, in turn, represent hundreds of thousands of women. There is agreement on some issues and a range of views, approaches, and strategies on others. Some groups put a greater emphasis on women's equity and rights as a road to sustainability, while others emphasize ecological integrity as foundational. Given the diversity of peoples, cultures, and worldviews and the complexity of issues, this is to be expected.

Historically, feminist views on sustainability come from two different directions: "women in development" (WID) approaches, and what came to be called ecofeminism. In the early twenty-first century these converged, and together they represent a complex overlay of concerns, analyses, approaches, and strategies.

Women in Development

Women in Development (WID) is an approach that came on the international scene in the early 1980s from those assessing the impact of development on women. After three decades of a development agenda for less industrialized countries—then termed the "third world"—it was evident that in many places women were not benefiting; oftentimes the programs made their lives more difficult. Organizations, such as Development Alternatives with Women for a New Era (DAWN) or the Association for Women's Rights in Development (AWID), assessed that many of the difficulties for women were rooted in a basic lack of equity, in the ideas and processes of development, and in capitalist and macroeconomic systems.

The United Nations (UN) Decade for Women: Equity, Development and Peace (1976–1985) culminated in a pivotal conference in Nairobi, Kenya, which recognized that the development agenda had failed women; as a result, the United Nations Development Fund for Women (UNIFEM) was established. The conference's final document, The Nairobi Forward-looking Strategies for the Advancement of Women, became a benchmark for systematic gender analysis, critiques, collective visions, and strategies for a sustainable life and livelihood for women, especially for poor women.

Enlarging Feminist Visions

This expanded vision of feminism was born of the experiences of activists who desired a process of economic and social development that was geared to human needs rather than financial gains. This also meant that development based on equity required access to economic and political power. If there was to be equality, peace, and development by and for the poor and oppressed, it was inextricably linked to the same objectives by and for women. As the WID efforts increased, it was evident that multiple issues intersected. The term WID changed to "gender and development" (GAD), expanding the focus to be able to tackle the social and ideological causes of women's subordination and the uneven power relations between women and men: women's rights were human rights. In practical terms, this enabled violence against women to be treated as a public-policy issue rather than a private domestic problem, insisting that there can be no development in situations of women's oppression. Sustainability had to address economic, cultural, and physical violence against women.

The women and development agenda soon enlarged again. GAD became WED—"women, environment, and development"—which later changed its emphasis to sustainable development. Environmental issues surfaced on global, development, and economic agendas, evidenced with the United Nations World Commission on Environment and Development and the publication of *Our Common Future*, or the Brundtland Report, in 1987. This report placed sustainable development—"development that meets the needs of the present generation without compromising the ability of future generations to meet their own needs"—on the political landscape. It activated a global search for alternative models and strategies to development. The call for sustainable development opened the door for cooperation and consultation between global, national, and local partners, bridging governmental and civic society. Women assumed it would include them.

Over these years, women's organizations sprang up all over the world. In addition to those mentioned, there were many more, including the African Women's Development and Communication Network (FEMNET, 1988), Women's Environment & Development Organization (WEDO, 1990), and Women in Development Europe (WIDE). Currently there are thousands of nongovernmental organizations addressing aspects of gender and feminism, development, environment, and sustainability.

The quantity of activities, research, conferences, and publications coming forth from these interconnecting national and international agenda was astonishing. The establishment of women's voices, networks, and collaboration represents colossal efforts of thousands of women, who also represent thousands of women's voices and views on sustainability. Many activists and scholars from all over the globe—such as Peggy Antrobus, Gita Sen, Rosi Braidotti, Wangari Maathai, and Vandana Shiva—spent years working on various issues. These included agriculture, trees, microfinancing, governance, food security and other development agenda.

At the same time, environmental issues were becoming more serious around the world. The United Nations launched a call to deliberate issues of the "environment and development." In consultation with a vast array of citizen's groups, experts, and national leaders, the United Nations proposed an agenda for sustainable development for the twenty-first century called Agenda 21. Before this, in 1991, as the world prepared for the 1992 United Nations Conference on Environment and Development (UNCED) in Rio de Janeiro, over one thousand women came from eighty-three countries to discuss and present an alternative and progressive feminist and ecological agenda. They held the World Women's Congress for a Healthy Planet in Miami, Florida, and produced the Women's Action Agenda 21, a document about the interrelated issues of women, development, sustainability, and environmental stability. It focuses on a critique of the forces underpinning the problems and offers solutions. The preamble, from which the following points are extracted, is candid about the intent and analysis.

> We speak on behalf of . . . the millions of women who experience daily the violence of environmental degradation.
>
> As long as Nature and women are abused by a so-called free-market ideology and wrong concepts of "economic growth," there can be no environmental security.
>
> We are outraged by the inequities.
>
> We will no longer tolerate the enormous role played by the military establishments.
>
> We . . . pledge our commitment to the empowerment of women, the central and powerful force in the search for equity.
>
> We demand our right, as half the world's population, to bring our perspectives, values, skills, and experiences into policy making.
>
> We equate lack of political and individual will among world leaders with a lack of basic morality and spiritual values and an absence of responsibility towards future generations.

The Women's Action Agenda 21 represents the first international feminist manifesto on sustainability, providing a useful representation of what was occurring in feminism and sustainability, predominantly from the developing countries. Although intended to influence UNCED and its outcomes, these enormous collaborative efforts were barely noticed. UNCED went ahead without much interest in the comprehensive analysis of the gendered dimensions of these issues. A comprehensive blueprint of action to be accepted globally, nationally, and locally, the official report of UNCED was a nine-hundred-page document entitled *Agenda 21*. Although the document included Chapter 24, "Global Action for Women Towards Sustainable and Equitable Development," and several additional references to women, most of the women's work from Women in Development (WID) to UNCED was omitted.

Since then, much has changed. Today most development or environmental institutions have specific areas of gender research and actions. The Women's Action Agenda 21 has been enormously useful. It is now called the Women's Action Agenda for a Healthy and Peaceful Planet 2015, and represents diverse experiences of thousands of women striving to bring the UNCED agreements to life. Generally, activists and academics from political science, international development, sociology, and feminism or gender studies have contributed to this feminist path toward sustainability.

Women, Environment, and Development (WED) or Ecofeminism?

Ecofeminists examine the sociopolitical and economic structures that restrict many women's lives to poverty, ecological deprivation, and economic powerlessness. This type of ecofeminism resonates with the general thrust of years of connecting women, environmental, and development work. Thus the path to sustainability involves equity, justice, and economic and political power for women.

In-depth ecofeminist research revealed the extent to which Western cultures were rooted in ideologies of domination, a central one being the interconnected domination of women and nature. While this work exposed the ideological substructure of the problem, however, it did not describe in a straightforward manner how to change it. A tension existed between those who developed ecofeminist theories, usually from affluent countries, and those working for political change in social movements, usually from developing countries.

The tensions between WED and ecofeminism became an explicit focus of conversation. Women reflected differently on the relationships between women and the natural world, and misogyny and the ecological crisis. Many from the WED side concentrated more on women's issues than environmental problems, and others more on ecological concerns. Spirituality or religion was central to some, and for others they were irrelevant or aroused suspicion. Some found the diversity unmanageable, and others rejoiced in the multitude of voices. Some kept the ecology–feminist connection but changed the words, using phrases such as *feminist ecology*, *feminist social ecology*, *feminist green socialism*, *feminist environmentalism*, and *feminist analyses of the environmental crisis* and WED.

It took time and effort for activists and academics to work together and to comprehend the complex relationships between the ideological analysis of the cultural-symbolic levels and the social, economic, political, and material difficulties. Yet throughout it all there was a mutual willingness to collaborate and to challenge. The issues are too difficult and complex for any one approach to be sufficient. All share the desire for a sustainable future.

Sustainability and Feminism

Debates continue on every topic: among transcultural or context-specific approaches, theory and social transformation, and in international conversations about democracy, globalization, and the meaning of sustainability. Different forms of inequity are increasingly part of any investigation of issues and effective responses.

Climate change is adding another level of ecological and social analyses, and most agree on the importance of increased awareness of sustainable solutions in an era of climate instability. In general, the link between feminism and sustainability is about a desire to heal the wounds caused by the splits between nature and culture, mind and body, women and men, reason and emotion, spirit and matter, theory and action, and ultimately between humans and the Earth.

Further Reading

Adams, C. (2005). *Ecofeminism and the eating of animals: Feminism and the defense of animals.* Sacramento, CA: Black Powder Press.

Association for Women's Rights in Development (AWID). (n.d.) Retrieved April 29, 2009, from http://www .awid.org

Cuomo, C. J. (1998). *Feminism and ecological communities: An ethic of flourishing.* London: Routledge.

Development Alternatives with Women for a New Era (DAWN). (n.d.). Retrieved April 29, 2009, from http://www.dawnnet.org

Eaton, H. (2005). *Introducing ecofeminist theologies.* London: T&T Clark International.

Eaton, H. & Lorentzen, L. A. (Eds.). (2003). *Ecofeminism and globalization: Exploring religion, culture and context.* Lanham, MD: Rowman & Littlefield.

Gaard, G. (1998). *Ecofeminist politics: Ecofeminists and the greens.* Philadelphia: Temple University Press.

Gebara, I. (1999). *Longing for running water: Ecofeminism and liberation.* Minneapolis, MN: Fortress Press.

Kheel, M. (2008). *Nature ethics: An ecofeminist perspective.* Lanham, MD: Rowman & Littlefield.

Leach, M. (Ed.). (2015). *Gender equality and sustainable development.* New York: Routledge.

Mies, M. & Shiva, V. (1993). *Ecofeminism.* London: Zed.

Nairobi forward-looking strategies for the advancement of women. (1985, July 26). Retrieved on May 9, 2009, from http://www.un-documents.net/nflsaw.htm

Ress, M. J. (2006). *Ecofeminism in Latin America: Women from the margins.* Maryknoll, NY: Orbis Books.

Ruether, R. R. (Ed.). (2005). *Integrating ecofeminism, globalization, and world religions.* Lanham, MD: Rowman & Littlefield.

Spring, O.; Hans G. B.; & Tidball, K. G. (Eds.). (2014). *Expanding peace ecology: Peace, security, sustainability, equity and gender.* New York: Springer.

United Nations Development Fund for Women (UNIFEM). (n.d.). Retrieved April 29, 2009, from http://www .unifem.org

Warren, K. (2000). *Ecofeminist philosophies.* Lanham, MD: Rowman & Littlefield.

Women's Action Agenda 21. (n.d.). Retrieved April 29, 2009, from www.iisd.org/women/action21.htm

Women's Environment and Development Organization (WEDO). (n.d.). Retrieved April 29, 2009, from http://www.wedo.org

Women and Social Change Leadership

Kathy ENGEL
New York University

Women have always taken on leadership roles in the fight for social change, equality, and peace. While their methods and leadership styles have differed, ranging from the use of hierarchical power to a commitment to collectivism, from identifying as caretakers to claiming power equal to that of men, women leaders in the fight for social justice have gained important changes that benefit not only women but all members of society.

Women have been in the vanguard of peace and social justice movements. Across cultures and throughout history, women have experienced ongoing systemic oppression, and they have responded with creative alternatives and progressive movements of protest. Examples include Harriet Tubman in the fight against slavery, Fannie Lou Hamer for voting rights, Ella Baker and Mary White Ovington in the Civil Rights Movement, Rosa Luxemburg in the German socialist movement, Winnie Mandela in the antiapartheid movement, Puerto Rican independence leader and poet Lolita Lebrón, and American Indian movement activists Anna Mae Aquash, Ingrid Washinawatok, and Winona LaDuke. Women have been pioneers in movements for labor rights, prison reform, reproductive rights, health, education, affordable housing, affirmative action and equal rights, human rights, and environmental safety—there is no single approach or characteristic that encompasses women as social change leaders. These women's leadership styles span a range—from soft to harsh, from espousing collectivism to wielding individual, hierarchical power, and from identifying as "caretaker of life" to calling for power equal to that of men.

Women have often, naturally, pushed to the forefront issues commonly identified as women's issues or feminist issues. Access to water, for example, an issue for women in many parts of the world is not always considered as such elsewhere and among different class groups, where the defining question for women might be identified as equal pay/equal rights, affirmative action, or reproductive choice.

There are those who are known publicly, who act as the spokespersons of change, such as Margaret Sanger (1879–1966), the American birth control activist, but there are also those who work day in and day out, in the midnight hours after the children have been fed, or not fed, put to bed, the laundry done, as writer and feminist Tillie Olsen (1912–2007) spoke of—writing at the ironing board. Some of these women take unimaginable risks overcoming physical, economic, social and emotional obstacles to "fix the world."

Ultimately, any obstacle to the fair treatment of women and girls—access to water, health, and safety—is a women's issue and a human rights issue. Some activist movements focus exclusively on issues directly affecting women. Since gender comes first in their analysis, they are primarily feminist or "womanist" in their actions and priorities. Women who have led in the arena of women's issues range from Gloria Steinem (b. 1934), an American journalist and activist known for her work in the feminist movement beginning in the late 1960s, and Nawal El Saadawi (b. 1931) of Egypt, a writer and physician known for her work against female genital mutilation. They have raised issues including reproductive rights, equal rights (including the fight for an amendment to the Constitution, the ERA, in the United States) and domestic and gender violence.

There has always been the challenge of developing a truly race- and class-inclusive movement of women, which would by definition address gender *and* race and class, with attention paid to the different realities faced by women from different ethnic, cultural, and economic backgrounds. It is the leadership of women of color and some "white" women that has consistently broadened the understanding of women's struggles to embrace pragmatically and in spirit the challenges faced by women who have lived racism and poverty. The lawyer, feminist, and civil rights activist Florynce Rae "Flo" Kennedy (1916–2000), a black woman from a working-class background in Missouri, became known for using "intersectionality" (the study of intersecting social identities) in her activism, highlighting the effects of what she called the "institutionally racist, sexist, classist society" of the United States.

In many places around the world, where people are struggling for national liberation from brutal dictatorships or foreign occupations, there is continuous debate about the level of priority of gender, or women's, rights in the context of the national struggle for freedom, human rights, and equality. The danger of identifying gender issues as less than top priority is that the reality and primacy of maternal mortality as a number-one oppressor and killer is then treated as secondary. The United Nations (UN) estimates that 35 percent of women have experienced physical or sexual violence at some point in their lives, and it is women who lead in making this an issue of global policy.

New Paradigms for Leadership

At the UN, women such as American activist Charlotte Bunch (b. 1944) have successfully campaigned for the principle that women's rights are human rights, as are civil rights. This is not a new post-Cold War effort. There are women who have worked for equal rights throughout history. Their struggle was not based on a quest for a different set of values and approaches, but access to what had historically been denied women. These questions run through any historical discussion about women's leadership and movements:

- What is a women's movement?
- What is "feminist" or "womanist" and does feminism speak to the needs of all women?

- What role does a women's movement play in a national progressive movement for economic justice, equality, peace, and human rights?
- What are the characteristics of women's leadership that contribute to a wider perspective on social change?

Women have historically insisted on the unity of civil rights, human rights, and women's rights. In the United States, Fannie Lou Hamer (1917–1977), who led a campaign for voting rights for African Americans in the 1950s and 1960s, is remembered as saying, "I don't want no equal rights any more. I'm fighting for human rights." Women in the civil rights movement got little attention, and indeed the prominent leaders were men. In recent years, however, there has been an effort to draw attention to people like Hamer and the educator and activist Dorothy Irene Height (1912–2010), whom President Obama called, "The godmother of the civil rights movement." In recent years, this wider focus on human rights continues. In 2013, Alicia Garza, Patrisse Cullors, and Opal Tometi founded the movement Black Lives Matter with a hashtag and a call to action on social media to address systemic racism and violence in the United States. These women and others are part of the new generation of women leading social change movements.

Change in Recent Decades

Phrases like "the personal is the political" and "everything is connected" emerged from the women's movement of the 1970s, when women leaders insisted that the needs and wants of the whole person in society be reflected in public policy. The ongoing contribution of women to global, national, and community politics and the embrace of connectedness as a worldview represent one of the most significant victories in the transformation of the struggle for human rights worldwide.

In the twenty-first century, we are emboldened by a powerful international movement of non-governmental organizations confronting governments and established ruling classes. The recognition of women's rights as human rights effectively gained credibility at the international level at the UN World Conference on Human Rights in Vienna, held in 1993, due largely to the work led by Charlotte Bunch of the Center For Women's Global Leadership at Rutgers University in the United States, and including the leadership of Betty Murungi of Kenya, Magalys Arocha of Cuba, Myrna Cunningham of Nicaragua, Tarcila Rivera of Peru, Viviana Figueroa of Argentina, Lepa Miedjenovic of Serbia, Loune Viaud of Haiti, Vivian Stromberg of the MADRE organization, Lucy Mulenkei of Kenya, Gladys Acosta of Peru, Pam Spees of the United States, Rhonda Copelon of the City University of New York Law Center, and the American activist Bella Abzug (1920–1998). These advocates, attorneys, and scholars have successfully campaigned on many issues, one important example being UN Security Council Resolution 1820, which states that rape and violence against women are crimes against humanity and war crimes.

Throughout history, movements led by women have sprung up organically and urgently in response to crises. In the United States, Sojourner Truth and Harriet Tubman were the most famous but not the only women who were heroes of slave resistance. Today, in countries across the world, the mothers of "disappeared" children and mothers against police violence and state tyranny lead the way to new movements for justice.

Lois Gibbs, a working-class housewife and mother, led the struggle in the late 1970s to clean up her neighborhood of Love Canal, built on a toxic waste dump, because of the danger to her children's health. Karen Silkwood (1946–1974), a worker at a nuclear facility, brought the danger of low-level radiation to a dramatically new level of consciousness. She was killed as she drove to meet a reporter with information she was about to release. Crystal Lee Sutton led the union struggle at J. P. Stevens in the early 1970s, outraged by her own experience of inequality and abusive working conditions. In 1955, Rosa Parks (1913–2005) dared to sit in the front of a bus in segregated Alabama, sparking a new phase in the freedom movement in the United States.

Nearly a century after the Triangle Shirtwaist Fire in 1911, which caused the deaths of 146 garment workers and led to the growth of the International Ladies' Garment Workers' Union (ILGWU), it was predominantly young women who worked to end sweatshop labor in lower Manhattan, where employees were still subjected to brutal working conditions. Sweatshop conditions continue to exist in New York City and around the world today.

In Argentina, El Salvador, South Africa, Israel, Palestine, and throughout the world, mothers have often been the most powerful advocates for peace and human rights, some driven by a demand for the recovery of their children who have "disappeared," or been tortured or killed, appealing to the moral conscience of the world. During the Vietnam War, Women Strike For Peace, Women's International League for Peace and Freedom, and the American Gold Star Mothers (an organization of mothers who have lost a child in military endeavors) helped to pierce the government propaganda at that time and spoke to Americans about the horror of the war. Women's International League for Peace and Freedom even sent a delegation to North and South Vietnam to advocate for peace.

It would be a serious mistake, however, to characterize the contribution and leadership of women in social change movements as based solely on the "moral power of mothers." Historically, women leaders for progressive social change have combined scholarship, analytic depth, and strategic and creative power with the willingness and ability to recognize and connect with moral and emotional vision and choices. In recent years, female activists like Malala Yousafzai, a Pakistani activist for female education and the youngest recipient of the Nobel Peace Prize, and the actress Emma Watson have worked with the UN to highlight the need for education, human rights, environmental protections, and other issues.

Further Reading

Arendt, H. (1969). *On violence.* New York, London: Harcourt Brace Jovanovich.

Bell-Scott, P. (Ed). (1991). *Double stitch, black women write about mothers and daughters.* Boston: Beacon Press.

Bell-Scott, P. (Ed). (1994). *Life notes, personal writings by contemporary black women.* New York, London: Norton.

Cook, B. W. (Ed.) (1986). *Women in culture and politics: A century of change.* Bloomington, IN: Indiana University Press.

Davis, A. (1981). *Women, race, and class.* New York: Vintage Books.

Gioseffi, D. (Ed.). (1988). *Women on war.* New York: Simon and Schuster.

Hooks, B. (1981). *Ain't I a woman: Black women and feminism.* Boston: South End Press.

Johnson, V. (1996). *Voices of the dream: African American women speak.* San Francisco: Chronicle Books.

Jordan, J. (2002). *Life after Lebanon. Some of us did not die.* New York: Basic/Civitas Books.

Randolph, S. (2015). *Florynce "Flo" Kennedy: The life of a black feminist radical.* Chapel Hill: The University of North Carolina Press.

Anthony, Susan B.

1820–1906—US social reformer

Denise R. JOHNSON
Independent Historian

Susan B. Anthony was one of the first US feminist leaders, a suffragette and campaigner for women's rights, the abolition of slavery, and alcohol temperance. She dedicated her life to these goals of reform, travelling the country to give speeches and attend reform meetings, often suffering backlash and criticism for overstepping the bounds of traditional femininity. A natural leader and free-thinker, Anthony also benefitted from the mentorship of other social reformers, both men and women.

Susan B. Anthony was a feminist leader and trailblazer for women's rights who spent her life working for positive social change. She dedicated her life to various reform movements, including abolition of slavery and temperance, which eventually gave way to her leading the fight against society's overall oppression of women. She sought legal reforms of restrictive marriage and divorce laws of the nineteenth century that left divorced women without property or means of support. Likewise, nineteenth-century laws denied divorced women custody of their children and afforded women little or no legal recourse over domestic disputes. Along with other like-minded early feminists, Anthony appealed to local and state legislatures of the northeast to consider the plight of women, especially the most vulnerable who had little or no means of support or way of seeking restitution in a society favoring men and restricting the lives of women. Anthony led the way for general social reforms and fought for equal voting rights for women against opponents who supported disenfranchisement of women. She demonstrated a tenacity and commitment to improving women's lives not typical of most nineteenth-century women, although throughout her long life Anthony did share the limelight with many notable figures such as the US women's suffrage leader Elizabeth Cady Stanton (1815–1902).

Anthony believed that obtaining voting rights would be the best first step in eradicating other oppressive conditions for women, and that women's public activism would help level the playing field in the domestic, social, economic, and political arenas. Everything she did was deemed to be for "the cause," which she regularly referenced as being the central force of her being—to gain the vote so that future generations of women could break free of the chains of oppression and openly participate in public life.

A National Heroine Is Born

Susan Brownell Anthony was born into a working-class household on 15 February 1820 in Adams, Massachusetts. Her father Daniel was a devout Quaker, and her mother Lucy Read was a Baptist. Anthony's father, like other Quakers, based his beliefs on egalitarian principles and valued education as a worthy endeavor for both boys and girls. With their father's guidance, the Anthony children briefly attended public school and then were homeschooled. As a young girl attending a public school, Susan was denied the opportunity to learn long division because the schoolmaster did not believe that girls should learn mathematics. Anthony's outraged father then removed her from public school and began the process of homeschooling under the tutelage of Mary Perkins. In 1837, Anthony's father enrolled Susan in a Quaker female seminary school run by Deborah Moulson. Anthony's formal schooling may not have been remarkable; however, her earliest written correspondence and diary reflect a personal rejection of the overemphasis placed on female piety and morality. Like all good Quakers, Anthony found these qualities acceptable within reason and practiced them personally; however, she became more interested in social and civil responsibility as a way of showing human morality. Throughout her long career as an activist against vice and the ills of society, Anthony demonstrated a natural inclination to stand by her convictions and take on roles of leadership in hopes of improving society.

Although the nineteenth century has been referred to as the "Era of the Common Man," the common woman gained little notice for her commonness. Economic dependency and restrictive marriages dictated woman's role in society, which led to Anthony's questioning the status quo at an early age. For example, as a girl of about eleven, Susan asked her father why a young and competent woman in his mill was not made overseer instead of a less-qualified man. Daniel Anthony explained that society simply would not accept such an arrangement and left her question largely unanswered. This vague reply did not appease Anthony, who continued to question the inequalities of society. Within a year, Daniel Anthony's business failed and Susan was forced to leave school. Soon after, she met Lucretia Mott (1793–1880), a Quaker and avid abolitionist, who was one of the founders of the Philadelphia Female Anti-Slavery Society. Although Anthony had grown up in an abolitionist household, Mott's fiery speeches stirred her soul and solidified her conviction to support the movement. During the early years of abolition reform, many Quakers remained ambivalent about the institution of slavery. As a result, the Hicksite Quakers, who supported abolition as well as other reforms, and with whom Mott had affiliated, became a more progressive group than mainstream Quakers.

Undoubtedly Anthony's new convictions regarding abolition posed a conflict within her family as to whether or not the cotton processed in her father's mills was produced by slave labor. Her father was spared the conflict because the business went bankrupt during the financial crisis known as the Panic of 1837, and he was forced to auction off the family's house, furnishings, and nearly all of their possessions. By 1839, Daniel Anthony had moved his family from Battenville, New York, to the impoverished town of Center Falls. In this small town, Anthony's family eked out a living by taking in boarders, while the senior Anthony earned a meager income as a postmaster. Susan B. Anthony took up teaching to assist her family, and although she wrote numerous letters and visited home as often as she could, she became a *femme sole* (woman alone) because marriage would take her sisters in one direction, while her career and life as a single women would take her in another. As a teacher, Anthony began to hone her skills of leadership by establishing herself as an individual and as an agent for social change.

Early Years of Leadership

Teaching was one of the few professions available to nineteenth-century women. Many of Anthony's contemporaries had taken up teaching but had abandoned the profession after marriage. Susan B. Anthony vowed never to marry and to encourage women to shun the social institution of marriage until full rights of citizenry were granted to women. Through teaching, Anthony gained a sense of autonomy and independence that she would have never realized as a married woman. Practicing her own advice and dedicating her life to reform, Anthony never allowed her personal life to interfere with her public ambitions. Until her death, she remained the staunch and principled leader of the women's suffrage movement, and continued to support other avenues of reform for the benefit of women and men alike.

By 1845, Anthony had carved out a life as a teacher and reform activist and had broadened her circle of friends to include many abolitionists and temperance reformers. During the 1840s, Anthony was involved with abolition work and with the Daughters of Temperance, which advocated for stronger liquor laws due to the effects of drunkenness on families. She soon gained pubic notice and was sought out to speak at temperance gatherings. Through these speeches and the many gatherings she attended, Anthony became acquainted with prominent leaders who helped her develop her natural inclination for leadership. One such person was Stanton, who became a lifelong friend and partner in the fight for equal rights. The duo attended temperance, abolition, and women's rights conventions together, and by 1855 Susan B. Anthony had become one of the nation's most outspoken leaders in the reform arena.

Until 1854, Anthony's work had been conducted in New York. As she became more active in the public sphere, her connection to prominent literati and reformers became extremely important to her leadership development. For example, prominent abolitionists William Lloyd Garrison and Samuel Joseph May sought her out as a traveling agent for their abolition society, which led her to widespread speaking engagements and national attention. Meanwhile, Anthony continued to work for temperance and women's rights, with women's suffrage at the epicenter of her work. Her leadership captured the attention of the nation, with many newspapers expressing opinions ranging from praise to condemnation that a woman would speak so forcefully in the public arena. Anthony humbly accepted the praise and steeled herself against the condemnations of newspaper editorials and outraged ministers who reminded Anthony to remember her place as a woman. At times she even had to deflect criticism from men who were members of reform societies to which she belonged.

Hope for Future Generations of Women

Although Anthony remained single her entire life, she had several suitors and turned down many proposals. Anthony felt that marriage would interfere with her beloved reform work. At times, she became frustrated with the women around her and often expressed deep regret when one by one most of her female friends married and had children. Yet married women such as Elizabeth Cady Stanton aided Anthony's rise to prominence as a leader. Many historians have noted that while Stanton was an eloquent writer, Anthony became a dedicated orator. Both women wrote and gave speeches; but Anthony, being single, could put more time and energy into her work. Anthony's growth as a leader was not an easy process. At times she felt ill at ease in the limelight; however, her dedication to reform gave her a strong voice and an air of dignified composure that was often noted by those who heard her speak.

As a Quaker, Anthony spoke directly to her audiences without mincing words. Whenever possible she spoke with other prominent reformers in order to add impact to speeches and public forums. She sought liaisons with important people who could impress their reform goals on society. After the Civil War and the abolition of slavery, she turned her full attention to women's suffrage and other women's rights issues. During the 1870s, women canvassed the nation in hopes of gaining support for the vote. Many women were heckled, some were arrested, and others became discouraged and abandoned the suffrage movement. Anthony refused to give up and again demonstrated her daring and leadership by illegally voting in a New York election in 1872. She was arrested and brought before Judge Hunt, who fined her for the infraction; Anthony refused to pay and appealed to the court. The outraged judge could not subdue the determined suffragette whose pleas for equality filled the courtroom. The case was dropped because the judge did not want Anthony tried by a jury who might have had sympathy for the plight of women who sought the vote.

By 1900, Anthony's leadership came full circle as she stepped down from her post as leader of the National American Woman Suffrage Association (NAWSA), which began in 1848 and lasted until 1921. Anthony quietly died in 1906 as her friend Anna Howard Shaw held her hand, but not before her leadership had inspired a nation of women to press on in order to gain the vote in 1920.

Further Reading

Anthony, K. (1954). *Susan B. Anthony: Her personal history and her era.* New York: New York University Press.

Archer, J. (1991). *Breaking barriers.* New York: Viking Penguin.

Auster, A. (1984). *Actresses and suffragettes: Women in the American theatre, 1890–1920.* New York: Praeger.

Barry, K. (1988). *Susan B. Anthony: A biography of a singular feminist.* New York: New York University Press.

Buechler, S. (1990). *Women's movements in the United States: Women suffrage, equal rights, and beyond.* Newark, NJ: Rutgers University Press.

Burns, K. et al. (1999). *Not for ourselves alone.* New York: Alfred A. Knopf.

Daley, C. & Nolan, M. (1995). *Suffrage and beyond: International feminist perspectives.* New York: New York University Press.

Davis, P. (1970). *A history of the national woman's rights movement.* New York: Source Book Press.

Dubois, E. (1992). *Elizabeth Cady Stanton/Susan B. Anthony correspondence, writings, speeches.* Boston: Northeastern University Press.

Edwards, T. (1990). *Sowing good seeds: The northwest suffrage campaigns of Susan B. Anthony.* Portland: Oregon Historical Society Press.

Flexner, E. (1975). *Century of struggle: The women's rights movement in the United States.* Cambridge, MA: Harvard University Press.

Ford, L. (1991). *Iron jawed angels: The suffrage militancy of the national women's party, 1912–1920.* Lanham, MD: University Press of America.

Frost, E. & Cullen-DuPont, K. (1992). *Women's suffrage in America: An eyewitness history.* New York: Facts on File.

Garner, L. (1984). *Stepping stones to women's liberty: Feminist ideas in the women's suffrage movement, 1900–1918.* Madison, NJ: Dickinson University Press.

Kraditor, A. (1965). *Ideas of the woman suffrage movement, 1890–1920.* New York: Columbia University Press.

Lutz, A. (1985) *Susan B. Anthony: Rebel, crusader, humanitarian.* Boston: Beacon.

Melder, K. (1977). Beginnings of sisterhood: The American woman's rights movement, 1900–1850. New York: Schocken Press.

Rawkow, L. & Kramarae, C. (1990). The revolution in words: Righting women, 1868–1871. New York: Routledge.

Sherr, L. (1995). Failure is impossible: Susan B. Anthony in her own words. New York: Times Books.

Solomon, M. (1991). A voice of their own: The woman suffrage press, 1840–1910. Tuscaloosa: University of Alabama Press.

Wells-Barnett, Ida B.

1862–1931—US journalist and activist

Caryn E. NEUMANN
Miami University of Ohio

Journalist and speaker Ida B. Wells-Barnett is best known for leading the fight against the lynching of African-Americans in the late nineteenth and early twentieth centuries. The "mother of clubwomen," she also helped form the first national organization of black women in the United States.

The civil-rights activist and journalist Ida Bell Wells, who came to national prominence with her crusade against and exposure of the lynching of African-Americans in the South, was born to former slaves, on 16 July 1862 in Holly Springs, Mississippi. Both of her parents succumbed to a yellow fever epidemic in 1878, forcing Wells to drop out of Shaw University (later Rust College) to support her five younger siblings. She taught in a rural school until she accepted an aunt's invitation in 1881 to move the family to Memphis, Tennessee. She eventually secured a teaching position in the Memphis public schools.

Resistance to Racism

A fiery woman unafraid to challenge authority, Wells began her activist career by defying the segregationist conventions of her day. On 15 September 1883, she refused to move to the segregated section of a railroad car. Dragged off a Chesapeake, Ohio, and Southwestern Railroad train after biting the conductor who tried to evict her, Wells won a lawsuit against the railroad in the lower courts only to see the Tennessee Supreme Court overturn the verdict in 1887. A request to write about this episode for a local Baptist weekly, the *Living Way,* launched her journalism career.

Using the pen name "Iola," Wells wrote articles on politics and race for black newspapers across the nation. She also became a co-owner of the Memphis militant weekly *Free Speech and Headlight* in 1889. Two years later, Wells lost her teaching position—her main source of income—for criticizing the local school system for its inadequate facilities and its toleration of instances of exploitative sexual relations between black female teachers and white board members.

The First Anti-Lynching Leader

Already established as a respected voice with the African-American community in Memphis, Wells risked everything when a close friend died, along with two other black men, at the hands of a lynch mob in 1892. Much more than a murder, a lynching was an organized attack by a mob of whites upon an individual or group of African-Americans, often with the complicity of local and state law enforcement agencies. As Wells grasped, the true purpose of a lynching was to intimidate an entire African-American community. Faced with white support for lynching and a dearth of black male leadership on the matter, Wells publicly counseled grassroots resistance in Memphis. She advised blacks to arm themselves for self-defense, and used her newspaper to strongly encourage African-Americans to abandon Memphis for the newly opened territory of Oklahoma.

This episode also transformed Wells into one of the nation's earliest investigative reporters. Conventional wisdom held that lynchings came in response to assaults by black men upon white women. Determined to end these brutal killings, Wells combed through newspaper accounts, visited death sites, and interviewed witnesses to determine that most lynchings were motivated by economic competition and racial control rather than a defense of southern white womanhood. In 1892, she published an editorial that revealed that most "rapes" were in fact often consensual liaisons between black men and white women. Wells wrote, "White men lynch the offending Afro-American, not because he is a despoiler of virtue, but because he succumbs to the smiles of white women." In response to the article, an angry mob of whites demolished Wells's newspaper office. Anticipating possible trouble, Wells had left Memphis before the offending editorial appeared in print. Warned of the probability that she would be lynched if she returned, she settled in New York City.

In the North, Wells continued her anti-lynching activism. Besides writing articles for the *New York Age*, she penned *Southern Horrors* (1892). The pamphlet's title mocks Southern honor as the commonly cited justification for lynching while documenting that only a third of the 728 lynching victims between 1884 and 1892 were even accused of rape. To spread her message, Wells took to the podium to denounce lynching.

A Public Woman

In the late Victorian era, women rarely ventured into the male public sphere. Wells changed this by spearheading the black women's club movement. To publish *Southern Horrors*, African-American women in New York, Boston, and Philadelphia held fundraising testimonials on Wells's behalf, thereby laying the groundwork for further organization. Meanwhile, in an attempt to apply international pressure upon the United States, Wells gave speeches in Europe about lynching. In response, a white Little Rock, Arkansas editor warned that no one should believe an African-American woman, since all black women were liars and prostitutes. In 1896, a furious Wells prompted the formation of the first nationwide black women's organization, the National Association of Colored Women (NACW), with a speech that challenged the women of the race to fight the widely reported claims of this bigoted editor. Later, in 1913, she would help organize the Alpha Suffrage Club,

Illinois's first black woman's suffrage organization, to agitate for tangible political power for women.

Wells married prominent Chicago attorney Ferdinand L. Barnett in 1895 and made the unusual choice to maintain her strenuous schedule. Although the births of her four children necessitated periodic withdrawals from the public, Wells-Barnett became one of the very few working mother activists of her time.

While she made lynching a political issue and established the groundwork for the eventual abolition of the practice in the mid-twentieth century, Wells-Barnett could not maintain effective leadership within the black community. Accustomed to battling for attention, she forged ahead with her own agenda and methods at the expense of relationships with her peers. In 1899, she left the NACW when she lost an election for presidency of the group. In 1909, she helped found the National Association for the Advancement of Colored People but ended her stormy relationship with the organization in the following year. By the 1920s, Wells-Barnett found herself and her vision of agitation out of favor among African-American reformers. She died of a kidney ailment on 25 March 1931, in Chicago.

During Wells-Barnett's lifetime, lynching did not stop but it did become a national source of shame as the result of her reporting. By exposing the white lies fabricated to justify murder and by organizing black resistance to racism, Wells served as a herald of the coming US civil rights movement. The radical and outspoken qualities that made Wells into a successful crusading journalist did not make her a successful leader. Unable to compromise with others who shared her ultimate goal of a just nation, she is remembered chiefly as a publicist of the horrors of black life in the United States.

Further Reading

Bay, M. (2010). *To tell the truth freely: The life of Ida B. Wells*. New York: Hill and Wang.

Duster, A. M. (1970). *Crusade for justice: The autobiography of Ida B. Wells*. Chicago: University of Chicago Press.

Giddings, P. (2009). *Ida, A sword among lions: Ida B. Wells and the campaign against lynching*. New York: Harper.

McMurry, L. O. (1998). *To keep the waters troubled: The life of Ida B. Wells*. New York: Oxford University Press.

Royster, J. J. (Ed.). (1997). *Southern horrors and other writings: The anti-lynching campaign of Ida B. Wells, 1892–1900*. Boston: Bedford Books.

Schechter, P. A. (2001). *Ida B. Wells-Barnett and American reform, 1880–1930*. Chapel Hill: University of North Carolina Press.

Thompson, M. I. (1990). *Ida B. Wells-Barnett: An exploratory study of an American black woman, 1893–1930*. Brooklyn: Carlson.

Goldman, Emma

1869–1940—US anarchist and feminist

Laurien ALEXANDRE
Antioch University

An anarchist and agitator for women's reproductive rights and freedom of speech, Emma Goldman remains a standard-bearer for leftist activists. A talented organizer and orator, she was the subject of much controversy during her lifetime, and was imprisoned and later deported for her activities. Today she is remembered not as "one of the most dangerous women" of her time, but as one of the first leaders in the radical and feminist movements.

Russian-born Emma Goldman, who immigrated to the United States in 1885, stands as a major figure in American radical and feminist history. As an impassioned advocate and intellectual leader, she used her pen and voice to influence, engage, and inspire others for social change in the early decades of the twentieth century. "Red Emma," as she was often called at the time, advocated for birth control and women's sexual emancipation, criticized mandatory conscription into the military during World War I, preached atheism, lectured on drama and the arts, fought for an eight-hour workday, and defended the ideals of anarchism in print and in lecture halls around the world. For this she was harassed, imprisoned, and ultimately deported.

Perhaps Goldman's greatest strength as a leader lay in her ability to inspire and influence society's disenfranchised; her domain was that of the "dissenting groups," in developmental psychologist Howard Gardner's terminology. While Goldman had limited crossover appeal to society's more privileged elements, the strength of her indirect leadership through her writing and speaking across the country gave her a reputation as "one of the most dangerous women" of her time. A visionary propagandist and activist, she promoted ideas aimed at liberating the body, spirit, and mind. Her story is one of a woman leader who used her skills, energy, and compassion tirelessly, and in the face of tremendous opposition, to bring forth an alternative vision, and an alternative story, for the "American century." Emma Goldman used her impassioned writing and speaking to spread a radical vision of a new social order. Her words affected and inspired those who heard her, as well as generations who read her words subsequently. The radical and feminist movements have spawned gifted leaders since her time, but few as influential and notable as Emma Goldman was for her generation and for those to come.

Early Years and Immigration

Born on 27 July 1869, Emma Goldman lived as a child in a small Russian city of Kovno, now in Lithuania. Her first experiences of injustice can be traced to her family's poverty and the ruthless and omnipresent anti-Semitism of the time. Her father's violent manner and authoritarian rule prompted Emma's earliest rebellions. At twelve, she moved with her family to St. Petersburg, where she glimpsed new movements for new social orders—Czar Alexander II was assassinated during Emma's brief stay in the city. She soon left Russia to pursue a "modern" education in Germany, where she developed an appreciation of classical music, drama, opera, and great literature. This early exposure gave her a lifelong appreciation for the role of the arts in elevating the human condition. Although Goldman was to be best known for her writings on behalf of anarchism, she would also write and lecture extensively on the arts, poetry, and literature. Among the writers she admired were George Bernard Shaw, Ralph Waldo Emerson, Walt Whitman, Anton Chekov, and Henrik Ibsen.

When she returned to Russia several years later, her father sent her to work in a corset factory and began pressuring her into an arranged marriage—whereupon, in 1885, sixteen-year-old Emma and her favorite half-sister Helena, set sail for the United States. Like so many immigrants of the time, she looked toward the new land as a place of hope, justice, and freedom. Upon seeing the Statue of Liberty, Emma Goldman was inspired by its symbols of hope and freedom for all. But her high hopes were dashed by the horrific working-class realities of her factory job in Rochester, New York. She also married a Russian immigrant and entered into a brief, unhappy marriage.

The Turning Point

The year 1886 was pivotal in Emma's evolution as an anarchist leader. Labor and radical activists held a rally in Chicago's Haymarket Square to protest the recent police brutality against McCormick Harvester workers striking for an eight-hour workday. A bomb was thrown at the rally, injuring people and killing one police officer. The media and authorities blamed Chicago's anarchist leaders and, amidst the hysteria of the times, condemned seven to death on flimsy evidence. Four were executed on 11 November 1887. Inspired by the stirring defiance of the imprisoned and doomed leaders, the outraged Goldman—still in her teens—became an active anarchist. Six years later, in 1893, the then-governor of Illinois, convinced of the Haymarket defendants' innocence, pardoned the remaining imprisoned anarchists. Goldman would fight for the rest of her years against the kind of hysteria that had led to the conviction and death of innocent people because of their unpopular political ideas. Indeed, the incident inspired her to a life-long commitment to freedom of speech and of the press.

With her political development came changes in her personal life as well. Risking the stigma of divorce, she left her husband in Rochester and moved to New York City, joining the anarchist community there. She quickly found a prominent place in the largely male labor and radical movements. Her eloquence and communication skills were soon apparent, and her speaking tours, for which she was known throughout her life, began during this period. She also met and fell in love with Alexander Berkman, a Russian émigré and "chum of a lifetime," in Goldman's words; together they vowed to dedicate their lives to anarchism. Although her love for Berkman was profound and public, she also had passionate affairs with other known radical men of the time.

Controversy and Deportation

In 1892, Carnegie Steel's manager Henry Clay Frick provoked a bloody confrontation with workers at the company's Homestead plant in Pennsylvania. Goldman and Berkman plotted to retaliate. When Berkman shot and injured Frick, he was convicted and sentenced to twenty-two years in prison. Although Goldman was involved in the plot, and verbally justified the attempted assassination, there was insufficient evidence to indict her. Berkman spent fourteen years in prison, and Goldman was tireless in her efforts to seek his release. In later years, she would denounce political violence.

The imprisonment of her colleague did not stop Goldman from her role as a spokesperson for unpopular ideas. Arrested in 1893 for urging a crowd of unemployed workers to demonstrate rather than rely on the electoral process for relief, she spent ten months in jail. Later, she chained herself to a podium to make it physically impossible for the police to remove her before she finished speaking. When President William McKinley was assassinated by Leon Czolgosz in 1901, police immediately tried to implicate Goldman because Czolgosz had attended one of her lectures. Although arrested, she was ultimately released, again due to lack of evidence against her.

After a brief withdrawal from public life, Goldman re-emerged with a strong presence, writing and editing her free-spirited monthly magazine *Mother Earth* from 1906 to 1917. She wrote and spoke on topics ranging from political theory and her own socialist brand of anarchism to drama and the arts to sexual emancipation. Her words inspired radicals across the country, but enraged and outraged authorities. Anti-radical, anti-immigrant hysteria was reaching a fever pitch.

As the United States moved toward war in late 1916, Goldman and others opposed the government's military preparations, believing that wars were fought on behalf of the rich at the expense of the poor. *Mother Earth* was Goldman's forum. In a government-sponsored pro-war crusade, however, *Mother Earth* and other antiwar periodicals were banned. Goldman wasn't silenced. She pressed on with her antiwar activities and within weeks of America's entry into World War I, she helped launch the No-Conscription League to encourage conscientious objectors.

In 1917, Goldman and her comrade Berkman were charged with conspiring against the draft and sentenced to two years in prison. Shortly after her release, she was re-arrested by a then young J. Edgar Hoover, who referred to Goldman as "one of the most dangerous women in America." On 21 December 1919, Goldman, Berkman, and over two hundred other foreign-born radicals were deported and forced to set sail for the Soviet Union.

Life in Exile

Goldman's remaining years were very difficult. With the exception of a ninety-day lecture tour granted during the Roosevelt administration, Emma Goldman never set foot on US soil again, spending the last twenty-two years of her life in Russia, Sweden, Germany, France, England, and Canada. The years in exile away from family and friends, the estrangement she felt in these countries, and the lack of money and legal rights, weighed heavily on Goldman. While exiled in her native Russia, she was outraged by the authoritarianism and over-bureaucratization of the Bolshevik state, as well as its repression of anarchists and limitations placed on individual freedom. Although she defended the Russian Revolution, she also argued against its excesses, most notably in her books *My Disillusionment in Russia* and *Further Disillusionment in Russia*. Her outspoken criticism of the Soviet state alienated her from many of her European and American radical colleagues. Hoping to secure a place to live with the rights and privileges of British citizenship, she married an elderly Welsh coal miner in the mid-1920s, despite her principled objections to the institution of marriage. In 1931, she published her two-volume autobiography *Living My Life*, which is still in print and read widely today.

At age sixty-seven, with the promise of an anarchist revolution in Spain, Goldman hurled herself into the Spanish cause. After Franco's triumph in 1939, she moved to Canada where she devoted the last year of her life to securing political asylum for the refugees of the Spanish war. Goldman died in Toronto on 14 May 1940. After her death, the US Immigration Service allowed her body to be readmitted to the United States, where she was buried at Waldheim Cemetery in Chicago near the Haymarket anarchists who had inspired her.

Legacy and Influence

Freedom of speech was a cause Emma Goldman championed throughout her life. As a powerful anarchist orator, she faced constant threats from police and vigilantes. Undeterred, she continued to find the courage of her convictions, although she paid dearly for her outspokenness.

The attempts to suppress Goldman and her unconventional views led many, even those who disagreed with her, to support her right to express her ideas. As a leader for "dissenting" groups, she promoted a broad range of issues and in so doing, influenced those even outside her immediate circle. Emma Goldman was unwavering and fearless; she stood up for unpopular causes and devoted her life's work to speaking and writing about injustice. Her vision was so profound that it inspired generations of women and men to come. For example, Goldman's unwavering and fearless commitment to freedom of expression influenced Roger Baldwin, founder of the American Civil Liberties Union, who heard her speak in 1908. Later he told Goldman in a letter, "You always remain one of the chief inspirations of my life, for you aroused in me a sense of what freedom really means" (*The Emma Goldman Papers* 2002). Emma Goldman's advocacy in defense of unpopular ideas (and her right to speak her views in public) helped keep secure the right of freedom of speech in the United States by inspiring others to champion such causes throughout the twentieth century.

But perhaps it was on issues of women's emancipation that Goldman spoke and exemplified the most unconventional opinions of the time. As an activist, she placed the personal sphere on a par with the economy, the state, and war. Goldman wrote about passionate love and reproductive freedom, advocating for birth control, which she believed was essential for women's freedom. She smuggled contraceptive devices into the United States and lectured frequently on the "right of the child not to be born." Several times she was arrested and charged with violating the Comstock Law, which prohibited the distribution of birth control literature and other articles of "immoral use." In Goldman's mind, only anarchism could set women free.

For her impassioned intellectual vision, Emma Goldman is also viewed as an influential leader of the feminist movement in the United States. The quote inscribed on the T-shirts of many 1960s young feminists was ascribed to her: "If I can't dance, I don't want to be part of your revolution." In reality, as she wrote in her autobiography after being reproached by a fellow radical who felt her dancing was inappropriate for an political agitator (Goldman 1934, 56), "I insisted that our cause could not expect me to behave as a nun and that the movement should not be turned into a cloister. I want freedom, the right to self expression, everybody's right to beautiful, radiant things. Anarchism means that to me."

Further Reading

The Emma Goldman Papers. (2002). Retrieved March 19, 2003, from http://sunsite.berkeley.edu/Goldman

Drinnon, R. (1982). *Rebel in paradise: A biography of Emma Goldman.* Chicago: University of Chicago Press.

Goldman, E. (1970). *Anarchism and other essays.* New York: Dover. (Original work published 1917.)

Goldman, E. (1934). *Living my life.* New York: Knopf. (Original work published 1931.)

Goldman, E. (1925). *My disillusionment in Russia.* London: C.W. Daniel.

Goldman E., & Shulman, A. (1998). *Red Emma speaks: An Emma Goldman reader* (3rd Edition). New York: Humanity Books.

Gornick, V. (2011). *Emma Goldman : Revolution as a way of life.* New Haven: Yale University Press.

Sanger, Margaret

1879–1966—Founder and leader of the US birth control movement.

Peter C. ENGELMAN
New York University

Margaret Sanger's devotion to and leadership of the cause for safe, legal birth control in the early to mid-twentieth century rivals more well-known US social reform leaders. She started and led the organizations that would coalesce into the Planned Parenthood Federation of America. In her late sixties, she led efforts to spread the movement internationally, helping to change the lives of women and families worldwide.

Margaret Louise (Higgins) Sanger led the successful campaign to make birth control legal, safe, and accessible. Sanger's law-defying tactics and shrewd public-relations maneuvers broke down long-standing anti-obscenity laws that prohibited the circulation of contraceptive information. Her activism educated and enlightened a repressive society and initiated a dramatic change in sexual mores. In a career spanning five decades, Sanger inspired a contentious alliance of radicals, society women, philanthropists, and medical professionals to open a network of birth control clinics, refine and develop contraceptives, and establish one of the most familiar and far-reaching women's health organizations in the world.

Early Life and the Call to Activism

Margaret Louise Higgins was the sixth of eleven children born to a freethinking Irish stonemason and his devout Catholic wife in Corning, New York. Margaret's mother weakened with each successive pregnancy, dying of tuberculosis at age fifty in 1899, a death Margaret blamed on excessive childbearing. Caring for her dying mother confirmed Margaret's interest in medicine, and she entered a nursing program the following year. She suspended her nursing career in 1902 to marry William Sanger, an artist and draftsman, and begin a family. From 1903 to 1910 Margaret gave birth to three children and lived a quiet suburban life, just outside New York City. Unsatisfied with the routines of family life, both Margaret and William sought to become more involved with socialist politics and to be nearer to the artistic and political radicalism of Greenwich Village. They moved to the city in 1911, joined the

Socialist Party, and immersed themselves in the burgeoning bohemian culture that was attracting creative dissenters and reformers from all over the country.

Radical Work as a Socialist

Sanger accepted a paid position as a lecturer for the Socialist Party and then moved on to an organizing role with the Industrial Workers of the World (IWW). While participating in IWW-led strikes in 1912–1913, Sanger closely observed the leadership styles of other organizers, including William ("Big Bill") Haywood (1869–1928) and Elizabeth Gurley Flynn (1890–1964), a highly effective orator who offered Sanger a model for an outspoken woman agitator. Sanger also admired the anarchist icon Emma Goldman (1869–1940), who delineated the link between women's empowerment and voluntary motherhood more than a decade before Sanger came on the scene.

Sanger returned to nursing on a part-time basis in New York, accompanying obstetricians into the immigrant neighborhoods of Manhattan's Lower East Side, where she witnessed the devastating effects of indiscriminate child-bearing, such as infant and maternal mortality, overcrowding, and dire poverty. She learned that the 1873 Comstock Act, which outlawed the dissemination of "immoral" articles, and associated laws that banned obscenity prohibited doctors from giving contraceptive information to patients, even when a woman's health was at risk. Sanger felt powerless to help; the only birth control methods she knew of at the time were condoms and withdrawal, which left the man solely in charge. "I resolved that women should have the knowledge of contraception. They have every right to know about their own bodies" (Sanger 1931, 56). Her nursing experience gave direction to her radicalism and later became her key credential when discussing the plight of poor women incapable of controlling their fertility.

Free Speech and Birth Control

In her informal lectures to women for the Socialist Party and before IWW groups, Sanger increasingly discussed sexual hygiene and health. The lectures led to a series of articles in the radical daily *The New York Call*, under the title "What Every Girl Should Know." In February 1913, the US Post Office banned publication of an article that discussed venereal disease. This act of official suppression made Sanger more militant in her speech. In 1914, she published an extremist monthly newspaper, the *Woman Rebel*. The paper amounted to a big dare: a challenge to its readers to oppose conformity and convention; an announcement to authority that women would defy the laws that banned the circulation of contraceptive information. Each woman, Sanger insisted, must be the "absolute mistress of her own body" (quoted in Baskin 1976, 25), and only through birth control—the term was first used in the *Woman Rebel*—could women ever achieve economic or political equality. The US Post Office confiscated six issues of the *Woman Rebel*, and federal agents indicted Sanger for violating the Comstock Act.

In the midst of her free-speech battle, Sanger prepared *Family Limitation*, a how-to manual that outlined and illustrated various forms of birth control, including condoms, diaphragms, douches, sponges, and withdrawal. She instructed friends to release the pamphlet after she fled the country in October 1914 to escape the *Woman Rebel* charges and a potential prison sentence. *Family Limitation* marked Sanger's emergence as the leading proponent of birth control in America.

Her self-imposed exile in Europe in 1914–1915 gave Sanger an opportunity to develop the intellectual framework she needed to broaden interest in a birth control campaign. She formed a lasting friendship with the great pioneer of sexual modernism, Havelock Ellis (1859–1939), who became her chief mentor, and with leading Malthusians (those who believed, following the writings of the nineteenth-century economist Thomas Malthus, that unchecked population growth would lead eventually to worldwide famine) in England. Ellis helped Sanger to soften her antiestablishment arguments, celebrate birth control as a precondition to women's sexual pleasure, and more clearly articulate eugenics-based arguments for smaller families.

Building a Movement

Sanger returned to the United States in the fall of 1915 to face trial on her *Woman Rebel* charges and take advantage of increased public interest in birth control following the arrest and imprisonment of her now estranged husband for distributing *Family Limitation*. On the eve of Sanger's trial in November 1915, her five-year-old daughter Peggy died of pneumonia. This personal tragedy intensified support for Sanger and prompted federal prosecutors to dismiss her case. In the spring and summer of 1916, Sanger crossed the country on a city-to-city speaking tour. Though still in mourning and unaccustomed to public speaking, she exhibited a disarming frankness in making emotional appeals for a woman's right to control her own body. Pretty, feminine, even vulnerable looking, she spoke in a clear, musical voice that provided an effective contrast to her blunt statements about biological ignorance and the revolutionary power of birth control to free women, reform the capitalist labor system, control poverty and disease, and end war.

Upon her return to New York, Sanger directly challenged the Comstock laws by opening the nation's first contraceptive clinic in Brooklyn in October of 1916. The Brownsville clinic served more than four hundred women in a period of two weeks before Sanger, her sister Ethel Byrne, and an assistant were arrested. The ensuing trials and thirty-day prison sentences served by Sanger and Byrne catapulted the cause of birth control onto the front pages of the nation's newspapers and brought a number of prominent society women on board. Though Sanger lost an appeal of her Brownsville conviction two years later, the courts recognized the health benefits of birth control and rendered a more liberal interpretation of the anti-obscenity laws, paving the way for legal, doctor-run clinics.

Sanger skillfully orchestrated these dramatic events to put her name and the issue of birth control into the newspapers and before the public. She even used the new medium of film, writing and starring in the silent "Birth Control" in 1917, to enhance her charismatic hold over a growing number of young women activists. She retold and revised accounts of her early activism throughout her life to justify her leadership and attract new followers.

Clinics and a New Coalition

Immediately following World War I, Sanger distanced herself from her antiestablishment roots and pulled the birth control movement into the mainstream, partly by choice and partly out of necessity. The war left the US radical movement in shambles, and Sanger recognized the need for a broader constituency to win over middle-class support needed to sustain the cause and change the laws. She sought alliances with doctors, advocates of population-control, and eugenicists, and worked to transform the birth control movement from a free-speech campaign into a medically sanctioned public-health program. It was no easy task, however, as her confrontational style alienated many in the medical and social-science communities. She relied heavily on leveraging the publicity generated by continuing government interference—the suppression of speech, the seizure of medical records, the confiscation of contraceptives and literature by Post Office and Customs agents—to compel prominent medical men to stand behind her. Methodically, but not without many set-backs, Sanger built an impressive coalition out of groups that largely distrusted each other and at times agreed on little more than that birth control was vital to human progress.

In 1921, Sanger organized a birth control conference in New York to attract greater academic and medical support and to launch the American Birth Control League (ABCL), the organizational and financial centerpiece of the movement. Her two books from this period, *Woman and the New Race* (1920) and *Pivot of Civilization* (1922), also attempted to redefine birth control along scientific lines and to draw the support of eugenicists, who enjoyed tremendous political influence in the 1920s. Sanger advocated a program of "negative eugenics" which sought to contain—largely through the voluntary use of birth control—those deemed "unfit" to procreate because of disease, mental deficiency, or delinquency. At no time did she define unfitness or inferiority in racial terms as did many leading eugenicists. Sanger opened the Clinical Research Bureau in New York in 1923, the first legal contraceptive clinic in the United States, and the model for physician-directed birth control clinics that opened across the country in the interwar years. She endorsed the diaphragm paired with a contraceptive jelly as the safest and most effective female birth control method. The diaphragm required medical fitting and instruction, further pushing the movement under medical supervision.

Leading the Movement to the Mainstream

Sanger further insulated her leadership position by becoming a woman of wealth and social stature in the 1920s. After divorcing her first husband in 1921, she married millionaire businessman J. Noah Slee in 1922, a decision that paid off handsomely for a movement always short on funds. Her new wealth allowed Sanger to travel the world in style and gain notoriety in Asia and Europe, strengthening her sway over the movement at home. No other birth control leader could draw the media and create publicity as effectively as Sanger, whom the newspapers were now referring to as world renown.

Sanger did not tolerate rivals and quickly defused attempts to undermine her authority as the movement's principal leader. She attacked and diminished the personalities and accomplishments of other birth control reformers, primarily the more deliberate, less provocative Mary Ware Dennett (1872–1947), who quickly faded from the movement. With few exceptions, Sanger surrounded herself with dedicated followers who worked to satisfy her goals but exhibited limited personal ambition. When a factional dispute did develop within the ABCL in the late 1920s, primarily over Sanger's leadership approach, Sanger decided to resign as president (in 1928) and reassert her leadership outside of an inhibiting organizational structure.

A year later she established a new organization, the National Committee on Federal Legislation for Birth Control (NCFLBC), and instituted a much looser organizational framework than the ABCL. The NCFLBC lobbied Congress from 1930–1937 to pass legislation lifting the bans on birth control. It failed to push a bill through, but once again Sanger managed to create sustained publicity, this time through dramatic congressional testimony. The committee disbanded soon after a significant court victory in 1936 in *United States v. One Package*, a case originated by Sanger in 1931 that opened the way for the legal distribution of contraception. By the end of the 1930s, a large majority of Americans—more than 70 percent—supported the legalization of birth control.

Having achieved many of her goals, including an American Medical Association endorsement of birth control in 1937, Sanger both stepped back from the movement and was pushed aside by an influx of younger public-relations professionals and medical bureaucrats. She facilitated a merger between the two branches of the movement, the ABCL and her Clinical Research Bureau, to form the Birth Control Federation of America in 1939 (it changed its name to the Planned Parenthood Federation of America in 1942), then retreated to her Arizona home, serving little more than an honorific role in the new federation.

International Birth Control and the Pill

After the war, in her late sixties, Sanger emerged from semiretirement to lead a new international coalition. Sanger had championed birth control abroad since the early 1920s. World tours in 1922 and 1935, along with her organization of several conferences fundamental to contraceptive research and population planning—including the 1927 World Population Conference in Geneva—had solidified her international leadership position. Challenged by European birth control reformers to help rebuild a viable postwar movement, and responsive to fears of population explosion in the developing world, Sanger played a pivotal role in organizing the International Committee on Planned Parenthood in 1948. This led to the International Planned Parenthood Federation (IPPF), which formed in 1952 with Sanger as its first president. She was unyielding, even imperious in steering the divisive organization through its first decade of existence, keeping it focused on contraceptive distribution through clinics and public health programs. A new generation of birth control activists complained about Sanger's peremptory manner and increasingly erratic leadership—she was in and out of hospitals with a heart condition and suffered from other infirmities. But none of them had a sufficient international following that would have enabled them to directly challenge her position. Sanger stepped down as president in 1959.

Both in the United States and abroad Sanger had instigated and encouraged contraceptive research in hopes of discovering cheaper, more effective, and less intrusive methods. In 1951, she convinced the philanthropist Katharine Dexter McCormick (1875–1967) to support the research of the biologist Gregory Pincus (1903–1967) on a hormonal method of inhibiting human ovulation. Sanger had envisioned an oral contraceptive pill as early as 1930, though few scientists had any confidence in the idea. It was largely Sanger's initiative and fund-raising skill that enabled and accelerated the research and testing that brought the birth control pill to market in 1960. The pill brought to fruition Sanger's controversial crusade to provide women with the opportunity for greater autonomy in both their private and public lives. Six years later Sanger died at age eighty-seven.

Impact and Legacy

The virtual elimination of religious, legal, and moral opposition to birth control during her career demonstrated Sanger's effectiveness as a leader. While she has been criticized for leading the movement away from a goal of woman-controlled healthcare that many feminists envisioned, the movement generated more momentous social change—as manifested in the changed role of women and the dynamic of the family—than any other twentieth-century social movement. A historical re-evaluation of Sanger is underway today, primarily because of her ties to the eugenics movement. Her leadership qualities and character should also be reexamined and compared with those of other US social reform leaders, such as the abolitionist William Lloyd Garrison (1805–1879), who shared with Sanger an uncommon, lifelong allegiance to a single cause.

Further Reading

Baker, J. (2011). *Margaret Sanger: A life of passion*. New York: Hill & Wang.

Baskin, A. (Ed.). (1976). *Woman rebel*. Stony Brook, NY: Archives of Social History.

Chesler, E. (1992). *Woman of valor: Margaret Sanger and the birth control movement in America*. New York: Simon & Schuster.

D'Emilio, J. & Freedman, E. B. (1988). *Intimate matters: A history of sexuality in America*. New York: Harper & Row.

Gordon, L. (1977). *Woman's body, woman's right: A social history of birth control in America*. New York: Penguin Books.

Engelman, P. (2011). *A history of the birth control movement in America*. Santa Barbara: Praeger.

Katz, E., Hajo, C. M., & Engelman, P. C. (Eds.). (2003). *The selected papers of Margaret Sanger: Vol. I. The woman rebel*. Urbana: University of Illinois Press.

McCann, C. R. (1994). *Birth control politics in the United States, 1916–1945*. Ithaca, NY: Cornell University Press.

Pincus, G. (1965). *The control of fertility*. New York: Academic Press.

Reed, J. (1978). *The birth control movement and American society: From private vice to public virtue*. Princeton, NJ: Princeton University Press.

Sanger, M. (1920). *Woman and the new race*. New York: Brentano's.

Sanger, M. (1922). *Pivot of civilization*. New York: Brentano's.

Sanger, M. (1928). *Motherhood in bondage*. New York: Brentano's.

Sanger, M. (1931). *My fight for birth control*. New York: Farrar & Rinehart.

Sanger, M. (1938). *Margaret Sanger: An autobiography*. New York: W. W. Norton.

Suitters, B. (1973). *Be brave and angry: Chronicles of the International Planned Parenthood Federation*. London: International Planned Parenthood Federation.

Tone, A. (2001). *Devices and desires: A history of contraceptives in America*. New York: Hill & Wang.

Carson, Rachel

1907–1964—US scientist and environmentalist

Maril HAZLETT
Independent Scholar

Despite the bias against women in the sciences, Rachel Carson succeeded in a career with the US Fish and Wildlife Service and as a science writer. Her 1962 book, *Silent Spring*, started the contemporary environmental movement. Warning about the dangers of DDT, she alerted people to the risks industrialized society posed to the environment and about the inextricable connection between humans and their environment.

With her 1962 book, *Silent Spring*, scientist Rachel L. Carson started the environmental movement by alerting postwar America to the hazards of synthetic chemical pesticides. *Silent Spring* focused primarily on the dangers DDT posed to wildlife and human health. Only eighteen months after the book's publication, Carson died from breast cancer, but her insights—in particular, that humans and nature are inextricably connected ecologically—have lived on. The first annual Earth Day in 1970 officially launched the current US environmental movement, and many successes followed—in environmental legislation and activism, conservation efforts, and the growth of organic agriculture, for example. Carson's ideas helped to guide these trends. Rachel Carson did not fit traditional models of leadership, however,.

Early Years

Carson grew up in western Pennsylvania and spent comparatively little time with other children her age; her mother, believing that Carson had a frail constitution, often kept her out of school. As a follower of the nature study movement—a teaching method that held that direct experience of nature could lead a child to both an aesthetic and scientific appreciation of the environment—Carson's mother tutored her according to these beliefs. The two spent hours roaming the land around their small farm, identifying birds, plants, and animals. This early upbringing later helped Carson to envision herself as not only a member of a human community, but also of the nonhuman environment.

When she entered Pennsylvania Women's College (now Chatham College), Rachel Carson decided to become a member of the scientific community as well.

She began college with the intention of becoming a writer, but then found herself fascinated by biology and the life sciences. With the encouragement of her mentor and science instructor, Mary Scott Skinker, Carson majored in English and biology. In 1929, Carson entered graduate school in zoology at Johns Hopkins University. However, at this time much bias and discrimination existed against women in the sciences. Most people believed that women were not intellectually or physically capable of pursuing scientific careers. In the scientific professions, few if any women ever rose to positions of power.

Her difficult family situation, compounded with this discouraging atmosphere, affected Carson's graduate career. As she started graduate school, the Depression had also just begun. Jobs and resources were scarce. Because of age or health problems, few of her family members could hold full-time jobs. At one point while a graduate student, Carson was financially responsible for five only partially able-bodied family members. To accommodate her outside employment, she was forced to drop to a part-time student status. As a result, her research moved slowly as well. She found herself more and more on the margins of academic life. Finally, Carson was forced to acknowledge that she could not both go to graduate school and support her family. After finishing her thesis and receiving a master's degree, Carson gave up her dream of pursuing a doctorate and started looking for a job instead.

A Scientist and a Writer

The gender bias against women in science followed Carson into employment. Luckily, however, given the dire economic climate, she did find a position. She began working in 1936 as a science writer for the US Bureau of Fisheries (later the US Fish and Wildlife Service). Although trained to perform scientific research, Carson instead found herself editing and summarizing the research of others. At this time, it was not uncommon for female scientists to find themselves supporting the work of male scientists rather than directly participating in or directing fieldwork or experimentation. The low-paying job did have some advantages, however. Carson had access to a vast realm of scientific literature, much of it unavailable to the general public. Later in her career as a writer, she would draw on the background and expertise provided by this job.

For more than fifteen years Carson stayed with the Fish and Wildlife Service. To help supplement her income—she now supported a household that included her aging mother and two young nieces—Carson also began writing science articles for local, regional, and eventually national publications. In her day job, she also began to move into positions of more responsibility, coordinating researchers, artists, and writers on various publication projects. While the career paths for a nonresearch scientist in government employment were limited, Carson still found opportunities to develop her leadership abilities. In particular, she learned to balance the often different perspectives of creative and scientific people.

To the casual observer, Carson's gender, upbringing, employment, and to some extent her personal inclination—she often displayed the solitude-loving characteristics of a writer—would seem to have worked against her becoming a leader. In fact, her life simply demonstrated a less traditional route toward leadership. Early in life, Carson assumed a guiding role within her family. Her mother took care of the home, and Carson became that home's primary connection with the outside world. Even within the somewhat constrained world of government employment, Carson developed many close friendships with other women in similar positions. Her most important connections were immediate, intimate, and supportive. She and her community of friends also learned to negotiate the hierarchical structure of the government bureaucracy that employed them. From these experiences, Carson developed a canny sense of politics and power.

These years immersed in scientific literature also added new dimensions to Carson's sense of membership in a larger ecological community. Moreover, the Fish and Wildlife Service was the home of the conservation movement in the federal government. This movement, begun around the turn of the century and focused primarily on issues of land and game management and wilderness preservation, was the precursor to the environmental movement. From these conservation contacts, Carson gained an in-depth understanding of the nature advocates whom she would eventually inspire with *Silent Spring*. When she did take on a leadership role, it would not be to exercise power over the natural world, but to become an advocate on its behalf.

Becoming a Leader

Carson made her first impression on the public mind as a science and nature writer. After the success of her 1937 article "Undersea" in the *Atlantic Monthly*, she wrote *Under the Sea-Wind* (1941). The book was published only one month before the attack on Pearl Harbor, however. In the rush of America's entry into World War II, it quickly disappeared from sight. Disappointed, Carson decided to focus on writing articles. In part because of her dissatisfaction with her job, by 1948 she had begun conceiving her second book, a natural history of the earth's oceans. *The Sea Around Us* (1951) was an enormous success. It won the National Book Award, and by the end of 1951 had sold over 250,000 copies. Carson was able to quit her job at the Fish and Wildlife Service and become a full-time writer.

As a best-selling author, Carson began her first ventures into public speaking. Some of her favorite themes included the beauty and complexity of nature, as well as the respect that it deserves from humanity. She also discussed the dangers of science and technology, and the need for science to be accessible to all citizens, so that they might make informed decisions on the risks posed by industrialized society. As she told one audience in 1952, "Mankind has gone very far into an artificial world of his own creation. He has sought to insulate himself, in his cities of steel and concrete, from the realities of earth and water and the growing seed. Intoxicated with a sense of his own power, he seems to be going farther and farther into more experiments for the destruction of himself and his world" (quoted in Lear 1997, 221).

Indeed, this statement introduced one of the major themes that would make Carson such an important intellectual leader for the contemporary environmental movement: the idea that humans were wrong to try to dominate nature. Such efforts would result in only self-destruction, she held, because humans too are a part of the environment. In her third book, *The Edge of the Sea* (1955), Carson emphasized the importance of humans gaining direct, immediate experience of the natural world. Such intimacy with nature, she believed, would make destroying the environment all but impossible.

Silent Spring

Carson originally intended her fourth book to focus on evolution, not pesticides. However, during the late 1950s, several events turned her attention toward these synthetic chemicals. Carson had first become interested in the environmental hazards of pesticides in the mid-1940s while working at Fish and Wildlife. After World War II, chemical manufacturers released the wartime chemical DDT (dichlorodiphenyltrichloroethane) into domestic markets. Several wildlife biologists had expressed worries over DDT's impact on wildlife populations. Other scientists were concerned with its potential effects on human health. As the public and agribusiness enthusiastically welcomed the chemical, however, such worries were pushed aside.

But a decade later the public mind, at least, had begun to change. Increasingly, the postwar environment seemed saturated with synthetic chemicals. These included food additives and various pollutants as well as pesticides. A group of Long Island residents sued their local government for an injunction to prevent aerial spraying of their homes, farms, and livestock. Disturbing reports began to surface from the South, where the US Department of Agriculture's aerial spraying campaign had wreaked devastation on wildlife and domestic animals. Grassroots antipesticide campaigns began to organize around the country.

Carson too found herself disturbed by environmental damage from pesticides. Originally she meant to write only an article on the topic, but could find no magazine to publish it. Thus the project evolved into a book. Beginning in 1957, Carson meant to write quickly, but instead *Silent Spring* took almost five years to complete. One reason was that the research fascinated and absorbed her. Carson, however, suffered many health problems during this time as well. The most severe came in late 1960: a diagnosis of advanced breast cancer.

When *Silent Spring* came out in 1962, the message of was alarming. As a scientist, Carson pointed to ecological principles to communicate the dangers of synthetic chemical pesticides. All living creatures, humans included, are made up of cells, she pointed out. All of them live embedded in habitats composed of air, water, soil, and plants. All depend on a fragile genetic code to perpetuate their communities. Pesticides disrupt and damage this fragile ecology. The long-term effects of pesticides on both wildlife and human health would prove the danger of humans dominating, rather than accommodating, nature.

The reaction to *Silent Spring* was immediate, enormous, and widespread. The public was horrified; few had realized the dangers of the pesticides that permeated their everyday lives. The chemical and pesticide industries were outraged, countering that their products *saved* lives by increasing agricultural production and preventing the spread of epidemic disease. Other reactions were more mixed. Scientists split over whether Carson was right. The Department of the Interior rejoiced at the opportunity to mitigate the effects of these chemicals on wildlife, but the Department of Agriculture dug in its heels at any new attempts to regulate agricultural chemicals. Politicians called Senate hearings, where pesticide policy reform found itself deadlocked.

In the controversy over *Silent Spring*, a public unnerved and alarmed by the potential long-term effects of pesticides—not only on their environment but on themselves—became Carson's followers. *Silent Spring* touched off a storm of debate that lasted long past Carson's 1964 death from breast cancer, barely eighteen months after the book's publication. Rachel Carson led a new way of thinking about the environment, one that launched a revolution in public opinion aimed at eliminating the hazards of industrial chemicals. Her example tells us that leadership does not only come from within organized groups, but also can come from the outside. Speaking truth to power—in this case, the entrenched powers of the agribusiness lobbies and government bureaucracies—is just as important as the exercise of power. Rachel Carson's leadership took the form of speaking up for nature.

Further Reading

Brooks, P. (1972). *The house of life: Rachel Carson at work*. Boston: Houghton Mifflin.

Carson, R. (1955). *The edge of the sea*. Boston: Houghton Mifflin.

Carson, R. (1951). *The sea around us*. New York: Oxford University Press.

Carson, R. (1962). *Silent spring*. Boston: Houghton Mifflin.

Carson, R. (1941). *Under the sea-wind*. New York: Simon & Schuster.

Dunlap, T. (1981). *DDT: Scientists, citizens, and public policy*. Princeton, NJ: Princeton University Press.

Graham, F. (1970). *Since Silent Spring*. Greenwich, CT: Fawcett.

Hynes, P. (1989). *The recurring silent spring*. New York: Pergamon Press.

Lear, L. J. (1997). *Rachel Carson: Witness for nature*. New York: Henry Holt.

Friedan, Betty

1921–2006—US feminist leader

Caryn E. NEUMANN
Miami University of Ohio

After publishing *The Feminine Mystique* in 1963, Betty Friedan became a leader for the women's movement, initiating the so-called second wave of feminism. She helped cofound the National Organization for Women (NOW) and became a fearless and combative spokesperson for reproductive rights and greater representation of women in the workforce.

Betty Friedan helped begin the second feminist movement in the United States in the 1960s by writing *The Feminine Mystique* and founding the National Organization for Women (NOW). Born Bettye Naomi Goldstein in Peoria, Illinois, on 4 February 1921, the future feminist displayed formidable intelligence and strong opinions in an era when beauty mattered most in girls. After graduating summa cum laude from Smith College in 1942, Friedan pursued graduate study in psychology at the University of California at Berkeley.

Rumblings of Discontent

In 1943, Friedan won the prestigious Abraham Rosenberg Research Fellowship, the largest grant available at Berkeley and one sufficient enough to last through the end of her doctoral studies. Rather than being overjoyed, she regarded the award with conflicting emotions. Noting that most women with doctoral degrees remained single, Friedan feared that accepting the fellowship would end her hopes of a family life. Adding to the pressure, Friedan's boyfriend reminded her that he would never win such an award and pushed her to decline the honor. She did so but would later use this episode in *The Feminine Mystique* as an example of the hostile forces weighing down women struggling to reach their full potential.

Moving to New York City in 1943, Friedan found work as a labor journalist with the left-wing Federated Press. In 1946, the United Electrical, Radio, and Machine Workers hired her away as a reporter for their official house organ. In June of the next year, she embarked on a tumultuous marriage to Carl Friedan, an entrepreneur and advertising executive. Pregnant with her second child in 1952, the union fired Friedan from her job. In 1956, she would bear her third and last child.

A community activist in her suburban New York City neighborhood, she spent the 1950s employed as a freelance author for mass-circulation women's magazines. Plagued by guilt that she had not lived up to the glorious future forecast for her, she sought a reason as to why so many of the best and brightest women of her generation also felt dissatisfied.

Birth of the Feminist Movement

Friedan's experiences of sex-based discrimination combined in 1957 to lay the groundwork for *The Feminine Mystique*. In this year, her Smith College class held its reunion and Friedan distributed a detailed questionnaire for classmates that would become the germ of the book. Most of the alumnae professed to be happy with their lives, but 60 percent did not find fulfillment in their role as homemaker. Friedan had discovered what she would term "the problem that has no name," the deep-seated and confused dissatisfaction her classmates felt but could not fully articulate. *The Feminine Mystique*, so-named because it challenged the myth of feminine fulfillment, appeared in print on 19 February 1963.

With a focus on white, middle class suburban women, Friedan provided a coherent explanation for the routine belittlement that women had experienced all their lives. She argued that the feminine mystique required women to renounce their brains and deny their senses, retreat to a childlike state and immolate themselves on the altar of their family's needs to find satisfaction in life. A distinctive aspect of the book was Friedan's use and gendering of contemporary psychology, particularly the theories of Abraham Maslow. She took what psychologists had written about men and turned it to feminist purposes by arguing that people developed a healthy identity not through housework but through commitment to purposeful and sustained effort.

The book became an instant bestseller. For years afterward, women would tell Friedan that reading it had changed their lives. But society as a whole did not receive Friedan's message warmly. Interviewers focused on her appearance, her personality, and her life story to trivialize her findings. Partly in response, she became defensive and combative.

Leader of the Feminist Movement

In 1966, the Equal Employment Opportunity Commission (EEOC) treated women's complaints about sex discrimination as a joke and instead focused on the problems of black men. Convinced of the need for an organization to fight on behalf of women's concerns, Friedan helped cofound the National Organization for Women (NOW). Already the public face of feminism, she served as the president of NOW until 1970. To make an impact, NOW made use of Friedan's boldness and disdain for rules, but once the organization had matured it had little use for what some called her temper and histrionics.

In 1969, a group trying to make abortion legal for doctors to perform invited Friedan to a meeting in hopes that her fame would bring publicity to their movement. At the founding of the National Association for the Repeal of Abortion Laws

(NARAL—later called the National Abortion Rights Action League), Friedan suggested that the right of a woman to control her body lay at the heart of the abortion rights movement and persuaded the group to change their focus to a woman's choice. NARAL, now known as Pro-Choice America, continues to advocate for women's reproductive freedoms but Friedan never played a big part in the organization..

The qualities of independence and combativeness that enabled Friedan to shatter societal presumptions about the proper place of women also made it impossible for her to work collaboratively to sustain her leadership of the women's movement throughout the 1970s. She simply managed to offend virtually everyone with whom she worked. Other women's activists, notably the more photogenic Gloria Steinem, assumed leadership of the movement as Friedan lost followers.

By the 1980s, Friedan had returned to her journalistic roots. Her 1981 book, called *Second Stage*, focused on working collaboratively with men to better the world. *The Fountain of Age*, about the myths of growing old that prompt some people to withdraw from life, made the bestseller list in 1993, while *Beyond Gender: The Real Politics of Work and Family* appeared in 1997. Enormously active as she grew older, Friedan published her memoir *Life So Far* in 2000. She died of congestive heart failure on her eighty-fifth birthday.

The mother of American feminism, Friedan had the vision and determination to establish the women's movement. She gave women the opportunity to choose the direction of their lives and encouraged them to reach their full potential.

Further Reading

Friedan, B. (2013). *The Feminine Mystique.* New York: W.W. Norton.

Friedan, B. (2006). *Life So Far: A Memoir.* New York: Simon & Schuster.

Hennessee, J. (1999). *Betty Friedan: Her life.* New York: Random House.

Horowitz, D. (1998). *Betty Friedan and the making of* The Feminine Mystique. Amherst: University of Massachusetts Press.

Sherman, J. (Ed.). (2002). *Interviews with Betty Friedan.* Jackson: University Press of Mississippi.

PART III

Women in Politics

An Overview of Women's Political Leadership

Karen O'CONNOR and Eric D. LOEPP
American University and University of Wisconsin–Whitewater

In the United States and other nations, the road to political leadership for women began with suffrage, followed by the slow acceptance of women in political office. Today, with many women leading governments in developed and less developed countries, they still encounter challenges when working to achieve their agenda both before and after attainting office. Yet women in positions of power are changing perceptions of who political leaders should be and how they should be as leaders.

Perhaps the most prevalent definition of political leadership is offered by the historian James MacGregor Burns. He describes political leadership as the power a leader exercises through his or her relationships. The people with whom the political leader interacts, and how he or she interacts with those people, become essential in defining the strengths and weaknesses of any political leader.

Political leaders include elected officials from mayors to senators and non-elected officials such as interest group officers and party activists. Historically, political leadership roles have been held by men; in the United States, the "conventional" politician has been a white, middle-aged male. Women have struggled to achieve both equal rights as well as equal access to political life; unwelcome in the board-room and the elected office, they were unable to build the necessary relationships to accrue the power necessary to lead.

In the 1960s, after years of groundwork laid by previous generations of female activists and other leaders, women were able to gain access to American political life and create social change from within governmental institutions. Outside the United States, female voters have increasingly gained the right to vote, and women are even holding elected office at higher rates than men in some countries like Bolivia and Rwanda. Yet modern social science research also shows that women continue to grapple with an uneven political playing field, even in democratic nations like the United States.

Nixon with Payton, Keller.. - "President Nixon meets with Jayne Spain and hosts one of the first press gatherings announcing appointments for women in the administration, April 21, 1971. Left to right: Vicki Keller, Dr. Valerija Raulinaitis, Jayne Spain, President Nixon, Barbara Franklin, and Sallyanne Payton". Courtesy of Barbara Franklin Papers, Penn State University Archives.

First Efforts at Political Leadership

The first American women political leaders got their start during the antislavery movement. When Lucretia Mott (1793–1880) and Elizabeth Cady Stanton (1815–1902) traveled to England with their husbands in 1840 to attend a meeting of the World Anti-Slavery Society, they were shocked when they could not participate as delegates. Instead, banished to the balcony, they reflected on their status vis-á-vis the slaves they were trying to free and vowed to hold a convention to address women's unequal treatment in all spheres of life.

When this meeting was finally held in 1848 in Stanton's home town of Seneca Falls, New York, over 240 women responded to their call. In what has come to be known as the Seneca Falls Convention, the women drafted a Declaration of Sentiments modeled after the Declaration of Independence, as well as a series of resolutions demanding greater social, religious, and civil rights for women. One of the rights the delegates viewed as most important was the franchise. Without the right to vote, women's voices would never be heard in the halls of government.

The meeting at Seneca Falls and the subsequent formation of groups that ultimately joined forces to become the National American Woman Suffrage Association (NAWSA) in 1890, immensely broadened opportunities for women's political leadership. These events also led to the creation of a new cadre of women political leaders, including Stanton and Susan B. Anthony (1820–1906), who led the women's movement through the rest of the nineteenth century.

Battle for Suffrage

In the late nineteenth and early twentieth centuries, women around the world began to press for the right to vote in earnest, an effort today referred to as first-wave feminism. In Australia in 1891, for example, Rose Scott (1847–1925) helped found the Womanhood Suffrage League. In the Netherlands, Aletta Jacobs (1854–1929) became the first woman in her country to study at university; in addition to becoming the nation's first female medical doctor, she would spend her life advocating for women's rights. In Great Britain, the move for suffrage was led by Emmeline Pankhurst (1858–1928) and her daughters Sylvia and Christabel. Because of Britain's unitary system of government, the British suffrage movement was able to target a single source of political power, the Parliament, in seeking the franchise. In the United States, with its federal system, however, at least until around 1915, the drive for women's suffrage was focused largely on winning the right to vote in each of the individual states. Because the suffragettes were better organized on the national level, they found the state-by-state battle to be a challenge; also, powerful entities such as the Roman Catholic Church mobilized to try to stop the efforts of women's rights activists.

Around 1915, leaders of the US suffrage movement shifted their focus. Spurred on by Alice Paul (1885–1977), who had recently returned from a stint working in the British movement, the NAWSA began to demand a federal constitutional amendment to enfranchise women. Around the same time, the General Federation of Women's Clubs endorsed woman suffrage, recognizing that the widespread reforms inspired by the progressive movement would be far easier to attain if women had the political clout of the franchise. These women, however, rarely spoke of the need for women political leaders, and instead wanted suffrage more to do good for society than as a way to increase leadership opportunities for women.

After the Victory of Suffrage

While many states afforded women the right to vote prior to the 1920s, the right was not federally protected until the ratification of the hard-fought Nineteenth or Susan B. Anthony Amendment, which gave women the right to vote in all state and federal elections. In an attempt to broaden the political power of women, many of NAWSA's leaders founded the League of Women Voters, a nonpartisan, good-government organization. A major task of the league was to encourage voter turnout and to provide the electorate with the information they needed to make informed electoral choices.

Despite the league's encouragement, few women rushed to become active participants in the government. This is likely because women, who had been denied political power for more than three hundred years, simply were not socialized to vote or run for public office. Interviews with women nonvoters in 1923 proved this theory, as many women stated that it was not their civic duty to vote. More than 10 percent of those surveyed believed women should not vote at all.

Once public opinion polling became common in the 1930s, it was clear that the road for women seeking political power would be a difficult one. Yet the public was not opposed to all forms of women's political leadership. Nearly half of those polled during the 1930s, 1940s, and 1950s said a woman would be preferred to a man as the head of the local Red Cross chapter or Parent Teacher Association. The public supported women in these positions because they were extensions of women's primary roles as mother and homemaker.

Still, some women held elective office during these years. The most common route to these positions was a practice known as "over his dead body," where widows were appointed to serve the remainder of their husband's terms, usually in state or federal legislatures. A small number of women, including actresses Helen Gahagan Douglas (1900–1980) and Clare Booth Luce (1903–1987) won seats in the US House of Representatives. Their actions paved the way for other women to run in their own right.

The Women's Movement

Just as a generation of women became politically active during the antislavery movement, the US civil rights movement of the 1960s created a new generation of women political leaders. Although these women still were not regarded as equal participants in American life, the women of the 1960s had greater liberties than their predecessors. In time, these would include, for example, access to more reliable contraceptives, including birth control pills, which helped to free women from the fear and consequences of unplanned pregnancies and the resulting childcare responsibilities.

Efforts to expand women's rights in the 1960s began with the creation of the Presidential Commission on the Status of Women (PCSW). This organization, commissioned by President Kennedy and chaired by former first lady Eleanor Roosevelt, was charged with assessing how women were treated in society and making policy recommendations to the president in domains like education and employment. Until this point in history, legislation concerning gender and the workplace was largely protectionist in nature, advocating different roles and responsibilities for male and female employees. These policies were ostensibly put in place to protect women from workplace injury and exploitation as well as to promote their health, but in effect provided a legal justification for paying women less than men or not hiring them at all. PCSW's final report, published in 1963, documented widespread discrimination and made several recommendations that would ultimately be incorporated into federal legislations like the Pay Equity Act of 1963.

Following the dissolution of the PCSW 1963, members of the commission went on to form the Citizens Advisory Council on the Status of Women (CACSW), a precursor to the National Organization for Women (NOW), which is today the largest group advocating for women's rights in the United States. The creation of NOW represented the beginning of second-wave feminism, an era in which women's rights advocates moved beyond voting enfranchisement and became increasingly active in combating gender-based discrimination across other areas of society. Evidence of these efforts is clear when we consider the growth in the number of women legislators that began in this era. In 1969, only 4 percent of all elected legislators were women. A change in attitudes about women in political leadership roles, especially among the educated elite, occurred between 1967 and 1975. By 1985, 15 percent of all legislators were women.

Women Form Political Organizations

Some of the dramatic change in the attitudes toward women in political leadership roles can also be attributed to the growth of organizations dedicated to increasing the number of women in elected and appointive positions of political leadership. For example, one of the first African American women to serve in Congress, Shirley Chisholm (1924–2005), joined forces with Gloria Steinem (b. 1934), Betty Friedan (1921–2006), and Representative Bella Abzug (1920–1988), to form the nonpartisan National Women's Political Caucus (NWPC) in 1971. The caucus' major goals included increasing support for women running for positions of political leadership, reforming political party structures to assure equitable representation of women, publicizing women's issues at stake in local, state, and national elections, and monitoring the selection of women as delegates to presidential nominating conventions. Although nonpartisan, the caucus immediately created Democratic and Republican task forces to press the parties for better treatment of women in the political process. Later, the NWPC also joined an ad hoc coalition of women's groups to press President Jimmy Carter (and subsequent presidents) to appoint more women to leadership positions.

Women Begin to Run for Office

While the first woman to serve in the US Congress, Jeannette Pickering Rankin (1880–1973) was elected in 1916, women's representation in Congress would not significantly increase for several decades. When they arrived on the political scene, however, it was not long before they took leadership roles on women's policy concerns. The women elected to the House of Representatives in the late 1960s and early 1970s "did not derive their public authority through the instrumentality of a man. Neither were they social mothers, as public women of the early twentieth century had (largely) been" (Witt, Paget, and Matthews 1994, 48). Although there were but fourteen women in the House in 1973, many of these women, including Patricia Schroeder (b. 1940), Elizabeth Holtzman (b. 1941), and Margaret Heckler (b. 1931), quickly took the lead in advancing women's issues. In fact, shortly after the election of President Carter in 1977, women in the US House of Representatives, bowing to pressure from women's groups including NOW and the NWPC, formed the bipartisan Congressional Women's Caucus. Fearing that some of the older women in the House might be reluctant to join, its founders agreed that the caucus would take no positions on any issues for which there was not unanimous agreement.

Women in several state legislatures also began to organize into bipartisan caucuses. This cadre of women, along with the newly elected women in the House during the 1970s and 1980s, provided young women with new role models. The creation of caucuses also helped bridge the gap between descriptive (simply being a woman) and substantive (representing women's interests) representation. These women not only became political leaders but also took the lead in advancing women's issues in state and the national legislatures.

Changes in Public Perceptions

It was not until 1992, however, that women made significant inroads into national positions of political leadership. In what became known as the Year of the Woman, the number of women members of the US Congress increased from 29 (6.7 percent) in 1991 to 48 (11 percent) in 1993. This election cycle also saw the election of the first women of color, Carol Braun (D-IL), to the US Senate. Since then, the number of women serving in the US Congress has continued to increase each year. In 2015, the US Congress included 104 female legislators, 20 in the Senate, and 84 in the House of Representatives.

In addition to a continuing revolution in public attitudes toward women in political office, the gains of the Year of the Woman were prompted by several events. First, the end of the Cold War led to a shift in national attention from foreign to domestic concerns, such as education and health, which long had been considered the domains of women. In addition, a congressional banking scandal forced many male members of Congress to retire, resulting in elections without incumbents, which are often easier for women candidates to win. Perhaps most importantly, the confirmation hearings in the early 1990s for Supreme Court Associate Justice Clarence Thomas (b. 1948) reminded Americans of the discrimination women faced in society. When law professor Anita Hill (b. 1956), a former employee, charged that Thomas had sexually harassed her, the entire nation watched a very hostile, all-male Senate Judiciary Committee grill Hill. Women were especially outraged, and many began to work toward electing more women to positions of political leadership. EMILY's List, a prochoice Democratic women's political action committee, which was founded in 1986 after Geraldine Ferraro's unsuccessful bid for the vice presidency, experienced an extraordinary increase in contributions. This new money allowed EMILY's List to train more potential candidates and campaign workers in 1992.

One group working to increase the number of women in executive leadership positions is The White House Project. This non-partisan group was first conceived at a 1997 dinner party hosted by Boston philanthropist Barbara Lee. At the time of this party, which was themed "Why Not a Woman," many other democratic countries, including Britain, India, and Israel, already had elected women prime ministers or presidents. America's failure to elect a woman president struck Lee, who joined forces with Marie Wilson, head of the Ms. Foundation for Women, and Laura Liswood (b. 1950), founder of the Council of Women World Leaders, to formally launch the project in June 1998.

Lingering Issues for Female Politicians

Despite important inroads women have made in politics, political science research tells us that electoral prospects and experiences are not the same for men and women, even today. Research comparing potential candidates, for instance, finds that women tend to view themselves as less qualified for holding office than do men with the same characteristics and professional credentials (Fox and Lawless 2004). When women do run for office, moreover, they face different challenges than men. For example, incumbent (current office holders) women are more likely to be challenged in their next election than are incumbent men (Lawless and Pearson 2008), and are also more likely to face strong challengers when they are (Milyo and Schosberg 2000). At the same time, women often have to work harder to raise money (Jenkins 2007) and tend to receive less support from political party organizations (Sanbonmatsu 2006). One encouraging pattern, however, is that when women who do run for office, they tend to win at similar rates as their male counterparts (Darcy et al. 1994).

Consequences of Women in Political Leadership

Beyond the simple question of gender equality, we must ask what women political leaders bring to governance that their male counterparts may not. Though this answer is controversial at best, political science research has shown that having women in positions of power improves the substantive representation of women and women's issues. And, while some may disagree with the assertion that women speak in a different voice, this view is strongly supported by researchers, who have found that women are more likely to use power for a desired end as opposed to gaining power for power's sake.

Social science has uncovered a good deal of evidence suggesting that women improve productivity. Groups that include women, for example, tend to work more effectively (Woolley et al. 2010). In politics, women have even been found to be stronger candidates (Milyo and Schosberg 2000) as well as more effective legislators than men (e.g., Volden, Wiseman, and Wittmer 2005). This may be due in part to the hurdles that women still face in winning elective office: "if it takes more talent and greater effort for female candidates to be taken seriously by voters, campaign contributors, and party gatekeepers, then the women who succeed in the electoral process are likely to be more talented and hardworking than the men who do the same" (Anzia and Berry 2011, 490). It is important to note that this research does not necessarily mean that women are inherently better leaders than men; instead, it suggests that because of discrimination and other challenges, only the most talented or hardworking individuals would likely win office in the first place.

Women as Political Leaders in State and National Legislatures

Significant research by political scientists indicates that the presence of women political leaders in legislatures makes a significant difference not only in what gets discussed, but also in what kinds of legislation are advanced. Female legislators, for example, are more likely to sponsor legislation concerning so-called women's issues—those relating to family and education, for instance—than are their male counterparts (Sanbonmatsu 2003, Swers 2002). These findings highlight the potential for women to represents citizens not only in a descriptive sense, but in a substantive fashion, as well, promoting issues and allocating resources to important policy areas that may not otherwise receive as much attention from legislators.

Generally speaking, women in legislatures are more willing than their male counterparts to work in a bipartisan fashion. Women in leadership roles may also utilize a more integrative leadership style, characterized by a tendency to reach out to others, make collaborative decisions, and educate colleagues. For example, when women chair committees, they generally attempt to facilitate interaction between committee members, witnesses, and others in attendance. In contrast, men are more likely to be aggressive leaders, who have a strong belief in majority rule and a self-interested citizenry. When a male member chairs a committee, he is often the dominant and controlling force in the room.

Integrative leadership also tends to translate into greater success for women legislators. For example, bills sponsored by women or indicated to be a priority among women tend to have a slightly higher pass rate than other legislation. Women may also conceptualize problems differently than men, perhaps making them more likely to offer solutions their predecessors have not considered.

Expanding Women's Political Leadership Around the World

Countries around the world have identified increasing women's presence in government as an important societal goal. At the Fourth World Conference on Women, held in Beijing in 1995, 189 governments agreed to take measures to ensure women's full access "to power structures and decision making to increase women's capacity for decision making and leadership" (The White House Project 2003, 27). Many countries have instituted quota systems in their national legislatures requiring a certain number of seats to be reserved for female representatives. These systems have been found to have a strong positive effect in increasing the presence of women in national legislatures (Schwindt-Bayer 2009, Tripp and Kang 2008). Today, in Rwanda and Bolivia, women make up more than half of legislators, with a further twelve countries' legislatures comprised of at least 40 percent female members.

Despite important progress being made in women's representation, gender parity has not yet been achieved. Indeed, objectives associated with first-wave feminism, with its emphasis on access to voting rights and basic legal protections, have only recently been realized in some countries, particularly in the Middle East. Women only achieved the right to vote in Saudi Arabia in 2015, while the United Arab Emirates granted these rights in 2006, and Kuwait in 2005. While these efforts to empower women are laudable, they also reiterate that extending even the most basic democratic rights to women remains an ongoing effort in some parts of the world.

Even in countries where women are actively involved in government, representation is not always equal. In many countries the proportion of women holding political office is considerably smaller than the proportion of women in the population, even in advanced democracies. In both South Korea and the United States, for instance, over half of the citizens are female yet fewer than 20 percent of national legislators are women. Women also make up fewer than 7 percent of elected heads-of-state around the world, and only 16 percent of the world's parliaments are led by female legislators.

Elected women also face unique challenges in office, such as being subjected to sexual harassment. In May 2016, a group of female legislators and activists in France publicly protested the sexual harassment, and even assaults, to which they argued women in French parliament are still routinely subjected. Female members of the British parliament have similarly reported being mistaken for researchers or assistants by their male counterparts. Some female legislators are also institutionally marginalized within their legislatures, such as being prevented from assuming leadership positions (Heath et al. 2005), compelled to focus only on "gendered" policy issues (Schwint and Bayer 2006), or generally facing hurdles to getting their bills passed (Franceschet and Piscopo 2008, Miguel 2012).

Prospects for the Future

It is fair to say that great strides have been made in increasing women's representation in governments around the world. The election of women to high-profile offices—such as the elections of Theresa May as Prime Minister of the United Kingdom, Angela Merkel as Chancellor of Germany in 2005, Kamla Persad-Bissessar as the first female Prime Minister of Trinidad and Tobago in 2010, and Kolinda Grabar-Kitarovic as the first and youngest female President of Croatia in 2015—represents an encouraging development for the future of women's leadership around the world. Still, systematic challenges unique to female leaders must be overcome to achieve gender parity in global politics. If societies want to continue increasing the number of women in positions of political leadership, young women must be socialized to take the lead as active participants in society and government. As more women enter into political leadership, antiquated notions of leadership as a male domain can be discarded and replaced by modern models that emphasize the important contributions of women to global democratic life.

Further Reading

Al-Rasheed, M. (2013). *A most masculine state: Gender, politics and religion in Saudi Arabia.* Cambridge: Cambridge University Press.

Anzia, S. & Berry, C. R. (2011). The Jackie (and Jill) Robinson effect: Why do Congresswomen outperform Congressmen?" *American Journal of Political Science, 55*(3), 478–493.

Boles, J. (2001). Local elected women and policymaking: Movement delegates or feminist trustees. In S. J. Carroll, (Ed.), *The impact of women in public office.* Bloomington: Indiana University.

Burns, J. M. (1992). The power of leadership. In A. Mughan & S. C. Patterson, (Eds.), *Political leadership in democratic societies.* Chicago: Nelson-Hall.

Carroll, S. J. (2001). Representing women: Women state legislators as agents of policy-related change. In S. J. Carroll, (Ed.), *The impact of women in public office.* Bloomington: Indiana University.

Carroll, S. J. (1985). Political elites and sex differences in political ambition: A reconsideration. *Journal of Politics, 47*(4), 1231–1243.

Clift, E. & Brazaitis, T. (2003). *Madam president: Women blazing the leadership trail.* New York: Routledge.

Dodson, D. & Carroll, S. J. (1991). *Reshaping the agenda: Women in state legislatures.* New Brunswick, NJ: Center for American Women and Politics.

Dolan, J. A.; Deckman, M.M.; Swers, M. L. 2015. *Women and politics: Paths to power and political influence.* Upper Saddle River, NJ: Pearson/Prentice Hall.

Fox, R. & Lawless, J. (2004). Entering the arena? Gender and the decision to run for office. *American Journal of Political Science, 48*(2), 264–280.

Henderson, S. & Jeydel, A. S. (2010). *Women and politics in a global world.* New York: Oxford University Press.

Jenkins, S. (2007). A woman's work is never done? Fund-raising perception and effort among female state legislative candidates. *Political Research Quarterly, 60*(2), 230–239.

Lawless, J. & Fox, R. L. (2010). *It takes a candidate: Why women don't run for office.* Cambridge: Cambridge University Press.

Lawless, J. & Pearson, K. (2008). The primary reason for women's underrepresentation? Reevaluating the conventional wisdom. *Journal of Politics, 70*(1), 67–82.

Little, T. H.; Dunn, D.; & Dean, R. (2001). A view from the top: Gender differences in legislative priorities among state legislative leaders. *Women & Politics, 22*(4), 29–50.

Mansbridge, J. (1999). Should blacks represent blacks and women represent women? A contingent yes. *Journal of Politics, 61,* 628–57.

McGlen, N. E., & O'Connor, K. (1983). *Women's rights: the struggle for equality in the 19th and 20th centuries.* Westport, CT: Praeger Publishers.

Milyo, J. & Samantha S. (2000). Gender bias and selection bias in House elections. *Public Choice, 105,* 41–59.

Raicheva-Stover, M. & Ibroscheva, I. (2014). *Women in politics and media : perspectives from nations in transition.* New York, NY: Bloomsbury.

Sanbonmatsu, K. (2006). *Where women run: Gender and party in the American states.* Ann Arbor: University of Michigan Press.

Schroeder, P. (1999). *Twenty-four years of house work and the place is still a mess: My life in politics.* Kansas City: Andrews McMeel.

Schwindt-Bayer, L. (2009). Making quotas work. *Legislative Studies Quarterly, 34*(1), 5–28.

Swers, M. (2002). *The difference women make: The policy impact of women in Congress.* Chicago: University of Chicago Press.

Thomas, S. & Wilcox, C. (2014). *Women and elective office: Past, present, and future.* New York: Oxford University Press.

Tripp, A. & Kang, A. (2008). The global impact of quotas. *Comparative Political Studies, 41*(3), 338–361.

The White House Project. (2003). *Why women matter: Lessons about women's political leadership for home and abroad.* New York: The White House Project.

The White House Project. (2000). *Pipeline to the future: Young women and political leadership.* New York: The White House Project.

Volden, C.; Wiseman, A.; & Wittmer, D. (2013). When are women more effective lawmakers than men? *American Journal of Political Science, 57*(2), 326–431.

Witt, L., Paget, K. M., & Matthews, G. (1994). *Running as a woman: Gender and power in American politics,* reprinted. New York: Free Press.

Woolley, A. W.; Chabris, C.; Pentland, A.; Hashmi, N.; & Malone, T. (2010). Evidence of a collective intelligence factor in the performance of human groups. *Science, 330*(6004), 686–688.

The Gender Gap in US Political Leadership

Laurien ALEXANDRE
Antioch University

The gender gap has particular importance for politics and affects the careers of both male and female politicians, and the make-up of the political parties in the United States. Researchers have sought to explain gender differences of political preferences, partisan leanings, styles of leadership, and values orientation, and studies are ongoing. Their findings will become even more important as women ascend to the highest level of political office.

The term *gender gap* is a catch-all phrase that refers to the existence and significance of gender differences in a variety of areas. Scholars, researchers, and analysts speak of a gender gap in employment and earnings, in education, in workplace authority, in leadership, and in opportunities available over the course of one's life, not to mention attendant social attitudes. This article identifies the social construction and interpretation of gender differences in one sphere in which leadership plays a highly visible role: politics.

Brief History of a Widening Gap

The term gender gap came into currency in the United States in the 1980s, with particular reference to electoral and partisan issues. Despite the political enfranchisement of women in the United States in 1920s, for the rest of the century women had less political power and fewer political leadership positions while having higher rates of political participation, and policy preferences that differed from those of men.

The 1980 presidential election brought voting women's political agenda to public and scholarly attention. Specific issues included the Equal Rights Amendment (ERA), the politics of the Republican Party, and the increasing feminization of poverty during the 1970s, as women became more dependent on and more supportive of social-welfare programs. Efforts to ratify the ERA in the states after congressional passage in 1972 witnessed intensive statewide electoral strategies throughout most of the decade. Pollsters began to cross-tabulate voting results by sex, and this became an important consideration from this time forward.

The notion of a "women's vote," was about to be taken seriously. Kathy Bonk, who has written on the gender gap, noted in "The Selling of the Gender Gap: The Role of Organized Feminism," a chapter in Carol Mueller's 1988 *The Politics of the Gender Gap,* that Ronald Reagan's 1980 presidential victory was characterized by an 8 percent gender gap: Women were almost equally divided, with 46 percent for Reagan and 45 percent for Carter, whereas men were 54 percent for Reagan and 37 percent for Carter. In looking to describe the difference in attitudes of men and women, the notion of a gap between men and women came to mind. The term first appeared in the *Washington Post,* on 16 October 1981, when the columnist Judy Mann wrote, "Last November there was a gender gap of 8% in the *New York Times/ CBS* exit poll in the presidential election." By mid-1982, the National Organization of Women (NOW), the nation's largest and most active women's advocacy group, began regularly using the term to describe gender-based differences in voting behavior. The organization started releasing a monthly column, *Gender Gap Update.*

Scholars and journalists continued to watch the gender gap, attributing it to Reagan's opposition to abortion and the ERA, which, they theorized, made women less likely than men to vote for him. Bonk noted that as Reagan's second-term campaign went into gear, one-third of all men stated they had a lot of confidence in Reagan's ability to provide leadership, whereas only 22 percent of women expressed similar confidence. An effort to widen the gender gap in favor of the Democrats became a major goal of the 1984 campaign, and the Democratic Party chose a female candidate for vice president: Geraldine Ferraro. But the expected gender landslide did not happen, perhaps because Americans cast their votes on the basis of presidents, not vice presidents. In addition, the Reagan Administration had made some symbolic actions, such as nominating Sandra Day O'Connor for the Supreme Court and filling several cabinet positions with women, which may have swayed some women voters.

The gender gap continued to be present in electoral and partisan participation in the subsequent decades. Women have voted at higher rates than men in every presidential election since 1984. Not only is voting behavior different, but the partisan gap continues to exist as well. As recently as November 2002, *Business Week* reported that the gender gap is "fast becoming a gender chasm" as the stalled economy has produced more uncertainty in women, who are more likely to reject Republican social conservatism.

It is an oversimplification, however, to say that more women vote Democratic and more men vote Republican. It is true that many studies of the gender gap have focused on the greater attraction the Democratic Party holds for women than for men, but there is more complexity than meets eye. First, there are regional differences in the gap, which mitigate against a straight male-female divide. Partisan preferences have been greater in the South than in the rest of the nation, which may override the gender gap there. Second, men have a greater tendency than women to self-identify as independents rather than as members of a political party. The political scientist Barbara Norrander discovered that an independence gap, in which men are more likely to consider themselves political independents and women are more likely to identify as partisan, averages six percentage points. Thus, women could be more prevalent in political party affiliation, but this majority in absolute terms would need to take into account the male independents and independent leaners.

Similarly, the political scientist Daniel Wirls, writing in the mid 1980s, suggested that the gap could be explained not by women's rejection of Ronald Reagan, but as the result of unequal rates of male and female defection from liberal values and the Democratic Party. From this perspective, the greater movement by men toward conservative positions and the Republican Party produced the gender gap and, consequently, the Republicans were not the victims of the gender gap but in fact beneficiaries of it.

The Gender Gap in Positions of Political Leadership

There is no question that a gender gap in positions of political leadership exists: Women do not hold office in numbers that reflect their percentage of the population; women face different challenges in campaigning; and there is debate over whether women lead differently or set different priorities from men once they win office. Whether those differences are the result of institutional barriers, long-held stereotypes, or women's personal choices, the fact remains that women are underrepresented.

Increasingly, however, since the time of 1984 campaign of Geraldine Ferraro, more women candidates have run and secured state and national office. The researcher Barbara Burrell noted in her 1994 book on women who successfully campaigned for the US Congress that in 1966, women accounted for 2 percent of congressional membership, while two decades later, in 1991–1992, they accounted for 6.6 percent. She further noted that globally, women on average made up 11 percent of democratically elected national parliaments.

The year 1992 was a significant historical moment with reference to gender and political leadership. The year was popularly referred to as the Year of the Women, and the climate was a favorable one for women candidates because a pool of experienced female politicians existed at local and state levels, and more female candidates were running for elected office. Nineteen women won major party nominations to run in California's fifty-two congressional districts. Significantly more women than men voted for the women candidates who were running in 1992. Burrell noted that the number of congressional women in California went to 11 percent and the number of women in state legislatures increased five-fold from 4 percent in 1971 to 20 percent in 1993. Yet despite these gains, the numbers remain low.

Why the gender gap in public office? Stereotyped gender roles reaffirm that while women's place may not be in the home, neither is it necessarily in office. Politics has been regarded as a male domain and political leadership as a masculine endeavor. Political leadership is often considered antithetical to women's roles, so female candidates have to persuade the public that they have the same leadership qualities as men, or else they have to transform public notions of leadership. A generation of studies show that public "support for the idea of women in public office has grown, [but] that gender-based stereotypes have not faded away."

If we consider political leadership only at the level of office-holding, however, we would be failing to take into account other aspects of gender-differentiated political behavior. Some scholars explore in depth how the gender gap in political activity has been exaggerated by the emphasis on particular modes of participation. Early findings that there are gender differences in political participation and activity indicated that men were more likely than women to take part in political life, but that finding should be viewed critically, because some of the studies failed to take into account factors such as access to political resources, lower levels of education, and less money or free time to devote. In addition, those early studies often failed to question the very definition of political involvement, overemphasizing office holding, for example, in which men are significantly more represented, and underestimating grassroots community activity, in which women have always taken part to an equal or greater degree than men

The Gender Gap in Political Values

Is there a gender gap in political values and policy preferences? Although women's influence ebbed and flowed during the twentieth century, the agenda that differentiated women's political behavior from men's showed a strong pattern of continuity around two broad concerns: equality for women and humanitarian social reform. Political scientists Robert Shapiro and Harpreet Mahajan analyzed twenty years of data in "Gender Differences in Policy Preferences: A Summary of Trends from the 1960s to the 1980s," published in 1986 in *Public Opinion Quarterly*. Their analysis reveals persistent differences in attitudes toward issues involving the use of force, and growing differences toward policies concerning regulation, social welfare, and traditional values. The increasing conservatism of men and women's greater support for so-called "compassionate" government programs may explain why men have become more attracted to the Republican Party while women feel more comfortable remaining within the Democratic Party.

Here too, the gap must be interpreted in ways that take into account its complexity. Some entertain the notion that women take a nurturing, caring stance, whether because of intrinsic biology or because of women's traditional roles as mothers. Instead of seeing this as a source of inadequacy, some scholars, such as Carol Gilligan, argue that women could be the source of higher-order values for society.

That approach, however, is controversial and open to debate. The feminist scholar Pamela Conover argues that there is no significant difference in value orientation between men and women when it comes to the principles of egalitarianism, individualism, and symbolic racism; however, women do differ from men in having, on average, greater sympathy for the disadvantaged. Conover suggests that the gap between men and women is really a gap between men and *feminist* women. "When men are compared to feminist women, there is a significant gender gap on every type of issue: however, on most foreign policy issues and many domestic issues, this gap evaporates when men are compared to non-feminist women." Thus, there are enough feminist women to create the appearance of a gender gap. The finding assumes that feminism is associated with distinctive values and policy preferences that both men and women can identify and can identify with; that feminism "awakens in both men and women support for a woman's perspective that consists of egalitarian values and generally liberal policies," as Elizabeth Cook and Clyde Wilcox put it in their article "Feminism and the Gender Gap: A Second Look," in *The Journal of Politics*.

Scholars have pursued this line of thinking and found only a limited gender gap in basic political values. Cook and Wilcox report that on policy issues, women were significantly more liberal than men on policy issues, women were more liberal than men on certain items, but the differences were relatively small. Gender differences were largest on support for spending to aid the unemployed, and on war and peace issues. In a study of gender-specific reactions to the 1991 Gulf War, Pamela Conover and Virginia Sapiro concluded that gender orientations toward war and foreign policy are more complex than many feminist and other theorists might have supposed. In their article "Gender, Feminist Consciousness and War" in the *American Journal of Political Science*, the authors say, "women are more afraid of the prospects of war and more wary of foreign involvements" though given justifications, they are as willing as men to ponder the use of force. When moved from the abstract to the concrete, an actual war, women reacted more negatively on every measure. The authors warn, however, that while the differences are important, they are not large enough to warrant sweeping statements differentiating women and men into stereotypic camps.

Understanding a gender gap in political values as well as partisan and electoral issues needs to be viewed also within the light of differences across groups defined by their race or ethnicity. For example, Burns noted that issues connected to civil rights are higher priorities among African-American and Latino men than they are for women as a whole. Men and women's agendas for political action were also differentiated along socioeconomic lines, and discrepancies of class, race, family status differentiate women's and men's experiences within gender categories.

Sources of the Gender Gap in Politics

As the sections above have indicated, gender gaps do exist in electoral behavior, partisan preferences, and political leadership. While the gaps' existence has become a permanent fixture of the US political, economic, and social landscape, the significance and explanation of the gender gap differences remains contentious. There is no agreement as to sources of gender differences on many of these issues. In fact, there is no single explanation for the varied sources, experiences, and manifestations of gender differences.

One approach to understanding value differences between the sexes takes as its basis biological differences and gender socialization. This would include the notion that women are biologically more cooperative than men (with the hypothesis being that this trait is evolutionarily desirable for the sex that bears children), and that the biological difference is reinforced by traditional socialization that goes along with women traditionally having primary responsibility for children. The result, according to supporters of this approach, is that women have a greater concern with preservation of life and a stronger tendency toward cooperative decision making than men. Gilligan, for example, posits that men and women have dissimilar conceptions of justice and that men are more oriented toward rights while women are more concerned with caring. Proponents of this view hold that men and women's political behavior will remain different even after controlling for other economic, cultural, and political variables. Certainly it is widely accepted that the fact that men and women are socialized differently has an impact on men and women's values.

Another explanation for gender gap differences is that socioeconomic status partially explains gender differences in political opinions and electoral behavior, in that women tend to earn less than men and are more likely to live in poverty. In other words, their situational constraints might explain why women and men differ on policies and values. The increasing number of women in the workforce and continued inequality of wages and employment may affect political attitudes.

A third explanation combines socioeconomic and gender variables and posits that women who are the most autonomous from men tend to differ the most from men in their political attitudes. Thus, women with higher education and occupational status, as well as unmarried women at all socioeconomic levels, diverged the most from men in their attitudes and voting behaviors. Relatedly, some explain the gap as connected to the growth in feminist consciousness—the growing awareness of inequalities and collective action to address these grievances. The argument here is that feminism increased to such a degree in the 1980s that there came to be noticeable gap, because feminist women were more liberal than men. The causal relationship in this explanation is difficult to determine, because it is unclear whether feminism exists prior to issue orientation or whether issue orientation is what leads to feminist consciousness. Conover and others do document, however, that the gender gap is greatest between feminist women and all men.

However one explains it, the gender gap in partisan leanings, political leadership, and values orientation does exist and has become a factor in the civil, political, and economic life of the United States. In the future, it will be important for scholars and students of the gender gap to continue to probe in which nations and among which women and men this gap is most evident, and in what life circumstance those men and women find themselves, and at what historical moment.

Further Reading

Adler, N. (1999). Global leadership: Women of influence. In G. Powell (Ed.), *The handbook of gender and work* (pp. 239–261). Thousand Oaks, CA: Sage.

Bonk, K. (1988). The selling of the gender gap: The role of organized feminism. In C. Mueller (Ed.), *The politics of the gender gap: The social construction of political influence* (pp. 82–101). Beverly Hills, CA: Sage.

Burns, N.; Schlozman, K.; & Verba, S. (2001). *The private roots of public action: Gender, equality and political participation.* Cambridge, MA: Harvard University Press.

Burrell, B. (1994). *A woman's place is in the house: Campaigning for congress in the feminist era.* Ann Arbor: University of Michigan Press.

Cook, E. A. & Wilcox, C. (1991, November). Feminism and the gender gap: A second look. *The Journal of Politics, 53*(4), 1111–1122.

Conover, P. J. (1988, November). Feminists and the gender gap. *Journal of Politics, 50*(4), 985–1010.

Conover, P. J. & Sapiro, V. (1993, November). Gender, feminist consciousness and war. *American Journal of Political Science, 37*(4), 1079–1099.

Dierst-Lahti, G. & Kelly, R. (Eds.). (1995). *Gender power, leadership and governance.* Ann Arbor: University of Michigan Press.

Dunham, R. (2002, November 11). A stalled economy is widening the gender gap. *Business Week Online.* Retrieved June 27, 2003, from http://www.businessweek.com/magazine/content/02_45/c3807076.htm

Gilligan, C. (1982). *In a different voice.* Cambridge, MA: Harvard University Press.

Goldin, C. (1990). *Understanding the gender gap: An economic history of American women.* New York: Oxford University Press.

Howell, S. & Day, C. (2000, August). Complexities of the gender gap. *The Journal of Politics, 62*(3), 858–874.

Kellerman, B. & Rhode, D. L. (2007). *Women and Leadership: The State of Play and Strategies for Change.* San Francisco, CA: Jossey-Bass.

Klein, E. (1984). *Gender politics: From consciousness to mass politics.* Cambridge, MA: Harvard University Press.

Manza, J. & Brooks, C. (1998, March). The gender gap in U.S. presidential elections: When? Why? Implications? *American Journal of Sociology, 103*(5), 1235–1266.

Mueller, C. M. (Ed.). (1988). *Yearbooks in Women's Policy Studies: Vol. 12. The politics of the gender gap: The social construction of political influence.* Thousand Oaks, CA: Sage.

Norrander, B. (1997). The independence gap and the gender gap. *Public Opinion Quarterly, 61*(3), 464–476.

Norrander, B. (1999, Winter). The evolution of the gender gap. *Public Opinion Quarterly, 63*(4), 566–577.

Rapoport, R.; Stone, W.; & Abramowitz, A. (1990, August). Sex and the caucus participant: The gender gap and presidential nominations. *American Journal of Political Science, 34*(3), 725–740.

Rhode, D. (Ed.). (2003). *The difference "difference" makes: Women and leadership.* Stanford, CA: Stanford University Press.

Ross, P. & Latta, M. L. (1999). Gender gap in earnings. In G. Powell (Ed.), *Handbook of gender and work* (pp. 95–123). Thousand Oaks, CA: Sage.

Shapiro, R. & Mahajan, H. (1986). Gender differences in policy preferences: A summary of trends from the 1960s to the 1980s. *Public Opinion Quarterly, 50*(3), 42–61.

Welch, S. & Hibbing, J. (1992, February). Financial conditions, gender and voting in American national elections. *The Journal of Politics, 54*(1), 197–213.

Whitehead, J. & Blankenship, M. (2000, Fall). The gender gap in capital punishment attitudes: An analysis of support and opposition. *American Journal of Criminal Justice, 25*(1), 1–13.

Wirls, D. (1986). Reinterpreting the gender gap. *Public Opinion Quarterly, 50*(3), 316–330.

Leading from the Fringes: Women's Paths to Political Power

Karen CHRISTENSEN
Berkshire Publishing Group

The scarcity of prominent women in historical records has kept us from seeing the various ways in which women have led from the sidelines, exerting (and rising to) power through husbands and lovers, brothers and sons. These methods of leadership can be found in historical records, in literature, and in research by scholars who are uncovering the multitude of ways these women exerted influence, from the distance past to the present day.

Women have found ways to exert influence and gain power through their relationships with men, even during times in which there were legal, social, and religious barriers to their achieving any independent public position. By looking at women's hidden or informal influence, we go beyond the view that women associated with powerful men were merely royal breeders, glorified servants, or sex workers, and acknowledge that they sometimes were, within the bounds of their time and place, leaders. And some women associated with powerful men rose in their own right to the pinnacles of power.

In the Tang dynasty, for example, a minor concubine used her intelligence, steely determination, and remarkable political acumen to become Wu Zetian (624–705), the only female emperor in the history of China. Other women have stayed on the sidelines, without official position and sometimes barely known in their own time, but nonetheless played a vital role in national and world affairs.

This is a universal phenomenon. Women have striven for status and influence across the world and throughout history: concubines became empresses, courtesans directed kings, and salonnières were the center of intellectual and political life in Enlightenment France and in London at the height of the British Empire. In the twentieth century, there were Washington hostesses who wielded power behind the scenes, and some recent national leaders, including Park Geun-hye (b. 1952) of South Korea and Cristina Elisabet Fernández de Kirchner (b. 1953) of Argentina, who came to power through a male relative.

Women who exert political power from the sidelines generally gain this power as a result of marrying a powerful man or being born into a powerful family without a strong male claimant. Sisters Song Qingling (1893–1981) and Soong Mei-ling (1898–2003) came from a well-connected Chinese family and married men who became world-famous leaders, Sun Yat-sen and Chiang Kai-shek. Others created a platform for themselves by using not only physical beauty but intelligence and artistic talents, even wit and social networking skills.

Of course women's looks and sexuality have often been central to their roles on the sidelines of power. Attractive women have sometimes achieved positions of power that would not have been available to other women. More importantly, women's ability, or inability, to bear (usually) male heirs has often shaped their destinies. For courtesans, some of whom, in both Europe and Asia, achieved considerable status, wealth, and influence, skill in lovemaking was prized, but in general women's sexuality was considered risky: Elizabeth I (1533–1603) of England was probably a more effective leader as the Virgin Queen.

Mothers have been even more important, and influential, than wives or other sexual partners. The mothers of kings or prospective kings have exercised both official and unofficial power, generally to benefit their sons but occasionally not. Irene (c. 752–803), mother of the Byzantium Constantine VI, "decided that her only child, Constantine VI, was not competent to rule . . . She had him blinded and then ruled in her own right" (Walthall 2008, 77).

The classic pattern was a beautiful or sexually attractive woman who used her personal attributes to attract or "catch" a man and thus to rise in the world, first by obtaining wealth and status but then by exerting power through her husband. Such women have often been regarded as mere gold-diggers, or as proxies for their husbands or families. They have been criticized and denigrated when they, like Edith Wilson (1872–1961), who took over many of husband Woodrow Wilson's executive duties as president after he suffered a stroke, claimed they were only carrying out their husbands' wishes—and, of course, maintaining their husbands' position and power. But the reality is that they often exerted their own ideas, and influenced the men whose names we know while theirs have faded from history.

In the twentieth century, there have been influential wives and daughters, some of whom became politicians themselves. Most notable among them is Eleanor Roosevelt (1884–1962), perhaps the wife who was most successful in achieving her own place in history, campaigning and participating in public policy during her husband Franklin's presidency and serving as a delegate to the United Nations General Assembly after his death. Beautiful young women like Imelda Marcos (b. 1929) or actresses like Madame Mao (1914–1991) or Eva Perón (1919–1952) are in the tradition of the ambitious concubine. Indira Gandhi (1917–1984), India's third prime minister, and the former Thai prime minister Yingluck Shinawatra (b. 1967) rose to power in countries that had previously been led by male family members.

Today, more and more nations are led by women. In Europe, they have generally risen without the help of a father or husband, but in Asia and Latin America it remains common for women to become leaders as a result of their relationships with a man, often following a husband or brother into office.

Women's Capacity for Leadership

A common English-language expression is that "behind every great man there's a woman." These women have been largely invisible, praised for their self-effacement and their tolerance of the sometimes less-than-admirable behavior of their great men. The British writer Edna Healey (1918–2010), herself the wife of a well-known politician, Dennis Healey, wrote a biography of the wives of Charles Darwin, Karl Marx, and David Livingstone, exploring the price women pay for loving a man with driving ambition or a sense of vocation that transcends ordinary concerns such as supporting a family or even being at home from one year to the next. Her own marriage, she wrote, was a perfect partnership, and her own ambition was satisfied by being a help-meet to her husband.

The idea of the "power couple"—an intimate partnership that pairs two people's strengths and weaknesses and enables one partner, and the couple, to achieve things he or she could not have achieved alone—goes back through the ages. There are numerous accounts of weak or sickly leaders bolstered by strong mothers, wives, or lovers. A 1885 collection of biographies entitled *Queenly Women, Crowned and Uncrowned* (1885), explains that "Josephine was exactly the partner [Napoleon] needed. Her courtly magnificence, her urbanity of manner, and her fascinating talents contributed scarcely less than his victories to the advancement of her husband."

But the woman was always subordinate, and in many cases there was no acknowledgment of the possibility of female leadership. In *Courtesans & Fishcakes: The Consuming Passions of Classical Athens*, author James Davidson cites the example of the orator Apollodorus addressing a court: "Hetaeras we keep for pleasure, concubines for attending day-by-day to the body and wives for producing heirs, and for standing trusty guard on our household property." But Davidson also points out that reality did not square with these neat divisions—women often stepped outside the boundaries set for them.

Women leaders often provoke accusations of weaknesses and susceptibilities, and questionable loyalties. In *Servants of the Dynasty: Palace Women in World History*, editor Anne Walthall points out in the introduction that, "For commentators around the world, women and power constitute an unholy mix. Women, it is assumed, do not know how to use power; they play favorites, corrupt officials if not the king, squander the state's financial resources, and lack the courage to resist enemies." Attacks on female rulers were often personal; gossip about female rulers' sexuality—from Catherine the Great to Hillary Clinton—has often overshadowed attention paid to their policies.

And stories about the incapacity of women are rife. The great Chinese military strategist Sunzi, to whom *The Art of War* is attributed, proved his methods to the King of Wu by using the king's two favorite concubines as commanders in a military drill. They were directed to lead 180 concubines but giggled instead of following Sunzi's orders; he therefore insisted that the king execute them. Two more concubines were chosen to lead the troops. All the "soldier" concubines then followed orders precisely. This fact convinced the king to appoint Sunzi as a general; if his rules would work with women, they would work with any common soldier.

On the other hand, there was a belief that women's taste, elegance, manners, and artistic accomplishments had a civilizing effect that wasn't only beneficial in the drawing room but in business and politics too, as Walthall (2008, 17) points out: "The historical sociologist Norbert Elias claimed that court societies are responsible for what he called the civilizing process, by which people learn to negotiate increasingly complex sets of interdependencies that require self-restraint and careful planning."

Women have often been seen as adept at what we now call social networking. In terms of political leadership, this networking focused on building alliances, soothing grievances, cementing loyalty, and sometimes encouraging intrigue. The traditional role of the female spouse of a male leader in Western countries has included acting as a hostess, not only as a social role model to other women, but as a help in building personal connections and promoting common feeling between distant leaders.

Influential Women in Eighteenth- and Nineteenth-century Europe

Women who led in other domains also came to prominence through men: fathers, husbands, and, occasionally, mentors. The French political philosopher Madame de Staël (1766–1817) was the daughter of a prominent minister. Harriet Beecher Stowe (1811–1896), whose anti-slavery novel *Uncle Tom's Cabin* "started this great war" according to Abraham Lincoln, was the daughter and sister of renowned preachers Lyman Beecher and Henry Ward Beecher.

Salons run by women were an important part of social, intellectual, and political life in pre-Revolutionary France. Salonnières, especially in Paris during the French Enlightenment, and also in Russia and in England, played an active role in intellectual and public life. Prominent salonnières include Madame Geoffrin, Princesse Mathilde, Empress Joséphine, Madame du Deffand, and Madame de Staël. Madame de Staël lived during the reign of Napoleon in the late 1700s. Her father was a rich banker, one of the richest men in France, and she was in her own right, as a writer and salonnière, one of the women in French post-Revolutionary history with the most political influence.

The French Sun King's mistress, courtesan Madame de Pompadour (1721–1764), was also a salonnière. She brought together great writers, artists, and the philosophers of the day, and cultivated discourse between influential men and women. As author and political scientist Susan Herbst (1994, 60–61) puts it in *Politics at the Margin*: "It would be an exaggeration to say that the salonnières—even those as famous as Madame Geoffrin—had power in the classic sense: It is not clear that they were able to make public men do what they otherwise would not do. What the salonnières did have was influence. . .Through the salons, women were able to set the discursive agenda, steering the conversation to subjects of interest to them. They set agendas by choosing whom to invite to their gatherings, encouraging certain lines of argumentation, and by promoting young men whose thought they favored."

Leadership in Literature

Literature is full of women rising due to their wits, charm, or pure goodness as Jane Eyre does in Charlotte Brontë's novel. Other women in fiction suffer when they break conventions—Hester Prynne, for example, in Hawthorne's *The Scarlet Letter* and Carrie Meeber in Theodore Dreiser's *Sister Carrie*. They also suffer because of their powerlessness. In English literature, for example, there is Thomas Hardy's *Tess of the d'Urbervilles* and Dorothea Brooke, the heroine of George Eliot's *Middlemarch*. Strong female characters also appear in much earlier works, including Chaucer's Wife of Bath; Hua Mulan 花木蘭, a fabled woman warrior in ancient China; and of course Shakespeare's ambitious Lady Macbeth. Most often, however, fiction shows women as happy followers of the status quo, with feisty characters like Jane Austen's Elizabeth Bennet happily marrying a very powerful man by the end of *Pride and Prejudice.*

More than any other novelist, the British Anthony Trollope (1815-1882) made women and political leadership a central thread, most notably in the six novels usually referred to as the Palliser series. The action takes place in and around the British parliament at the height of the British Empire, in the middle of the nineteenth century. Although all the politicians are men and his female characters eschew what was then called "rights for women," the plots are sometimes driven by women who are in the thick of political life, consulted by friends in government as well as by their own relations. Trollope was a realistic novelist, conventional in his politics, and he considered marriage and motherhood a sufficient and fulfilling career for women. But his female characters come close to breaking with the author who created them. One can imagine that Trollope was portraying the women of his time, who like the *hetaeras*, concubines, and wives in ancient Greek society, did not stick to the roles that the authorities of the day had defined for them. Alice Vavasor, the heroine of *Can You Forgive Her?* the first novel in the series and set in the 1860s, breaks off an engagement because her fiancé wants a quiet country life. She cannot bear the idea of retreating from London and public life. In fact, she is often teased for her political interest. Another character, Lady Laura Standish, persuades her father to join the government. "That women should even wish to have votes at parliamentary elections was to her abominable, and the cause of the Rights of Women generally was odious to her; but, nevertheless, for herself, she delighted in hoping that she too might be useful,—in thinking that she too was perhaps, in some degree, politically powerful."

In an unusual twist, Trollope also had a prominent male character, for whom two books in the series are named, who has particularly close relationships with women and rises in large part because of his beauty and charm. Using one's gifts, whatever they may be, when trying to succeed without advantages of birth or position, is not reserved only to women, even in Victorian England.

Wives, Hostesses, and Politicians in the Twentieth and Twenty-first Century

After women gained the right to vote, in 1920 in the United States, they began to run for office. Yet women with no position except that of wife (or sometimes daughter) to a powerful man remained central to the Washington political scene until late in the twentieth century. Some were ambitious only for status and influence, while others were more policy oriented. Katharine Graham (1917–2001) became both a hostess and a powerful businesswoman after taking over the *Washington Post* after her father and husband died. Other famous hostesses include Pamela Churchill Harriman (who married three influential men), Evangeline Bruce (wife of Ambassador David Bruce), and Lorraine Cooper (wife of Senator John Sherman Cooper of Kentucky).

Few people rise to influence without help from someone they are intimately connected to, whether a marriage partner or a wealthy family connection. But more and more we see women leaders who have worked their way up in the same way men have traditionally done. By 2016, a growing number of the world's countries are or have been led by a woman—including Angela Merkel (b. 1954) of Germany and Tsai Ing-wen (b. 1956) of Taiwan—with few sharing the path to power of so many female leaders of the past: the result of their connection with a man. That pattern, however, is far from absent in the twenty-first century, especially in Latin America and Asia. Even Hilary Clinton (b. 1947), the Democratic candidate for president in 2016, is the wife of a former US president. Indeed, after the Indiana primary vote in 2016, she was referred to by an MSNBC reporter as "the former first lady." And yet Clinton's success has created a surprising question for twenty-first-century women, as shown when reporters asked First Lady Michelle Obama, as if it were the most natural thing in the world, if she planned to run for president.

The story of business leader and philanthropist Teresa Heinz (b. 1938), on the other hand, could have come straight from a Trollope novel: She married a Republican senator and inherited much of his family fortune, then went on to marry the rising politician John Kerry. In the UK, Margaret Thatcher (1925–2013) married a wealthy older man who called her "The Boss" and funded her early political campaigns.

Another phenomenon garnering considerable attention in popular culture is that of the "power couple," in which two educated, ambitious professionals combine forces. This term can be used admiringly, or it can be a way to denigrate a relationship as almost unnatural, because warm love and sexual intimacy are supposed to determine our choice of life partners. One such power couple is central to the television series *House of Cards*, in which a beautiful and clever wife has devoted herself to making her husband a political success. Once he becomes president, however, she demands to be appointed to a position that she deems herself qualified for through having been at her husband's side and intimately involved in his work behind the scenes. Pillow-talk power and frustrated female ambition is one of the dramatic threads. (In 2016, in fact, a husband and wife, Daniel Ortega and Rosario Murillo, were elected president and vice president of Nicaragua.)

The ways in which women have sought and achieved power over the past millennia offers a more expansive perspective on women and leadership than we get from merely looking at the handful of women who have attained the kind of positions that characterize any standard list of male leaders in history. Long before the murmurings of "rights for women," individual women in all walks of life were demonstrably strong, intelligent, and effective. Some achieved positions of real power from the sidelines and demonstrated true leadership. These women were of their time and ahead of their time, too: women who wanted to live to their fullest capacity. One of Trollope's politically inclined fictional heroines, Lady Glencora Palliser, wife of the prime minister, wants "a niche for herself in history." Women have often sought a niche in history and a bigger world for themselves, as well as the ability to control their own destiny, and to manage the destiny of their family, tribe, or nation, and did so long before the women's movement of the twentieth century opened a much wider door to leadership

Further Reading

Schmid, S. (2013). *British literary salons of the late eighteenth and early nineteenth centuries.* New York: Palgrave.

Brown, K. (Ed.). (2014.) *Dictionary of Chinese biography.* Great Barrington, MA: Berkshire.

Goodman, D. (Spring 1989). Enlightenment salons: The convergence of female and philosophic ambitions. *Eighteenth-Century Studies,* Vol. 22, No. 3, Special Issue: The French Revolution in Culture, pp. 329–350. The Johns Hopkins University Press.

Graham, I. (2016). *Scarlet women: the scandalous lives of courtesans, concubines, and royal mistresses.* New York: St. Martin's Press.

Halperin, J. (1977). *Trollope and politics: A study of the Pallisers and others.* New York: Barnes & Noble Books.

Healey, E. (1986). *Wives of fame: Mary Livingstone, Jenny Marx and Emma Darwin.* London: Sidgwick & Jackson.

Herbst, S. (1994). *Politics at the margin: Historical studies of public expression outside the mainstream.* New York and Cambridge: Cambridge University Press.

Marton, K. (2001). *Hidden power: Presidential marriages that shape our history.* New York: Pantheon.

Orth, M. (2007, September). The Washington hostesses: Susan Mary Alsop, Oatsie Charles, Evangeline Bruce, Kay Graham, and Pamela Harriman. *Vanity Fair.* Retrieved June 15, 2016, from http://www.vanityfair.com/news/2007/12/socialDC200712

Sunzi, R. D., Sawyer, M. (2005). *The Essential Art of War.* New York: Basic Books.

Trollope, Anthony. (2012). *Can you forgive her?* Oxford: Oxford University Press. (Original work published 1864)

Trollope, Anthony. (2011). *Phineas Finn.* Oxford University Press. (Original work published 1869)

Trollope, Anthony. (2011). *Phineas Redux.* Oxford University Press. (Original work published 1874)

Walthall, A. (Ed.). (2008). *Servants of the dynasty: Palace women in world history.* Berkeley: University of California.

Williams, S. W. (1885). *Queenly women, crowned and uncrowned.* Cincinnati, OH: Cranston and Stowe, Cincinnati.

Women in International Diplomacy

Douglas MO
Berkshire Publishing Group

Traditionally male arenas, leadership positions in the fields of international diplomacy and commerce have become available to women only relatively recently. Women in senior diplomatic roles are still a scarcity in many countries, while in others, such as China, the United States, Great Britain, and Russia, individual women have ascended to the highest levels, with roles of paramount responsibility, and have left lasting impressions.

D espite the majority of the world's diplomats being male, the number of women making their presence felt on an international scale has been increasing. This aspect of women in political life is rather unique, since the heart of diplomacy is being able to cooperate and negotiate with those from drastically different cultural backgrounds, particularly during times of dissension. Yet female diplomats around the world have challenged the status quo by demonstrating their capacity to represent and negotiate for their nations even under trying circumstances.

Women Representing Nations

In a few countries, women have reached the upper echelons of commerce and the foreign service as career diplomats, some aided by historical circumstance or new governmental policies. The countries of Great Britain, Russia, China, and the United States have been leaders in this regard, beginning as early as 1923 in Russia.

Russia

Alexandra Kollontai was one of the first-ever female diplomats, appointed as Soviet Union ambassador to Norway in 1923. Kollontai was raised in both Russia and Finland, and consequently became well versed in a multitude of languages—making her the perfect diplomatic candidate. Kollontai was a prominent figure during the Russian socialist movement and was responsible for spearheading mass movements of working-class women. In addition, Kollontai contributed to the political recognition of the USSR. Kollontai is in every sense of the word a trailblazer among all women in politics.

Following Kollontai's death in 1952, the Soviet Union saw no women in diplomacy. Maria Zakharova, the Russian Foreign Ministry spokesperson, stated that it was impossible for women to enter the realm of international relations, as they were simply not welcomed. This trend changed in the late 1990s, when the Soviet embassy in Laos chose Lyudmila Vorobyeva to be an interpreter. Vorobyeva worked in Laos for thirteen years, was Russia's mini-state counselor in Thailand from 2005 to 2007, and Russia's ambassador to Malaysia from 2010–2015.

Great Britain

Women joined the ranks in diplomacy for the United Kingdom beginning in 1946, when labor force shortages were such that the Foreign and Commonwealth Office had no choice but to send capable women to carry out quasi-diplomatic work abroad. Diplomacy was considered to be different in nature compared to other occupations, since it relied on building relationships with foreign countries that may have different values about gender roles—in Latin American nations, where Catholicism has a far-reaching influence, or in conservative nations like Japan. Cicely Mayhew was one of the first women to be appointed to the British diplomatic service, serving as the King's first female emissary in 1947. Another pioneer, Dame Anne Warburton, became Britain's first woman ambassador to Denmark. After Warburton's time in Denmark, she went on to serve as the UK's permanent representative to the United Nations and other international organizations in Geneva from 1983–1985. Eleanor Emery joined the diplomatic service in 1966, and went on to become the first British women to head a foreign mission as high commissioner to Botswana in 1973.

The long-standing notion in Britain regarding women taking up diplomatic careers was that no favorable accommodations existed for child rearing; in fact, there was a marriage ban in place for women until 1973. With that in mind, British female diplomats often had to pursue their professional ambition at the expense of a private life. Mayhew and Warburton possessed a forthright outlook and were unwilling to leave a job that they came to love, which perhaps, did not represent the outlook of all women.

Several women followed Warburton as ambassadors, but the numbers were conspicuously miniscule—fewer than a dozen women through the 1970s and 1980s. Until Veronica Sutherland took office in 1987, every female ambassador was unmarried and childless. In a *Financial Times* article entitled "Britain's First Female Diplomats," former ambassador to Luxembourg Juliet Campbell conceded that future generations may wonder why female pioneers in diplomacy acquiesced to such a patriarchal system. Yet the anomalous nature of women in diplomatic positions was sewed into the fabric of British gender ideology.

As far as statistics goes, the number of female diplomats in Britain has been increasing relative to decades ago. This is in part due to job sharing—a husband and wife currently head the mission to Zambia. Anne Pringle, the first female ambassador to Moscow, epitomizes today's generation of feminist women in diplomacy; her Moscow posting is the first time in twenty years that she has worked in the same country as her husband (Barker 2009).

China

Despite theoretical equality under Mao Zedong's famed phrase "women hold up half the sky," few women have ascended to the upper echelon of politics after the establishment of the People's Republic of China in 1949. Since then, four vice premiers have been women, with two out of these four, Wu Yi and Chen Muhua, involved in international trade and commerce.

Chen Muhua's political career started when she enrolled as a student at Chinese People's Anti-Japanese Military and Political College in Yan'an, Chinese Communist headquarters during the war years. Chan's career highlights include her positions as vice minister and minister of International Liaison Department of the Central Committee of the CPC, and president of the People's Bank of China. Chen achieved the highest government position for a woman at the time when she became vice premier in 1978. As president of the People's Bank of China, she established financial reform policies. Chen was also responsible for China's foreign aid to African countries during her time in the Foreign Economic Relations Office during the 1960s.

Wu Yi's political career took off when she was elected deputy mayor of Beijing in 1988, where she remained until 1991. Wu then served the posts of deputy minister of Foreign Economic Relations and Trade, minister of Foreign Trade and Economic Cooperation, and was a member of the fourteenth and fifteenth central committees of China's Communist Party. Wu became state counselor in 1998 and was subsequently appointed to be vice premier of the State Council in 2003. Wu is remembered for her presence and direct persona. More specifically, Wu's

Wu Yi, Madeline Albright, and Bob Kapp in 2004.

negotiation skills were admired globally, especially during her defense of China's interests at international trade talks.

One of Wu's most distinguished moments as a politician occurred during the 1996 Sino-US negotiations on intellectual property rights. Two days before negotiations, the head of the Chinese delegation fell ill, and Wu stepped into the leadership role. Due to Wu's efforts, China and the United States reached an agreement and signed a bilateral memorandum in China's favor regarding intellectual property rights. Wu has also played a pivotal role in discussions regarding China's efforts to expand exports, Sino-US trade deficits, and debates on China's entry into the World Trade Organization.

Wu's negotiation style is shaped her by "tenacity, candor, self-confidence, and tough image" (china.org.cn 2008). This was evident during the SARS outbreak when Wu displayed an activist and hands-on-approach after replacing Zhang Wenkang as health minister in 2003. Many lives were lost both in China and abroad due to the lack of government transparency, and many overseas offices of multinationals were closed during this time. Yet Wu's leadership instilled a sense of comfort and confidence among people in China. *Time* magazine even dubbed Wu the "goddess of transparency" in 2004 for her leadership during these difficult years.

Charlene Barshefksy, a former US trade representative, spoke highly of Wu and her ability to get things done in an efficient manner: "If one was looking for a minister to help China regain international trust, she would be the person." Barshefsky continues, "Her directness undercuts the notion that there's guile or any attempt to deceive. Also, she means business" (The Age 2003).

Domestic policy assistants Bobbie Kilberg and Sallyanne Payton meeting with Barbara Franklin (center). Courtesy of Barbara Franklin Papers, Penn State University Archives.

United States

From 1969 to 1973, the United States experienced a period of heightened feminist activism. One of these activists was business leader Barbara Hackman Franklin (b. 1940), who would be recruited by President Nixon in 1971 to help bring more women into high-level positions in the federal government. Responsible for seeking potential female appointees and also identifying vacancies, Franklin was able to recruit more than three times as many female executives for the government than in any previous administration. The focus of the Nixon administration on appointing qualified women for policy-making jobs marked a turning point for women's rights, specifically because rules and practices were reformed, and "agencies were directed to begin to hire and promote women at the middle grade and to set up training programs for those below" (Stout 182). As a result of Franklin's dedication and advocacy for women, a long-standing tradition was established; the Nixon program to recruit more women continued under President Gerald Ford.

In 1975, he appointed Carla Hills as secretary of Housing and Urban Development; she would go on to be a US trade representative from 1989 to 1993. President Carter appointed three women to be in his cabinet—one of them, Juanita Kreps (1921–2010) as secretary of commerce in 1977. President Reagan appointed Sandra Day O'Connor to the Supreme Court in 1981, and like Carter, had three women in his cabinet. The trend continued when President George H.W. Bush appointed two consecutive women for secretary of labor, and Barbara Franklin as secretary of commerce in 1992. President Clinton appointed Madeline Albright as the first female secretary of state, along with five other women to his cabinet. To date, the United

Wen Jiabao and Carla Hills in 2003.

States has had three past female US trade representatives, two female secretaries of commerce, and three female secretaries of state, the most senior cabinet position.

Initially a lawyer, Carla Hills became involved in government work when she accepted the role of assistant to the attorney general (which ironically was intended for her husband, who refused the job). In 1988, President George H.W. Bush appointed Hills to be the first female US trade representative (USTR)—despite lack of experience in trade, she was unanimously approved by the Senate when she declared: "We will open foreign markets with a crowbar where necessary, but with a handshake whenever possible." It is no surprise that Hills's nickname was "velvet crowbar," due to the combination of her toughness and a soft-spoken demeanor. She was known for her hard work in educating herself about the workings of international trade. Hills' most prominent achievements as USTR were opening Japanese markets to American goods and fighting European Community Trade Barriers.

Juanita Kreps was the first female secretary of commerce, serving in President Jimmy Carter's cabinet from 1977–1979 (Kreps was one of two women in Carter's cabinet at the time). As secretary of commerce, Kreps became the "nation's traveling saleswoman, taking trade missions to the Soviet Union, Europe, Asia, and Africa" (McFadden 2010). In fact, Kreps was credited with negotiating a historic trade agreement with China in 1979—China had just opened to the West in 1976. She advocated for businesses to act on principle and with responsibility toward employees, the public interest, and the environment. Although Kreps only served for three years, her legacy left an indelible impact and paved the road for women in diplomacy and politics.

Barbara Hackman Franklin became the next female secretary of commerce. She led a historic mission to China in 1992 (she was the first cabinet officer to visit China following the 1989 protest at Tiananmen Square in Beijing), from which she was able to bring back one billion worth of trade for American companies.

Madeline Albright was nominated by President Bill Clinton to be the first female secretary of state in 1996—the Senate confirmed her in 1997. Albright's family, originally from Czechoslovakia, immigrated to Denver, Colorado following the communist coup in 1948. Albright has had a profound influence on the nature of American diplomacy, and is most remembered for her promotion of the NATO expansion eastward into the former Soviet bloc nations.

Condoleeza Rice was the first African American woman to serve as the nation's secretary of state, from 2005 to 2009. She is remembered for dedicating her department to "transformational diplomacy," its mission being to encourage well-governed states around the world. In particular, Rice was responsible for relocating American diplomats to Iraq and Afghanistan, which were deemed turbulent areas. The next secretary of state, Hillary Clinton, went on to become the Democratic Party's nominee for president.

Further Reading

Barker, A. (2009, November 6). Britain's first female diplomats. *Financial Times*. Retrieved July 15, 2016, from https://next.ft.com/content/8e936c88-c9ad-11de-a071-00144feabdc0

Condit, T. Alexandra Kollontai. Retrieved July 5, 2016, from https://www.marxists.org/archive/kollonta/into .htm

Dame Ann Warburton, diplomat—obituary. (2015). Retrieved July 5, 2016, from http://www.telegraph.co .uk/news/obituaries/11662733/Dame-Anne-Warburton-diplomat-obituary.html

Department of Commerce. Retrieved June 24, 2016, from https://www.commerce.gov/page/commerce-history

Global Diplomatic Forum. (2016, March 22). Women in diplomacy. Retrieved June 22, 2016, from http://www.gdforum.org/women-in-diplomacy-2016

Huang, J. (2008, November). Chen Muhua. Retrieved June 22, 2016, from http://www.womenofchina.cn/womenofchina/html1/about/9/5488-1.htm

International Herald Tribune. (2012, March 6). Holding Up Half the Sky. Retrieved July 6, 2016 from http://www.nytimes.com/2012/03/07/world/asia/holding-up-half-the-sky.html

MacLeod, C. (2013, March). China's women struggle to breach male-heavy politics. Retrieved June 22, 2016, from http://www.usatoday.com/story/news/world/2013/03/11/china-women-politics/1972109

McCarthy, H. (2014). The rise of the female diplomat. *Prospect Magazine.* Retrieved June 23, 2016, from http://www.prospectmagazine.co.uk/opinions/the-rise-of-the-female-diplomat

McFadden, R. D. (2010). Juanita M. Kreps, commerce secretary, dies at 89. *New York Times.* Retrieved July 5, 2016, from http://www.nytimes.com/2010/07/08/us/08kreps.html

National Committee on U.S. China Relations. 2016 Annual Members Program: Leaders Speak. Retrieved June 24, 2016, from https://www.ncuscr.org/content/2016-annual-members-program

Office of the Historian. Retrieved July 5, 2016, from https://history.state.gov/departmenthistory/people/albright-madeleine-korbel

Office of the US Trade Representative. Retrieved June 24, 2016, from https://ustr.gov/about-us/history/list-past-ustrs

Soft Power: The Professional Secrets of Russia's Top Female Diplomats. Retrieved July 15, 2016, from http://sputniknews.com/russia/20160308/1035957966/russia-diplomacy-women-secrets.html

Stout, L. (2012). *A matter of simple justice: The untold story of Barbara Hackman Franklin and a few good women.* University Park, PA: The Pennsylvania State University Libraries.

US Department of State. Retrieved June 24, 2016, from http://www.state.gov/secretary/former

Wang Z.; Zhou J.; Yang X.; & Zhang T. (2008, March 8). Iron lady—Wu Yi. Retrieved June 22, 2016, from http://china.org.cn/china/2008-03/08/content_12000268.htm

When the going gets tough, China calls its top woman in red. (2003, May 10). Retrieved June 22, 2016, from http://www.theage.com.au/articles/2003/05/09/1052280440543.html

Wu Yi, always remembered by Chinese people. (2008, March). Retrieved June 23, 2016, from http://www.womenofchina.cn/womenofchina/html1/people/officials/9/1801-1.htm

Your dictionary. Retrieved July 5, 2016, from http://biography.yourdictionary.com/carla-anderson-hills

Yuen, L. (2013). China's glass ceiling: Women still excluded from high-level politics. *The Atlantic.* Retrieved June 22, 2016, from http://www.theatlantic.com/china/archive/2013/06/chinas-glass-ceiling-women-still-excluded-from-high-level-politics/276589/

Biography. Retrieved July 18, 2016 from http://www.biography.com/people/condoleezza-rice-9456857

Imperialism and Gender

Heather STREETS-SALTER
Washington State University

Imperialism in the nineteenth century and early twentieth century had lasting and sometimes surprising effects on perceptions of gender and the welfare of women within colonial societies. The colonizers brought their standards of gender to bear on societies that had lived quite differently for thousands of years. Recent research is investigating the complex and varied ramifications of these gender ideals and biases on such populations, and discovering how colonization affected the perception of gender of those in the home countries.

Attitudes about "appropriate" sexual behaviors of both men and women were central to imperial endeavors beginning in the late 1800s; such ideals allowed colonizers to categorize and divide indigenous peoples into distinct and knowable groups. Colonial encounters between rulers and ruled often changed local gender relationships and standards in ways that deeply affected culture in the colonies and in imperial metropolises.

From the late nineteenth century until the end of World War II, the most powerful nations (along with others that aspired to great power) pursued the strategy of imperialism in an attempt to achieve national political and economic goals. Although imperialism was not new (Great Britain and Spain are notable examples of countries where pursuit of empire began centuries earlier), this period is historically unique because so many nations became involved in imperial ventures and because the territories they claimed were so extensive. Between 1885 and 1914 alone, European countries added 2.8 billion hectares to their imperial territories, the United States and Japan joined European countries in the pursuit of empire, nearly all of Africa came under colonial domination, and the British Empire grew to include one-quarter of the world's population.

Societies and systems established by imperial nations varied greatly across time and space. Some became settler colonies, where colonizers would establish large, permanent communities. Others were created because of the resources that could be extracted or because of their strategic location and were ruled by small numbers of administrators backed by military force, or even by indigenous groups overseen by colonial administrators. Whatever form imperial societies took, they all profoundly affected both rulers and those ruled economically, socially, culturally, and politically. Moreover, during the last two decades scholars have begun to understand that imperial systems around the world were maintained and legitimized, at least in part, through the use of language and policies based on gender ideals. These ideals included beliefs about the appropriate behaviors and sexualities of both men and women and were frequently used to mark distinctions between colonizing and indigenous cultures. They were also frequently inseparable from beliefs and attitudes about racial difference and were often used to shore up notions about the inherent inequality of colonized peoples. In addition, colonial encounters between rulers and ruled—varied though they were—changed local gender relationships and ideals in ways that deeply affected culture in the colonies as well as in imperial metropolises. These changes were not uniform in all colonies, or even within the various "national" empires. Rather, they depended on existing indigenous cultures, the presence or absence of natural resources, the presence or absence of colonial settlers, the degree of incorporation into the global economy, access to land, and many other factors. When examined from a global perspective, then, the relationship between imperialism and gender emerges as a complex phenomenon. At the same time, we can also detect several broad similarities that elucidate global connections and patterns.

Gender as a Means of Marking Hierarchy

Beliefs about gender, sexuality, and gender roles were central to imperial endeavors around the world because such beliefs provided legitimation for preserving distinctions between rulers and the ruled, and because they helped colonizers categorize—and hence divide—indigenous peoples into distinct and knowable groups. Although the precise form that such beliefs took varied across time and space, the need to clearly mark the boundaries between colonizer and colonized through language and practices associated with gender and gender difference was widely shared across many imperial systems.

Nearly every imperial system sought to justify the unequal distribution of power between rulers and ruled—and even the existence of colonies themselves—by concerning itself with the sexual behaviors, appetites, and attitudes of colonized men and women. One recurring theme in French Indochina, British India, the Dutch East Indies, and British South Africa—to name only a few—was the idea that white women were in constant danger from the voracious and perverse sexual appetites of colonized men. The fear of rape, and the need to protect white women from it, hence came to justify the strict separation between colonizers and colonized as well as the careful control of both colonized men and white women. As a result, white women often found their lives in colonies paradoxically quite comfortable (because of servants, privilege, and leisure time) as well as quite restricted. Colonized men, for their part, were routinely excluded from positions in which they might have even a remote chance of exercising power over white women. They also found themselves at risk of severe punishment if they transgressed the boundary between themselves and colonizing women. Perhaps not surprisingly, rhetoric about the need to control colonized men and to protect white women grew more intense during times of high colonial tension.

One example of the ways in which gender could be employed to maintain distinctions between rulers and ruled was the 1883–1884 Ilbert Bill controversy in

British India. The bill had been designed to concede a small amount of power to Indian civil servants by allowing Indian judges jurisdiction over some European cases. Britons in India vehemently opposed even the slightest suggestion that Indians might be able to pronounce judgment over Europeans, and openly attacked the bill on the grounds that it threatened the safety of white women. Although the bill itself said nothing about women, opponents argued that it opened the door for Indian civil servants—whose ultimate fantasy, they asserted, was the possession of a white woman—to use their new power to take sexual advantage of British women. Moreover, opponents claimed that Indian men could not be expected to treat British women with decency because they were said to treat their own women so poorly. In the end, opposition to the bill among the British community in India was so strong that it had to be dropped. Indian men had been kept firmly in a subordinate role through rhetorical claims about the gendered consequences of conceding power to colonized men.

Anxieties about racial mixing—miscegenation—also echoed widely across imperial systems during the last half of the nineteenth century, and here again beliefs about gender and sexuality played critical roles in maintaining the separation between rulers and ruled. Most imperial systems were predicated on the belief that colonizing men needed sex in order to be satisfied. The problem, however, was a shortage of colonizing women in many colonial societies—even those that encouraged settler families. As a result, colonizing men frequently established sexual relations with indigenous women through prostitution, concubinage, or, less commonly, marriage. Such relationships were rarely based on true partnership: even when colonized women entered into them of their own choice (abundant evidence suggests that the use of force and manipulation was quite common), they enjoyed few rights or privileges and could be discarded at will. Moreover, these sexual relationships produced a whole set of new problems. Chief among these was how to maintain distinctions between colonizers and colonized given the existence of such intimate relationships. Even more problematic was how to classify and treat the mixed-race children who resulted from these relationships.

In the East Indies, Dutch efforts to confront these issues illustrate both the centrality of sex management to imperial projects as well as the ways state policies about the regulation of sex could change over time. Prior to the twentieth century, the Dutch East Indies Company sharply restricted the immigration of Dutch women to the East Indies. The company reasoned that Dutch men would be more likely to remain in the East Indies if they established long-term relationships with indigenous women. Moreover, indigenous women were less expensive to maintain than European women and could be expected to perform domestic labor in addition to their sexual functions. For these reasons the company advocated that Dutch men keep concubines—women who shared all of the duties of wives without the legal protections and entitlements of marriage. By the 1880s, concubinage was the most common domestic arrangement for European men in the Indies, a situation that produced tens of thousands of mixed-race children. Yet, by the turn of the twentieth century, the existence of this large mixed-race population had begun to worry the Dutch East Indies Company and the Dutch government because it threatened to blur the divide between the colonizers and the colonized. To which group did these children belong? Were they Dutch or Indonesian? Would they support Dutch rule, or would they try to subvert it? As part of these worries, Dutch officials increasingly began to argue that Indonesian concubines had neither the skills nor the morals to raise their mixed-race children to be adults worthy of Dutch citizenship. As a result, during the early twentieth century the Dutch government reversed earlier policy by seeking to ban the practice of concubinage and to encourage instead the immigration of Dutch women to the Indies. These women, the government now believed, would provide a civilizing influence on Dutch men and would have the cultural skills to raise their children to be proper Dutch citizens. For European men who could not afford Dutch wives, the government now encouraged prostitution as a means of side-stepping long-term, family-style liaisons with indigenous women. In both the pre- and post-twentieth-century East Indies, government concerns with the sexuality and sexual behaviors of both men and women, colonizers and colonized, highlight the central importance of sex management—and the gender relationships such management depended upon—to the imperial state.

Beliefs about gender also contributed to imperial policies of divide and rule—that is, policies that emphasized differences between subgroups of colonized peoples as a way of minimizing unified opposition to imperial rule. In places as far-flung as India, Indonesia, South Africa, and French West Africa, to mention only a few, such policies encouraged preferential treatment of certain groups, which tended to pit these groups against less-preferred groups. Moreover, colonizing powers often bestowed favor on groups who seemed to embody colonizers' own notions of ideal masculinity. In French Algeria, for example, French colonial administrators articulated stark divisions between the two major ethnic groups in the region: Kabyles and Arabs. Kabyles, the administrators argued, were superior to Arabs in nearly every way. Kabyles were sedentary rather than nomadic; they lived in mountains rather than the plains; they spoke an Aryan language rather than a Semitic one; and they were secular rather than religious. Gender ideals were also central to Kabyle superiority. The French, for instance, perceived Kabyle men as tall and athletic and likened their bodies to French ideals of the male physique. Kabyles were also said to be brave and fierce warriors who had proven themselves worthy foes of the French. Finally, despite their ferocity, Kabyles were said to treat their women with respect, which again resonated with French notions about themselves. Arabs, on the other hand, were perceived as physically small, lazy, slovenly, and cowardly people who brutally oppressed their women. These perceptions of gendered difference were neither trivial nor matters of simple representation. Rather, they encouraged preferential treatment for Kabyles, imposed a strict division between two indigenous groups, and deeply influenced French-Arab interactions in Algeria. Indeed, the language of gender difference in imperial situations served not only to maintain distinctions between rulers and ruled, but also to maintain distinctions between different groups of colonized people.

Gender and the Colonial Encounter

Colonial encounters between rulers and ruled had profound social, cultural, political, and economic effects all over the world. In terms of gender, such encounters frequently disrupted local ideologies, relations, and traditions and often led to changes in all three. In virtually every colonial encounter, the gender ideals of the colonizing powers helped to shape colonial practice, law, and culture. The way

173

such ideals were translated into policy, however, depended upon the response of colonized peoples, and thus the effect of such ideals was neither uniform nor predictable. Moreover, the disruptive effects of the colonial encounter on gender ideals were not a one-way street because they influenced gender ideals in imperial home countries as well.

Nineteenth-century Hawaii illustrates the ways colonial gender ideals could interact with indigenous gender ideals in unexpected ways. Prior to contact with Westerners during the eighteenth century, Hawaiian culture had imposed sexual separation between men and women and had mandated that women follow certain eating taboos. In other respects, however, Hawaiian women played important social, economic, political, and spiritual roles and maintained a large degree of personal autonomy. As Western—especially US—influence increased in Hawaii during the nineteenth century, Hawaiian women were criticized as being sexually immoral, were consistently written out of US-dominated politics, and were increasingly defined as legally subordinate to Hawaiian and US men. Thus, as a result of US intervention into Hawaiian society, Hawaiian women's legal and social positions deteriorated. Yet, these same interventions also led to an improvement in Hawaiian women's position as landholders during the last half of the nineteenth century. This unexpected improvement was the result of the Great Māhele of 1848, when the Hawaiian government—under duress by US interests—divided Hawaiian land into salable pieces. The overall result for Hawaiians in general was massive dispossession from the land. For Hawaiian women, however, the results were much more ambiguous because the number of women who inherited land in the post-Great Māhele period dramatically increased. In part, this increase was a result of indigenous choices and beliefs about women as effective guardians of Hawaiian land. The net effect was the preservation of Hawaiian women's economic and social importance even as their legal status diminished as a result of discriminatory US policies.

Further cases illustrating the interaction of colonial and indigenous gender ideals abound in colonial Africa. In northern Ghana, for example, the implementation of the British judicial system caused indigenous women's legal status to deteriorate. In particular, colonial rule sought to introduce and enforce the notion that wives were the property of their husbands—a notion that, although foreign to Ghanaian gender ideals, allowed men to claim increasing legal control of their wives. In colonial Tanganyika, European authorities instituted policies—such as taxation and the conversion of cattle sales to cash—that increasingly defined Masai men as heads of households and allowed them privileged access to the political domain. Masai women, who had long played vital economic and social roles within their communities, were thus increasingly marginalized by colonial policies that clearly favored men as political and economic actors. At the same time, African women were not merely passive victims of a patriarchal partnership between colonizers and indigenous males. Rather, African women in many colonial states manipulated colonial court systems for their own benefit, ventured into independent economic enterprises, and moved into new occupations—as teachers or midwives—opened up to them by the colonial encounter.

Colonial encounters could also shape gender relations in imperial home countries. In Britain, imperialism informed the gender identities of both women and men and often provided the context within which claims about appropriate gender roles were made. A case in point was the British feminist movement, which developed and grew during the last half of the nineteenth century—and thus coincided with the massive expansion of the British Empire. British feminists advocated equal legal rights with British men, but they justified their claims to equality by arguing for the need to represent and civilize colonized—especially Indian—women. Indeed, feminists argued that the oppressed condition of Indian women necessitated their own political participation so they could utilize their superior moral authority to "uplift" their Indian "sisters." In this context British feminists' sense of themselves as women depended heavily on their perception of gender relations in the wider imperial world.

Gender and the Nationalist Response to Imperialism

Given the centrality of gender ideologies to imperial projects around the world, we should not be surprised that they were similarly central to a variety of nationalist responses to imperialism. Yet, gendered responses to imperialism did not follow set patterns across time or space and varied widely in relation to both the colonial power and local culture. One pattern that did emerge in places as diverse as post-1945 India and Indonesia, 1960s and 1970s Zimbabwe, and 1950s and 1960s Algeria was the formulation of an aggressive, hypermasculine nationalist rhetoric. Where this pattern emerged, colonized women sometimes became targets of nationalist violence. In other cases, they were idealized and made to stand as symbols of purity and tradition. Both strategies tended to marginalize women's roles in nationalist struggles and tended to complicate post-imperial gender relations. A second, paradoxical, pattern was the active participation of women in most nationalist movements all over the world. Indeed, women from French Indochina to Jamaica to Angola served in critical roles as messengers, providers, and even as soldiers.

The case of Zimbabwe in Africa illustrates the complex ways gender could help constitute the language and practices of anti-imperial nationalist movements. Under colonial rule Zimbabwean men felt increasingly emasculated as they lost status to white Europeans, were treated as children, and were unable to protect Zimbabwean women from the sexual advances of colonizing men. Emasculation took more material forms as well because colonial rule had made it progressively more difficult for Zimbabwean men to achieve those goals that were thought to mark ideal masculinity—including especially taking a wife, buying land, and providing for a family. As a result, Zimbabwean nationalism during the 1960s and 1970s took on an aggressively masculine posture (the two main parties styled themselves after the cock and the bull) that emphasized the importance of being manly, virile, and heterosexual. Incidents of violence against women increased dramatically during this period, evidenced by a spike in the number of rapes and attempted rapes. At the same time, women's actual participation in the Zimbabwean nationalist movement was crucial to its eventual success. They provided information to nationalist guerrillas, gave food and shelter to nationalist fighters, and, after 1975, were trained as guerrilla fighters themselves. Yet, in spite of such active women's participation, Zimbabwean independence in 1980 did not lead to equality for Zimbabwean women. Instead, like many other states that emerged in the wake of successful anti-imperial movements, patriarchy was simply reconfigured in new ways—boosted and encouraged by the aggressively masculine ways that many colonized men responded to their colonial overlords.

The Indonesian nationalist movement during the immediate post–World War II period shared the hypermasculine tone of the Zimbabwean nationalist movement. As in Zimbabwe, Indonesian men had long endured denigration by Dutch colonizers, who consistently referred to Indonesian—and especially Javanese—men as weak and effeminate. Moreover, Dutch men had gained privileged access to Indonesian women. To combat this sense of emasculation, Indonesian nationalists in the anticolonial war of 1945–1949 consciously adopted an aggressively masculine ethos by celebrating toughness, virility, and militarism and broke with established (Javanese) cultural traditions of courtesy and gentleness. In this revolutionary movement, women and female sexuality were seen as dangerous and even traitorous. Women's colonial roles as concubines (*nyais*) had made them suspect as potential spies, and weakness associated with women was viewed as a potential drain on, and distraction from, the cause of revolution. Indeed, because so many Indonesian nationalists felt it necessary to fight European imperialism with a new, hypermasculine gender identity, the movement turned against its female supporters in a bid to create a new sense of masculinity on the European model.

Implications of a Gendered History

The relationship between global imperialism and gender was complex. It was not uniform across space and time, and its precise form varied widely according to local conditions, the colonial culture being imposed, and the specific issues involved. Moreover, the consequences of gender ideals in imperial situations often worked themselves out in unintended, ambiguous, and unexpected ways. What is clear, however, is that beliefs about gender were central to imperial projects around the world and that they had real, observable effects in the material world as well as in the realm of representation, discourse, and psychology. In addition, gendered responses to imperial control played a role in shaping gender relations in many newly independent nations, with effects that can still be felt in the present.

Further Reading

Allman, J. & Burton, A. (2003). Destination globalization? Women, gender and comparative histories in the new millennium. *Journal of Colonialism and Colonial History, 4*(2), 1–10.

Allman, J., Geiger, S., & Musisi, N. (2002). *Women in African colonial histories.* Bloomington: Indiana University Press.

Ballhatchet, K. (1980). *Race, sex, and class under the Raj: Imperial attitudes and policies and their critics.* London: Weidenfield and Nicolson.

Burton, A. (1994). *Burdens of history: British feminists, Indian women, and imperial culture, 1865–1915.* Chapel Hill: University of North Carolina Press.

Chaudhuri, N. & Strobel, M. (1992). *Western women and imperialism: Complicity and resistance.* Bloomington: Indiana University Press.

Clancy-Smith, J. & Gouda, F. (1998). *Domesticating the empire: Race, gender, and family life in French and Dutch colonialism.* Charlottesville: University Press of Virginia.

Cooper, F. & Stoler, A. L. (1997). *Tensions of empire: Colonial cultures in a bourgeois world.* Berkeley and Los Angeles: University of California Press.

Dawson, G. (1994). *Soldier heroes: British adventure, empire, and the imagining of masculinities.* London: Routledge.

Epprecht, M. (1998). The "unsaying" of indigenous homosexualities in Zimbabwe: Mapping a blindspot in an African masculinity. *Journal of Southern African Studies, 24*(4), 631–651.

Hodgson, D. (1999). "Once intrepid warriors": Modernity and the production of Maasai masculinities. *Ethnology, 38*(2), 121–150.

Holden, P. & Ruppel, J. (2003). *Imperial desire: Dissident sexualities and colonial literature.* Minneapolis: University of Minnesota Press.

Kleeman, F. Y. (2003). *Under an imperial sun: Japanese colonial literature of Taiwan and the South.* Honolulu: University of Hawaii Press.

Levine, P. (2003). *Prostitution, race, and politics: Policing venereal disease in the British Empire.* New York: Routledge.

Linnekin, J. (1990). *Sacred queens and women of consequence: Rank, gender, and colonialism in the Hawaiian Islands.* Ann Arbor: University of Michigan Press.

Lorcin, P. (1999). *Imperial identities: Stereotyping, prejudice, and race in colonial Algeria.* London: I. B. Tauris.

Midgley, C. (1998). *Gender and imperialism.* Manchester, U.K.: Manchester University Press.

Sangari, K. & Vaid, S. (1990). *Recasting women: Essays in Indian colonial history.* New Brunswick, NJ: Rutgers University Press.

Sinha, M. (1995). *Colonial masculinity: The "manly Englishman" and the "effeminate Bengali" in the late nineteenth century.* Manchester, U.K.: Manchester University Press.

Stoler, A. L. (2002). *Carnal knowledge and imperial power: Race and the intimate in colonial rule.* Berkeley and Los Angeles: University of California Press.

Streets, H. (2004). *Martial races: The military, masculinity, and race in British imperial culture, 1857–1914.* Manchester, U.K.: Manchester University Press.

Wu Zetian

625–705 CE—China's only female emperor
(r. 690–704)

N. Harry ROTHSCHILD
University of North Florida

Wu Zetian, better known as Empress Wu, ruled in tandem with her husband Emperor Gaozong, then presided as Grand Dowager after his death. In 690, she assumed the throne as China's first and only female emperor. Recent historical scrutiny reveals her as a woman possessed of tremendous creativity and political virtuosity. She was an eminently capable ruler who dominated the Chinese court during a half century of relative stability and prosperity.

In patriarchal traditional China, where "men were venerated and women denigrated," it took a favorable confluence of circumstance, opportunity, ambition, and prodigious talent for Wu Zetian to assume the dragon throne. Wu Zetian had decades of political seasoning and training. She became eminently familiar with court politics and administration over thirty-five years, first ruling in tandem with husband Emperor Gaozong (r. 655–683), then presiding over the court as Grand Dowager (684–690) after his death. In 690, she assumed the throne and ruled as emperor, establishing her own Zhou dynasty (690–705).

With neither precedent nor sequel, Wu Zetian's remarkable achievement of becoming China's lone woman emperor stands as testament to her historical significance. Yet her contribution to Chinese history is far greater. Her reign was innovative. Her deft use of propaganda and rhetoric shed light on the nature of statecraft and emperorship in traditional China. She played a seminal role in the development of East Asian Buddhism. To standardize skills and knowledge expected of military officers, she created the *wuju*, a military examination in 702. During her reign the registered population grew substantially. In short, she was an eminently capable ruler and a shrewd politician who dominated the Chinese court for the better part of a half-century of relative stability and prosperity.

Historical Serendipity

Born at the dawn of the Tang dynasty (618–907 CE), a true multiethnic and cosmopolitan empire that enfolded many lands, peoples, and religions, Wu Zetian emerged in the right place and at the right time. Such an era was ideally suited for the rise of a historical anomaly. During the Period of Disunity (220–581 CE), four centuries of chaos and warfare, non-Chinese peoples like the Toba Turks dominated northern China. The nomadic culture of the steppe blended with the sedentary, agrarian ways of the Chinese heartland. The Silk Roads carried endless caravans of new fashions, goods, and ideas from Persia, India, and Central Asia. This hybrid culture often challenged cultural assumptions, loosening the hold of Confucian mores on women of the early Tang.

Influenced by the freewheeling lives of Central Asian women among hide yurts and grazing flocks of the steppe, who were culturally not restricted to the domestic realm, Tang women enjoyed greater freedom than their counterparts from earlier dynasties. They were able to divorce husbands rather freely. Bold and self-assured, Tang women rode unveiled through city markets, flaunting their femininity with low-cut necklines or mingling with men at Buddhist temple fairs. In addition, in the decades leading up to Wu Zetian's accession, there were powerful female rulers in Korea and Japan. Also, beyond the western borderlands of the empire, a powerful matriarch presided over a matriarchy that Tang records called the Eastern Kingdom of Women.

Another important precondition to Wu Zetian's ascendancy was the pervasive Buddhist presence. Popular among commoners and elites alike, Buddhism was a cultural common denominator pervading a wider pan-Asian continuum, linking India, Central Asia, China, Korea, and Japan. Buddhist temples, pagodas, and statuary filled the twin capitals, Luoyang and Chang'an, and dotted the surrounding countryside. Wu Zetian lent her patronage and support to the Buddhist establishment, sponsoring the construction of many Buddhist temples. In return, the Buddhist monks ardently supported her emperorship.

All of these circumstances of this distinctive era served to facilitate Wu Zetian's rise. Given the distinctive nature of the era—the ethnically diverse and ideologically pluralistic empire into which she was born—Wu Zetian's historical arrival was serendipitous. Descended from mixed Central Asian–Chinese bloodlines, derived from her background as the offspring of provincial merchants rather than literati aristocrats, and steeped in Buddhist learning, she had the perfect background and disposition to preside over such a cosmopolitan empire.

Rise to Empress

As a young girl, Wu Zetian followed her father, Wu Shiyue, from one provincial official appointment to the next. After his death, she left her widowed mother to enter the women's quarters of the imperial palace as a "talent," one of nine fifth-ranked concubines in the harem of famous Emperor Taizong (c. 599–649 CE; r. 626–649). Though she never gained Taizong's favor, he was impressed by her dazzling pulchritude and bestowed upon her the nickname Enchanting Miss Wu.

While on his deathbed Taizong instructed his ill-prepared son and successor, Gaozong, in the arts of statecraft. As the heir apparent spent more time in the inner (women's) quarters, Wu Zetian and he formed a deep emotional bond. Still, after Taizong's death in 649, in accord with ritual practice, Wu Zetian and the rest of the harem were sent to a nearby Buddhist convent. Lonely, Wu Zetian wrote a poem expressing her keen desire for her lover that began with the verses:

I look upon your disc of jade and my thoughts scatter in disarray,

As haggard from grief, sundered and separate, I so keenly miss my Sovereign.

Later, Gaozong recalled her to the inner palace and promoted her to Lady of Luminous Demeanor, a higher position. After she bore several sons, Gaozong elevated her to become Empress Wu in 655, displacing Empress Wang, a barren woman of a far more eminent background.

Sharing Emperorship: The Two Sages

After a serious stroke early in his reign, Gaozong shared his imperial responsibilities with Wu Zetian. Beginning in 660, she jointly deliberated upon administrative decisions with her imperial husband from behind a curtain in the audience hall. People of the time called them the "Two Sages." As empress, she played an active and visible political role. Her involvement in state ceremonial rites acclimated court and country to her political presence. In 676, after heir apparent Li Hong died of tuberculosis, an ailing Gaozong offered to abdicate the throne to Wu Zetian. Though she declined, to justify her growing open political role, she gathered a private band of talented Confucian scholars of low rank known as the Scholars of the North Gate. These unofficial advisors compiled a series of literary works geared toward consolidating Wu Zetian's political authority.

Grand Dowager, Sage Mother

After Gaozong's death in 683, Wu Zetian's eldest remaining son, the inept and frivolous Emperor Zhongzong, rapidly fell under sway of his Empress Wei. Wu Zetian summarily deposed him in 684, and moved to consolidate her political authority. Now Grand Dowager, she also assumed the role of regent, overshadowing her tractable and timid youngest son Li Dan, Emperor Ruizong. Ministers addressed her as "Your Majesty." As one of the Two Sages, while seated in court Wu Zetian had remained hidden behind a purple curtain, heard but not seen. Now the curtain was removed and she alone "oversaw the court and issued edicts." To impress her distinctive signet upon the court, she changed the colors of official robes and banners to accord with the Zhou dynasty of antiquity and altered names of offices to follow ornate archaic precedent. Distancing herself from the Tang capital Chang'an, she designated Luoyang her divine capital.

Wu Zetian had many enemies. In 684 and 688, separate rebellions led by princes from the imperial Li family sputtered and failed. To discourage further uprisings and to intimidate potential rival factions, she began to use a group of cruel officials during this regency. Lai Junchen, the most notorious of these men, authored the *Manual of Entrapment*, a work detailing the arts of ensnaring the innocent, fabricating circumstances of conspiracy, and forcing confessions through torture. Once she felt secure in her power as emperor in the mid-690s, Wu Zetian distanced herself from these cruel officials. When Lai, called by one official "the foremost evil of state" was executed at her command, the jubilant populace gouged out his heart and trampled his corpse into a bloody pulp.

Though she wielded de facto power and her feckless son Ruizong offered to abdicate, Wu Zetian declined, feeling the time was not yet ripe. Incrementally, though, she took steps toward assuming emperorship. In 688, her propagandists "discovered" a white stone in the Luo River with amethyst characters that read, "When the Sage Mother is among the people, the realm will enjoy eternal prosperity." Later that year, in an occasion tantamount to a dress rehearsal for her coronation, Wu Zetian staged a grand rite with pomp and ceremony, publicly and sensationally casting herself as a caring "Sage Mother" nurturing myriad "sons" within a wider empire. Shortly thereafter, she assumed the title "Sage Mother, Divine and August." The character for "August," *huang*, was part of the compound for emperor, *huangdi*. To mark the occasion, civil ministers, military officers, and foreign dignitaries paraded before an altar set along the Luo River. Guests honored the Sage Mother with an unrivalled abundance of tribute: an exotic array of gifts including splendid birds, miraculous beasts, precious gemstones, and other exquisite rarities.

China's Only Woman Emperor

On the ninth day of the ninth month of 690, Wu Zetian ascended the dragon throne as the first and only female emperor in Chinese history. She built her Divine Capital Luoyang into an international metropolis rivaling Chang'an. In military affairs and foreign relations, Wu Zetian was neither soft nor weak. She balanced a policy of embracing those who voluntarily submitted with punitive campaigns against the recalcitrant. Unlike rulers of some later dynasties who denigrated the martial arts and prized civil courtly culture, Wu Zetian attached great importance to recruiting capable generals. In 692, General Wang Xiaojie defeated the Tibetans and reclaimed the Four Garrisons, rich oasis states along the Silk Roads in western China, which strengthened Chinese control over Silk Road commerce and increased her prestige among Central Asian peoples. Under her guidance, troops also staved off a series of fierce incursions from the Khitan and Turks.

Wu Zetian's later years were unremarkable. A tired and careworn septuagenarian, she realized that her Wu nephews had alienated court and country alike, and named her son heir apparent in 698, a decision that determined that the Zhou dynasty would not outlive her reign. She was unable to maintain her strong-willed and perspicacious management of court. Progressively, as she grew increasingly infirm, Wu Zetian turned to Daoism, performing rites of expiation and seeking, like many Chinese emperors before and after her, an elixir of immortality. She frequently withdrew from her court at Luoyang and headed for the hot springs and Daoist temples of Mount Song. Sensing a previously unseen weakness in the tired woman emperor, a group of court ministers staged a coup in 705, killing the Zhangs and forcing Wu Zetian into retirement in the Imperial Park outside the walls of the imperial city. The Tang dynasty was restored. Wu Zetian died ten months later, disheveled and weary. She was interred with her husband Gaozong at Qianling, the only tomb in Chinese history to house two emperors.

A Retrospective Look at Wu Zetian

In the didactic Confucian historiography, Wu Zetian has been consistently demonized. Confucian historians in subsequent dynasties referred to her as Empress or

Grand Dowager, but almost never as Emperor. She is often accused of inhuman and barbarous acts of dubious historicity: smothering her infant daughter and blaming it on Empress Wang, killing several of her sons, or practicing witchcraft to incapacitate her husband Gaozong. Confucian historians judged her as an anti-heroine, a regicide where the ideal male ruler was duly filial; corrupt and lewd where he was virtuous; self-aggrandizing where he was austere. In the Ming dynasty (1368–1644) novella, *The Lord of Perfect Satisfaction*, she is cast as a lust-driven, insatiable wanton relentlessly seeking pleasure from her prodigiously endowed lover while utterly neglecting matters of state. Such tales reflect the longstanding Confucian vision of the whimsical, willful, and self-indulgent character of a woman in power.

Yet some Confucian historians showed a certain begrudging admiration for Wu Zetian's statecraft. Song dynasty (960–1279) historian Sima Guang (1019–1086) expressed reluctant respect for her governance in his remark that, "Even though the Grand Dowager excessively used emolument [i.e., payment] and rank to gain the hearts of the people, those not responsible in office were eventually dismissed and punished. The Grand Dowager grasped the handle of punishment and reward in order to administer the empire. Government issued from her alone. She possessed enlightened oversight and good judgment of character. Therefore, at that time outstanding and sagely men competed to be employed by her" (*Zizhi tongjian* 205.6478).

This more generous assessment tallies with historical reality: by most objective criteria, Wu Zetian's rule was successful. Economically and culturally, her achievements rival those of the best Tang emperors. There were no major peasant rebellions. Two uprisings—one in 684 and another in 688—gained no widespread popular traction. In addition, Wu Zetian held on to the vast territories of the Tang empire, re-establishing control of the Four Garrisons along the Silk Road and staving off the aggression of the great Turkish Khan, Qapaghan. She also fostered commerce and economic growth. The significant growth in the registered population—from 3.8 million family households in 652 to 6.15 million (roughly 31 million people) in 705—reflects stability and economic prosperity.

Wu Zetian Today

In recent decades, there has been a concerted effort to redress the negative and static Confucian interpretation and to provide a more balanced and nuanced vision of Wu Zetian's person and her political career. Internationally, China's only female emperor has received growing attention outside of academia. She is prominently featured in Civilization V, a computer-based strategy game, and her story has been told, and often reimagined, in a number of novels, documentaries, television mini-series, and movies.

Further Reading

Bokenkamp, S. (1998). A medieval feminist critique of the Chinese world order: The case of Wu Zetian, *Religion, 28*, 378–390.

Chen J. (2002). *Monks and monarchs, kinship and kingship: Tanqian in Sui Buddhism and politics.* Kyoto, Japan: Scuola Italiana di Studi sull'Asia Orientale.

Chen J. (1994). Empress Wu and proto-feminist sentiments in T'ang China. In *Imperial Rulership and Cultural Change in Traditional China* (pp. 77–114). Seattle: University of Washington Press.

Dien, D. S. (2003). *Empress Wu Zetian in fiction and in history: Female defiance in Confucian China*. Hauppage, NY: Nova Science Publishers.

Fitzgerald, C. P. (1955). *The Empress Wu*. Melbourne: Cheshire.

Forte, A. (2005). *Political propaganda and ideology at the end of seventh century China*. Kyoto, Japan: Italian School of East Asian Studies.

Gao S. (Ed.). (1995). *The chalice and the blade in Chinese Culture*. Beijing: Social Sciences Press.

Guisso, R. (1978). *Wu T'se t'ien and the politics of legitimation in T'ang China*. Bellingham: Western Washington University Press.

Hu J. (1998). Wu Zetian benzhuan 武则天本傳 [The essential biography of Wu Zetian]. Xi'an, China: Shaanxi Normal University Press.

Lewis, M. (2009). *China's cosmopolitan empire: The Tang dynasty*. Cambridge, MA: Harvard University Press.

Rothschild, N. H. (2008). *Wu Zetian: China's only female emperor*. New York: Longman.

Sima G. (1956). *Zizhi tongjian* 资治通鉴 [Comprehensive mirror for aid in government]. Beijing: Zhonghua shuju. (Original work published 1086)

Tong, J. (2000). *Fables for the Patriarchs: Gender politics in Tang discourse*. Lanham, MD: Rowman and Littlefield.

Twitchett, D. (Ed.). (1979). *The Cambridge history of China, vol. 3: Sui and Tang China*. Cambridge, UK: Cambridge University Press.

Yang L. (1960–1961). Female rulers in imperial China. *Harvard Journal of Asiatic Studies, 23*, 47–61.

Zetian W. 趙文潤 & Wang S. 王 雙怀. (2000). *Wu Zetian pingzhuan* 武则天評傳 [A critical biography of Wu Zetian]. Xi'an, China: Sanqin.

Elizabeth I

1533–1603, Queen of England

Margaret COLLINSON and David COLLINSON
Lancaster University

Queen Elizabeth ascended to the throne during a time of turmoil and bankruptcy and ruled for the era known as the Age of Enlightenment. A skilled leader and effective ruler, she relied on counselors, whom she trusted implicitly, but mostly utilized her knowledge of foreign policy and the language of her neighbors to get her way abroad, while at home she effectively employed what we would now call political spin and the cult of personality.

Elizabeth I was Queen of England from 1558 to 1603. During her reign she demonstrated considerable leadership skills, surviving in an environment that was often extremely hostile and threatening. Popular culture flourished during her reign, and her court was a focal point for writers, musicians, and scholars such as William Shakespeare (1564–1616) and Francis Bacon (1561–1626), and explorers such as Francis Drake (c. 1540–1596) and Walter Raleigh (c. 1554–1618). Elizabeth encouraged a spirit of free inquiry that in turn facilitated the scientific revolution and the Age of Enlightenment. During her reign the English economy expanded massively. The queen herself came to be known as Gloriana, a name that reflected the triumphs of the age she oversaw.

The England Elizabeth had inherited was blighted by bankruptcy, roaring inflation, disastrous wars, and religious conflict. Poverty, disease, and deprivation were rife. From childhood, Elizabeth's life was fraught with danger. When she was only two years old, her father (Henry VIII, 1491–1547; reigned 1509–1547) executed her mother Anne Boleyn (his second wife) and Elizabeth was declared illegitimate. After her father died, her brother Edward (1537–1553; reigned 1547–1553), the son of Henry's third wife, inherited the throne but only lived for a short time. In 1553, Elizabeth's Catholic half-sister Mary (1516–1558; reigned 1553–1558), Henry's daughter by his first wife, became queen. In March 1554, Elizabeth was incarcerated in the Tower of London, accused of plotting against Mary and of refusing to embrace the Catholic faith. She was released in May but remained under suspicion and was carefully watched until Mary died childless in 1558.

In the context of these threats, deprivations, and indignities, it is remarkable indeed that Elizabeth ever became Queen of England, let alone that she then reigned for forty-five years. Elizabeth had been forced to learn the arts and skills of survival at a very early age, and this knowledge stayed with her throughout her life, significantly influencing her approach to leadership. The life of Elizabeth tells us a great deal about leadership and about the effective exercise of power and authority.

Elizabeth and Government

Elizabeth recognized that, unlike her father, she could not adopt an autocratic approach to leadership based on absolute power. She would have to lead in a rather more sophisticated way. Her powers of oratory (which age did not diminish) became legendary and enabled her to obtain the support of the Privy Council, the bishops, Parliament, and the people. Elizabeth's speech to a deputation from Parliament about her repeal of monopolies in 1601 became known as her "Golden Speech." In 1601, Parliament debated the outlawing of monopolies. This constituted a significant challenge to the Queen's royal prerogative to grant monopolies. However, aware of the strength of feeling within Parliament on this matter, Elizabeth decided to pre-empt any unwelcome legislation by sending a message to Parliament that she herself would reform affairs. Her superb timing defused the agitation, "the House was overjoyed...not by its own victory, but at their Queen's magnanimity" (Williams 1967, 346). Parliament requested leave to send deputation to thank her and it was to this deputation that Elizabeth gave her Golden Speech. Elizabeth's consummate skill as a leader had turned the possibility of a humiliating defeat into a great victory.

Still a relatively young woman of twenty-five when she took the throne, Elizabeth recognized the value of wise counsel. She created a small circle of trusted advisers, the most influential of whom was William Cecil (1520–1598). On formally appointing Cecil as her secretary of state, she told him, "This judgement I have of you, that you will not be corrupted by any manner of gift, and that you will be faithful to the state, and that without respect of my private will, you will give me that counsel you think best, and if you shall know anything necessary to be declared to me of secrecy, you shall show it to myself only" (Luke 1973, 28). She relied on Cecil to speak frankly and to give his opinion even when it conflicted with her own. Together, they forged a unique partnership. Over the next forty years the queen rarely took an important decision without consulting Cecil first, although she did not always defer to his advice.

Highly intelligent, Elizabeth made herself thoroughly familiar with all aspects of policy within and outside her realm. Accordingly, it was very difficult to deceive her. Being multilingual, she was able to converse directly with ambassadors from many different countries, and this ensured that no information could be accidentally or deliberately lost in translation. Cecil's admiration and respect for his queen's grasp of policy and politics can be clearly seen from his remark that "there never was so wise a woman born, for all respects, as Queen Elizabeth, for she spake and understood all languages; knew all estates and dispositions of Princes. And particularly was so expert in the knowledge of her own realm and estate as no counsellor she had could tell her what she knew not before" (Somerset 1997, 64).

Although Elizabeth never left the shores of England, she was by no means an insular queen. Indeed, she was an expert on foreign policy, and one of her legacies was the establishment of England as a maritime nation. Although she never formally condoned piracy on the high seas, Elizabeth informally encouraged (partly through financing) Francis Drake and other sailors to plunder and pirate on her behalf. During her reign, English merchant ships challenged Spain's seafaring pre-eminence, and the first English settlers were sent to North America.

Elizabeth maintained a pragmatic approach to international affairs. Very careful with money, she was highly reluctant to fight wars, as their cost inevitably drained her treasury. When forced into battle against the Spanish Armada, however, Elizabeth was an unflappable leader. Her inspirational speech to the troops at Tilbury Docks again demonstrated her oratory skill and great courage.

Elizabeth appreciated the value and indeed necessity of managing her reputation. Courtiers frequently used propaganda and "political spin" on her behalf. In matters of international politics monarchs were always very aware of their image. Their position and status within the international arena also reflected directly on their courtiers, especially ambassadors who were resident in foreign courts (i.e., "prestige by association"). As a female, Elizabeth was at a disadvantage within the international hierarchy. However, her intellect, judgment, and grasp of foreign policy became legendary. Consequently, as Elizabeth's reign unfolded, the reputation of both the Queen and of England increased significantly. Visual images of Elizabeth were also tightly controlled, with paintings presenting Elizabeth as a very powerful and glorious ruler. These images cultivated the idea of Elizabeth as an eternally youthful virgin queen who was married to England and her subjects. Elizabeth used her yearly progresses around the country to make herself visible to her subjects. Her courtiers were often amazed at how she allowed the common people to approach her.

Along with these great strengths, Elizabeth, like all great leaders, also had weaknesses. She was very vain and could be extremely temperamental. She had a furious temper, and many of her courtiers lived in fear of her rebukes. As one ambassador noted, "She seems to me incomparably more feared than her sister, and gives her orders and has her way as absolutely as her father did" (Somerset 1997, 60). She could also be very indecisive, a trait that frustrated her close advisers. Two of the great issues of government that dominated much of Elizabeth's reign were the question of religion and of Elizabeth's possible marriage. In both cases, Elizabeth was able to manage the ambiguities of her situation in highly effective ways.

Elizabeth and Religion

Throughout Elizabeth's reign religious divisions were a central concern. Elizabeth's father, Henry VIII, had rebelled against the pope and rejected the Catholic Church, which at that time dominated Europe. Subsequently, Queen Mary, Elizabeth's half-sister, had returned England to Catholicism and married the Catholic King of Spain. Mary had persecuted those who resisted the Catholic faith. Elizabeth was acutely aware of the religious polarities within England and sought to walk the more inclusive, less extreme path of toleration. Although she returned England to Protestantism, Elizabeth recognized the dangers of encouraging the extreme elements of Protestantism. Despite insisting on changes in church services, she retained many trappings of Catholic worship, including candlesticks, crucifixes, and clerical robes. Forging a religious middle ground, she brought a degree of peace to England that was not echoed in continental Europe, where religious fanaticism and turbulence ran rampant. In Spain there were the Inquisitions, while in France heretics were being burned at the stake. By contrast, Elizabeth attempted to defuse religious tensions by gaining outward compliance with the Protestant services. Anyone not attending church was subject to a fine. In the first part of Elizabeth's reign those Catholics who either attended the parish church, or paid their fines for non-attendance, could usually still practice their faith privately without fear of persecution. In contrast with the Queen's more relaxed attitude toward religious matters, Elizabeth's counselors were fearful that Catholic religious extremists would attempt to assassinate the queen. Francis Walsingham (c. 1532–1590), acting under the direction of Cecil, was in charge of information gathering through the extensive network of spies considered necessary to obtain information about any potential threats to the queen. Walsingham, who held extreme Puritan views, operated a sophisticated counterespionage organization using double agents and torture to obtain information. Although Elizabeth considered Walsingham to be an extremist in terms of religion, she admired his shrewdness and never doubted his commitment to her well-being.

Elizabeth's policy of religious moderation was tested to its limits when her cousin Mary Queen of Scots (1542–1587) sought sanctuary in England in 1568 following an uprising in Scotland. Mary was Catholic, and there were some Catholic factions at the national and international level who believed that she was the rightful queen of England. Cecil and Walsingham were concerned that Mary's presence in England threatened Elizabeth's safety. After almost twenty years in captivity in England, Mary was executed for treason in 1587.

Elizabeth and Marriage

Like many leaders, Elizabeth had a strong sense of destiny. She had no doubt that her rise to the throne was God's doing. When informed that her half-sister Mary had died and she was now queen, Elizabeth stated, "This is the Lord's doing; and it is marvelous in our eyes" (Marshall 1991, 47). Elizabeth viewed the advantages she derived from her sovereign status as far outweighing the disadvantages that she saw accruing from her sex. For Elizabeth, being a woman was not so much a handicap as an irrelevance, as she stated "my sex cannot diminish my prestige" (Somerset 1997, 60). In the sixteenth century, the first duty of a monarch was to marry and have children, thereby ensuring the succession. Cecil in particular was very keen to secure the succession and create a Protestant heir to the throne.

Elizabeth's experiences in childhood and her knowledge of international politics led her to believe that marrying would be disadvantageous both to her and the realm. As a queen it was expected that she would marry someone of royal blood. Elizabeth understood that marriage to a foreign prince offered some security from other hostile states within Europe. She knew, however, that the English people were notoriously suspicious of and antagonistic toward foreigners. Mary Tudor's marriage to Philip of Spain had caused great disruption within the realm. The other option was marriage to an English nobleman. Elizabeth considered that such a marriage would create jealousies within the nobility and could lead to civil war. From the queen's perspective, having to share power with a husband conflicted with her sense of her own destiny. Although at that time an unmarried queen was considered unnatural, Elizabeth turned her single status into a strength. With great leadership skills, she created the image of the virgin queen who sacrificed personal happiness for the welfare of her people.

Elizabeth's policy of remaining single did leave the problem of who would succeed her. The loss of such a charismatic leader as Queen Elizabeth left a vacuum that resulted in deep-seated internal conflict. On her death, Elizabeth was succeeded by the son of Mary Queen of Scots, James I of England (1566–1625; reigned as James VI of Scotland 1567–1625 and as king of England 1603–1625), who had been raised a Protestant. This subsequent period in English history was characterized by religious strife, social turmoil, and a civil war.

Respected abroad and celebrated at home, Elizabeth I was an extraordinary woman. Four hundred years after her death we still recognize the legacy she bequeathed. Elizabeth became one of the greatest monarchs in English history—perhaps the greatest. Her reign was a time of increasing prosperity, peace, and a significant strengthening of England's international interests. Many consider the Elizabethan era to have been a golden age. After the highly turbulent years of Henry VIII's reign, the relative stability that England enjoyed during Elizabeth's long reign was of enormous benefit to the development of English society and culture. Elizabeth's reign led to the emergence of the British Empire. This included the colonization of Virginia (named after the virgin queen). Sailors such as Drake and Raleigh took the English language abroad; today it is the preeminent language of world communication. A highly skilled and progressive leader, Elizabeth utilized strategies of religious and political tolerance effectively. She encouraged learning and merriment, which in turn facilitated free speech and creativity. Her policies encouraged further development of parliamentary democracy, a moderate Church of England and, for the times in which she lived, a relatively prosperous, peaceful, and stable society and economy.

Further Reading

Anthony, K. (1929). *Queen Elizabeth*. New York: Literary Guild.

Cecil, D. (1973). *The Cecils of Hatfield House*. London: Constable and Co.

Compton, P. (1933). *Bad Queen Bess*. Tonbridge, UK: Tonbridge Printers.

Collinson, P (1994). *Elizabethan essays*. Oxford, UK: Oxford University Press.

Erickson, C. (1999). *The first Elizabeth*. London: Robson Books.

Fraser, A. (1992). *The six wives of Henry VIII*. London: Weidenfeld and Nicholson.

Guy, J. (1988). *Tudor England*. Oxford, UK: Oxford University Press.

Haigh, C. (1988). *Elizabeth I*. Harlow, UK: Longman

Hibbert, C. (1992). *The virgin queen: The personal history of Elizabeth 1st*. Harmondsworth, UK: Penguin Books.

Irwin, M. (1962). *Elizabeth and the prince of Spain*. London: Chatto and Windus.

Jenkins, E. (1958). *Elizabeth and Leicester*. London: Panther Books.

Jenkins, E. (1958). *Elizabeth the great*. Bungay, UK: Richard Clay and Co.

Luke, M. (1970). *A crown for Elizabeth*. New York: Coward McCann.

Luke, M. (1973). *Gloriana: The years of Elizabeth*. Toronto, Canada: Longman Canada.

Marshall, R. K. (1991). *Elizabeth I*. London: HMSO.

Miles, R. (1994). *I, Elizabeth*. London: Pan Books.

Milton, G. (2000). *Big chief Elizabeth: How England's adventurers gambled and won the New World*. London: Hodder and Stoughton.

Neale, J. E. (1953). *Elizabeth and her parliaments, 1559–1581*. London: Jonathon Cape.

Neale, J. E. (1958). *Essays in Elizabethan history*. London: Jonathon Cape.

Plowden, A. (1973). *Danger to Elizabeth*. London: Macmillan.

Plowden, A. (1980). *Elizabeth Regina, 1588–1603*. London: Macmillan.

Ross, J. (1994). *The Tudors*. London: Artus Books.

Rowse, A. L. (1971). *The Elizabethan renaissance: The life of the society*. Harmondsworth, UK: Penguin.

Somerset, A. (1997). *Elizabeth I*. London: Phoenix.

Sitwell, E. (1946). *Fanfare for Elizabeth*. London: Macmillan.

Starkey, D. (2000). *Elizabeth: Apprenticeship*. London: Chatto and Windus.

Strickland, A. (1906). *The life of Queen Elizabeth*. London: J. M. Dent and Sons.

Thane, E. (1932). *The Tudor wench*. New York: Brewer, Warren and Putnam.

Watkins, S. (1998). *In public and in private: Elizabeth 1st and her world*. Singapore: C S Graphics.

Weir, A. (1999). *Elizabeth the queen*. London: Pimlico

Williams, N. (1967). *Elizabeth: Queen of England*. London: William Clowes and Son.

Williams, N. (1972). *The life and times of Elizabeth I*. London: George Weidenfeld and Nicolson.

Williams, P. (1998). *The later Tudors: England 1547–1603*. Oxford, UK: Oxford University Press.

Catherine the Great

1729–1796—Empress of Russia

Lori A. FELDSTEIN
Independent scholar, Philadelphia, Pennsylvania

Although she was well known for her skilled foreign policy, the German-born Catherine the Great, who ruled Russia from 1762 until 1796, is also known for her promiscuity and the controversy surrounding her seizure of power. She opened schools to women and granted freedom to the wealthy but refused to abolish serfdom.

Catherine II, also called Catherine the Great, was a German princess who married into the Russian royal family. She is known in the Western world because of her extramarital love life and because she is speculated to have taken over Russia's throne by killing her husband, Peter III (1728–1762). She was, nonetheless, one of most important leaders in Russia's history During her thirty-four-year reign (1762–1796), Catherine the Great ruled as the most powerful autocrat in Russia since Peter the Great (1672–1725).

Accession to Power

Sophie Friederike Auguste von Anhalt-Zerbst, later Catherine the Great, was born in 1729 to two minor German royals. She frequently enraged her tutor by trying to find logical explanations for sacred dogmas. Later, this way of thinking manifested itself in Catherine's passion for Enlightenment philosophy.

In 1744, Sophie's life changed forever when she was invited to St. Petersburg by Empress Elizabeth (1709–1762), who reigned as Russia's czar from 1741 to 1762, to meet her nephew, Karl Peter Ulrich, later Peter III, the heir to Russia's throne. Upon meeting Sophie, the empress found many reasons to choose her for Peter's bride. Sophie's family was obscure, and the empress thought that Sophie would easily renounce her German allegiance. In addition, Sophie was Protestant, and therefore thought to be more willing to convert to the Russian Orthodox faith. True to the empress's supposition, Sophie willingly converted to Russian Orthodoxy and was given the new name Yekaterina (Catherine) Alekseyevna.

In 1745, Catherine married Peter III. Peter III had grown up in Germany and considered himself to be German in every respect. He had an intense dislike for all things Russian. He also hated his wife, who, although of German blood, considered herself to be Russian. Catherine, in return, hated her husband. They had one child, Paul (1754–1801), who was raised entirely by Empress Elizabeth. With no real purpose at home or at court, Catherine became restless. She began to take extramarital lovers. There is even some debate as to whether Peter III was Paul's biological father.

On 25 December 25 1761, Empress Elizabeth died and Peter III was crowned czar. Peter spoke mostly German. He made horrible jokes about Russians. He even changed the Russian army's uniform to look more German. The worst of Peter's early actions, however, came in 1762. Before her death, Empress Elizabeth had been fighting a war with Prussia; after her death, Peter III signed a treaty restoring power to the Prussian king. This stolen victory cemented Peter III's unpopularity with the Russian people.

On 28 June 1762, Catherine initiated an instant, bloodless, and popular coup d'état. Peter, who did not try to resist, was captured and placed under house arrest. Several days later, he was mysteriously assassinated. Catherine denied complicity. There are a plethora of theories about the circumstances under which the deposed czar was murdered. One speculation is that Peter's guards strangled him to death. Another hypothesis is that Catherine's lover killed him on Catherine's orders. Although the truth is not known, those closest to Catherine held that when Catherine received the news of her husband's death, she fainted. She later said, "My reputation is ruined! Never will posterity forgive me for this involuntary crime" (Troyat 1980, 137). It was not that Catherine was sad about her husband's death; she was merely nervous about its repercussions on her political career. Publicly, the czar was said to have died of natural causes. Not one person disputed this claim.

Accomplishments and Policies

When Catherine II came to power, she made it abundantly clear that she would not give up the throne to her son when he came of age. Catherine's first real success was in foreign policy when she successfully used the Russian-Prussian alliance. In 1763, King Augustus III (1696–1763) of Poland died. The Russian-Prussian alliance backed the election of Catherine's former lover, Stanislaw II Augustus Poniatowski (1732–1798) to replace him. Because he had no royal ties, Poniatowski remained loyal to his Russian backers. This was a brilliant foreign policy move on Catherine's part. The first of three partitions of Poland had occurred. The second partition occurred in 1793. In 1795, the final Polish partition took place, and Poland ceased to exist. Catherine carried out additional military victories in Turkey, where she led two successful wars in 1768–1774 and in 1787–1791. Those wars, in conjunction with the annexation of the Crimea in 1783, effectively removed the Tartar threat to Russian security and established Russian control over the northern coast of the Black Sea.

Catherine also initiated many influential domestic policies. She improved the dismal situation of women when, in 1783, she put Princess Dashkova (1744–1810) in charge of the Academy of Arts and Sciences. Princess Dashkova was the first woman who was not a part of the royal family to hold any position of power in Russia. In addition, Catherine opened up the first schools for women.

Catherine's main goal for Russia was to reorder and systemize its class structure. To that end, Catherine set out the 1785 Charter of the Towns, which stated that the more wealthy the individual, the more rights that individual would be granted. On the same day, she put out the Charter of the Nobility, which granted various freedoms to the nobility, including freedom from corporal punishment. While Catherine gave a great many rights and freedoms to the nobility, she did not free the serfs. About 90 percent of Russia's peasant class was serfs, and although Catherine was against serfdom, she did not abolish it. Catherine knew that the nobles would stop at nothing, including killing the czar, to prevent the end of serfdom.

On November 6, 1796, Catherine died and was succeeded by her son, Paul I. Throughout Catherine's life, there had been a deep hatred between mother and son. When Paul came to power, his goal was to exact revenge on his mother. He did this with his Law of Succession, which eliminated the possibility of any woman ever ruling Russia again. Catherine the Great, therefore, was truly the first and last of her kind, a unique leader in both Russian and world history.

Further Reading

Alexander, J. T. (1989). *Catherine the Great: Life and legend*. New York: Oxford University Press.

Anthony, K. (1925). *Catherine the Great*. Garden City, NY: Garden City Publishing Company.

Cowles, V. (1971). *The Romanovs*. New York: Harper & Row.

De Madariaga, I. (1990). *Catherine the Great: A short history*. New Haven, CT: Yale University Press.

Dixon, S. (2001). *Catherine the Great*. Harlow, UK: Longman.

Dmytryshyn, B. (1974). *Modernization of Russia under Peter I and Catherine II*. New York: John Wiley & Sons.

Gooch, G. P. (1966). *Catherine the Great and other studies*. Hamden, CT: Archon.

Gribble, F. (1942). *The comedy of Catherine the Great*. New York: E. P. Dutton.

Haslip, J. (1977). *Catherine the Great: A biography*. New York: G. P. Putnam's Sons.

Kaus, G. (1935). *Catherine: The portrait of an empress*. New York: Viking.

Masson, C. (1970). *Secret memoirs of the court of Petersburg* (2nd ed.). New York: Arno.

Thomson, G. S. (1950). *Catherine the Great and the expansion of Russia*. London: English Universities Press.

Troyat, H. (1980). *Catherine the Great*. New York: Meridian.

Waliszewski, K. (1905). *The romance of an empress*. New York: D. Appleton.

Cixi, Empress Dowager

1835–1908—Chinese Regent for Qing emperors

L. Shelton WOODS
Boise State University

Serving as the empress dowager and regent for two young and ineffectual emperors, Cixi rose to fill a gap in power during the waning years of the Qing dynasty in China. She overpowered feuding officials to appoint and control the emperor of her choice and struggled to preserve the monarchy through decades of conflict, rebellions, and war. A complicated and mysterious woman, she was often maligned and blamed for the ills and eventually dissolution of imperial rule.

One of the most famous women in Chinese history, Cixi served as regent for her unruly biological son, Emperor Tongzhi, as well as for her struggling nephew, Emperor Guangxu. She played a key role in steering these two emperors and was the center of much controversy throughout her life. She was blamed for many of China's problems as the period of the imperial system came to an end. The many firsthand testimonies of Cixi's friendliness did not help to change her negative public image; it was much easier, and sensational, to place all of China's maladies on one person. China's imperial system ended three years following her death, and Cixi was a convenient scapegoat for China's great humiliation. She was, in the end, a tragic figure who served as a symbol of a dying institution that defined China for more than two millennia.

A Humble Origin

Cixi was born on 29 November 1835, but little is known of her early years. She moved from obscurity to the center stage of one of the world's largest countries when she entered the Forbidden City as one of Emperor Xianfeng's concubines in 1852. She became known as Lady Yehenara, a combination of her family and clan names. Yehenara gave birth on 27 April 1856 to Emperor Xianfeng's first son, Tongzhi. One of Emperor Xianfeng's concubines gave birth to a daughter in 1855; these were the only two children of the emperor. China's imperial system dictated that even though the emperor's first wife, Lady Niuhuru, was not these infants' biological mother, she was still the queen mother with the responsibility of raising the children; in short, she adopted the concubines' offspring.

Becoming Cixi

As Xianfeng neared death in 1861, protocol dictated that the regents for the five-year-old future emperor were to be his biological mother, Lady Yenehara, and Empress Niuhuru. At twenty-three and twenty-one years old respectively, these young women lacked the requisite education and political savvy to properly steer China away from the dangers in its immediate path; in addition, the emperor's advisors began to plot to seize control of the imperial court. It was at this point that Lady Yenehara's willpower and strength of character became evident. Collaborating with her brother-in-law, Prince Gong, Yenehara brought her son to the Forbidden City in Beijing and subsequently approved, if not planned, the execution of those who stood in her way.

As regents for the boy emperor, the two women acquired new names based on their living quarters in the Forbidden City: Empress Niuhuru became Dowager Ci'an (Empress of the East), and Lady Yenehara became Dowager Cixi (Empress of the West). United States officials in China informed the US government that China was now ruled by the two female regents along with Prince Gong; in official communications, Dowager Cixi was identified as simply a symbol rather than a true power in the Manchu political machinery.

For the next ten years, the two dowagers served as mere approval stamps for the policies generated by Prince Gong and the Qing bureaucratic machine. Some assert that Cixi made an agreement with Prince Gong that she would control domestic affairs while he directed China's foreign policy. Foreign biographers also claimed that during this period Cixi brought in multiple lovers and had sexually active men posing as eunuchs so she could spend her days and nights indulging in palace orgies. In truth, Cixi was not in a political or ceremonial position to dictate orders to Dowager Ci'an and Prince Gong. Furthermore, her continued position in the Forbidden City was predicated on remaining a chaste widow of the former emperor. Any hint of sexual promiscuity on the dowager's part would have been grounds for punishment and loss of her titles and position within the Qing imperial system.

Cixi's First Regency

Dowager Cixi occupied her days as her son's guardian, carrying out imperial ceremonies, gardening, expanding her wardrobe, and playing with her Pekinese dogs. She was waited on hand and foot by an army of eunuchs (up to three thousand in number) who made sure the dowager's life was comfortable. Eunuchs also tutored Cixi and she struggled throughout her life to master reading and writing Chinese. She was secluded from the public and certainly removed from any interaction with foreigners. But learning calligraphy and living in isolation were not her biggest difficulties; the main trial for Cixi during her first regency was that she had given birth to a son who grew up to become a young man whose addiction to sex was widely known. The dilemma that Dowager Cixi faced was that although she was the biological mother, she was not the official mother of the future emperor—the Son of Heaven. So as her son matured, her influence in his life was limited. At the age of nineteen, his health gave out, officially due to smallpox, though syphilis reportedly compromised the emperor's health in his final days. Based on unreliable sources, some writers attribute the emperor's death to the Dowager Cixi. The sensational story claims that Cixi encouraged her son to waste his energies in orgies and then poisoned him when he fell ill. In this way, she could supposedly continue her court dominance.

Cixi's Second Regency

Emperor Tongzhi died without leaving an heir, and Cixi was once again in the middle of the succession debate. Her brother-in-law, Prince Chun, had married Cixi's younger sister, and they had a three-year-old son, Guangxu, who fit the generational requirement to be the next Qing Emperor. Cixi ordered that the boy be brought to the palace and she presented her nephew as the next emperor. Consequently, the pattern of the dowagers and Prince Gong regencies would resume until Guangxu reached the age when he could officially rule.

While the reliability of the sources regarding Cixi is suspect, this incident shows an undeniable pattern. This was the second time Cixi took control of a situation that determined China's future. While she might have been motivated by self-preservation when insisting that her child was the rightful heir, it is probable that her decision to place her nephew on the throne was based less on self-preservation than on self-interest. Furthermore, Cixi could not have merely been a background player in the Forbidden City if she possessed the political capital to decide who the next emperor would be.

Cixi as Sole Regent

Between 1881 and 1884, power-sharing between the two dowagers and Prince Gong ended due to Ci'an's untimely death and Gong's dismissal from his official position. Both incidents were unsubstantially blamed on Cixi. After Dowager Ci'an died, rumors circulated, and are accepted even to this day, that Dowager Cixi was responsible for her colleague's death. Cixi was now the lone regent for Guangxu. Yet thousands of eunuchs and scores of Manchu and Chinese bureaucratic officers managed the day-to-day affairs of the ancient imperial system. She also called upon Guangxu's father, Prince Chun to serve as chief minister and relied on Li Hongzhang, the highest Chinese official in the Qing bureaucracy, to help guide China in its international relations.

The Hundred Days Reform

China was desperately in need of a wise, virtuous, and mentally strong emperor, yet Guangxu was not that man. The moribund Qing court led by a fragile emperor and his aging aunt appeared incapable of making needed changes to save China. After an 1895 disastrous attempt by Emperor Guangxu to modernize China's bureaucracy, Cixi reportedly placed him under house arrest while publicly declaring that the emperor was ill and she would once again serve as regent until the sovereign recovered. Although her motives were suspect, Cixi returned to her role as regent, while the mentally fragile Guangxu was removed from a position of responsibility.

The Boxer Rebellion

In 1898, when an anti-West Boxer Army of Chinese peasants-turned-vigilantes reached Beijing, the dowager, under pressure from her advisors, chose not to oppose them. It is probable that Cixi had the preservation of the imperial institution in mind. It would not have taken much provocation for the Boxers to turn on the Manchu officials, since in some sense the Manchus were foreigners themselves. The industrialized countries were outraged by the Boxers' actions, which included the killing of missionaries and diplomats, and formed a large multinational army that slowly but deliberately made its way to Beijing during the summer of 1900. Cixi decided to flee for her life. Many legends surrounding Cixi's flight remain to this day. Two of these are that Cixi disguised herself as a peasant as she fled the capital, and that she had one of Emperor Guangxu's consorts thrown into a well as they departed the Forbidden City.

For fourteen months Cixi remained in the Xi'an area, returning to Beijing only after a negotiated treaty with the foreign powers. But the Boxer Rebellion and its immediate aftermath finally served to liberate Cixi. For more than a decade, the court had cowered behind anti-foreign rhetoric of its officials. Now the victorious foreign powers insisted that anti-foreign generals be executed or exiled. For those foreigners who best understood China, the root of China's problem in 1900 was not a dictatorial, reclusive woman; rather, it was a radical fringe group whose bold actions gave them inordinate power. Now that they were gone, Cixi returned to the Forbidden City free from the need to placate these anti-foreign officials.

Cixi Revealed

When the dowager returned to Beijing following the Boxer uprising she was much more open to meeting with foreigners and gave them unprecedented access. Consequently, the period between 1901 and 1908 is crucial in forming the most accurate understanding of Cixi. Several foreign women spent enough time with Cixi after 1902 to each write books about the dowager. These books, written during the first decade of the twentieth century, parallel each other in their assessment of Cixi. In essence, they describe her as a reserved but affable woman who exhibited benevolence toward the emperor and regret for the anti-foreign sentiments by her former advisors. The value of these testimonies is not only in their independent corroboration of Cixi's benevolence, but also in their actual relationship with Cixi. These were not writings based on distant memory or unsubstantiated gossip.

But these biographies, for the most part, were not well-received. The authors were women who had minimal publishing experience, and there were no sensational tales to be told of orgies or a diabolical fiend who cared only for her own comforts. Still, it would seem that firsthand testimony would have helped shape Cixi's public image; it did not. It was much easier, and sensational, to place all of China's maladies on one person. Metaphorically, the dowager had very wide skirts behind which all of China's problems could be placed.

Cixi's physical appearance was also less secretive during the last years of her life. The famous Dutch painter Hubert Vos was commissioned to paint Cixi's portrait. While spending time with the posing dowager in 1905, Vos reiterated the sentiments of other firsthand accounts regarding the benevolence and affability of Cixi.

The Final Years

Two crises engulfed Cixi's last three years. In 1904, Japan declared war on Russia, and much of the fighting occurred in Manchuria, disrupting any semblance of normalcy that the Qing tried to maintain in their homeland. Following Japan's surprising victory over Russia in 1905, many within China surmised that if Japan could modernize to the point of fighting Russia to at least a stalemate, then perhaps there was hope for China. Cixi approved a mission wherein Qing officials traveled around the world to bring back ideas of how China might survive in a modern, industrialized world.

Cixi accepted the recommendations of the returning officials, and then faced her final crisis in a life full of challenges. Emperor Guangxu had never enjoyed robust health. During the summer of 1908, the emperor's health deteriorated; he suffered from acute abdominal pains. Several Western doctors attended to his symptoms but they were unsuccessful in stemming his rapid decline.

Throughout October 1908, Guangxu teetered at death's door. Then at the beginning of November, the dowager's health also rapidly deteriorated as she seemed to be suffering from the flu and related symptoms. On 14 November 1908, the emperor died. The following day his aunt, the seventy-three-year-old Dowager Cixi, followed him in death.

Rumors about the dowager's cruelty did not die with her; in fact, many sensational stories spread immediately after her death. A persistent tale that emerged from the last weeks of the dowager's life was that Guangxu was rejoicing over the impending death of his aunt, so she conspired to poison the emperor—reportedly insisting that Guangxu had to die before she did. While this story, like many others about Cixi, is sensational, it ignores the more mundane facts surrounding the life of this Manchu woman who tried to hold China together despite her limited training and education.

For most of her life, Cixi had to maneuver through political minefields for basic self-preservation. She was manipulated and she did her share of manipulating. Three years following her death, China's imperial system ended and it was easy to point to a woman now unable to defend herself as the cause for China's great humiliation. But she was, in the end, a tragic figure who served as a symbol of a dying institution that defined China for more than two millennia.

Further Reading

Chang, J. (2013). *Empress Dowager Cixi: The concubine who launched modern China*. New York: Knopf.

Chung, S. F. (1979). The much maligned Empress Dowager: A revisionist study of the Empress Dowager Tz'u-Hsi (1835–1908). *Modern Asian Studies, 13*(2), 177–196.

Cohen, P. A. (1997). *History in three keys: The Boxers as event, experience, and myth*. New York: Columbia University Press.

Collis, M. and Society China. (1944). *New sources for the life of the Empress Dowager Tz'U Hsi.* London: China Society.

Der, L. (1911). *Two years in the Forbidden City.* New York: Moffat, Yard and Co.

Haldane, C. F. (1966). *The last great empress of China.* Indianapolis: Bobbs-Merrill.

Kwong, L. S. K. (1984). *A mosaic of the Hundred Days: Personalities, politics, and ideas of 1898.* Cambridge, MA: Council on East Asian Studies, Harvard University: Distributed by Harvard University Press.

Lin H. (2010). Some questions concerning the high tide of the Boxer Movement. *Chinese Studies in History, 20*(3–4), 137–155.

Liu T. (2010). On the K'ang-Hsi Emperor. *Chinese Studies in History, 14*(4), 76–107.

Seagrave, S. & Seagrave, P. (1992). *Dragon lady: The life and legend of the last empress of China.* New York: Knopf.

Warner, M. (1972). *The Dragon Empress: Life and times of Tz'U-Hsi, 1835–1908, Empress Dowager of China.* London: Weidenfeld and Nicolson.

Roosevelt, Eleanor

1884–1962—Humanitarian and political leader

Maurine H. BEASLEY
University of Maryland

Eleanor Roosevelt is best remembered for her work before, during, and after her husband Franklin Roosevelt's presidency to influence policy and improve the lives of less fortunate Americans. Her causes included women's rights, civil liberties, equal treatment of African-Americans, and especially human rights as a delegate to the United Nations. She transcended the constraints placed on patrician women in the early and mid-twentieth century, and forged a path that still inspires leaders around the world.

Anna Eleanor Roosevelt (she did not use her first name, perhaps to avoid confusion with her mother) was born in New York City, the oldest child of Elliott and Anna Hall Roosevelt. During her twelve years as first lady and seven years as a US delegate to the United Nations, Eleanor Roosevelt manifested leadership on behalf of the disadvantaged in a variety of public and private ways. Her style of leadership, which embraced the ability to communicate ideas of compassion and caring to a mass audience, was instrumental in making her one of the most admired American women of the twentieth century. The niece of one president of the United States, Theodore Roosevelt (1858–1919), and the wife of another, Franklin D. Roosevelt (1882–1945), Eleanor Roosevelt charted a new activist course for presidential spouses during her years in the White House, from 1933 to 1945. She was also the guiding spirit, in 1948, behind the United Nations' adoption of the Universal Declaration of Human Rights, one of the world's most important statements of human equality.

Overcoming the constraints that surrounded women's roles in the late nineteenth and early twentieth centuries, Roosevelt became the most prominent woman of her day by breaking through the bounds of her patrician social class. As a political wife, she played an important role in Democratic politics, becoming known for her advocacy of better treatment for women, African-Americans, youth, and underprivileged segments of society. As the widow of a president, she displayed remarkable diplomatic and political skills. She represented the United States at the United Nations from 1945 to 1952, during a time of Cold War tensions, and she spoke up for civil rights and free expression at home. Through her writings, public speaking, and broadcasting, she stood out as a strong voice for peace and justice; she saw herself as a spokesperson for the liberal ideals of her husband and his New Deal administration.

Understanding Eleanor Roosevelt's influence requires an examination of her life in the context of family influences, personal relationships, and involvement in the events that marked the twentieth century. Her emergence as a leader dramatized the sweeping changes that had taken place in women's roles—from the nineteenth-century ideal of Victorian *noblesse oblige* to the modern concept of women as full participants in society.

Childhood and Education

Both of Eleanor Roosevelt's parents had inherited wealth and were socially prominent descendants of influential families. Her paternal grandfather, Theodore Roosevelt Sr., known as "Greatheart," helped found the Metropolitan Museum of Art and the Newsboys' Lodging House for homeless youth. Her maternal grandmother was a Livingston, whose great-great grandfather, Philip Livingston, had signed the Declaration of Independence. Eleanor's father Elliott was the younger brother of Theodore, president of the United States from 1901 until 1909.

Eleanor Roosevelt endured a troubled childhood. Her mother, known for her beauty, rejected Eleanor because she considered her plain, but her father, noted for his charming personality, adored her and she, in turn, worshipped him. He introduced her to charitable endeavor by taking her with him to serve Thanksgiving dinner at the newsboys' home. Experiences of this sort, however, were rare for young Eleanor because her parents' marriage crumbled. Elliott Roosevelt suffered from mental instability. Depressed and addicted to alcohol and drugs, he was unfaithful to his wife and was sent away from the family, leaving his daughter, a shy, solemn child, to grieve for his absence.

Before she was ten years old, both her parents had died, resulting in Eleanor and Hall, her younger brother, being reared by their maternal grandmother, Mary Ludlow Hall, a stern widow who lived both in Manhattan and at Tivoli, the family estate in the Hudson River Valley. In the Hall household, Eleanor Roosevelt watched her two aunts and two uncles indulge in the excessive lifestyle of the leisure class. Yet her upbringing did have a moral dimension. Mrs. Hall believed upper-class women had a duty to aid the less fortunate as well as to keep up social appearances. In later years, Eleanor Roosevelt wrote that her grandmother had taught her important lessons of self-discipline and conscientious performance that remained with her, even though she had moved far outside her grandmother's narrow world.

The happiest period of Eleanor's girlhood came at Allenswood, an English boarding school for wealthy girls, where she studied from 1899 to 1902. Her quick mind and concern for others made her a favorite of the headmistress, Maria Souvestre, a liberal Frenchwoman. In 1902, Eleanor returned home to make her formal debut into society. Spurred by Souvestre's ideas of social conscience, she joined the Junior League, a social service organization for debutantes, and volunteered at the Rivington Street Settlement House. She also helped investigate sweatshops for the National Consumers League.

Marriage, Motherhood, and the Political Life

In 1903, Eleanor became secretly engaged to her fifth cousin once removed, the handsome Franklin D. Roosevelt, a Harvard student who lived on a Hudson River estate at Hyde Park, New York. After overcoming initial objections from his widowed mother, Sara Delano Roosevelt, the young couple was married on 17 March 1905 in New York City. While Franklin pursued a political career, his wife was occupied with motherhood, bearing six children, one of whom died in infancy, between the years 1906 and 1916. Uncertain of herself, she tried to please her mother-in-law, who controlled the family finances. For instance, she gave up working at the settlement house because of family fears that she might bring home germs and she settled into the restricted life of an upper-class matron. After serving in the New York legislature, Franklin Roosevelt became the assistant secretary of the Navy and the Roosevelts moved to Washington, DC, in 1913, where they remained until 1920.

In the capital, Eleanor Roosevelt began to mature, slowly and painfully, into a self-confident individual. At first she took part in the activities expected of the wives of political figures, making routine calls on other women and organizing successful social events. The entry of the United States into World War I in 1917 provided scope for more fulfilling pursuits as a volunteer for the American Red Cross and the Navy Relief Society. She improved conditions at St. Elizabeth's Hospital, a federal psychiatric institution, by persuading a friend, Secretary of the Interior Franklin Lane, to set up a congressional investigating committee that increased funds for the hospital.

Eleanor's world shattered in 1918 when she discovered that Franklin had been carrying on a long-term romance with Lucy Mercer, her social secretary. Although the couple decided to stay married for the sake of their children and Franklin's political career and they continued to function as political partners, they no longer lived together as man and wife After the family's return to New York, Eleanor nursed Franklin when he contracted polio in 1921, and she worked under the direction of Louis Howe, Franklin's political mentor, to salvage his political career while he recuperated from the disease.

Women's Networking

In the 1920s, Eleanor Roosevelt threw off her mother-in-law's domination and widened her circle to include women's organizations. Although she had initially opposed women's suffrage, after women won the right to vote in 1920, she pushed for a greater role for women in politics. She involved herself in the League of Women Voters and the Women's Trade Union League, which brought her into contact with Jewish and immigrant women. She became a leader in the Women's Division of the New York State Democratic Party, edited the *Women's Democratic News*, and began to write on women's issues for national magazines.

In charge of women's activities for the Democratic National Committee in 1928, she was forced to resign for fear of conflict of interest when her husband was elected governor of New York that year. Yet she kept on writing articles such as "Women Must Learn to Play the [Political] Game as Men Do" (*Redbook*, April 1928). She became part owner of Todhunter, an exclusive girls' school in New York City, and also taught there. While she campaigned for Franklin's election as president in 1932, when the country was experiencing the Great Depression, she expressed reservations about becoming first lady to her intimate friend, journalist Lorena Hickok. Eleanor was afraid that the conventional social demands of the position would impede her career interests.

Leadership as First Lady

Once in the White House, however, Eleanor Roosevelt redefined the traditional role played by the president's wife. Using skills developed in her work with women's organizations, she reached out to the public, unlike her predecessors. She held press conferences for women reporters, providing news of special interest to women. Traveling widely, she went on paid lecture tours and gave sponsored radio broadcasts, giving the proceeds to charity. While she stopped teaching, she continued writing magazine articles and advice columns for women's magazines. In 1935, she started a daily newspaper column, "My Day," a diary-like account of her activities that continued until the year of her death. Although her public communication generally was not billed as political—a sample lecture topic, for example, was "Problems of Youth"—it had political overtones that obviously benefited the Roosevelt administration. In 1937, she published the first volume of her well-received autobiography, *This Is My Story*, one of two dozen books she wrote on subjects related to her travels, life experience, and political views.

Eleanor played a major behind-the-scenes role in a variety of New Deal programs. She backed the establishment of the National Youth Administration to help Depression-stricken young people and championed the resettlement of unemployed coal miners in West Virginia. As war loomed in Europe, she pressed for passage of legislation to admit refugee children but Congress did not act. Unlike her husband, who feared Southern conservatives in Congress, she spoke up for the rights of African-Americans, unsuccessfully urging her husband to support anti-lynching legislation. When Marian Anderson, an African-American singer, was denied the use of a hall owned by the Daughters of the American Revolution because of her race, Eleanor resigned from that organization. Surprisingly, she did not make a public protest about the forced resettlement of Japanese-Americans in internment camps during the war years, although she did disagree with the policy.

Sometimes she endured intense hostility—for her looks, for not staying home, for her friendships with those of different races and ethnic groups. Newspaper criticism forced her to resign as the unpaid assistant director of the Office of Civil Defense in 1942, but she publicized the World War II war effort by visiting service personnel in England, the South Pacific, and Latin America.

Work in the United Nations

Following Franklin Roosevelt's unexpected death in 1945, President Harry S. Truman appointed Eleanor Roosevelt as US representative to the United Nations, where she served until Eisenhower became president in 1953. Her unsurpassed devotion to the organization, which she saw as essential to maintaining world peace, and her work as chair of the Human Rights Commission, which drafted the Universal Declaration of Human Rights, added to her international reputation.

After she left her official position, she continued to work as a volunteer on behalf of the United Nations. As a leading liberal in the Democratic party, she attacked McCarthyism (a period from about 1950 to 1956 during which supposed American communists were persecuted), pressed for civil liberties, backed the civil rights campaign, and was a strong supporter of the new state of Israel.

Although she did not support the Equal Rights Amendment for most of her political life, on the grounds that it would negate protective legislation for working women, her last public service was to chair President John F. Kennedy's Commission on the Status of Women. Commission activities set the stage for the women's movement of the 1960s and 1970s.

She died in New York City in 1962. Among the outpouring of sympathy were the words of U Thant, acting secretary-general of the United Nations, who called her the "First Lady of the World."

Implications for the Twenty-first Century

Eleanor Roosevelt's leadership at the United Nations laid the foundation for contemporary attempts to establish the legal concept of basic human rights. Her career continues to inspire both men and women because she transformed the circumstances of her privileged life into help for humanity. She took Victorian concepts of charity and duty and turned them into modern statements of hope for all people.

Further Reading

Beasley, M. H. (1987). *Eleanor Roosevelt and the media: A public quest for self-fulfillment.* Urbana, IL: University of Illinois Press.

Beasley, M. H. (2010). *Eleanor Roosevelt: Transformative first lady.* Lawrence, KS: University Press of Kansas.

Beasley, M. H., Shulman, H. C., & Beasley, H. R. (2001). *The Eleanor Roosevelt encyclopedia.* Westport, CT: Greenwood Press.

Black, A. M. (1996). *Casting her own shadow: Eleanor Roosevelt and the shaping of postwar liberalism.* New York: Columbia University Press.

Black, A. M. (Ed.). (1995). *What I hope to leave behind: The essential essays of Eleanor Roosevelt.* New York: Carlson Publishing.

Burns, J. M., & Dunn, S. (2001). *The three Roosevelts: Patrician leaders who transformed America.* New York: Atlantic Monthly Press.

Caroli, B. B. (1998). *The Roosevelt women.* New York: Basic Books.

Cook, B. W. (1992). *Eleanor Roosevelt, 1884–1933,* Vol. 1. New York: Viking.

Cook, B. W. (1999). *Eleanor Roosevelt, 1933–1938,* Vol. 2. New York: Viking.

Emblidge, D. (2001). *My Day: The best of Eleanor Roosevelt's acclaimed columns, 1936–1962.* New York: Da Capo Books.

Gerber, R. (2002). *Leadership the Eleanor Roosevelt way: Timeless strategies from the first lady of courage.* New York: Prentice Hall Press.

Glendon, M. A. (2001). *A world made new: Eleanor Roosevelt and the universal declaration of human rights.* New York: Random House.

Goodwin, D. K. (1994). *No ordinary time: Franklin and Eleanor Roosevelt: The home front in World War II.* New York: Simon & Schuster.

Lash, J. P. (1971). *Eleanor and Franklin: The story of their relationship based on Eleanor Roosevelt's private papers.* New York: W. W. Norton & Company.

Roosevelt, E. (1984). *The autobiography of Eleanor Roosevelt.* Boston: G. K. Hall. (Original work published 1961)

Scharf, L. (1987). *Eleanor Roosevelt: First lady of American liberalism.* Boston: Twayne.

Soong Mei-ling

1897–2003—Fundraiser for war efforts; wife
of Chinese leader Chiang Kai-shek

Hannah PAKULA
Independent scholar, New York City

Soong Mei-ling was the first and most famous woman of her day to break through the barriers of traditionally male-dominated Chinese society. She became known internationally as Madame Chiang Kai-shek, but was a force in her own right. Although she never held an official position during her extraordinarily long life, she played an important diplomatic role for China during World War II and afterward, challenging the traditional role of women in Chinese society.

Soong Mei-ling (often spelled May-ling), did not follow the traditional path of a female born in China in the late nineteenth century. Educated in the United States, she found it difficult to assimilate back into Chinese society as a young woman. After marrying Chinese leader Chiang Kai-shek (1887–1975), she helped advance the agenda of the National Party by pursuing diplomatic relations, making use of the press, and advising on foreign affairs. She was the first and certainly most famous woman of that time to challenge the stereotypical role of females in Chinese society.

An American Childhood

The children of an aristocratic mother and a peasant father who would go on to become a tycoon, Soong Mei-ling and her five siblings were educated in the United States. (Soong Mei-ling will be referred to by her given name, Mei-ling, throughout this article to distinguish her from the other members of her large and famous family.) The eldest, Ai-ling (1890–1973), attended the first women's college, Wesleyan, in Macon, Georgia. The Shanghai gentry were shocked that her father had chosen to, in their view, waste money educating a daughter. Money-oriented, Ai-ling married Kong Xiangxi (H. H. Kung; 1881–1967), a banker and politician. Qingling, the second sister, followed Ai-ling to Wesleyan. She later ran off to marry Sun Yat-sen (1866–1925), the leader of the Chinese revolution and her father's closest friend, who was already married with three children. Devout Methodists, the Soong parents tried but failed to get the marriage annulled.

Mei-ling, the Soongs' fourth child and third daughter, followed Qingling to Georgia when she was only ten years old. A smart, willful child, her pre-college education included public and private schooling as well as private tutoring. When Qingling graduated from Wesleyan, Mei-ling transferred to Wellesley College in Massachusetts to be near her older brother, Soong Tzu-wen (T. V. Soong; also spelled Tse-ven), who was at Harvard, since their parents would not allow her to remain alone in Georgia.

After graduating and returning to China, Mei-ling was put in charge of the large family residence in Shanghai, a job that included supervising its twelve servants. Mei-ling found many differences between the Chinese and American social cultures, especially when it came to the role of women. In the early twentieth century, young Chinese women, even from the best families, were considered inferior to men, and good only for procreating and playing parlor games like mahjong. Although she took part in the social whirl of Shanghai's upper crust, she also looked for work to keep her busy and interested. Having observed the "dirty, ragged swarming humanity" in Shanghai's slums, Mei-ling jumped at the chance when the Shanghai Municipal Council asked her to join the Child Labor Commission, on which no Chinese person, male or female, had ever served.

Meeting Chiang Kai-shek

There are conflicting stories about how Mei-ling and Chiang Kai-shek met and married, but it is obvious that they became attracted to each other during visits Mei-ling made to Guangzhou and the Nationalist Party headquarters in Wuhan in the winter of 1926–1927. He first mentions missing her in his diary in March 1927. Shortly after that, Ai-ling took charge, arranging to meet him on a boat anchored near Shanghai. During their long conversation she proposed that Chiang marry Mei-ling and that both Ai-ling's husband and their brother be given important positions in his government.

Chiang sent his current wife Jennie to the United States, whereupon he claimed that she was not his wife. Mei-ling accepted his proposal of marriage, and he then sailed for Japan to obtain her mother's permission. An ardent Methodist, Madame Soong asked him to convert to Christianity; when he said he would read the Bible and decide, she agreed to the marriage. Chiang and Mei-ling were married on 1 December 1927. Their wedding aroused a good deal of speculation as to the motives of the participants: was it love, attraction, the melding of power and family status, or all of the above?

Recognition of Chiang's Government

While her husband was preparing to continue what is known as the Northern Expedition, meant to unify China under his rule, Mei-ling had to get used to a life in the new Nationalist capital of Nanjing that was very different from any she had ever known. She was the rare wife of an official who followed her husband into a primitive city with no comfortable accommodations, heat, or sewage, moving into army headquarters in Nanjing and seeming to revel in the discomforts of her choice.

By early July 1928, Chiang had overcome the warlords in his path and made a triumphal entry into Beijing. During that summer, Great Britain recognized

Chiang's government and sent its ambassador to Nanjing. With the diplomatic community based in Nanjing, Mei-ling's role became essential. Chiang spoke no English, and she did all the translating, acting both as his official interpreter and chief advisor on foreign affairs.

Chiang's military victories, however, had not solved his problems with either of his opponents: the Communists or the warlords. Throughout her husband's battles, Mei-ling continued to provide help, and it was clear that she, like her sister Qingling, had found a man to love and serve.

Second Sino-Japanese War and American Aid

By the early 1930s it was clear that Japan, in search of men and raw materials, was preparing to invade China, which it did in September 1931, attacking and overrunning Manchuria. As the Japanese cut a bloody path through China, Mei-ling assumed the voice of the victim, crying out for help to the rest of the world.

After the Soviets signed a neutrality pact with Japan in 1941, the Japanese were free to do anything they wanted in China since they no longer had anything to fear from the Russians. The Chiangs, who had done "everything possible" to push Russia into war against Japan, were shocked. Mei-ling was particularly disappointed, as she had taken "an active part in troublemaking," supplying "misinformation" to the Soviets and telling them that "the greatest support the Soviet Union could render China would be to declare war on Japan" (Chuikov 2004, 80–81).

In the autumn of 1942, President Roosevelt sent Wendell Willkie, his recent opponent for the presidency, on a foreign tour. Chiang regarded Willkie's visit as an opportunity to get more funds and armaments from the United States and to impress the man who might one day become the American president. It is rumored, however, that Mei-ling and Willkie had an affair during his visit. With an invitation from First Lady Eleanor Roosevelt to visit the United States lying on her desk, Mei-ling allegedly followed Willkie back to the US under the pretense of consulting with American doctors about her ever-failing health.

Her American interlude started in a New York hospital, where she was diagnosed with nervous ailments. From there she proceeded to Washington, DC, where she wowed both houses of Congress with her looks, her speaking prowess, and her ability to raise huge amounts of money without ever seeming to ask for it. Unfortunately, Mei-ling's public persona was coupled with an imperious nature, which turned the White House staff against her and worried the president. Roosevelt was afraid that Mei-ling's dismissive behavior with reporters would damage his pro-China policy, already jeopardized by her fabulous jewels and furs that sat incongruously on a woman begging for supplies for starving citizens of her country. He tried to get her to leave the United States ahead of schedule, but she embarked on a lengthy tour that took her to Hollywood and lasted eight months.

Political Decline of Chiang's Government

By the beginning of January 1948, it was apparent that Chiang's government, with ten million Chinese on the verge of starvation, was falling apart politically, militarily, and financially. When Chiang failed to get more supplies from the United States, Mei-ling, thinking she could accomplish what he could not, left again for America.

Her trip—dubbed by a 1948 *Washington Post* article "a frantic, hopeless mission to woo back the Chinese supply line"—was a failure. To counter recent bad publicity, Mei-ling had brought only one fur coat—which was out-of-date and showing wear—and a minimal amount of luggage. But President Truman, who accused her family of stealing $750,000 of the money the United States had given to China, refused to give her any more. She then set to work to see what she could do to counter rumors that her husband was about to make peace with the Chinese Communist Party. Chiang had already moved gold, soldiers, gunboats, and his entire air force to Taiwan, and just months after Mao Zedong proclaimed the establishment of the People's Republic of China on 1 October 1949, Chiang flew to Taiwan. In January 1950, Mei-ling followed, explaining that, although she had been urged to stay in the United States, God ("an ethereal Voice") had spoken to her and told her to "return to share the fate of my husband and my people on Formosa" (Chiang 1955, 23–24). (*Ilha Formosa* means "beautiful island" in Portuguese.)

As soon as Mei-ling arrived on the island, she tackled the problem of the current rift between the Nationalists and the US government, assuring the Americans that the Nationalist government was not asking for American troops, but only advice on technical matters. She then toured the military hospitals, where she discovered that soldiers wounded in battle were not being paid. Within a few weeks she had visited Chiang's troops on the island of Quemoy, bearing cigarettes, food, and Bibles. A 1950 *New York Times* article noted that "more frequent and effective Nationalist air raids on coastal cities didn't coincide accidentally" with Mei-ling's return home.

Two years later Mei-ling again made what she hoped would be "a triumphal return to the American spotlight" (Li 2006, 373), speaking out against the Communists and writing articles to back up her speeches. As if to underscore her complaints, the mainlanders lobbed fifty thousand shells in two hours at the island of Quemoy, an attack that continued for five days. Although Secretary of State John Foster Dulles had once suggested that the Nationalist government leave the island, he and Chiang issued a joint statement saying that the Nationalist government was the "authentic spokesman for free China" (Crozier 1976, 368–369). This was not enough for Mei-ling, who appeared on *Meet The Press* saying that a Taiwanese invasion of the mainland was "growing nearer and nearer" (Newsweek 1958). The statement was a precursor to a full-fledged campaign started by Chiang in Taiwan, informing the mainlanders that "the time for collective action is here" (McHugh 1962) and guaranteeing the readiness of the Nationalist Army to back up the Taiwanese.

She left Taiwan in the summer of 1965 and stayed away for over a year, during which time she gave eighteen major speeches. During this visit she made a number of enemies, people who claimed she must be trying to get the United States government "to support nationalist troop landings on the Chinese mainland as part of a general escalation of the war in South Vietnam." In October 1966 Arkansas Senator J. William Fulbright (for whom the Fulbright scholarship is named) asked the State Department to explain "under what auspices she has come to seek to influence our foreign policy," (*New York Times* 1966) and by the end of the month she was gone.

Chiang Kai-shek was convinced that a combination of the Cultural Revolution and the escalation of the Vietnamese War would give him opportunities to attack the mainland. It fell to his wife, however, to make one last-ditch effort to get American support for a Nationalist invasion of the mainland—a plea that was strongly discouraged, first by Virginia Senator Harry Byrd on a visit to Taiwan and then by Richard M. Nixon, who visited Taipei the year before he became president. Nixon, however, was so impressed with Mei-ling's "intelligence, persuasiveness, and moral force" that he said she could have become "an important leader in her own right."

Later Years and Legacy

After Chiang suffered a cardiac arrest, Mei-ling assumed his role, along with her own, of outraged spokesperson against the Communists. Chiang died in April 1975, and five months later his widow left for the United States with more than a dozen aides and nurses. From then on she made her home in New York.

She returned to Taiwan only twice—once to say goodbye to her favorite niece and once to try to halt reforms that Chiang's son, Chiang Ching-kuo, now premier, was effecting. In 1995, at the age of ninety-eight she was guest of honor at a senate reception in Washington, DC, celebrating the fiftieth anniversary of the end of World War II. She always enjoyed celebrating her birthday in March, when friends and relatives gathered at her apartment for dinner. Mei-ling's last party was for her 105th birthday in 2002. Hospitalized with pneumonia on her 106th, she died on 12 October 2003.

Further Reading

Academia Historica, Taipei. (2010). Homepage. Retrieved December 5, 2011, from http://www.drnh.gov.tw

Anders, Leslie. (1965). *The Ledo Road: General Joseph W. Stilwell's highway to China.* Norman: University of Oklahoma Press.

Ch'en Chieh-ju. (1993). *Chiang Kai-shek's secret past: The memoir of his second wife, Ch'en Chieh-ju.* Boulder, CO: Westview Press.

Chiang, May-ling Soong. (1955). *The sure victory: By Madame Chiang Kai-shek.* Westwood, NJ: Revell.

Chiang, May-ling Soong. (1977). *Conversations with Mikhail Borodin: By Madame Chiang Kai-shek.* Taipei, Taiwan: World Anti-communist League, China Chapter.

Chuikov, Vasilii I. (2004). *Mission to China: Memoirs of a Soviet military advisor to Chiang Kai-shek* (David P. Barrett, Trans.). Norwalk, CT: EastBridge.

Corcoran, Thomas G. (1980). Rendezvous with democracy. (Unpublished manuscript.)

Crozier, Brian. (1976). *The man who lost China: The first full biography of Chiang Kai-shek.* New York: Scribner.

Dorn, Frank. (1973). *Walkout: With Stilwell in Burma.* New York: Pyramid Books.

Li, Laura Tyson. (2006). *Madame Chiang Kai-shek: China's eternal first lady.* New York: Atlantic Monthly Press.

McHugh, James Marshall. (1930–1965). James Marshall McHugh papers, #2770. Ithaca, NY: Cornell University Library, Division of Rare and Manuscript Collections.

Nation Archives and Records Administration (NARA). (2011). Homepage. Retrieved December 5, 2011, from http://www.archives.gov

Taylor, Jay. (2000). *The Generalissimo's son: Chiang Ching-kuo and the revolutions in China and Taiwan.* Cambridge, MA: Harvard University Press.

Wedemeyer, Albert C. (1958). *Wedemeyer Reports!* New York: Holt.

Wellesley College Archives. (n.d.). Homepage. Retrieved December 5, 2011, from http://web.wellesley.edu/web/Dept/LT/Collections/Archives

Jiang Qing

c. 1914–1991—Leader of the Chinese "Gang of
Four"; wife of Mao Zedong

Natascha GENTZ
The University of Edinburgh

Jiang Qing was at various stages in her life a prominent Shanghai actress, the wife of Mao Zedong, and the most prominent female leader of the Cultural Revolution. Many consider "Madame Mao," as she is commonly known in the West, to be among the most evil people in history for her leading role in the purges of the Cultural Revolution.

Jiang Qing became most well known in the West probably through the broadcasting of her show trial in 1981, during which she was sentenced to death as a counterrevolutionary attempting to overthrow the Chinese government. She was held responsible for the worst excesses of the Cultural Revolution, a ten-year period (1966–1976) of political turmoil and upheavals that led to the deaths and suffering of millions of people in China. As a leader of the "Gang of Four," a powerful faction of the upper echelon put on trail for their misdeeds, she was the only one to vehemently defend both her case and the Cultural Revolution, protesting loudly against any accusations by a tribunal she did not recognize as legitimate.

Only a few years earlier, Jiang Qing had been the only female leader to figure prominently on propaganda posters across the country. As the wife of Mao Zedong (1893–1976) and a member of the Cultural Revolution Group, the leading central radical organization, some believed she would be the future successor of the Great Chairman Mao. Her sudden downfall was the outcome of the most dramatic coup d'état in the Chinese Communist Party's (CCP's) history following Mao Zedong's death in September 1976, resulting in the arrest of the Gang of Four and the official end of the Cultural Revolution. Jiang Qing's death sentence was commuted to life imprisonment in 1983. In 1991, she committed suicide in a hospital, allegedly not her first attempt since being imprisoned.

Jiang Qing is one of the most prominent and controversial women in modern Chinese history. She is alternately hailed as a true revolutionary and model to follow and listed among the top ten most evil humans in the world on popular websites; one such site ranks her fifth, after Joseph Stalin, Adolf Hitler, Heinrich Himmler, and Pol Pot. Her life and public persona provide rich material to explore a wide range of issues in modern Chinese history and society: a truthful assessment of the

Cultural Revolution, elite power struggles, women and politics, communism and feminism, but also more trivial matters of intrigues, power, and sex.

Early Years

Jiang Qing was born, most likely in 1914, as Li Yunhe in Zhucheng, a county in Shandong Province. Her grandfather was a rich landlord but the family fortune was lost by Jiang Qing's father, who became a carpenter. Jiang Qing grew up in poverty and only received six years of education. Due to her poor education, her early years were marked by a constant search for ordinary jobs and money, and she decided to start training as an actress, a popular route for young unemployed girls to choose—particularly in the 1920s and 1930s, when a booming modern theater and film industry was growing in new and cosmopolitan urban centers.

Star Actress in Shanghai

During the 1930s, Shanghai's film industry was thriving, particularly with the development of a national film industry, which increasingly turned away from Hollywood as a model. In this period, modern Chinese drama, (the "spoken drama" in contrast to the traditional opera-style drama) had matured into a respected and popular new art form, producing a large number of dramatic pieces that are still part of the Chinese literary canon today. Translations of Western authors also played a crucial role in the development of this new art, and among these, Ibsen's *A Dollhouse* was one of the most prominent.

Jiang's performance as Nora on Shanghai's Golden City Great Stage in June 1935 was an instant success and ran for an unprecedented two months. It attracted large public attention: numerous articles, stage photographs, and interviews with Jiang Qing in the Shanghai papers. In China's drama circles, the year 1935 was later celebrated as "the year of Nora."

Although newspapers and magazines soon filled with gossip about Jiang's relationships or quarrels with film companies about roles, status, or payment, this publicity ironically did not help her career. She also might have lost interest in life as a celebrity. In a public letter written in June 1936, she declared her decision to leave film and pursue a more meaningful life. After the Japanese occupation of Shanghai in the summer of 1937, Jiang Qing left and made her way to Mao's Communist revolutionary base in Yan'an.

Revolutionary Wife

Jiang Qing enrolled in the Central Party School at Yan'an, and the Lu Xun Academy of Fine Arts, which trained actors, writers, musicians, and artists. Jiang Qing seems to have attracted Mao's attention when she raised a question after one of his speeches and asked for personal lessons. They quickly became friends and lovers, which was problematic, as Mao Zedong was still married to his third wife, He Zizhen

(1909–1984). In 1937, she had moved from Yan'an to Xi'an, but was still his official wife, although sources differ about the exact date of their divorce.

Jiang Qing's relationship with Mao met with considerable resistance within the CCP leadership in Yan'an. According to the rules and stipulations, the Central Party Committee had to approve divorces and marriages of leading cadres. It was decided that Jiang Qing was not to appear in public as "wife of Mao Zedong" but as "Comrade Jiang Qing." Her main purpose was to look after Mao Zedong's well-being, and she was to stay out of politics for the next twenty years.

Accepting these terms and conditions, Mao Zedong and Jiang Qing married in November of 1938. Jiang Qing did not figure prominently in the early period of the People's Republic, due to these limitations, but mainly worked as Mao's secretary and looked after their daughter, Li Na, who was born in 1940. The marital relationship seems to have deteriorated shortly after the CCP moved out of Yan'an.

Comrade Jiang Qing

Even after the twenty years' restriction from politics, Jiang Qing did not easily find a way back into the public arena. Most biographers correlate her political rise to the decline of Mao Zedong after the mass mobilization of labor and agriculture in the late 1950s called the Great Leap Forward that resulted in a famine costing millions of lives. Under increasing criticism, Mao had to resort to his closest allies and supporters, and thus gave more leeway to Jiang Qing to engage in cultural politics. During the early 1960s, Jiang Qing started to work on "revolutionizing" Peking Opera, advocating the replacement of traditional content with modern works on contemporary and revolutionary themes, which was in line with the official policy to suspend ghost themes, and generally criticize "feudal" and "reactionary" drama.

In July 1964, at the Festival of Peking Opera on Contemporary Themes, she gave her first public speech, "On the Reform of Peking Opera," endorsed by Mao Zedong, and from then on developed model operas, *yangbanxi*, for which she is probably most known. The model operas were a selection of dramas of different genres, which under the guidance of Jiang Qing were remolded into revolutionary plots with heroic roles and melodramatic pathos. Only these dramas were to be played during the Cultural Revolution, and thus permeated the entire country over several years as the only form of entertainment. In February 1966, Jiang Qing was officially and publicly commissioned "advisor on questions in literature and art of the People's Liberation Army." It was from then on that Jiang Qing started to appear in military uniform in public.

More important was her rise in the party nomenclature, as a member of the Central Cultural Revolution Group (CCRG) formed in May 1966. With increasing numbers of top leaders being purged from office, the CCRG played an increasingly important role in politics. Jiang Qing joined the group as vice chairperson in May, but effectively took control a few months later. Jiang Qing and the CCRG became deeply involved in the Red Guard movement (in which young people formed paramilitary units attempting to enforce Mao's directives), and established personal alliances with leading Red Guard members. Most notably, Jiang Qing and the CCRG resisted any attempts to scale down the excesses of violence during these years. Jiang

Qing was also well known for leading special investigation groups to purge hig party leaders and high-profile figures of the cultural fields, identified by her as the leaders of the "black line" in art and literature. She now regularly appeared in public at receptions of Red Guards on Tiananmen Square in Beijing or gave speeches during mass rallies or important party meetings.

While Jiang was certainly not in the position to launch any cult of personality of her own—even if she was the only female political figure to appear on propaganda posters of the Cultural Revolution—she chose other symbolic attributes to mark her leadership role. In 1974, she convened a national design conference with the objective of creating a national dress for all women to wear, though with little success. Some biographers see this as evidence of an ambition to become a new empress of China, since she followed the model of the only female emperor (i.e., not an "empress" but an emperor who was female) in Chinese history, Wu Zetian (625–705 CE), who also designed a national dress as described in the *History of the Tang* (Tangshu).

White-Boned Demon

The last years of the Cultural Revolution were marked by a continuous power struggle between the radicals around the Gang of Four and reformers, including Deng Xiaoping (1904–1997) and Zhou Enlai, who aimed at setting the country onto the path of modernization. These splits extended to factionalism also within the People's Liberation Army. When Zhou Enlai died in January 1976, people gathered at Tiananmen Square on the national day of mourning, the Qingming Festival, to pay tribute to one of their most respected politicians. This soon developed into open criticism of the radical policies of the Cultural Revolution and most of all Jiang Qing, in the form of allegorical poems and caricatures about the "Late Qing Empress" and other female leaders. While the demonstrations were immediately stopped, it was clear that popular support for Jiang Qing was waning.

With the death of Mao Zedong in September of the same year, she and the Gang of Four had lost their final backing, and only a month later they were arrested. The trial began about four years later, in November 1980, after the Special Court had prepared a meticulous documentation of their crimes. Lasting until January 1981, parts of the indictments were published in the Chinese press, and some of the trial scenes were also broadcast nationwide to give a clear signal that the Cultural Revolution had ended and the culprits had been found. Jiang Qing was the only one among the accused who did not repent, but protested loudly against all accusations, explaining that all she did was follow Mao's instructions.

By then, the public verdict had clearly turned against her. Along with the trial, and during the emerging Democracy Wall movement (during which for a brief period posters expressing dissent were allowed to be put up on a wall in Beijing), a very explicit hate campaign against Jiang Qing had started, denouncing and exposing her as a "White-Boned Demon," a counterrevolutionary, an ambitious empress in disguise, or a petty bourgeois at heart.

Jiang Qing was sentenced to death in 1981, although two years later this was changed into life imprisonment. Little information is available about her last years in prison and later in the hospital, as the CCP and Chinese press were keen to let the

Cultural Revolution and Jiang Qing fade into obscurity. Both topics are included in the PRC's list of taboo topics of public discussion. Suffering from throat cancer, she was released to a hospital in May 1991, where she committed suicide. She is buried at the Fukuda cemetery in Beijing under her birth name, Li Yunhe.

Remembering Jiang Qing

There are very few neutral biographical sources about Jiang Qing; most are either apologetic or condemnatory, containing judgments about her progressive and visionary spirit or her evil and selfish nature. While such a judgmental approach is very much in line with traditional Chinese biographical writing, which often followed a principle of "praising or blaming" that continued through Communist biographical writing, it is also true for most sources written about Jiang outside of mainland China. Jiang Qing has also served as a source of inspiration for fictional novels and dramas, both in China and in the West.

The official verdict on Jiang Qing by the Communist Party came in the form of a "Resolution on Party History" (Resolution 1981), which had to solve the dilemma of how Mao could not have recognized her evil character or why he should have involved himself with such a person. It was decided that Mao Zedong was aware of Jiang Qing's evil character, yet was not able to stop her in her ruthless ambitions.

After this official verdict, CCP statements about Jiang Qing were rarely to be found, and after the public hate campaign of the past, the new strategy was to lapse into silence. A continuing public interest in Jiang Qing in China, however, is reflected in the numerous unofficial biographies and popular semi-fictional accounts of her life, which to a large degree concentrate on her early years in Shanghai, various love affairs, and subsequent marriage with Mao. In English, the most cited is Professor Ross Terrill's *The White-Boned Demon: A Biography of Madame Mao Zedong*. Chinese historians like Ye Yonglie and Cui Wanqiu present more material-based studies of Jiang Qing, which focus on the early years of her life while still emphasizing her selfish part in a historical tragedy—with Mao being a rather passive male counterpart overwhelmed, seduced, and then deceived by her sexual attraction (Ye 1993; Cui 1987; Terrill 1984).

The advent of the Internet in China revealed that not all popular sentiments condemned Jiang Qing univocally, as there are indeed websites to be found in which she is addressed as a "martyr" and presented as a model hero (Yang 2007). Decades after her death, Jiang remains a divisive and controversial a figure in Chinese history.

Further Reading

Brief introduction of Comrade Chiang Ch'ing. *Survey of China Mainland Press* 4089 (29.12.1967), pp.1–2. Originally published in *Guanyin hongqi* (29.10.1967), Canton

Cui W. (1987). *Jiang Qing qian zhuan* 江青前传 [Jiang Qing's early years.] Hong Kong: Cosmo Books Ltd.

Listverse. (2010). Top 10 most evil humans. No. 5: Jiang Qing. Retrieved December 24, 2013, from http://listverse.com/2010/12/31/top-10-most-evil-humans

Miller, A. C. & Chung, H. (1968). *Madame Mao—A Profile of Chiang Ching*. Hong Kong: Union Press Ltd.

Min, A. (2000). *Becoming Madame Mao*. New York: Mariner Books.

Resolution on CPC History, 1945–1981. Beijing: Foreign Language Press, 1981.

Terrill, R. (1984). *The White-Boned Demon. A biography of Madame Mao Zedong.* London: Heinemann.

Vittinghoff, N. (1995). *Geschichte der Partei entwunden—Eine semiotische Analyse des Dramas Jiang Qing und ihre Ehemänner (1991)* von Sha Yexin [History and the Party—A semiotic analysis of the drama of *Jiang Qing and Her Husbands* (1991) by Sha Yexin.] Bochum, Germany: Projekt Verlag.

Wei Shaochang. (1987). *Jiang Qing waishi* 江青外史 [Unofficial history of Jiang Qing.] Hong Kong: Zhongyuan chubanshe.

Witke, R. (1977). *Comrade Chiang Ch'ing.* Boston and Toronto: Little, Brown and Co.

Yan J. (1986). "*Wenhua da geming" shi nian shi* "文化大革命" 十年史 [History of the Ten Years of the "Cultural Revolution."] Tianjin, China: Tianjin Renmin chubanshe.

Yang G. (2007). A portrait of martyr Jiang Qing. The Chinese Cultural Revolution on the Internet. In K. L. Ching & G. Yang. (Eds.), *Re-envisioning the Chinese Revolution. The politics and poetics of collective memory in Reform China* (pp. 287–316). Stanford, CA: Stanford University Press.

Ye Y. (1993). *Jiang Qing zhuan* 江青传 [Biography of Jiang Qing.] Beijing.

Zhang Chunqiao, Jiang Qing sanshi niandai heiwen. Gongpi shiyong 张春桥，江青 三十年代黑文。 公批使用 [Black materials of the '30s by Zhang Chunqiao and Jiang Qing, use for criticism.] (1977).

Zhong, H. (1967a). *Jiang Qing zhengzhuan* 江青正传 [Authentic account of Jiang Qing.] Hong Kong: Youlian yanjiusuo.

PART IV

The Spectrum of Women's Leadership

The Gender-based Structure of Work

Deborah M. FIGART and Heidi I. HARTMANN
Stockton University and George Washington University

Gender norms have always affected the work that women do, but with industrialization came a gender-segregated structure that still applies to many workplaces. Often in lower-paying jobs with fewer advancement opportunities, many women have struggled to escape traditional occupations only to find that their new careers have become devalued. Solutions lie in improved labor-market information, more family-friendly workplaces, and equitable pay and opportunity for all. Both public policies and private actions can help.

In the pre-industrial period, most people worked in homes, small workshops, and on farms close to home. Although tasks were divided along age and gender lines, nearly everyone was considered a worker. With the rise of the Industrial Revolution beginning in the late 1700s and early 1800s in the United States and Europe, paid labor markets developed on a large scale, as businesses increasingly separated from homes and new types of employers sought new sources of labor—people who were free to work for wages. In general, since industrialization, labor markets have been divided, structured, or segmented along gender and racial-ethnic lines. Labor markets are "rife with hierarchical distinctions between different categories of work and different groups of workers" (Figart 2003, 379).

In the United States, some of the earliest wage workers were young, single, white daughters of farmers, since they could be spared from the farm. In the early factories, they often performed work that they had been doing in the home, such as spinning thread. But with the development of so-called "heavy" industry (i.e., iron, steel, railroads, and oil refining), paid employment was increasingly considered a male domain. Being a breadwinner became central to (white) men's identity. White women, if they could afford to, were expected to focus on home and family. Marriage bars, or employer policies or practices that terminated women's employment upon marriage, remained common up through the 1930s and helped to enforce the norm that married women should focus on home and family care (Amott and Matthaei 1996, Hartmann 1976).

In large part, this cultural mandate never applied to married working-class women, many of whom were recent immigrants or the daughters of immigrants. Nor, even after slavery, did the dominant ideal of male breadwinner and full-time homemaker reach African-American women, either working class or middle class.

217

The scholar Jacqueline Jones (1986) has effectively shown that black women typically began paid work as teenagers, remained in the paid labor force when they married and had children, and worked through middle age. Few African-American men earned a family-sustaining wage and even today their wages are typically lower than white men's (Landry 2000, Institute for Women's Policy Research 2016a).

Gender-Based Job Segregation in the Twentieth Century

Over the course of the twentieth century in the United States, women of all racial-ethnic groups, but especially white, married women during and after World War II, increased their participation in the labor force. Yet most paid work is still segregated along gender lines, and many specific race and ethnic groups can also be found in specific clusters of jobs. Occupations and industries typically employ predominantly women (for example, nursing), men (truck driving), or are gender mixed (retail). Today, nearly two-fifths of women are employed in occupations that are at least 75 percent female , while nearly half of men work in male-dominated occupations (Institute for Women's Policy Research 2016b). Often, those occupations that are integrated on the surface (for example, waiting on tables), become less so as specific jobs titles and tasks across different businesses are examined, with men often working at better-paying firms while women work in lower-paying firms even in the same industry (restaurants, for example).

Private household work has remained well over 90 percent female for the past century. Clerical work, previously done mainly by men, who were called clerks, became increasingly female-dominated secretarial work over the course of the twentieth century. Blue-collar work in the skilled trades—electrical work, plumbing, painting, and carpentry, for example—has remained a male domain; trade work is still less than 10 percent female. Management and the professions are integrated when the general, aggregate category is considered, but many specific managerial and professional jobs are performed predominantly by men or women, with, for example, more women than men being English teachers and more men than women being engineers.

In addition to limiting an individual's opportunity to pursue the work that may be of greatest interest to him or her, segregation in the labor market affects pay and promotion prospects, with members of socially disadvantaged groups generally working in less appealing jobs and earning less. The economists Francine Blau and Lawrence Kahn have found that half of the wage gap between women and men is due to occupational and industrial segregation by gender (2016). Studies have shown that as the percentage of an occupation's incumbents who are female rises, the average wage falls, even when controlling for other factors affecting wages (Baron and Bielby 1980). Thus the gendered structure of labor markets can refer just as much to the structure of pay in the labor market as to who works where. In the twentieth century, women have frequently challenged the tendency for women's jobs to have lower pay, and advocates have developed the concept of comparable worth, also called pay equity, as shorthand for the demand that women's jobs not be devalued because women do them. Advocates of comparable worth argue that jobs should be compared on the basis of the skill, effort, and responsibility they require as well as the working conditions under which they are performed, and pay set accordingly, rather than by custom or tradition, which likely incorporates the effects of discrimination on pay rates (Figart and Hartmann 2000).

One of the most puzzling aspects of the gender-based wage gap and job segregation in labor markets is that they remain strong despite enormous economic changes. Entire occupations and industries come and go, competition increases on a global scale, labor markets are continuously changing and restructuring, yet the phenomena of segregation and the wage gap remain, re-forming themselves in new labor market conditions. In fact, both white women and women of color have often entered professional and technical fields as those fields were changing. Women of color became computer operators for large mainframe computers as those were being phased out and computing was moving to individual desktops; similarly, they became telephone technicians as more of that work became automated. White women increased their representation in medical schools and law schools in the 1970s, just as autonomy in these professions began to decline. A major study by social researchers Michael Carter and Susan Carter, published in 1981, documents how large law firms, medical and legal clinics, and health maintenance organizations (HMOs) tend to push out sole practitioners, reducing their autonomy and profit margins. Men retain the best positions in the profession (partnerships at Wall Street law firms, for example), while women take the newly open jobs in the less privileged part of the profession. The field of pharmacy also changed as women entered, as large chain store pharmacies employing more women replaced local pharmacist entrepreneurs, who had been mostly men. As many law and medical schools now approach or exceed 50 percent in female student enrollment, well-educated men are moving on to greener pastures elsewhere, particularly in high tech, which has been resistant to greater integration.

Within management, men predominate in line positions in financial management and production management, areas on the fast track to the executive suite. Women managers, and especially African-American women, are disproportionately concentrated in specialties such as human resources, public relations, and marketing, fields which lead less readily to the top executive positions. This phenomenon is one reason that women have hit a "glass ceiling" in corporate America.

Causes For Gender Segregation

Occupational segregation and wage discrimination can be the result of overt actions by employers or subtle forms of institutional discrimination or even unconscious decision-making. Institutional discrimination connotes a situation in which structural features of labor markets and employment practices, while limiting opportunities, are seen as normal. Of course, what is normal in one period can be challenged and changed in another. For example, prior to the passage of the Civil Rights Act in 1964 and subsequent litigation, help-wanted classified ads were routinely listed under the headings "Help Wanted Female" and "Help Wanted Male." And overt discrimination can be transformed into less overt discrimination, as when women are offered less overtime, less responsibility, or fewer cross-department assignments that would increase their visibility and help prepare them for promotions. According to feminist scholars, discrimination is deeply embedded in social institutions and culture. Indeed the roots of occupational segregation can be seen to predate industrialization.

The anthropologist Margaret Mead (1901–1978) has famously said that although the jobs women and men do differ from society to society, in all societies men and women do different work and everywhere the work women do is valued less.

The extent of sex segregation and the size of the wage gap have both fallen since the 1960s. The index of segregation, frequently used to assess women's progress in the US labor market, fell some 18 percentage points, from 68 to 50, between 1972 and 2011 (Hegewisch and Hartmann 2014). The wage gap, using data from the US Current Population Survey, fell from about 40 percent in 1960 to 23 percent in 2002 and has remained at a similar proportion ever since. (That is to say, women who work full-time, year-round, used to earn 60 percent of what full-time, year-round working men did; in 2014 they earned just less than 79 percent of what men do. See Institute for Women's Policy Research 2016a). While these declines certainly represent progress for women in breaking out of narrow confines in the labor market, progress has not been steady and is even slowing down. With both segregation and the wage gap, for example, far more progress was made in the 1980s than has been since.

Competitive market forces alone are not likely to cause institutional discrimination to evaporate in the long run. In fact, employers may even profit from engaging in discrimination. If discrimination lowers the wages of less powerful groups of workers, rather than (or in addition to) raising the wages of preferred groups, many employers likely profit from the situation and would have to increase the wages of underpaid workers to eliminate pay discrepancies.

Feminist economists and sociologists have advanced several theories of institutionalized discrimination: crowding, queuing, dual labor market, and segmentation theory. Implicit bias is a recent entry in the field that helps explain how these practices continue.

Crowding

In a ground-breaking 1974 article, the feminist economist Barbara Bergmann proposed that discrimination "crowds" women and racial minorities into a smaller subset of occupations. According to the crowding hypothesis, the oversupply of workers in these occupations depresses their wages, due to the competition for limited job openings. Women, especially women of color, are overcrowded into female-dominated occupations; these occupations pay less, on average, than jobs with similar education and experience requirements that are not open to them. White male workers have always had more occupational choices, so they do not face crowding, but they are even more concentrated in virtually single-sex occupations than women are, perhaps because they have little reason to give up these better jobs. Since women face barriers to moving into these jobs, the limited labor supply keeps wages high in the male sector.

Queuing

Queuing theory, developed by the sociologists Barbara Reskin and Patricia Roos (1990), treats the hierarchy between groups of workers as an institutionalized aspect of the social fabric. According to this approach, employers rank workers by order of preference and workers rank jobs based on their desirability. The workers higher up on an employer's queue get first choice at the most desirable jobs.

Dual Labor Market

According to dual labor market theory, pioneered by the economists Peter Doeringer and Michael Piore in 1971, the economy is divided between a primary sector and a secondary sector that do not allow much mobility of workers between them. The primary sector comprises traditional manufacturing jobs and skilled trade occupations. These jobs are often unionized and offer promotion opportunities, in a well-organized internal labor market. In contrast, occupations in the secondary sector are low-wage and dead-end and lack benefits. Male workers, especially white men, are concentrated in the primary sector and female workers, men of color, and immigrants in the secondary sector, where jobs are also often temporary with irregular hours. Dual labor market theory complements the image of separate labor markets in crowding models. Dual labor market literature is largely inductive, drawing inferences from case studies of specific firms and analyses of the structure of labor markets in the economy of a particular time and place. While labor markets in the United States have changed significantly since this theory was first developed (the unionized work force has declined as a share of the labor force, for example), the basic idea of good jobs and bad jobs still provides a perspective for understanding labor markets that appeals to many.

Segmentation Theory

Segmentation theory has been developed to explain why the labor market is divided (Figart, Mutari and Power 2002). Employers are motivated to maintain gender and race hierarchies in order to "divide and conquer" workers. Employers benefit from mirroring the local culture's race and gender hierarchies and keeping workers divided against one another: Their union densities are less, their wage bills are lower. One strand of segmentation theory implies that white male workers could be better off if they joined with their coworkers to demand higher wages for all. Theorists have also examined the role of alliances between employers and white male workers in the establishment of discriminatory employment practices.

Task Segregation and Gendered Valuation

Within the social sciences, gender theory has augmented these heterodox, mainly economic, theories by acknowledging the cultural devaluation of female-dominated occupations, the tasks and skills associated with "feminine" qualities, and workers with family responsibilities. These cultural values lead employers to create segregated jobs and informal task segregation. Employers maintain gender and race hierarchies, and thus occupational segregation, because cultural assumptions about women of all races and about men of color shape their economic decisions. Many of these processes occur, and can be observed, at the level of the organization. For example, even if women and men are employed in a position with exactly the same job title, employers may structure their work differently by task. This is task segregation.

Studying clerks in supermarkets, the sociologists Martin Tolich and Celia Briar (2003) uncovered informal forms of discrimination that do not show up in hiring statistics or paychecks, but do result in differential promotional opportunities and quality of working life. Male supermarket clerks, they found, have more freedom of movement on the job; they leave the checkout lanes to restock products and clean the aisles. Access to more varied tasks is the gateway to a possible promotion. Female supermarket clerks, on the other hand, are more tied to their registers and more often assigned to the "express lane." Employers treat the male and female clerks differently not because it is necessarily profitable or divides their work force. They simply carry, and act out, unspoken assumptions about men's impatience with staying in one place, women's greater emotive skills, and which employees need to be cultivated for promotions.

Implicit Bias

More recently, psychologists have developed the theory of implicit bias to account for these unacknowledged discriminatory behaviors in workplaces. Many managers deny having any discriminatory intentions. Nevertheless, the culturally dominant ideas of which work is appropriate for which workers often become so automatic that when asked to imagine a political leader, for example, many respondents (including women and people of color) will see a white male in their mind's eye (American Association of University Women 2016). Mahzarin Banaji (2013) and others are developing workplace interventions which can short circuit these automatic choices and help managers be more mindful when making decisions that affect hiring and promotion.

Gender-Related Work Preferences

Increasingly in the labor economics and business literature, women's and men's preferences and private decisions about family care are cited as the main causes of segregation and other differential outcomes observed in the labor market. Suppose women want to work fewer hours, travel less, or have less responsibility on the job because they want to have more time and energy available to take care of children, other family members, homes, and communities? If women prefer less-demanding positions on average, then are employers discriminating when they assume all women want such positions and structure their personnel decisions accordingly (see Sandberg 2011)? And since much preparation for the labor market takes place before people enter the labor market, especially in schools and colleges, are employers responsible for there being few male nurses and few female engineers in the United States today? Questions such as these suggest that many aspects of the gendered structure of labor markets are influenced by what happens outside the labor market, yet employers cannot be excused from the roles they play in perpetuating stereotypical ideas through employment policies and practices.

Just as what women do in the workplace may be conditioned by decisions made elsewhere, what happens in the workplace can affect women's and men's decisions concerning how to divide their energies between paid employment and family care. Lower pay for women in the labor market, an expectation of greater discrimination or harassment in male-dominated fields, a lack of publicly funded child care and paid family leave, and income tax policies that discourage second earners in families all help steer many men and women toward decisions regarding career choice and work and family care that support the status quo.

Solutions to Gender Segregation

Like the causes, the remedies needed to reduce the gendered structure of labor markets and to increase opportunities for women are many and intertwined (Reskin and Hartmann 1985; McCall 2001; Figart, Mutari and Power 2002; Hegewisch, Bendick, Gault, and Hartmann 2016). Active enforcement of antidiscrimination and equal-opportunity laws in both employment and education is essential. Access to many jobs is still essentially denied to women. Young women making educational and career choices often do not have adequate knowledge of future pay and benefits and may simply pursue what they see other women doing. Better information and improved career coaching could help women as well as immigrants and men of color pursue jobs that take their interests and talents into account but provide better pay and prospects. Employers, too, can learn that workers in jobs considered "less skilled" may actually have the skills and talents needed to move into better jobs. New laws to encourage comparable pay in women's and men's occupations would more fairly compensate women for working in traditionally female jobs and at the same time encourage more men to take those jobs. Subsidized child care, paid family leaves, and flexible work arrangements would all help families to mesh work and family demands and to divide family care more equitably. While some employers are making their workplaces more family friendly on their own, usually to attract and retain highly skilled employees, and a few states have implemented paid family leave, many other workers have no such benefits at work and reaching these workers will likely require that national laws be put in place (McCrate 2005, Boushey 2016). Tax policies that treat dual-earner and single-earner couples more equitably are also needed. In short, the gendered structure of labor markets results from both internal and external factors, and both need to be addressed for change to occur. While much remains to be done if the labor market is to provide equal opportunity for everyone, social changes as profound as increasing gender equity can be expected to take a long time. In the United States, women organized actively for seven decades before gaining the vote, and by 2016, they still had only 19.4% percent of the seats in the US Congress (MAKERS 2014). From the long-term perspective, a surprising amount of change has occurred in the labor market in a relatively short time period.

Further Reading

American Association for University Women. (2016). Are you biased against women leaders? http://www.aauw.org/article/implicit-association-test/Amott, T. & Matthaei, J. (1996). *Race, gender, and work: A multi-cultural economic history of women in the United States* (Rev. ed.). Boston: South End Press.

Banaji, M. & Greenwald, A. (2013). *Blindspot: Hidden biases of good people*. New York: Delacorte Press.

Baron, J. N. & Bielby, W. T. (1980). Bringing the firm back in: Stratification, segmentation, and the organization of work. *American Sociological Review, 45*(5), 737–65.

Bergmann, B. R. (1974). Occupational segregation, wages and profits when employers discriminate by race or sex. *Eastern Economic Journal, 1*(2–3), 103–110.

Blau, F.D. & Kahn, L.M. (2016). The gender wage gap: Extent, trends, and explanations. Working Paper. Cambridge, MA: National Bureau of Economic Research.

Boushey, H. (2016). *Finding time: The economics of work-life conflict*. Cambridge, MA: Harvard University Press.

Doeringer, P. B. & Piore, M. J. (1971). *Internal labor markets and manpower analysis*. Lexington, MA: D. C. Heath and Company.

Figart, D. M. (2003). Policies to provide non-invidious employment. In M. R. Tool & P. D. Bush (Eds.), *Institutional Analysis and Economic Policy* (pp. 379–409). Boston: Kluwer Academic Publishers.

Figart, D. M. & Hartmann, H. I. (2000). Broadening the concept of pay equity: Lessons for a changing economy. In R. Baiman, H. Boushey, & D. Saunders (Eds.), *Political economy and contemporary capitalism: Radical perspectives on economic theory and policy* (pp. 285–293). Armonk, NY: M. E. Sharpe.

Figart, D. M., Mutari, E., & Power, M. (2002). *Living wages, equal wages: Gender and labor market policies in the United States*. London: Routledge.

Hartmann, H. I. (1976). Capitalism, patriarchy, and job segregation by sex. *Signs, 1*(2 supplement), 137–169.

Hegewisch, A.; Bendick, M.; Gault, B.; & Hartmann, H. (2016). *Pathways to equity: Narrowing the wage gap by improving women's access to good middle-skill jobs*. Washington, DC: Institute for Women's Policy Research.

Hegewisch, A. & Hartmann, H. (2014). Occupational segregation and the gender wage gap: A job half done. Scholar's paper to commemorate the 50th anniversary of the publication of the report of President Kennedy's Commission on the Status of American Women. Washington, DC: US Department of Labor.

Institute for Women's Policy Research (2016a). The gender wage gap: 2015; earnings differences by race and ethnicity. Washington, DC: Institute for Women's Policy Research.

Institute for Women's Policy Research (2016b). The gender wage gap by occupation 2015 and by race and ethnicity. Washington, DC: Institute for Women's Policy Research.

Jones, J. (1986). *Labor of love, labor of sorrow: Black women, work, and the family from slavery to the present*. New York: Vintage Books.

Landry, B. (2000). *Black working wives: Pioneers of the American family revolution*. Berkeley and Los Angeles: University of California Press.

MAKERS. (2014). White House Summit: MAKERS Talk Women in Leadership. Retrieved July 7, 2016, from http://www.makers.com/blog/white-house-summit-makers-talk-women-leadership

McCall, L. (2001). *Complex inequality: Gender, class and race in the new economy*. New York: Routledge.

McCrate, E. (2005). Flexible hours, workplace authority, and compensating wage differentials in the U.S. *Feminist Economics 11*(1), 11–39.

Reskin, B. F. & Hartmann, H. I. (Eds.). (1985). *Women's work, men's work: Sex segregation on the job*. Washington, DC: National Academy Press.

Reskin, B. F. & Roos, P. A. (1990). *Job queues, gender queues: Explaining women's inroads into male occupations*. Philadelphia: Temple University Press.

Sandberg, S. (2011). Transcript and Video of Barnard College Commencement. Retrieved July 7, 2016, from http://barnard.edu/headlines/transcript-and-video-speech-sheryl-sandberg-chief-operating-officer-facebook

Tolich, M. & Briar, C. (2003). Just checking it out: Exploring the significance of informal gender divisions among American supermarket employees. In E. Mutari & D. M. Figart (Eds.), *Women and the economy: A reader* (pp. 248–56). Armonk, NY: M. E. Sharpe.

Women in Business Leadership: Challenges and Development

Candida G. BRUSH and Eliana CROSINA
Babson College and Boston College

Women's role in business leadership is growing, affected both by legislation and education gains, which have shaped societal expectations. Despite important gains, women's progress into the upper echelons of leadership has not progressed as quickly as many hoped. In addition to the *glass ceiling* (the invisible barriers that keep women from rising to the top), new discussions refer to the so-called *glass cliff* (or, women's increased access to high-level, but risky, leadership positions).

When asked to name a successful business leader, most people think of individuals like Mark Zuckerberg (CEO of Facebook), Elon Musk (CEO and CTO of SpaceX and Tesla Motors), or Jeff Bezos (CEO of Amazon). Often, the first image one has of a business leader is that of a man. Over the past thirty years, many women have also become successful business leaders, including, for example, Sheryl Sandberg (COO of Facebook), Mary Barra (CEO of General Motors), Indra Nooyi (CEO of PepsiCo) and Meg Whitman (CEO of Hewlett-Packard) – to mention a few. These women, just like their men counterparts, have made a significant impact on the US economy.

At the same time that women have progressed in business leadership and entrepreneurship, a debate has risen in research and the popular press as to whether, and if so how, gender matters in leadership.

- Are women less assertive?
- Are men more decisive?
- Are men better at numbers and women better at managing people?
- Can women make the "tough" decisions?

Answers to these questions vary, largely depending on one of two perspectives people generally take: 1) that men and women are similar in how they lead; or 2) that women lead differently. Given a general definition of leadership as the ability to inspire and influence beliefs, attitudes, and the behavior of others, (Kotter 2001), it is worth exploring these two perspectives about women in business leadership.

225

The Numbers of Women in Business Leadership

Since 1960, the percentage of women in the workforce has risen from 38 to 57 percent in 2014, with women accounting for 52 percent (a historically high number) of all workers in management, professional, and related occupations (Bureau of Labor Statistics 2015). As more women have entered the workforce, many moved into executive positions across industry sectors, either by rising through the ranks of existing organizations, or founding their own ventures. To illustrate, in 2013, one out of five Fortune 500 companies reported 25 percent or more women as their executive officers (Catalyst 2013). Research also shows that women currently make up approximately 20 percent of the boards of S&P 500 companies, and that they occupy about a quarter (25.1 percent) of executive and senior level positions at these organizations (Catalyst 2016). However, only 17.9% of board members for Fortune 1000 companies are female. These numbers have not changed dramatically in the last few years. By contrast, many countries have adopted laws that require companies to increase the number of women on their boards to 40 percent representation, including Sweden, Germany, France, Norway, Iceland. There is also research showing that when companies have women corporate directors, they experience better financial performance.

The growing representation and influence of women in already established businesses is paralleled by their rising involvement in entrepreneurial ventures. To illustrate, between 1997 and 2014 the number of women-owned businesses increased by 68 percent (compared to a national average of 47 percent). This led to an 11 percent increase in employment, and a 72 percent growth in revenues in women-owned organizations (NAWBO 2014). The National Association of Women Business Owners estimates that in 2014 there were 9.1 million women-owned businesses in the United States, generating more than $1.4 trillion in revenue, and employing approximately 7.9 million people.

Factors Influencing Women's Rise in Business Leadership

What accounts for the growth in participation of women in business leadership positions? There is no single answer, but, at a broad level, the environment for women's participation in business leadership is more acceptable today than twenty years ago due to a combination of regulatory changes and educational progress. These, in turn, have come to shape societal expectations around, and ultimately women's roles as leaders.

Legislative Changes

Legislative changes such as the Civil Rights Act of 1964, and the Affirmative Action Act of 1978, were pioneering efforts to address some of the challenges that women faced in rising to the top of corporations. In particular, Title VII of the Civil Rights Act prohibited discrimination against women based on their sex. As such, employers could no longer deprive women of any benefits available to men, including, for instance, promotions. In 1978, this act was amended to make it clear that discrimination based on pregnancy was also unlawful, as well as to provide for a process by which complaints may be filed with the Equal Opportunity Commission.

The Equal Pay Act of 1963, as its name suggests, required employers to pay men and women equally for the same work, skills, responsibility, and working conditions. In addition, the Family Medical Leave Act of 1993 allowed workers to take time off for bearing, adopting children, and/or taking care of seriously ill family members. By making it possible for women to pursue their occupation of choice, be fairly compensated for their work, and be in a position to entertain both a career and a family, these legislative changes, in their aggregate, helped remove some of the institutional barriers that had long inhibited women's progress in the workplace.

The passing of the Equal Credit Opportunity Act of 1975, which permitted women to acquire loans and credit in their own name, marked an important milestone for the financial independence of women, and especially for that of women entrepreneurs. Ten years later, the Women's Business Ownership Act provided set-asides for women business owners, created the National Women's Business Council, and established new federal capacities to guarantee loans to women-owned organizations. Moreover, the Small Business Administration's (SBA) preferential procurement program (known as section 8[a]) made it easier for women to obtain government contracts; and the SBA's microloan program (the 7 M program), together with the Women's Pre-qualification Loan Program, offered qualified women entrepreneurs faster access start-up capital. In 2012, thanks to the Women-Owned Small Business Federal Contract Program in particular, WOSBs were granted 182,791 contracts, worth, in their aggregate, $11.5 billion. Taken together, these various initiatives have, and should continue to, improve access to lending, training, as well as federal contracting for women-owned businesses. (NWBC 2014)

Educational Progress

Today more women have a business education than in the past, which better qualifies them for leadership roles. Specifically, the Association to Advance Collegiate Schools of Business (AACSB) reports that in 2013 approximately 43 percent of all undergraduate business degrees were awarded to women; that nearly 47 percent (46.7 to be exact) of all master students were female; and that the percentage of women receiving MBAs was 36.3—a historically high figure. (AACSB 2013)

When it comes to entrepreneurship, many options for training exist—including more than seven hundred schools offering entrepreneurship courses at each the MBA and undergraduate levels. Today women account for more than 35 percent of the students taking entrepreneurship-related courses. Several colleges and universities have created summer curricula or courses focusing on women entrepreneurs (e.g., Stanford Business School, Babson College, and Barnard College). In addition, it is estimated there are at least twelve accelerators providing training, funding and mentoring for start-up women entrepreneurs, notably Women's Startup Lab in California, The Brandery in Cincinnati, and Mergelane in Colorado. Further, the Tory Burch Foundation, in partnership with the Goldman Sachs 10,000 Small Businesses and Babson College provides a specialized program to help women entrepreneurs grow their businesses. The three month program includes one-on-one business advising, practical skill development and mentoring.

Shifting Roles of Women in the Family and Society

Since World War II, some of these educational and legislative changes created opportunities for women to develop business knowledge and expertise. As a consequence, traditional family expectations and social norms, which had largely cast women as homemakers and men as income providers, started, slowly, to shift. The increasing prevalence of dual-career couples, and greater participation of working fathers in child care speak to these important changes that have made it possible (and arguably more acceptable) for women to entertain leadership roles within their organizations, including as CEOs or as other top-level executives.

Moreover, women's organizations such as 2020 Women on Boards, the Committee of 200, the National Association for Women's Business Owners, the National Association of Female Executives, and a multitude of other groups have been founded to advocate for women in business leadership, and to provide them business and networking support. Publications offering specialized information for women have also been burgeoning, and major business outlets such as *Entrepreneur,* the *Wall Street Journal,* or *Fortune* are increasingly featuring stories about companies led by women. Such accounts both increase the visibility of successful business women, and provide role models for other women to consider.

Even the academic press has taken more and more interest in issues of gender and leadership, addressing, in particular, the opportunities and challenges female leaders are confronted with. To illustrate, more than 3,000 journal articles that discuss gender and leadership have been published since 1970, of which 38 percent in 2010 and after (Eagly and Heilman 2016, 349). Despite this focus, important questions remain with respect to gender differences in leadership.

Are There Gender Differences in Business Leadership?

As the number of women in leadership positions increased, debates followed. Do men and women lead differently? Almost everyone has an opinion on this subject, depending on where they have been raised, worked, attended school, and, more broadly, what they learned from their experiences. The degree to which men and women business leaders may be perceived as similar or different in their approaches to leadership, and on which dimensions, are rooted in longstanding assumptions about men and women (Maier 1992). In the paragraphs that follow, we provide a brief overview of various gender perspectives that have informed management scholars' thinking and theorizing on the subject over the years.

In the early 1950s and 1960s, *masculinism* (sexism) assumed that women were essentially different from men; that they made different (often less important) contributions to society; and, as such, they were largely excluded from management. The 1970s brought *feminism,* which assumed that women and men were essentially the "same," and, therefore, that women should or could take on masculine roles. A *feminine-ism* view rising in the 1980s also sought sex-based inclusion, but celebrated instead the unique contributions of women rather than invoking their conforming to traditional male-roles. More recently, *transformative feminism* has called for role-based inclusion, androgyny, and the acceptance of diversity as ways to reduce gender-driven social, political, and economic inequity (Warren 2000).

All these views, with their underlying assumptions around women's capabilities vis-à-vis men's, provide the foundations for debates around gender similarities and differences in leadership. As alluded to earlier, two of the most prevalent views are that: 1) "women lead like men," or that there are no or only negligible differences among men and women leaders that may be accounted for by their sex; and 2) that "women lead differently," or that there are unique tactics, practices, styles that set women apart from men as leaders. We explore these perspectives, by bringing to the fore their theoretical underpinnings, as well as examples from existing literature.

Women Lead Like Men

Liberal feminism advances that female subordination is perpetuated by some of the institutional (political and social) structures that regulate social life (Greer and Greene 2003). As such, by removing the institutional obstacles (through political and legal reform) that have traditionally hindered women in their social and economic advancement, gender equality may be furthered (Tong 1989). This way, factors affecting leadership have more to do with the set of organizational and socio-cultural constraints that leaders are confronted with, rather than with their sex.

A key argument espoused by those who assume that women and men are not different as leaders is that women who pursue leadership positions have needs, ambitions, style, demographics and a career pathway similar to their men counterparts (Hasalam and Ryan 2008). Moreover, because leaders are socialized into their roles, no differences between men and women leaders, if ever present, persist (see Powell 1990, De La Rey 2005 for review). The assumption that women leaders are similar to men may be extended to expectations for behavior, because status expectations state theory. Status expectation states refer to the cultural beliefs organized along the lines of social status differences, like gender, that set individual expectations about how the self or others will perform at a given task (Foschi 2000, Ridgeway and Correll 2000). This implies that leadership behaviors in organizations are assumed to be "male" in nature, which means women leaders are expected behave in a masculine manner, having the same ambitions and motivations.

Over the years, scholars have taken fine-grained and more contingent approaches to understand how, and under which conditions, women may lead like men. Moreover, when comparing men and women leaders they have looked at aspects such as: their motivation to pursue leadership positions, their emergence as leaders, as well as their perceived effectiveness. For example, Donnell and Hall (1980) found that female managers are just as motivated as male managers, but that they are more driven by autonomy and opportunities for growth, and less so by pay than their male counterparts. In a recent study on leadership emergence, Lanaj and Hollenback (2015, 1488) showed that irrespectively of their sex, individuals who engage in social behaviors have a similar tendency to under-emerge as leaders (although engaging in social behaviors contributes to their perceived effectiveness). Similarly, Kushnell and Newton (1986), found that a leader's sex does not shape followers' satisfaction, but that the leader's style does. In exploring conflict management styles and leadership effectiveness among experienced men and women leaders, Korabik and colleagues (1993) showed no sex-specific differences in self-reported conflict management. Finally, in his review of the literature, Powell

(1990, 71) noted that "...sex differences are absent in task-oriented behavior, people-oriented behavior, effectiveness ratings of actual managers, and subordinates' responses to actual managers..." We turn next to examining how, when, and why men and women may differ in how they lead, and the factors that may contribute to such perceived differences.

Women Lead Differently

Social feminism posits that the organizational and institutional contexts in which women are embedded shape the tactics and practices that they deploy to assert their leadership (Greer and Greene 2003). As such, women's backgrounds, experiences, and respective work environments impact their way of perceiving, thinking, and ultimately leading others (Carter and Williams 2003). This way, social feminism inherently invokes gender, among others, as a socially constructed category that women and men must negotiate in order to exercise influence and induce compliance (rather than being taken for granted).

These notions have been explored, over the years, by a number of scholars who have taken different perspectives to explain how men and women differ in how they lead. For example, Margaret Henning and Anne Jardim in their landmark book *The Managerial Woman* (1977) focused on the leadership and management skills of businesswomen in male-dominated environments. In particular, the women in their study, as ways to fit in and induce compliance in their hierarchical and male-centered organizations, exhibited more flexibility, eagerness to learn, and cooperative behaviors compared to their male counterparts. Sally Helgesen (1990) replicated a study by Henry Mintzberg conducted on men in 1973 examining the "work" of women leaders. In contrast to Mintzberg, who showed men executives working at an unrelenting pace, controlling information, and being task-oriented, Helgesen found that women were intuitive in their decision making, shared information, emphasized inclusion and cooperation, and had more of a networking, rather than an authoritarian, style. Building on this work, Judith Rosener (1990, 1995) found men more likely to describe their work as leaders in "transactional" ways, and women seeking to be more inspirational with their followers, in ways that traditionally distinguish "transformational" leadership. Eagly and Carli (2003), using interviews and a meta-analysis, explored the changing context of female leadership, proposing that the female disadvantage was eroding and the female advantage was growing.

Studies of women entrepreneurs show similar patterns. For example, Bird and Brush (2002) noted that women practice shared control and participation in decision making, develop policies that encourage learning and employee well-being, seek cooperation and participation in strategy, and facilitate development of policies that help balance family and work (Bird and Brush 2002). Moreover, compared to men executives and entrepreneurs, women have been found to score lower on vision formulation (analysis, planning), and higher on innovative realism (Bird and Brush 2002).

Others have claimed differences in men and women leadership styles, along the lines of women being less hierarchical, more focused on enhancing their followers' self-worth, and overall more cooperative and interpersonal (e.g., Hegelsen 1990). Questions have been raised around the extent to which some of these insights, developed partly in laboratory settings, and partly based on self-reported data, may be broadened to account for the actions of leaders (women and men) in organizational contexts (e.g., Eagly and Johannesen-Schmidt 2001). Moreover, while noting patterns of differences in leaders' styles, the research we alluded to so far says little about where such differences originate from, how and why.

By problematizing gender and its construction, emerging scholarship regarding women leaders has become more nuanced in addressing the conditions under which, and the reasons underlying men and women's different leadership styles (see the 2016 *The Leadership Quarterly* special issue on gender and leadership for a comprehensive review). For example, research on women entrepreneurs shows that, confronted with the challenges of being taken as legitimate and as serious as their male counterparts, female entrepreneurs engage in a range of gender (and identity-related) practices to assert their leadership (e.g., Díaz García and Welter 2013, Lewis 2013, Marlow and McAdam 2015). In their study of Spanish women entrepreneurs, for example, Díaz García and Welter's (2013) described women engaging in a host of behaviors to both support existing gender differences, and to draw attention to their unique expertise and contributions, ultimately to establish themselves as leaders. Similarly, Lewis (2013) showed women entrepreneurs either rejecting a "masculine" approach to work, accentuating their femininity, or emphasizing their professionalism as ways to exercise their leadership while preserving their self-authenticity.

The idea that women pursue leadership positions for reasons comparable to men's, and that they share similar needs and ambitions, also has been problematized. To illustrate, Jennings and Brush (2013), in summarizing the various ways in which gender influences entrepreneurial intention and action, showed that women may be driven by different motives (compared to their men counterparts) in their entrepreneurial efforts—including starting their firms to achieve better work-family balance (see also Powell and Eddleston 2008, Eddleston and Powell 2012, Powell and Greenhaus 2012).

On the whole, emerging research embraces leadership as a socially-embedded process. Thus, differences in how men and women lead, and the reasons why, are attributed to a host of closely interconnected social and individual factors, including how individuals express and negotiate their gender (Eagly and Karau 2002).

Challenges and Opportunities for the Future

Women continue to rise in their roles as leaders. The 2016 candidacy of Hillary Clinton as president of the United States, constituted a rudimentary but telling indicator of some of the remarkable strides women have made rising through the ranks of organizations—political as well as others. Despite important advancements, however, "...the perpetual question remains: Why aren't there more women leaders?" (Eagly and Hellman 2016, 349)

The answer to this question is clearly not simple (as attested by the myriad of articles and books on the topic). On the whole, however, research shows that environments of organizations and institutions tend to be more "masculinized"—a characteristic that inherently creates obstacles (practical and psychological) for women (e.g., Jennings and Brush 2013, Marlow and McAdam 2015). While on the whole these obstacles have decreased since the 1980s, those that remain reflect the way that leaders are recruited and selected (through personal networks), and evaluated (using policies rooted in male norms such as task accomplishment and authoritarian control). These, in effect, manifest a subtle "glass ceiling," which the still comparatively small number and slow progress of women reaching the corporate boardrooms and executive suite of Fortune 500 companies reflects.

This glass ceiling, defined as preconceptions, stereotypes, or assumptions those in power hold about women and their abilities and/or commitment to careers (Smith 2000), inhibits progress. For example, if it is perceived that a fast-track young woman will be likely to become pregnant, she may be passed over for a promotion. Similarly, if a woman who leads a fast-growth high-technology company is seen as not capable of making tough decisions, she may not receive any equity financing to grow her venture. The fact that only 15 percent of venture capital funded businesses between 2011–2013 had one woman on the executive team (an increase from 5 percent in 1999), and only 2.7 percent of the 6,793 invested companies had a woman CEO speaks volumes about ongoing perceptions of women's leadership capabilities. Further, the number of women partners in the venture capital industry has declined from 10 percent to 8 percent over the same period (Brush et al. 2014).

To make matters worse, research shows that the relatively small percentage of women who do break through the glass ceiling are likely to take on precarious and arguably risky leadership positions (Ryan and Haslam 2005, 2007)—something also known as "the glass cliff." Over the past decade, the glass cliff has largely been framed as a problem that pertains to women, rather than explored as men being favored for specific high-potential leadership positions. Thus, one possible way to "…get women off the glass cliff may be to start focusing our attention on men's privileged access to the glass cushion" (Ryan et al. 2016, 453).

For progress to continue, misguided perceptions and stereotypes must ultimately be dismantled. Scholars may contribute to this end with research that takes contextualized views of leadership, looking closely at the opportunities and constraints that influence leaders' actions. This may involve attending both across and within gender differences (Eddelston and Powell 2012), as well as reporting on possible non-differences. Much work still lies ahead. The growing incidence, impact, and strength of women business leaders and entrepreneurs (which are only expected to increase over time) motivate us, and indicate that the field is ripe for more promising research work.

Further Reading

AACSB. (2013). Degrees conferred percentage by gender, level, and region. Retrieved June 14, 2016, from http://www.aacsb.edu/knowledge/data/frequently-requested/degrees-conferred/degrees-by-gender

Bem, S. (1993). *The lenses of gender.* New Haven, CT: Yale University Press.

Bennis, W. & Nanus, B. (1985). *Leaders: Strategies for taking charge.* New York: Harper & Row.

Bird, B. J. & Brush, C. G. (2002). A gendered perspective on organizational creation. *Entrepreneurship Theory & Practice, 26*(3), 41–65.

Book, E. W. (2000). *Why the best man for the job is a woman.* New York: HarperCollins.

Brush, C. G. (1992). Research on women business owners: Past trends, a new perspective, and future directions. *Entrepreneurship Theory and Practice, 16*(4), 5–30.

Brush, C. G. (1998). A resource perspective on women's entrepreneurship: Research, relevance, and recognition. *Proceedings of the Organization for Economic Cooperation and Development Conference on Women Entrepreneurs in Small and Medium-Sized Enterprises.* Paris, France.

Brush, C. (1999). Women's entrepreneurship. *Proceedings of the Second International Labor Organization Enterprise Forum*. Geneva, Switzerland

Brush, C. G. & Edelman, L. F. (2000). Women entrepreneurs opportunities for database research. *Databases for the Study of Entrepreneurship, 4,* 445–484.

Brush, C.G.; Greene, P.G.; Balachandra, L.; & Davis, A. (2014). *The Diana Report Women Entrepreneurs 2014: Bridging the Gender Gap in Venture Capital*. Wellesley, MA: Babson College

Bureau of Labor Statistics. (2015). *Women in the Labor Force: A Databook. Report 1059*. Retrieved June 14, 2016, from www.bls.gov

Calas, M. & Smirchich, L. (1992). Re-writing gender into organization theorizing: Directions for feminist perspectives. In M. Reed & M. Hughes (Eds.), *Re-thinking organizations: New directions for organizational research*. London: Sage

Carter, N., & Williams, M. (2003). Comparing social feminism and liberal feminism: The case of new firm growth. In J. Butler (Ed.), *Women entrepreneurs: A volume in research in entrepreneurship and management* (pp. 25–50). Greenwich, CT: Information Age Publishing.

Catalyst. *Catalyst Census: Fortune 500*. New York: Catalyst, December 10, 2013.

Catalyst. *2015 Catalyst Census: Women and Men Board Directors*. New York: Catalyst, 2016.

Catalyst. *Pyramid: Women in S&P 500 Companies*. New York: Catalyst, June 14, 2016.

De la Rey, C. (2005). Gender, women and leadership. *Agenda, 19*(65), 4–11.

Díaz García, M. C. & Welter, F. (2013). Gender identities and practices: Interpreting women entrepreneurs' narratives. *International Small Business Journal, 31*(4), 384–404.

Donnell, S. M. & Hall, J. (1980). Men and women as managers: A significant case of no significant difference. *Organizational Dynamics, 8*(4), 60–77.

Dubrin, A. (2001). *Leadership: Research finding, practice, and skills* (3rd ed.). Boston: Houghton-Mifflin

Eagly, A. H. & Heilman, M. E. (2016). Gender and leadership: Introduction to the special issue. *The Leadership Quarterly, 3*(27), 349-353.

Eagly, A. H. & Karau, S. J. (2002). Role congruity theory of prejudice toward female leaders. *Psychological review, 109*(3), 573.

Eagly, A. H. & Johannesen-Schmidt, M. C. (2001). The leadership styles of women and men. *Journal of social issues, 57*(4), 781-797.

Eagly, A. & Johnson, B. (1990). Gender and leadership style-a meta-analysis. *Psychological Bulletin, 108,* 233–256

Eddleston, K. A. & Powell, G. N. (2012). Nurturing entrepreneurs' work–family balance: A gendered perspective. *Entrepreneurship Theory and Practice, 36*(3), 513-541.

Envick, B. (1998). Behaviors of entrepreneurs: A gender comparison. *Journal of Business and Entrepreneurship* 106–115.

Foschi, M. (2000). Double standards for competence: Theory and research. *Annual Review of Sociology,* 26:21.

Gilligan, C. (1982). *In a different voice: Psychological theory and women's development*. Cambridge, MA: Harvard University Press

Goleman, D. (2004). What makes a leader? *Harvard Business Review, 82*(1), 82–91.

Grant, J. (1988). Women as managers: What can they offer organizations? *Organizational Dynamics,* 16, 56–63.

Greene, P. G.; Brush, C. G.; Hart, M.; & Saparito, P. (2001). Patterns of venture capital funding: Is gender a factor? *Venture Capital Journal, 3*(1), 63–83.

Greer, M. & Greene, P. (2003). Feminist theory and the study of entrepreneurship. In J. Butler (Ed.), *Women Entrepreneurs: A Volume in Research in Entrepreneurship and Management* (pp. 1–24). Greenwich, CT: Information Age Publishing.

Haslam, S.A. & Ryan, M.K. (2008) The road to the glass cliff: Differences in the perceived suitability of men and women for leadership positions in succeeding and failing organizations. *The Leadership Quarterly,* 19:5, 530–546

Helgesen. S. (1990). *The female advantage: Women's ways of leadership*. New York: Currency/Doubleday

Henning, M. & Jardim, A. (1977). *The managerial woman*. Garden City, NY: Anchor Press/Doubleday.

Jennings, J. E. & Brush, C. G. (2013). Research on women entrepreneurs: challenges to (and from) the broader entrepreneurship literature?. *The Academy of Management Annals, 7*(1), 663–715.

Kotter, J. P. (2001). What leaders really do. *Harvard Business Review, 71*(11), 3–11

Kushell, E. & Newton, R. (1986). Gender, leadership style, and subordinate satisfaction: An experiment. *Sex Roles, 14*(3-4), 203–209.

Korabik, K.; Baril, G. L.; & Watson, C. (1993). Managers' conflict management style and leadership effectiveness: The moderating effects of gender. *Sex roles, 29*(5–6), 405-420.

Lanaj, K. & Hollenbeck, J. R. (2015). Leadership over-emergence in self-managing teams: The role of gender and countervailing biases. *Academy of Management Journal, 58*(5), 1476-1494.

Lewis, P. (2013). The search for an authentic entrepreneurial identity: Difference and professionalism among women business owners. *Gender, Work & Organization, 20*(3), 252-266.

Maier, M. (1992). Evolving paradigms of management in organization: A gendered analysis. *Journal of Management Systems, 4*(10), 29–45.

Mintzberg, H. (1973). *The nature of managerial work.* New York: Harper & Row

Marlow, S. & McAdam, M. (2015). Incubation or induction? Gendered identity work in the context of technology business incubation. Entrepreneurship Theory and Practice, *39*(4), 791–816.

National Women's Business Council. (2014). Building Bridges: Leveraging Research and Relationships to Impact the Business Climate for Women, Annual Report. Retrieved April 5, 2015, from https://www .nwbc.gov/sites/default/files/Building%20Bridges.pdf

NAWBO. (2014). State of women-owned businesses. Retrieved April 5, 2015, from https://nawbo.org/sites /nawbo/files/2014_state_of_women-owned_businesses.pdf

Powell. G. (1990). One more time: Do female and male managers differ? *Academy of Management Executive, 4*(3), 68–75.

Powel, G., & Graves, L. (2003). Women & men in management (3rd ed.). Thousand Oaks, CA: Sage

Powell, G. N. & Eddleston, K. A. (2008). The paradox of the contented female business owner. Journal of Vocational Behavior, *73*(1), 24-36.

Powell, G. N. & Greenhaus, J. H. (2012). When family considerations influence work decisions: Decision-making processes. Journal of Vocational Behavior, *81*(3), 322-329.

Ridgeway, C. L. & Correll, S.J. (2000). Limiting inequality through interaction: The end(s) of gender. In *Contemporary Sociology,* (Vol. 29, pp. 110–120). American Sociological Association.

Rosener, J. (1995). *America's competitive secret: Utilizing women as management strategy.* New York: Oxford University Press

Rosener, J. (1990). Ways women lead. *Harvard Business Review, 68*(6), 119–120.

Ryan, M. K. et al. (2016). Getting on top of the glass cliff: Reviewing a decade of evidence, explanations, and impact. *The Leadership Quarterly, 27,* 446–455.

Ryan, M. K. & Haslam, S. A. (2007). The glass cliff: Exploring the dynamics surrounding the appointment of women to precarious leadership positions. *Academy of Management Review, 32*(2), 549-572.

Ryan, M. K. & Haslam, S. A. (2005). The glass cliff: Evidence that women are over-represented in precarious leadership positions. *British Journal of Management, 16*(2), 81–90.

Schein, V. (1973). The relationship between sex role stereotypes and requisite management characteristics. *Journal of Applied Psychology, 57,* 95–100.

Smith, D. (2000). Gender and leadership style. In D. Smith (Ed.), *Women at work: Leadership for the next century.* Upper Saddle River, NJ: Prentice Hall.

Tannenbaum, R. & Schmidt, W. (1958). How to choose a leadership pattern. *Harvard Business Review, 36*(2), 95–102.

Tong, R. (1989). *Feminist Thought: Comprehensive Introduction.* San Francisco, CA: Westview.

The Evolution of Women Leaders in the Film Industry

Donna HALPER
Lesley University

While the movie industry has depended on visionary and hard-hitting leaders to usher films into production, not all of these visionaries were men. Some women innovators were written out of history, while others were able to make inroads in this highly competitive environment. A growing number have also taken advantage of the rise of independent filmmaking and new media outlets, helping to change the status quo that has existed in Hollywood since its inception.

In 2016, the Women's Media Center, a non-partisan organization founded in 2005 to raise the visibility, viability, and decision-making power of women and girls in media, released the results of a ten-year study of gender and Oscar nominations. The data showed that from 2006–2015, nominations of women accounted for just 19 percent of all non-acting nominations (327 women compared to 1,387 men). The Oscars, awarded by the Academy of Motion Picture Arts and Sciences, offer prestige and high-profile recognition to their winners and their nominees. The lack of representation of women among Oscar nominees over the last decade both demonstrates and contributes to women's under-representation in behind-the-scenes roles in film—particularly those with the greatest decision-making power (Women's Media Center 2016).

The lack of adequate participation by women in the movie industry is not new; it is a problem that has gone on for more than a century. Women have served in a number of key roles in movie-making, yet their contributions have often been minimized or ignored. And yet, since the dawn of the film industry, there were important women who demonstrated leadership and who served as role models for the women who came after them. When the women's movement of the 1960s brought new interest to feminist scholarship, efforts were made to revisit some of the pioneering women of early film. In 1972, the first International Festival of Women's Films was held in New York City; it featured 120 films, some classics and some contemporary, all made by women. But most film critics, who were overwhelmingly white and male, did not show much enthusiasm for the idea, and they ignored the event (Rosen 1972, 31).

Today, there is more attention being paid by film historians to the contributions women have made to the movie industry. But it wasn't until the 1990s when many film history textbooks began to give more than a passing mention to the role of women in the industry; and to this day, many of the female pioneers remain forgotten or underappreciated, while contemporary women in film, including actresses in blockbuster hit movies, still do not receive the recognition (or the compensation) given to their male counterparts (Rogers 2015).

In the Beginning

Five men created the Hollywood system—Carl Laemmle, Adolph Zukor, William Fox, Louis B. Mayer, and Benjamin Warner—and developed the first film studios which still operate today (Universal Pictures, Paramount, Fox, MGM, and Warner Brothers respectively). Although they did not know each other before arriving in Hollywood, it is striking how much they had in common: they were predominantly Jewish immigrants or sons of recent immigrants of Eastern European origin. Most of their relatives were in retail businesses so that they had some basic familiarity with the concept of public taste, merchandising, market swings, and competition. They were eager to assimilate in an anti-Semitic and xenophobic post-World War I American climate.

> Something drove them to a ferocious, even pathological, embrace of
> America . . .[and] to deny whatever they had been before settling here. . .within
> the studios and on the screen, they could simply create a new country—an empire
> of their own, so to speak—one where they would not only be admitted, but would
> govern as well. They would fabricate their empire in the image of America as they
> would fabricate themselves in the image of prosperous Americans. They would
> create its values and myths, its traditions and archetypes. It would be an America
> where fathers were strong, families stable, people attractive, resilient, resourceful
> and decent. This was their America, and its invention may be their most enduring
> legacy. (Gabler 1998, 4–6)

But while the founders of the American film industry were men (and in other countries, the same was true—for example, the French film industry was created by such innovators as Auguste and Louis Lumière and Georges Méliès), women were there almost from the beginning, serving not just as hair stylists and costume designers but as actresses, directors, and screenwriters. In fact, screenwriting would become an especially welcoming profession during the movie industry's formative decades: half of all films copyrighted between 1911 and 1925 were written by women (Beauchamp 1997, 11).

The first female director was Alice Guy (later Alice Guy Blaché), whose career began at the Gaumont Studios in France, where she started as the secretary to studio owner Léon Gaumont. She directed her first short feature, "La Fée aux Choux," in 1896, and during the period from 1896 through 1905, she directed every film that came from Gaumont Studios (Slide 1996, 16). As a result of her prolific output, many historians today acknowledge her as a pioneer in the development of narrative storytelling (Taubin, 2010, 54). Determining the exact number of films she directed during her long career, first in France and later in the United States (where from 1910–1914, she ran her own studio, Solax, the first woman to do so), has been problematic, however, since most of her work has not survived. Film historians estimate she may have been involved with as many as one thousand films (Kilston 2010, 155). While most of them were silent, she was also an early experimenter with sound (McBane 2006, 187), and she experimented with hand-tinted color at a time when most films were black-and-white (Taubin 2010, 54).

Another female innovator during the film industry's early days was Lois Weber. A former evangelist, singer, and theater actress, she was encouraged by her husband, actor and director Phillips Smalley, to get involved with the movie industry. Weber first worked as a scriptwriter before becoming a director. By 1912, she and her husband were the heads of production for the Rex Company, a subsidiary of Universal Pictures, where she wrote, directed, and even starred in a number of films (Slide 1996, 33). It was a time of transition for moviemaking, as films were now longer and more complex, featuring intricate plots and more thought-provoking stories. Weber soon became well respected for her skill in advancing conventions of filmmaking, as well as for her willingness to explore controversial subject matter such as birth control, religious hypocrisy, adultery, and domestic violence. And while romance was often part of the plot, her female characters did not always adhere to the stereotypical gender norms of that era (Stamp 2015, 30–31). Among those who sang her praises was Carl Laemmle, head of Universal Studios, who once said that he always trusted Weber's instincts and willingly gave her the budget she asked for when making a movie because "[s]he knows the Motion Picture business as few people do" (Slide 1996, 39).

When silent films transitioned into the talking-picture era and tastes began to change, Weber was unable to duplicate her previous success. But another female director was gaining critical acclaim during this time —Dorothy Arzner, whose directing career included four silent films and thirteen sound features, during the period between 1927–1943. In her personal life, she was more unconventional than Lois Weber or Alice Guy Blaché, both of whom were married and worked closely with their husbands. Arzner never married, nor did she adopt the typical mode of dress for women of her day—she preferred to wear pants, and kept her hair in a boyish style. And while her sexual orientation was never openly discussed, she lived with a female companion, choreographer Marion Morgan, for forty years (Thompson 2015). But her non-conformity did not impede a career that included such achievements as directing Clara Bow, Katherine Hepburn, Joan Crawford, and Lucille Ball. The men who ran Hollywood had very definite, and very stereotypical, ideas about what the female audience wanted, and Arzner was often expected to make "women's pictures," yet she was able to transcend the stereotypes and create compelling plots with interesting female protagonists. Although she always denied encountering discrimination (Slide 1996, 111), she did acknowledge that more was expected of her as Hollywood's only female director. She told one reporter that "…I knew if I failed [to make a successful picture], I did not have the kind of fraternity men had one for another to support me" (Rosen 1972, 34). Arzner was also the first woman admitted to the Directors Guild of America, in 1937.

But despite the groundbreaking work of Guy Blaché, Weber, Arzner, and several others—including Frances Marion, the first woman to win an Academy Award for screenwriting in 1930 and the author of more than three hundred Hollywood movie scripts during her career (Beauchamp 1997, 11)—these pioneering women were written out of film history for generations. The reasons are not surprising: in a culture were power and authority were gendered masculine, the accomplishments of men were considered more important and more newsworthy.

From the beginning of Hollywood, leadership was connected to the perception that the audience shared a gendered belief that men were the stars, the brave onscreen heroes who rescued the damsel in distress or won the war or made the important decisions. A number of women in the studio system became successful actresses, but their main purpose in the typical film was to be beautiful and to serve as the object of the male star's desire. As feminist scholar Laura Mulvey has pointed out, Hollywood films have historically been told from the male perspective, thus making the female the subject of the "male gaze." The action in the story is his, while she is there to be acted upon, and her role has often been written to maximize an erotic impact (Sassatelli 2011, 123–124). With few exceptions, female characters were rarely permitted to be independent, and a happy "Hollywood ending" was when they found the right man to marry. The moguls who ran Hollywood in its golden age reflected and promoted the patriarchal myth of the powerful and successful man—someone who owned lavish homes and glamorous cars, knew all the right people, and had his pick of beautiful women.

Meanwhile, as the concept of the director as "auteur" was gendered masculine, this marginalized the work of Arzner and other women (Stevens 2015). It also meant that the women still trying to break into directing would find it increasingly difficult to get budgets from the major studios. This is what happened to Ida Lupino, a popular Hollywood actress during the 1940s. When she decided in the late 1940s that she wanted to direct, the only way for her to do so was to start her own independent production company. And now that Dorothy Arzner had left to work in academia, Lupino was Hollywood's only female director. Her films were low-budget and critical reviews were mixed, but she made her presence felt, directing six feature films from 1949—1953. And like Lois Weber had done years before, Lupino explored controversial social issues, including rape, bigamy, and unwed motherhood (Georgakas 2000, 32). She enjoyed directing, but noted that female directors had unique challenges, such as the need to win over a skeptical male crew which was unaccustomed to taking orders from a woman (Flint 1995, 10).

Leadership Spheres in Modern Hollywood

There are three primary spheres within contemporary Hollywood that are pertinent to a discussion of where and how leadership exists within the industry. The first is the business itself: the studios (which finance and distribute much of the world's feature films), producers, and talent agencies. The second is the "talent." The third is the film set, with the director at the top. In each of these spheres, men (and usually white men) have played the dominant role, although in recent years there has been considerable discussion and debate about sexism, discrimination, and how to make the industry more inclusive and reflective of the contemporary world.

The second arena involves the talent: the writers, directors, and actors who regularly think up ideas for films and are responsible for putting them on screen. Even though they often have no intention of being leaders, these people can take on leadership roles in the community. This is especially true of movie stars: because of their popularity and their celebrity status, they often are given a platform they might not have had otherwise. For example, actress Anne Hathaway has long been an advocate for gay rights, and actress/director Natalie Portman has frequently spoken out on behalf of environmental causes and the protection of wildlife.

The third sphere of leadership is the film set, whose hierarchy places the director at the top. Whether or not this director actually is or remains the leader for the duration of production largely depends on his/her leadership abilities and how much power the movie stars, the studio executives, and the producers have. Aside from his or her talent, a director's passion, clarity of vision, and ability to make decisions (even if they turn out to be wrong) are perhaps the most important traits when it comes to inspiring and leading on the set. But as some successful women in Hollywood have found, whenever a woman is in charge, there is an extra level of complexity she must navigate: since most bosses historically have been men, the norms of management have long been based on masculine modes of communication. Thus, even today, women need to find a style that is natural to them, without seeming as if they are trying to be "one of the boys."

Hollywood's Women Executives

Nearly all of the studios in Hollywood (and in other countries as well) were historically run by men, although Alice Guy Blaché's Solax Studio was one exception. The women who were able to carve out their own niche in Hollywood as actresses, screenwriters, or directors did so knowing there was just so far they could rise. That did not change until 1980, when Sherry Lansing became the president of film production at 20th Century Fox, the first woman to ever hold such a key post at a major studio. As was still typical of that time, the newspapers focused as much on her physical appearance as they did on her qualifications, noting that Lansing was an attractive women with "flowing dark hair, a come-hither stare, and high cheekbones" (Baltake 1980, B-7). But Lansing was much more than a pretty face; she had astute business sense and knew which kinds of stories would resonate with large audiences. As a partner in the production company of Jaffe/Lansing, she was instrumental in such blockbuster hits as "Fatal Attraction," "Indecent Proposal," and "The Accused." In 1992, she became chairman of Paramount Pictures' Motion Picture Group, a post she held for twelve years. During her tenure, Paramount produced some of the industry's biggest hits, including "Forrest Gump," "Braveheart," and "Titanic." In addition to being a successful Hollywood executive, Lansing has consistently used her position of power to raise money for countless charities. After leaving the movie industry, she started a foundation devoted to cancer research.

One area of the film industry where women have found success is in producing. According to a 2012 study conducted by the *Los Angeles Times,* only 18 percent of the members in the producers' branch of the Academy of Motion Picture Arts and Sciences (AMPAS) are female; but that is a much higher percentage than the number of women directors, writers, or cinematographers. And the women working as producers have been involved with such major hits as "E.T.," "The Color Purple," "12 Years a Slave," and "Zero Dark Thirty." Producing is a multi-faceted job that encompasses everything from optioning manuscripts to hiring screenwriters, managing budgets, getting financing, and finding the right talent (Sperling 2014, 32). Among the most successful women working as producers is Kathleen Kennedy, whose career blossomed after she went to work for Steven Spielberg in the late 1970s. By 1981, she had started her own production company, and in the years that followed, she produced more than sixty films; in addition to working with Spielberg, she has collaborated with such directors as Martin Scorsese, Clint Eastwood, and Robert Zemeckis. In 2012, she was named president of LucasFilm, as well as the brand manager for the Star Wars franchise.

But despite the success of individual women in Hollywood, including director Kathryn Bigelow, who became the first woman to win an Academy Award for Best Director in 2009, Hollywood remains overwhelmingly male-dominated. A study done by the Women's Media Center showed that in 2014, 85 percent of films had no female directors, 80 percent had no female writers, 33 percent had no female producers, 78 percent had no female editors and 92 percent had no female cinematographers (Lang 2015, "Women"). And a 2016 analysis of twenty-three independent film festivals, done by the Center for the Study of Television and Film, showed that women are more likely to direct documentaries than narrative films—35 percent of documentaries had a female director, as opposed to only 19 percent of narrative films (Lauzen 2016). On the other hand, for up-and-coming directors, independent film festivals provide an opportunity to have audiences and film critics see their work, and a good reaction can lead to wider distribution. A good example is the 2010 indie hit "Winter's Bone," directed by Debra Granik, produced by Anne Rosellini, and starring Jennifer Lawrence. The film was well received at the Sundance Film Festival, and it ultimately received four Academy Award nominations in 2011.

One area of the movie industry where improvements are still greatly needed is participation by women of color. While Hollywood has been criticized for the scarcity of good roles for actresses of color, there are even fewer opportunities for black women who want to be directors. A 2016 study from the University of Southern California's Annenberg School for Communication and Journalism found that "out of 407 directors who premiered major movies and shows during 2014–2015, only 53 were people of color. And only two, Amma Asante and Ava DuVernay, were black women" (Strachan 2016). Often, women of color find that even when they make a successful or critically acclaimed film, as Julie Dash did with her 1991 independent work "Daughters of the Dust," which won an award for excellence in cinematography at Sundance, it never leads to a motion-picture deal. Dash has also noted that Hollywood executives seem to expect black filmmakers to only do stories about specific topics, such as the civil rights movement. Lacking opportunities to make Hollywood movies, Dash and others have focused on productions for cable television and even on making music videos.

In order for women to continue to lead and to change the status quo in Hollywood, more attention must be paid to the subject matter of film. There have been a few positive signs over the past decade in increasing the presence of women on screen: One good example is happening at Walt Disney Pictures, which (after decades of animated features with stereotypical plots about the courageous Prince Charming seeking to rescue his beautiful but helpless princess) has begun offering young movie-goers female characters who are not passively waiting for their hero to arrive. In the 2012 movie "Brave," Princess Merida was the one doing the choosing and the rescuing, and in the 2013 movie "Frozen," directed by Jennifer Lee (who also wrote the screenplay), both Princess Elsa and Princess Anna were actively involved in advancing the plot and resolving the challenges they face. Also presenting positive female role models are movies like the 2014 fantasy/science fiction hit film "The Hunger Games." But while the presence of strong female characters is encouraging, the overall number of females in leading roles has not increased; only 12 percent of the protagonists in the top-grossing 2014 films were women (Lang 2015, "Study").

Studies repeatedly show that women comprise the majority of movie-goers, yet Hollywood's overwhelmingly male executives still prefer to produce action-adventure films featuring strong male protagonists; this continues their belief that men do not want to see a "women's movie" but women will see an action-adventure. In order for this mindset to change, it will become increasingly important in the future for Hollywood's women directors and studio executives to advocate for more interesting and varied plots for female characters.

Further Reading

Baltake, J. (1980, February 7). 20th Century-Fox production chief is aware of the woman's role. *Lexington Herald*, p. B-7.

Beauchamp, C. (1997). *Without lying down: Frances Marion and the powerful women of early Hollywood*. Berkeley, California: University of California Press.

Flint, Peter B. (1995, August 5). Ida Lupino, film actress and director, is dead at 77. *New York Times*, p. 10.

Gabler, N. (1988). *An empire of their own: How the Jews invented Hollywood*. New York: Anchor Books/Random House.

Georgakas, D. (2000). Ida Lupino: Doing it her way. *Cineaste*, Vol. 25, issue 3, pp. 32–36.

Halper, D. L. (2014). *Invisible stars: A social history of women in American broadcasting* (2nd ed.). Armonk, NY: M.E. Sharpe.

Harp, D. (2007). *Desperately seeking women readers*. Lanham, Maryland: Lexington Books.

Kilston, L. (2010). Alice Guy Blaché. *Art in America*, vol. 98, issue 5, pp. 155–156.

Lang, B. (2015, February 9). Study finds fewer lead roles for women in Hollywood. *Variety*. Retrieved June 17, 2016, from http://variety.com/2015/film/news/women-lead-roles-in-movies-study-hunger -games-gone-girl-1201429016

Lang, B. (2015, October 27). Women comprise 7 percent of directors on top 250 films (Study). *Variety*. Retrieved June 17, 2016, from http://variety.com/2015/film/news/women-hollywood-inequality-directors -behind-the-camera-1201626691

Lauzen, M. M. (2016). Women in independent film. Center for the Study of Women in Television and Film. Retrieved June 17, 2016, from http://womenintvfilm.sdsu.edu/files/2016 percent20Indepen-dent_Women_Report.pdf

Linson, A. (1993). *A pound of flesh: Perilous tales of how to produce movies in Hollywood*. New York: Grove Press.

McBane, B. (2006). Imagining sound in the Solax Films of Alice Guy Blaché. *Film History*, vol. 18, no. 2, pp. 185–195.

McMahan, A. (2002). *Alice Guy Blaché: Lost visionary of the cinema*. New York: Continuum.

Merritt, G. (2000). *Celluloid mavericks: A history of American independent film*. New York: Thunder's Mouth Press.

Morton, E. (2015, July 8). Dorothy Arzner, hidden star maker of Hollywood's golden age. *Atlas Obscura*, Retrieved June 17, 2016, from http://www.atlasobscura.com/articles/dorothy-arzner-hidden-star -maker-of-hollywood-s-golden-age

Phillips, J. (1991). *You'll never eat lunch in this town again*. New York: New American Library.

Rensin, D. (2003). *The mailroom: Hollywood history from the bottom up*. New York: Ballantine Books.

Rogers, K. (2015, October 13). Jennifer Lawrence speaks out against gender pay inequality. *New York Times*. Retrieved June 17, 2016, from http://www.nytimes.com/2015/10/14/arts/jennifer-lawrence-speaks -out-against-gender-pay-inequality.html

Rosen, M. (1972, August 12). Women, their films, and their festivals. *Saturday Review*, pp. 31–36.

Sassatelli, R. (2011, September). Interview with Laura Mulvey: Gender, gaze and technology in film culture. *Theory, Culture & Society*, vol. 28, no. 5, pp. 123–143.

Slide, A. (1996). *The silent feminists: America's first women directors*. Lanham, Maryland: Scarecrow Press.

Sperling, N. (2014, October 10). Successful female directors are still a rarity in Hollywood. *Entertainment Weekly*, pp. 32–34.

Stamp, S. (2015). *Lois Weber in Early Hollywood*. Oakland, California: University of California Press.

Stevens, I. (2015, October). Women with a movie camera. *Sight & Sound*, vol. 25, Issue 10. Retrieved June 17, 2016, from http://www.bfi.org.uk/news-opinion/sight-sound-magazine/features/pictures/women-movie -camera

Strachan, M. (2016, February 26). What it's like to be a black woman in white Hollywood. *Huffington Post*. Retrieved June 17, 2016, from http://www.huffingtonpost.com/entry/female-black-directors -hollywood_us_56cfbde9e4b0bf0dab31a4b9

Taubin, A. (2010). Coming up on the outside: Male directors are so last year. *Film Comment*, Vol. 46, issue 1, pp. 54–55.

The female gaze: 100 overlooked films directed by women. (2015, October). *Sight & Sound*, vol. 25, issue 10, pp. 18–37. Retrieved June 17, 2016, from http://www.bfi.org.uk/news-opinion/sight-sound-magazine /october-2015-issue

Thompson, H. (2015, July 13). Why was one of Hollywood's first female film directors, Dorothy Arzner, forgotten? *Smithsonian.com*. Retrieved June 17, 2016, from http://www.smithsonianmag.com/smart -news/1920s-dorothy-arzner-paved-way-female-directors-today-180955904

WMC investigation: 10-year analysis of gender and Oscar nominations. (2016). Women's Media Center. Retrieved June 17, 2016, from http://wmc.3cdn.net/440567c9ba6cd7b984_5am6ihlui.pdf

Women and Leadership in Literature

Claudia M. HUIZA
National University

Despite limited access to education, leisure time, recognition, and opportunities to be published, women have contributed to world literature since the flourishing of the earliest civilizations. The women's movement has helped to bring more of these writers to light, especially those from underrepresented communities and from developing countries. Despite an endless variety of themes and subject matter, the writing of women is shown to question the status quo and challenge oppression.

Although the world's earliest-known writer (Enheduanna, c. 2300 BCE) was a woman, women's literature has often been disregarded or trivialized, at least until the twentieth century's feminist wave focused more attention on it. From ancient Greece's Sappho to contemporary authors from the developing world, the subjects, styles, and stories are varied; women's literature, however, often does challenge boundaries and confront oppression. In this way, women found a voice and ways to influence their societies without necessarily having the opportunity to assume roles of leadership.

Historically, women have both penned and been the subject of literary works since ancient times, but their relationship to the literary realm has been mediated by their struggle to become literate—to be able to write, read, and critique literary works—and by their insufficient participation in the production process. They have largely been stereotyped or downright ignored, and rarely presented as autonomous agents of history. Furthermore, women writers historically have been marginalized by their male counterparts, and many of their works either remain unacknowledged or tokenized by literary critics. With the rise of the global women's movement, and the feminist movements in the West in the last millennium, male and female scholars alike are rediscovering and celebrating foundational works of women's literary production from ancient times to the present.

Ancient Women Writers

Some of the earliest writings and evidence of women's literacy have been found in excavations of the ancient cities and cultural centers of Egypt, Mesopotamia, Greece, Asia, and the Americas. The earliest known female writer, and the earliest known author, Enheduanna, lived and wrote around 2300 BCE, in an area that is today part of Iraq. She was an Acadian writer, priestess, poet, and princess, daughter to King Sargon I of Akkad, who created the first historical empire. The paucity of writing about this important author and poet as well as her exclusion from world literature and women's literature anthologies is not surprising given that her works have only recently resurfaced. All of the artifacts upon which translations of Enheduanna's work are based come from the old Babylonian period nearly a half millennium after her existence, and include at least two and possibly three major hymns directed to the goddess Inanna, the goddess of battle.

Although no evidence has been unearthed so far of literary works written by ancient Egyptian women, they did have a goddess of writing—the goddess Seshat, the "female scribe." High-ranking or royal women, such as Neferura, the female pharaoh Hatshepsut's (reigned 1503–1482 BCE) daughter, were sometimes provided a private tutor.

The Greek poet Sappho, born toward the end of the seventh century BCE, during the Greek Archaic Period, remains one of the most well-known poets of all time. A native of the island of Lesbos, Sappho was one of the two (with Alcaeus) great leaders of the Aeolian school of lyric poetry. She was widely acclaimed for the originality of her brilliant lyric poetry and lived to be honored by her people for her literary gift; she was even referred to as the tenth muse.

The first recorded female playwright, Hroswitha of Gandersheim, was born in 932 CE to the Saxon aristocracy. She became a Benedictine cloister nun early in life and was known for her witty and farcical plays. A century later, Anna Comnena became the first known female historian. Born in 1083, Comnena detailed the reign of her father, Alexius I, and the exchanges between the Byzantines and western crusaders of the first crusades in her fifteen-volume history of her family, titled *Alexiad*. Comnena lived in an era when women chiefly were expected to remain secluded in their quarters (called *gyneceum*) attending solely to family matters. In her writings, however, it is evident that she was allowed to express her own thoughts and serve an important role in preserving her family's history.

In the realm of theology, composition, and visionary writing, Hildegard von Bingen, born in 1098, published the visionary *Scivias*. Known as "Sybil of the Rhine," she was highly revered for her treatises about natural history and medicinal uses of flora and fauna as well as minerals and stones. She founded several convents, and after beatification has been referred to as Saint Hildegard. She wrote, composed, and was a respected leader and wise woman at a time when few women were accorded these privileges.

Japanese writer Murasaki Shikibu is credited with writing the world's oldest novel and one of the finest, *The Tale of Genji*. Written in the Heian period (794–1185) in Japanese history, when prose and poetry by women scarcely existed in the West, the work followed a tradition of romances depicting life among the court nobility of Japan. Shikibu was born into the Fujiwara family, daughter of the governor of a province, who allowed her to study with her brother, even letting her learn some Chinese classics, which was considered improper for females at the time. In its length (more than one thousand pages in the English translation), complexity, realism, psychological depth, and literary distinction, *The Tale of Genji* is considered a masterpiece of Japanese literature.

The First Feminists

With the publication of her poetry in the fourteenth century, poet and philosopher Christine de Pizan became the first woman to earn her living through writing. She is widely believed to be the first feminist writer in the history of literature. Many of de Pisan's works urged that women be allowed to participate more fully in society. She also denounced the way women were portrayed in medieval literature. For example, in her long poem "Letter to the God of Love," she complained that women were often described as dishonest and unreliable. She openly criticized misogynous literature in a controversial debate known as the *Querelle des Femmes* (the women question), and is thought to have also inspired many British women writers who came after her.

Indeed, British women writers argued strongly for women's literacy, even as they were forced to use pen names so as to avoid scandal. The first known feminist argument published in English is credited to one Margaret Tyler, whose true identity remains a mystery. In 1578, Tyler argued that women have the same capacity to research and write as men do, and that they should be allowed not only to write, but also to choose their own subjects. A decade later, another writer who went by the pen name of Jane Anger became the first major female polemicist in English. In a lengthy tract called *Jane Anger: Her Protection for Women* (1589), she challenged the misogyny present in Elizabethan culture and asked, "Was there ever any so abused, so slaundered, so railed upon, or so wickedly handeled [*sic*] undeservedly, as are we women?" Other "first feminists," as the scholar Moira Ferguson calls them, include Aphra Behn, the first female British playwright and a spy for the British government; Mary Collier, author of *The Woman's Labour* (1739); Ann Cromartie Yearsley, author of "A Poem on the Inhumanity of the Slave-Trade" (1788); Catherine Sawbridge Macaulay Graham, who in 1790 published *Letters on Education*; and the most influential British feminist thinker of her time, Mary Wollstonecraft, who said, "It would be an endless task to trace the variety of meanness, cares and sorrows, into which women are plunged by the prevailing opinion, that they were created to feel than reason, and that all the power they obtain, must be obtained by their charms and weakness." Her persuasive and passionate call for human justice is exemplified in her most famous work, *A Vindication of the Rights of Woman*, written in 1792.

Following in the line of daughters of the nobility around the world who had access to literacy, the Indian poet Mira Bai, a devotee of Krishna and a princess who renounced her royal family, was the only female among the sixteenth-century Bhakti poets. Her poems celebrate women's songs and folk traditions, and are often directly addressed to a female friend or an audience of women. At a time when infringement of the rules of chastity, modesty, and seclusion for married women was an insult to the family of a noblewoman, her writings showed a remarkable sensuality and were considered to be quite subversive.

In the Americas, there is also a rich history of women authors that has only recently begun to be rediscovered and celebrated. Societal and cultural attitudes resulting from the legacy of colonization, genocide, and the undermining of indigenous people's traditions and values have led to a literary canon that is characterized by the inadequate representation of female-authored works. Of the autonomous ancient peoples of Mesoamerica, it is the Aztec princess Macuilxochitl "5-Flor"

(5-Flower) who stands as the lone female voice in a rare compilation of poems by thirteen Aztec poets published by Miguel León-Portilla, Mexico's leading indigenous scholar, in the 1960s. Daughter of the great adviser to seven Aztec emperors, Tlatoani Tlacaelel, Princess Macuilxochitl 5-Flor exemplifies the high status that the daughters of the ancient Aztec nobility could achieve. The first feminist, and undoubtedly the greatest poet of the Americas in the seventeenth century, the Mexican poet and Jesuit nun Juana Inés de la Cruz, was a self-taught woman of genius who spoke out against the injustices done to women and called for their education. She wrote secular lyrical poetry, of which her most famous are her *Redondillas*, as well as comedic plays that criticized the passive role that was expected of women in the Middle Ages and challenged the female archetypes in medieval literature. When she refused to stop writing secular works, she was forced by the archbishop to turn over her books, scientific instruments, and other possessions, and died of an unknown epidemic that swept her convent. She is often compared to the Greek Sappho and has influenced countless writers after her.

The 1800s and Early 1900s

The late eighteenth and nineteenth centuries saw a proliferation of publications by women. After centuries of calling for greater access to literacy and education, to legal rights and labor rights, the international women's struggle for human and civil rights intensified and reached new heights. An influential group of American women, including Elizabeth Cady Stanton and Lucretia Mott, composed the "Declaration of Sentiments and Resolutions," outlining the main issues and goals for the emerging women's movement, at the First Women's Rights Convention at Seneca Falls, New York, in 1848. In 1866, Elizabeth Cady Stanton and Susan B. Anthony formed the American Equal Rights Association, an organization for white and black women and men dedicated to the goal of universal suffrage. It was in this environment of division and cooperation that African-American women's writings began to proliferate. The works of these writers spanned several literary genres, including poetry, essays, short stories, histories, narratives (including slave narratives), autobiographies, novels, theological works, social criticism, and economic and philosophical treatises. Although the first known book of poetry by an African American, *Poems on Various Subjects, Religious and Moral* by Phillis Wheatley, appeared in 1773, it was not until the mid-nineteenth century that novels like Harriet Beecher Stowe's *Uncle Tom's Cabin* (1852) and *Our Nig* by Harriet Wilson (1859) appeared. Sojourner Truth once remarked, in reply to an allusion to the late Horace Greeley, "You call him a self-made man; well, I am a self-made woman." Indeed, what may be considered the first testimonial work by an African American woman, *The Narrative of Sojourner Truth: A Northern Slave,* a dictated memoir by Sojourner Truth, was published in 1850, and the first collection of essays by an African American, Ann Plato's *Essays,* was published in 1841.

Harriet Jacobs published her *Incidents in the Life of a Slave Girl* in 1861, though the book was thought to be written by a white woman until the rediscovery of Jacobs's works in the 1980s. Nancy Prince, who published *Narrative of the Life and Travels of Mrs. Nancy Prince* in 1850, provided the first autobiographical account of life as a free black woman in antebellum America. It is also an important contribution to the genre of autobiographical travelogues, since she documents her travels to Russia, Jamaica, and different parts of the United States over the course of eighteen years. Elizabeth Keckley, who wrote *Behind the Scenes, or, Thirty Years a Slave and Four Years in the White House* as a personal account of life in the White House, challenged the predominant stereotypes of women, and African American women in particular, in the nineteenth century. A friend and confidante of Mary Todd Lincoln, she was highly criticized for claiming that she was a friend of a white woman, and the wife of a president at that. The oldest son of President Lincoln, Robert Lincoln, waged a campaign against the book, and was successful in having it withdrawn from publication. Ellen Craft's amazing account of her and her husband's escape from slavery, *Running a Thousand Miles for Freedom*, detailed how she was able to pass as a white male in order to travel by train and boat with her husband, William Craft, posing as her slave. And since William's narrative voice actually tells the story, *Running* also shows how difficult it was, even for a woman bold and daring enough to escape slavery in this way, to find a public voice as a black woman. Indeed, like her disguise, which involved poultices that "muffled" her and allowed her to avoid conversation, Ellen's voice is given through the filter of William's perspective.

The mid-nineteenth century also saw the publication of one of the earliest precursors to contemporary Chicana (Mexican-American) literary tradition. With the publication of her novels *Who Would Have Thought It?* in 1885 and *The Squatter and the Don* (under the pseudonym C. Loyal) in 1872, Maria Amparo Ruiz de Burton became the first writer to publish a novel from the perspective of the Californios, the dispossessed population living in Alta California at the end of the US invasion of Mexico that began in 1846 and ended with the Treaty of Guadalupe-Hidalgo in 1848. Ruiz de Burton's novels and personal writings provide a scathing condemnation of the new rulers and the forms of ruling imposed upon the conquered population and give balance to mainstream histories of this period of American history.

In Spain, the nineteenth century produced the most celebrated female author of her time, and arguably one of Spain's most important literary figures. Emilia Pardo Bazán, born in 1852, was a Spanish countess who wrote over five hundred short stories and essays, more than forty novels, and seven plays. Of all her works, perhaps her best known piece is *La cuestión palpitante* ("The Critical Issue"), written in 1883. A polemical essay that discusses naturalism, it introduced the French and Russian literary movements to Spain and started an important literary controversy in which she championed the free will of the individual.

Born in 1882, Virginia Woolf, is credited, along with Marcel Proust and James Joyce, with developing a new kind of modernist prose, which she associated with female consciousness and with precise evocations of states of mind and body. A supporter of the suffrage and feminist movements, her famous extended essay, *A Room of One's Own*, examines the history of literature written by women and argues for women's economic independence and the privacy of a room in which to write.

Contemporary Women Writers

The French writer Simone de Beauvoir, with the publication of her book *The Second Sex* in 1953, is considered by some to have inspired the second wave of the feminist movement with her in-depth discussion of women's oppression and of their role as "other." Indeed, her comprehensive treatise on women weaves together history, philosophy, economics, and biology and postulates on the power of sexuality. The 1970s and 1980s were enormously important in feminist literary theory and women's studies, with major contributions by such writers as Hélène Cixous of France, Teresa De Lauretis of Italy, and Bengali exile Gayatri Chakravorty Spivak, among others. Then, in the late 1980s, women of color and women from Third World countries, such as Kumari Jayawardena of Sri Lanka, Chandra Talpade Mohanty of India and the United States, Paula Moya of the United States, Trinh T. Minh-ha of Vietnam and the United States, and Cherrie Moraga of the United States published powerful writings that theorized, challenged, and expanded discussions of feminist theory, LGBT/queer theory, black feminist theory and Chicana/Latina feminist theory, and enriched the fields of postcolonial and Third World women's literature.

Women writers in the twentieth and twenty-first centuries have continued to speak out against oppression, to redefine the boundaries of what are considered acceptable literary forms and subjects, and to gain more widespread recognition of their works. But the literary canon is still in need of revision that must insist upon the incorporation of women writers who have been ignored and omitted from literary history.

One example of such inclusiveness is Shirley Geok-Lin Lim and Norman A. Spencer's *One World of Literature*, originally published in 1993, which offers an array of twentieth-century male and female authors, and one of the most complete collections of full texts and excerpts by women writers from around the world. The anthology represents the works of brilliant female authors seldom known outside their own countries as well those known worldwide. According to the editors, "we live in an age in which an understanding of global cultures is more critical than ever. . . [W]e are all affected by individuals, events and ideas from other cultures and countries, a truth the late twentieth century has brought home to almost everyone." It is with this spirit in mind that works such as theirs are beginning to bring balance to a literary world where women's literacy, women's writing and its assessment, and the representation of women as autonomous subjects has tended to suffer under the weight of homogeneity, unilateralism, patriarchy, ethnocentrism, and the Western gaze.

Further Reading

Archer, L. J., Fischler, S., & Wyke, M. (Eds.). (1994). *Women in ancient societies: "An illusion of the night."* Basingstoke, U.K.: Macmillan.

Arkin, M., & Shollar, B. (Eds.). (1989). *Longman anthology of literature by women: 1875–1975.* New York: Longman.

Barnard, M. (1986). *Sappho: A new translation.* Berkeley: University of California Press.

Barnstone, A. B. & Barnstone, W. (Eds.). (1980). *A book of women poets: From antiquity to now.* New York: Schocken.

Bruner, C. H. (Ed.). (1983). *Unwinding threads: Writing by women in Africa.* London: Heinemann.

Brusky, S. (2000). The travels of William and Ellen Craft. *Prospects, 25,* 177–192.

Capel, A. K., Markoe, G. E., & Markoe, G. (Eds.). (1997). *Mistress of the house, mistress of heaven: Women in ancient Egypt.* New York: Hudson Hills.

Cranston, E. A. (1983). Heian literature. In *Kodansha Encyclopedia of Japan: Vol. 5. Literature* (p. 33). Tokyo: Kodansha.

Craft, W. (1860). *Running a thousand miles for freedom.* London: William Tweedie.

Damrosch, D. et al. (2004). *The Longman anthology of world literature* (Vols. A–C). New York: Longman.

Flores, A. & Flores, K. (1986). *Hispanic feminist poems from the Middle Ages to the present: A bilingual anthology.* New York: Feminist Press.

Gilbert, S. M. & Gubar, S. (1996). *The Norton anthology of literature by women: The traditions in English.* New York: Norton.

Hallo, W. W. (1968). Individual prayer in Sumerian: The continuity of a tradition. *Journal of the American Oriental Society, 88.*

Hallo, W. W. & Van Dijk, J. A. (1968). *The exaltation of Inanna.* New Haven, CT: Yale University Press.

Hirschfield, J. H. (1988). *The ink dark moon: Love poems by Ono No Komachi and Izumi Shikibu, women of the ancient court of Japan* (M. Aratani, Trans.). New York: Scribner's.

Kato, S. (1979). *A history of Japanese literature.* Tokyo: Kodansha.

Kourilsky, F. & Temerson, C. (Eds.). (1988). *Five plays by contemporary French-speaking women playwrights from different cultural backgrounds: Denise Bonal (Algeria); Michele Fabien (Belgium); Abla Farhoud (Lebanon and Quebec); Fatima Gallaire-Bourega (Algeria and France); Simone Schwarz-Bart (Guadeloupe and France).* New York: Ubu Repertory Theater Publications.

Lawall, S. (Ed.). (2002). *The Norton anthology of world literature.* New York: Norton.

Lesko, B. (1987). *Women's earliest records: From ancient Egypt and western Asia.* Atlanta, GA: Scholars Press.

Lim, S. G.-L. & Spencer, N. (1993). *One world of literature.* Boston: Houghton Mifflin.

Meyer, D. & Fernandez, M. (1983). *Contemporary women authors of Latin America: New translations.* New York: Brooklyn College Press.

Plant, I. M. (2004). *The women writers of ancient Greece and Rome.* Norman: University of Oklahoma Press.

Rayor, D. J. (Trans.). (1991). *Sappho's lyre: Archaic lyric and women poets of ancient Greece.* Berkeley: University of California Press.

Rexroth, K. & Chung, L. (Trans. & Eds.). (1972). *The orchid boat: Women poets of China.* New York: McGraw-Hill.

Seidensticker, E. G. (1979). Tale of Genji. *Kodansha Encyclopedia of Japan* (Vol. 7, p. 331). Tokyo: Kodansha.

Zgoll, A. (1997). *Der Rechtsfall der En-hedu-Ana in dem Lied nin-me-sar-ra.* Munich, Germany: Ugarit Verlag.

The Brighton Declaration and Women's Leadership in Sports

Anita WHITE
Chair of the Organizing Committee of the Brighton Conference on Women and Sport

The Brighton Declaration, drafted in 1994 at the World Conference on Women and Sport in Brighton, England, was a landmark document that called for equal opportunity and resources on a variety of levels for women in sports. The declaration has since been adopted by international organizations as well as national councils and sporting federations. The work primarily of women leaders, the declaration has had a powerful impact on gender equality in sports.

The Brighton Declaration is a statement of principles about equality for women in sports, and has gained worldwide acceptance since it was first developed in 1994. The document calls for the commitment and the resources needed to bring equality to women in sports in terms of opportunity, facilities, support for high-level athletes, and research inclusion, among other factors. It is an example of leadership in the genesis of an international women and sports movement that aims to change sporting culture to one that enables and values the full involvement of women in every aspect of sports.

Development of the Brighton Declaration

In 1994, the first World Conference on Women and Sport, aimed at policy and decision makers in sports, was held in Brighton, England. Organized and hosted by the British Sports Council, the conference was also supported by the International Olympic Committee (IOC). It aimed to accelerate the process of change in the interests of women and sports and to redress the imbalances women faced in sports. The conference was attended by 280 delegates from 82 countries, representing governmental and non-governmental organizations, National Olympic Committees, international and national sport federations, and educational and research institutions.

The conference agenda covered a range of issues, including culture, gender, disability, and sexuality along with discussions on leadership, the management of change, marketing, mentoring, and networking. One major outcome of the conference was the Brighton Declaration, which conference organizers believed would raise awareness of gender issues in sports and help to gain the commitment of governmental and non-governmental organizations to work toward gender equity in sports.

The Brighton Declaration benefited from input by conference delegates through feedback in workshops, collective discussion of a draft declaration, and individual submissions to a drafting group. An initial draft was developed by Sue Baker Finch of the Australian Sports Commission before the conference, and she was then joined by Julia Bracewell and John Scott of the British Sports Council, and the Honourable Pendukeni Ivula-Ithana, Minister of Youth and Sport from Namibia, on the drafting group. Revisions and amendments were made to align the document with other international women's and human rights agenda as well as to include issues and concerns of conference delegates from all parts of the world. This small drafting group demonstrated a consultative style of leadership in the way they worked to gain input and ownership of the document from conference delegates. The four members of the group brought different skills and experience to the table. Sue Baker-Finch had considerable experience of women and sports policy development in Australia, Julia Bracewell was a former international fencer and a practicing lawyer, John Scott had significant experience of international relations in sports, and Pendukeni Ivula-Ithana had knowledge of the struggle for human rights in Africa and the workings of the United Nations. A final draft was distributed to delegates on the last day of the conference and unanimously endorsed.

The British Sports Council, a governmental organization and the organizer of the conference, had been active not only in developing national sports policy and programs but also in international sports policy (e.g., anti-doping measures) and had strong links with both European and Commonwealth networks. In the early 1990s, Briton Margaret Talbot provided leadership of the European Women and Sport working group, and this group had already embarked on a series of biannual conferences in Europe. By enlisting the support of its Commonwealth networks, the Sports Council was able to widen the conference to make it a world event. During the previous decade, partner sports councils in Canada, New Zealand, and Australia had developed national policies and programs to combat gender inequality in sports. Their experience together with that of the Europeans, particularly the Scandinavian countries, provided the expert resource base needed to establish a globalized women and sports movement at the first World Conference on Women and Sport.

The success of the conference was due to the vision and determination of a number of influential women leaders in Europe and the Commonwealth, backed by organizations that had the power, networks, and human and financial resources to stage a successful conference. Women provided the necessary leadership—working collectively (though not without some conflict) and being supported by men in powerful institutional positions who respected the ideology of their work and recognized the need for the sports world to address gender issues.

Adoption of the Brighton Declaration

A measure of the success of the Brighton Declaration is the extent to which it has been adopted and endorsed. Adoption of the declaration is monitored by the International Working Group on Women and Sport (the IWG), and national and international organizations that have endorsed the declaration are listed on its website (www.iwg-gti.org).

It is useful to consider the range of organizations that have adopted the declaration. Within the governmental sector, European ministers of sports and the Council of Europe together with Commonwealth heads of government, Commonwealth ministers of women's affairs and Commonwealth ministers of sports were among the first to adopt the declaration. Arab ministers of youth and sports, and the Supreme Council for Sport in Africa were also early signatories. Within the international non-governmental sector, both the International Olympic Committee and the International Paralympic Committee (IPC) adopted the declaration, as did the Commonwealth Games Federation. The declaration initially had less impact with international sports federations (IFs), though by 2016, twenty-eight IFs including the International Federation of Football Associations (FIFA) had adopted it. Many leaders in the women and sports movement had come from a background in physical education and sports research and education, so it is not surprising that they have taken the declaration to their lead international organizations for adoption, such as the International Council for Sports Science and Physical Education. This organization was active in the implementation of the declaration by drawing up a gender equality plan and monitoring progress. By 2016, over 441 organizations from all parts of the world had adopted the declaration (iwg-gti.org/iwg-signatories). They include national Olympic committees; international and national sports federations; ministries of sports, culture, youth and women; and women's sports associations.

In nearly every case, adoption of the declaration has been due to the initiative, determination, and persistence of individuals who are part of the women and sports movement. Their cause has been bolstered by an increasing awareness by the governmental sector of human rights and women's issues. Although the sports world has sometimes been slow to shed its "malestream" culture, the example of the IOC in adopting the declaration and developing women and sports initiatives has set an example that others have followed.

Adoption of the declaration, however, is only the first step—implementation and action to make the changes that are needed to translate the principles of the declaration into practice are what is required to make lasting social change. This is much more difficult to monitor, though an attempt has been made by the IWG, which publishes quadrennial progress reports on its website.

Development of the International Women and Sports Movement

Leadership of the international women and sports movement is diverse and shared by many women working in different organizations in different parts of the world. At the international level, the IWG was established at the Brighton Conference to provide coordination and leadership to the movement. This group has continued since 1994. It has been led by co-chairs from all five continents, and directly supported by organizations in the UK, Canada, Japan, Australia, Finland, and Botswana. The group is made up of representatives from each continent, the two international voluntary organizations for women and sports (WomenSport International and the International Association of PE and Sport for Girls and Women), as well as individually co-opted members. The IWG has deliberately adopted feminist styles of leadership with an emphasis on sharing, cooperation, openness, informality, networking, and mentoring. Since the first World Conference on Women and Sport, regional networks, groups and associations have been set up in Africa, Asia, and the Arab nations. Formed by women leaders from a range of different sports and backgrounds, these organizations are examples of the development of new structures addressing the challenges of bringing about change in sports and improving the status of women. The Women's Sports Foundation in the United States (est. 1974) continues to be a leader in this field, along with the Canadian Association for the Advancement of Women in Sport (est. 1981) and both have been generous in sharing resources and ideas internationally, such as the United States' Title IX legislation, which ensures equality for women in collegiate sports.

A different but complementary strategy has been to mainstream gender equality within existing sporting organizations and structures. The IOC and IPC both have working groups or commissions on women and sports that report to their respective executive boards, and many national Olympic committees and federations of sports have followed suit. Their work focuses on raising awareness and bringing about change within exiting sporting culture and practice.

Momentum from the first World Conference on Women and Sport has been sustained not only by the activities of these organizations, groups and networks, but also though quadrennial world conferences held under the auspices of the IWG. The second conference was held in Windhoek, Namibia, the third in Montreal, Canada, the fourth in Kumamoto, Japan, the fifth in Sydney, Australia, and the sixth in Helsinki, Finland. In all these activities, the Brighton Declaration has remained the cornerstone statement of values and guiding principles. In 2014, the declaration was reviewed, revised and updated, two decades after its launch, during the sixth World Conference for Women and Sport in Helsinki, Finland to better reflect the progress made and continuing issues women encounter in sports. It continues to gather endorsements as "The Brighton Plus Helsinki Declaration on Women and Sport." The seventh world conference is scheduled to take place in Gaborone, Botswana in October 2018.

A Model for the Development of Women's Leadership in Sports

The development of the Brighton Declaration in 1994 is a good example of strategic feminist leadership in a field that is traditionally male-dominated. Women leaders throughout the world have used the Brighton Declaration as a political tool to raise awareness of women and sports issues, and to gain the commitment of powerful institutions to gender equity in sports. The timing of the declaration was crucial, for although there were pockets of women and sports activism in the early 1990s, there was little international co-operation and communication on the issues. As a result of the conference and the declaration, women and sports is now firmly on the agenda of sporting and other agencies throughout the world and a strong network has been created. Some creative tensions exist between different factions, for example governmental and non-governmental organizations, radical and liberal feminists, and between different cultural approaches. These tensions and the diversity within the movement are managed through the agreement on fundamental principles set out in the Brighton Declaration, and the acknowledgement that there are different ways of working to achieve the universal aims and principles contained within it.

Further Reading

Canadian Association for the Advancement of Women and Sport and Physical Activity (CAAWS). (2003). Retrieved June 19, 2003, from www.caaws.ca

Christensen, K., Guttman, A., & Pfister, G. (Eds.). (2001). *International encyclopaedia of women and sports*. New York: Macmillan Reference.

Fasting, K.; Sand, T.S.; Pike, E.; & Matthews, J. (2014). *From Brighton to Helsinki. Women and sport progress report 1994–2014*. Helsinki: IWG/Finnish Sports Confederation.

Hargreaves, J. (2000). *Heroines of sport: The politics of difference and identity*. London: Routledge.

Hartmann-Tews, I. & Pfister, G. (Eds.). (2003). *Sport and women: Social issues in international perspective*. London: Routledge.

International Olympic Movement. Retrieved June 19, 2003, from www.olympic.org.

International Working Group on Women and Sport (IWG). (2003). Retrieved June 19, 2003, from www.iwg -gti.org

The Women's Sports Foundation. Retrieved June 19, 2003, from www.womenssportsfoundation.org

Women in Utopian Religions and Cults

Susan J. PALMER
Dawson College

From heretical movements in the early Church, to American Utopian sects and communes, to end-of-time cults, the presence of women and female imagery has always been strong outside of mainstream religion. Especially since the nineteenth century, women have founded religious movements and led apocalyptic cults. Such heterodox movements share in a search for new cosmologies and meaning, often celebrating fertility and "feminine" traits.

U topian religious movements, marginal religions, and contemporary cults reveal an overwhelmingly feminine presence. A wealth of utopian literature has appeared in the 1980s and 1990s that exalts women as world saviors and rulers of future utopias. Eschatologies in many marginal religions feature goddesses as well as gods presiding over the new age. The earth is revered as a pregnant planet contracting in birth spasms, and comics depict Amazon warriors defeating all-male armies. Within the leadership structure of many groups, there are an abundance of female messiahs, and mediums; feminine leadership, or equal opportunity, is taken for granted. Even among the rank and file members there seems to be a prevailing notion that their women will play a key role in the end time—as midwives assisting the birth of a new age, as mothers of a future *Homo superiorus*, or as usherettes in a cosmic theater.

Women in the History of Millenarian Heresies

This situation is unexpected—perhaps unprecedented—if one considers the male-oriented millenarian visions that arose from the Middle East; the Jewish Messiahs, the Muslim Mahdis, the Christian Son of Man. These traditions envisage equestrian sky gods, male demons erupting from earth, and cosmic battles starring warrior-heroes.

A gnostic mystical-apocalyptic movement threatened the Church of Rome during the High Middle Ages in southern Europe, known as the Brethren of the Free Spirit. This movement was organized in secret cells that were loosely affiliated, connected by itinerant preachers who circulated mystical tracts and poetry that were highly sophisticated. A lay order was composed of the Beghards (male) and the Beguines (female), who took vows of celibacy and served the poor; and many lived communally, loosely attached to the Franciscan monasteries.

There is evidence that the overwhelming majority of members were unmarried women from the wealthy merchant class, who had no other role in life that would win them status and respect in society. Many of these, upon becoming Beguines, wore a hooded gray robe and a veil, but continued to live with their parents or were anchorites enjoying a private income, and many moved into communes. The historian Norman Cohn suggests that many of the Beguines were attracted to the intense mystical experience cultivated within this lay order that brought with it a sense of belonging to a superhuman elite, as well as to the amoral, sexually permissive relationships offered by the wandering Beghard charismatic preachers; and that once the movement was driven underground by persecution, around 1320, the "Free Spirit had become an invisible empire, held together by the emotional bonds—which of course were often erotic bonds—between men and women" (Cohn 1970, 162).

In 1310, an outstanding Beguine from northern France, Marguerite Porete, was burned at the stake with her Beghard companion and "guardian angel" for her book of mystical theology, *The Mirror of the Simple Souls*. She had many followers, and her book circulated among the upper classes in France and England. The Free Spirit came to the attention of Pope Clement V at the Council of Vienna in 1311, where he decided that they were heretics who must be curbed. Hundreds of Beghards and Beguines were subsequently captured and burned at the stake in the south of France. The doctrines and mystical quest of the Brethren of the Free Spirit was never completely extinguished, and many of the essential features of the mystical anarchical sect continue to appear on the margins of orthodox religion.

Women in the Radical Reformation

An interesting kind of androgynous messianism emerged from Martin Luther's (1483–1546) insistence that monks and nuns leave the monasteries and marry, and his concern for the Christian, loving quality of familial relations whereby the family hearth, as opposed to the church, became the focal point of the community. While Luther had denied the sacramental and covenantal status of marriage, those bishops who attended the Council of Trent (1545–1563) sought to make celibacy and marriage equally sacramental and valid. They rejected the esteem for celibacy that had influenced the Catholic Church since the second century, arguing that the original Hebraic values placed a strong emphasis upon conjugal love and the divine injunction to be fruitful and multiply.

The radical reformers, however, insisted that marriage was even more holy and sacred; it was a covenant with Christ. Drawing upon images in Revelation of the bride of Christ and the "woman clothed in the sun," they discovered a new theological basis for marriage as well as a new sexualized language for millennial rhetoric. These eventually led to certain excesses and aberrations in the communal and familial experiments launched by prophets.

This new androgynous messianism was preached by William Postel (1510–1581) from Normandy, who moved beyond covenantal marriage to propound elaborate theologies of spiritual marriage as a path to redemption. In Venice he became converted to a kind of feminist spirituality through his association with an illiterate Venetian virgin of the age of fifty, who spent her life in ministering to the poor and sick and was a known psychic and faith healer, respected for her spiritual discernment. When she died in 1551, Postel felt her "spiritual body and substance descended unto him" and began to claim he was now reborn as the Holy Spirit incarnate. He wrote and distributed many millenarian books and broadsheets in which he prophesized a return of the Golden Age that Noah had supposedly presided over.

Sexual Solutions to Social Disorder

Since myths must mirror their social worlds, one would expect the apocalyptic myths of budding religions to reflect current trends and cultural tensions. Utopian communities of the nineteenth century, for example, expressed the Victorians' deep concern for reconstructing family life and clarifying gender roles. The Oneida Perfectionists, whose founder, John Humphrey Noyes held himself to be the *Third* Coming, rejected monogamous marriage and procreation and considered woman to be a "female man." The Shakers who followed Mother Ann Lee sought to purify their brothers and sisters from sin through ritual shaking, a celibate life, and egalitarian gender roles. The early Mormons built their kingdoms in heaven through "celestial marriage," polygamy, and procreation. All these groups considered their utopian forms of "ordered love" (Kern 1981) to offer spiritual solutions to the decline and fragmentation of the lineage family in the antebellum period.

The suspenseful eschatologies of new religious movements (NRMs) reflect our own preoccupations with issues of sexual identity, women's power, and the disintegration of the nuclear family. For many NRMs, reconstructing relations between the sexes in correct alignment to the divine cosmos is an essential step in preparing for the millennium, or the one thousand years Christ will reign before the final judgment. There are groups that exalt woman as world savior, humanity's only hope for averting nuclear destruction. Other groups are resigned to the prospect of a worldwide holocaust, but see women as the builders of a new society, or rulers in the golden age, as in the case of the Brahma Kumaris, founded by Dada Lekraj, who foresees women reigning as goddesses in the *satyug,* a golden age after the present world has been destroyed.

Radical lesbian spirituality advocates a rejection of and separation from male hegemony so that women can bond in a just and loving sisterhood and excavate their true metaphysical identity. At the other extreme are neoconservative groups and racialist religions that tell woman to return to her rightful place as wife and mother, "covered" by her husband in order to prepare her children for the Second Coming, or to breed and rear a new, sinless, wholly human race.

Gender, Genesis, and Ecofeminism

Some feminist theologians and scholar-critics of patriarchal religions have challenged misogynistic extrapolations of the doctrine of original sin and struck a rich millenarian vein in their writings. Mary Daly (1928–2010) who describes herself as a "post-Christian feminist," finds the "original sin of sexism" wreaking its destructive effects upon women throughout history and proposes a "Fall into freedom"

257

as the only means whereby Eve will learn to "name herself, to become all she can be" (Daly 1974, 67–68). Daly's millenarian vision depicts a psychic war between the sexes based on their metaphysical proclivities. She regards males as "gynaecidal" and life-hating, in contrast to women, whom she defines as "biophilic" and creative. Also speaking from the margins of radical feminism, is Sonia Johnson (b. 1936), an ex-Mormon radical feminist. In her book, *Wildfire* (1989), she preaches a message of lesbian apocalypticism.

Another genre of feminist apocalypticism is found in NRMs that venerate the powers in nature, such as neoshamanic healing circles, Wicca, and various schools of ecotheology. Gaians espouse the notion of the planet as an integral, living, maternal organism. Wiccans have adopted the anthropologist Margaret Murray's (1863–1963) mythologized history of witchcraft as the original religion of the human race that went underground to withstand the onslaught of Christianity and has survived in fragmented covens of Goddess-worshippers who continued to stimulate the agricultural cycle through reenacting the parthenogenic birth and violent death of the vegetation deity. Starhawk (b. 1951), a famous witch, author, and ecological activist orchestrated protest demonstrations in the late eighties to pit women's natural magic against the marauding masculine forces of industry and war; as when in 1987 her witches in Vancouver saved up their menstrual blood for two years in freezers, then gathered, chanting, to throw it against nuclear reactors.

Other large, international and well-known NRMs have evolved their own idiosyncratic "sexual solutions" to pollution or the nuclear threat that almost *parody* trends in the feminist movement. Profeminist prophets Rajneesh, Raël, and Ramtha, are striking examples of this. Bhagwan Shree Rajneesh (1931–1990), Indian-born eclectic philosopher and founder of Rajneeshpuram, a communal utopian city in Oregon that lasted from 1981 to 1985, proclaimed: "My own vision is that the coming age will be the age of woman. . .Feminine energies must be released!" (Rajneesh 1987, 18). In Rajneeshpuram he appointed women as leaders, "the pillars of my commune," and they filled over 80 percent of executive positions. He explained that woman is "a female Buddha," more receptive and spiritually advanced than man, and less inclined towards aggression and "power trips." In 1983, Rajneesh emerged from a vow of silence and announced that after the world was decimated by AIDS in 2000, that women would take over and build a new age based on love, harmony with nature, meditative consciousness, and superior technology.

Raël, a former racing car driver from France who founded the Raëlian Movement after claiming he was contacted by extraterrestrials in 1973, has announced that "the Age of Apocalypse will be the age of women!" He urges men to develop the feminine qualities of love, peace, tolerance, and empathy if humans are to avoid self-destruction through nuclear weapons. Humanity must learn to "make love, not war" in the Raëlian Movement's fun-loving international, multiracial, "quadrasexual" community.

The Ramtha Foundation also espouses a feminist apocalyptic theory. JZ Knight (b. 1946), a petite blond businesswoman, began in 1977 to function as the mouthpiece for Ramtha, the invisible two-meter, 4000-year-old "Lemurian" warrior. Based in Yelm, Washington, she has traveled across the country renting out hotel ballrooms to hold weekend "dialogues" wherein Ramtha takes over her body, expounds his gnostic philosophy, and dispenses advice. In a manner reminiscent of nineteenth-century female mediums, JZ Knight channels an entity that defends the rights of women and challenges male hegemony. Ramtha condemns males for their omnivorous sexual appetite and encourages the empowerment of women.

A "Comic" Ending For the Future

While these leaders promote what feminist scholar Rosemary Radford Reuther (1988) calls a "radical romantic feminism," other groups emphasize cooperation and harmony between the sexes, and in all these groups the notion of reconciling the sexes and achieving the "right" balance of power as a prerequisite for ushering in a successful millennium is importantly present. Messiahs and prophets often form a charismatic duo with their wife or mistress, for androgyny is a potent ingredient that enhances the charisma, not only of shamans and rock stars, but of charismatic leaders as well.

Bo and Peep, the founders of Heaven's Gate, a UFO religion, were a charismatic duo composed of an homosexual choir director and an unhappily married nurse, prepared their followers for the extraterrestrials' descent when they would all become immortal, flying androgynes. The younger consorts of male prophet-founders occasionally take over the reins of leadership upon their death. Reverend Moon and his wife represent the male and female aspects of God, the "One True Parent of Mankind" for members of the Unification Church, and Moon had anointed Mrs. Moon to preside over the movement before his death in 2012. David Berg, the "Lord's Endtime Prophet" and founder of the Children of God, before his "homecoming" in 1994, anointed his consort, Maria, to succeed him as the "Endtime Prophetess." Women have always assisted the dying. In their intimate proximity to dying gurus they may ask favors, manipulate mythologies, and mold the succession so as to create more egalitarian or "uxor-friendly" patterns of authority.

One notable feature of "feminized" millennia is a tendency towards optimism and peaceful resolutions—what Stephen D. O'Leary (1994) would term the *comic* frame of apocalyptic discourse. He identifies two frames that interact, each dramatizing its own resolution of the problem of evil: the *tragic* (dualistic and anticipating a redemptive climax marked by catastrophic suffering), and the *comic*, that espouses an open-ended or cyclic view of the future that can be influenced by human agency. Feminist apocalyptic dramas appear to be reacting against what they perceive to be the male-generated *tragic* mode of narrative. Nevertheless, the widespread assumption that humanity can finally enjoy the fruits of peace with women in charge is belied by some prophetesses' fascination with weapons and the themes of war.

Elizabeth Clare Prophet (1939–2009) of the Church Universal and Triumphant (CUT) is one of the outstanding millenarian prophets of our age. After the death in 1973 of the original founder, her husband and "twin flame" Mark Prophet, she succeeded him as the Messenger. From the church's headquarters in Montana, she delivered high speed oral "dictations," relaying messages to humanity from the Ascended Masters. Some of these were apocalyptic in content, particularly the prophecies of one Saint Germain, who was expected to succeed Christ when the Piscean Age moves into the Age of Aquarius.

In a 1986 dictation, Saint Germain warned that the Soviet Union was planning a nuclear attack on America, and members should prepare by building bomb shelters. Members moved to Montana in the hundreds and incurred enormous debts building bomb shelters. On 11 March 1990, Saint Germain again predicted that the Soviets attack was imminent, and urged members to withdraw their money from banks, to move out of urban areas, stockpile food and weapons, and move into underground tunnels to prepare for the tribulation. Over seven hundred of the commune's staff and two thousand members gathered at this time to pray. The ensuing disconfirmation in prophecy resulted in many defections and bankruptcies. Despite these classic ingredients of a "tragic" survivalist agenda, anthropologist Jocelyn Dehaas (1994) argues that CUT conforms rather to religious scholar Catherine Wessinger's model (1993) of "progressive millennialism"—not unlike O'Leary's comic frame.

The Order of the Solar Temple, notorious for their 1994 mass suicides/homicides staged in Quebec and Switzerland, espoused an ecofeminist apocalyptic theory and cultivated a female avatar. Joseph Di Mambro was their grandmaster in Switzerland, and he raised his daughter, Emmanuelle, to be the "cosmic child" of the New Age. Di Mambro's young mistress was immaculately impregnated by the Ascended Master Manatanus in a public "rite of conception" involving laser beams and special lighting effects. Luc Jouret, the Quebec grandmaster, claimed it was necessary to balance positive "feminine energies"—which they associated with the French culture, art, and Nature—with the extant negative "male energies"—associated with the English, industrial powers, and materialism. To this esoteric end, the OTS imported eleven Francophone members from Martinique to Quebec to combat the Anglo influence.

Meaning Amidst New Mythologies

That the apocalyptic imagination in America is resplendent with or (depending upon one's perspective) alarmingly polluted by feminine images, is a phenomenon easy to prove. To guess its meaning is a more difficult task. Sexual imagery has always been a strong element in end-time narratives, as it is in the world's creation myths. Cosmogonies usually recount the origins of life from the union of the first Man and Woman, to their eventual separation through the Fall into mortality through infanticide, parricide, or incest. Millenarians through the ages seem to be particularly set on reconstructing the primordial drama in Eden and exonerating Eve. Norman Cohn describes the Brothers of the Free Spirit movement (circa 1550) that attracted many wealthy unmarried women who emulated Eve in practicing ritual nudity, thus "asserting . . . that they were restored to the state of innocence which had existed before the Fall" (Cohn 1970, 180).

Apocalyptic narrations of destruction and regeneration must, of necessity, include the symbols of creation common to its culture. Western monotheistic patriarchal religions tend to show a dearth of creation myths that depict woman's life-giving creativity or explicit images of the birth process. Judy Chicago, the feminist artist and sculptress claims she could not find any adequate iconography of creation in Western art, only masculine images she found utterly unconvincing—"unless you believe in God touching Adam on the finger!"

Since the 1970s, there has been a trend to make childbirth a public event—to film it, to invite friends into the labor room. At the same time, there has been a corresponding trend to hide the ugly intimate details of the deathbed—to "medicalize" death, as historian Phillippe Ariès (1988) argues. Ariès laments the decline of the traditional *artes moriendi*, the public deathbed scene, of farewells and religious testimonials. It might be argued that this lost art has been replaced by the art of birth, a new public ritual; and that when one contemplates the grim, "scientific" possibility of a global holocaust, earth goddesses presiding as midwives over a planet's accouchement are considerably less scary than sky gods in battle.

Today we find a profusion of feminine imagery and a strong female presence in the millennial dreams of the late twentieth century. As students of religion and culture we are aware that myths and symbols mirror society and its natural environment, and that a people's mythology will respond to changing social and ecological conditions. It appears reasonable, therefore, to assert that millenarian movements today are feeling the impact of feminism, and that the contemporary eschatologies featuring cosmic interplay between polar forces, good versus evil, light versus dark, sky versus earth, will express our deep preoccupation with issues of gender, identity, and power.

Further Reading

Aries, P. (1988). *The hour of our death*. New York: Oxford University Press.

Balch, R. (1982). Bo and Peep: A case study of the origins of messianic leadership. In *Millennialism and Charisma*, edited by Roy Wallis. Belfast: Queen's University, 13–22.

Cohn, N. (1970). *The pursuit of the millennium*. London: Oxford University Press.

Daly, M. (1973). *Beyond God the father: Toward a philosophy of women's liberation*. Boston: Beacon Press.

Daly, M. & Jane C. (1987). *Websters' first new intergalactic wickedary of the English Language*. Boston: Beacon Press.

Dehaas, J. H. (1994). Apocalyptic prophecy and the notion of non-linear time in the Church Universal and Triumphant. Paper presented at a meeting of the Society for the Scientific Study of Religion, Albuquerque, NM.

Foster, L. (1981). *Religion and sexuality: Three American communal experiments of the nineteenth century*. New York: Oxford University Press.

Johnson, S. (1989). *Wildfire: Igniting the she/volution*. Albuquerque, NM: Wildfire Books.

Kern, L. (1981). *An ordered love*. Chapel Hill: University of North Carolina Press.

Lee, M. (1995). *Earth first! Environmental apocalypse*. Syracuse, NY: Syracuse University Press.

Marrs, W. (1989). *New Age lies to women*. Austin, TX: Living Truth Publishers.

Melton, J. G. (1992). *Encyclopedic handbook of cults in America*. New York: Garland.

Milne, Hugh. (1986). *Bhagwan: The god that failed*. New York: St. Martin's Press.

Palmer, Susan J. (1996, October). Purity and danger in the Solar Temple. *Journal of Contemporary Religion, 11*(3), 303–318.

Prophet, E. C. (1986). *Saint Germain on prophecy*. Livingstone, MT: Summit University Press.

Raël. (1989). *The message given to me by the extraterrestrials*. Tokyo: Raëlian Foundation.

Rajneesh, B. S. (1987). *A new vision of women's liberation*. Poona, India: Rebel Press.

Ramtha. (1987). *Intensive changes: The days yet to come*. Eastsound, WA: Sovereignty.

Reuther, R. R. (1988). *Women in religion in America*. New York: Beacon Press, vol. 1.

Rudolph, K. (1987). *Gnosis: the nature and history of Gnosticism*. San Francisco: Harper & Row.

Wessinger, C. (1993). "Annie Besant's millennial movement: Its history, impact, and implications concerning authority." *Syzygy: Journal of Alternative Religion and Culture, 2*, pp. 55–70.

Wessinger, C. (Ed.). (1993). *Women outside the mainstream: Female leaders in marginal religions in nineteenth century America*. Urbana, IL: University of Illinois Press.

Women in the Missionary Movement

Hyaeweol CHOI
Australian National University

Women have played an important role overseas as Christian missionaries. Oftentimes they alone had access to women and children in missions in Asia and the Middle East; and as doctors and teachers they wielded unprecedented power while they organized, "modernized," and even helped to shape or alter the role of women in societies where they worked.

Women missionaries constituted an indispensable workforce in the foreign missionary enterprise, representing almost 60 percent of the entire mission personnel by 1890. The largest organized women's movement in North America in the early twentieth century was the women's missionary movement, whose expansive involvement reached across the globe into Asia, Africa, Latin America, and the Middle East. Despite the significant role of women in the foreign missionary enterprise, only from the 1980s did women missionaries and their subjects of conversion begin to draw scholarly attention. Since then, much research has shown that although women were precluded from clerical rights because of highly patriarchal church organizations, the unique experiences of women missionaries in the separate sphere called "woman's work for woman" made significant impact on mission methods and strategies. It also reveals the complex intersections of gender with race and class in transcultural encounters between missionaries and the members of non-Christian societies.

American women's engagement in the foreign missionary enterprise was largely governed by two prevailing ideologies. One was the nineteenth century's singular notion of civilization primarily informed by a worldview based in Christian and Enlightenment ethics. The other was the Victorian concept of True Womanhood, which privileged religious piety and domesticity. In line with these dominant ideologies, women were called upon to undertake "woman's work for woman" to rescue "heathen sisters." Women missionaries adventured into the unknown world, regarding it as their "household" where they would practice the feminine virtues of care, sacrifice, and devotion. The mission field in turn provided them with unprecedented opportunities to exercise power and authority in their own separate female sphere in which women were empowered but at the same time constrained while they struggled to find their enhanced role and status within the male-centered church organizations.

Separated Into a Female Sphere

In the nineteenth century, the status of women became an important criterion in measuring the level of civilization a society had achieved. Numerous missionary writings reported the oppressed life of women in "heathen" lands who were confined to the inner chambers, received no formal education, and were bound by longstanding customs, such as foot-binding, early marriage, concubinage, and slavery. Set against the idealized position of women in the Christian West, who presumably enjoyed freedom, honor, and dignity, the exaggerated image of downtrodden women in "heathen" societies compelled many American Christian women to feel obliged to engage in rescuing their unfortunate sisters and to spread the gospel as a sure sign of liberation.

Where the custom of the separation of genders prevailed in the Middle East and Asia, male missionaries could not have access to women. Therefore, as theology professor Dana Robert points out, the "strongest public justification for including women in the foreign mission enterprise at all was not to be companions and helpmates to their husbands, but rather to reach the otherwise unreachable women and children" (Robert 1996, 36). Given the role of women as mothers for the future generation, the conversion of women was considered of special importance to ensure the success of the foreign mission. The creation of the Woman's Foreign Missionary Societies (WFMS) in various denominations from the 1860s further spurred a greater involvement of women, providing better-educated women of the time with an outlet to use and discover their talents and leadership. Especially for single women, who were prevented from becoming missionaries earlier, the WFMS served as a means to legitimize their religious and professional commitment (Thorne 1999).

In line with the prevailing gender ideology based on the Victorian notion of "separate spheres," women missionaries were channeled into the "feminine" domestic arena as teachers and doctors for women and children, while men missionaries assumed leadership roles in the religious, evangelical domain through preaching and organizational supervision. Although most women missionaries readily accepted their status as the subordinate sex, the separate "woman's work for woman" proved to be a fertile ground for many of them to learn and exercise leadership, organizational skills, independence, and professionalism. They organized their own women's conferences with significant autonomy. Women's mission journals, such as *Heathen Woman's Friend* (later *Woman's Missionary Friend*), *Woman's Work for Woman*, and *Woman's Missionary Advocate*, were crucial media for them to propagate their unique contributions to the foreign mission as well as to develop a growing sense of professionalism. Along with the significant changes in political and cultural milieu especially after World War I, a greater number of women missionaries were able to pursue personal and professional ambitions that went beyond the traditional gender boundaries (Brouwer 2002).

Gender and Race in Transcultural Encounters

The experience of women missionaries as the subordinate gender in the American cultural context can be contrasted with their status as the presumably "superior" race vis-a-vis the Other, and this tension reveals a more complicated picture of the legacy of women missionaries. There are various interpretations of the role of women missionaries in shaping new womanhood in "heathen" lands, ranging from their functioning as liberators on one end to cultural imperialists on the other. Missionary-led social and cultural reforms, such as educational and occupational opportunities for women and the prevention of early marriage and concubinage, point to the liberator role that women missionaries played. On the other hand, the Euro-centric colonialist views of "the Other" and their sense of racial and religious superiority render them as cultural imperialists.

The wide range of activities and experiences of women missionaries in the culturally diverse foreign mission fields cannot be understood in a clear-cut, binary fashion, however. While they were significantly influenced by the prevailing religious doctrines and Western-centered worldview of the time, they were in a position to confront much more complex cultural dynamics with indigenous people, who were far from passive recipients of a foreign religion and culture. Rarely compromising the fundamental tenets of Christian teachings, missionaries tried to adapt to the particular local situations that demanded more flexible and innovative ways of distributing the gospel. For example, American missionaries were shocked by the extreme degree of separation of genders in Korea, where boys and girls began to be segregated after age seven. Respecting the custom, missionaries came up with the idea that they put a paper screen in the middle of the church so men and women could attend together but would not see each other (Choi 2009). Professor of theology Kwok Pui-lan points out how Christian symbolism was feminized in the Chinese cultural context. Missionaries saw Chinese women not only as the victims of the Chinese patriarchal system but also as the catalyst for sociocultural changes in China, and thus gave more emphasis to the close relationship between Jesus and women, especially oppressed women (Kwok 1992, 29–57).

While spreading the gospel was the ultimate goal of all missionaries, the gender-specific division of labor drove women missionaries toward more cultural and secular activities. The scholar Leslie Flemming notes that "because of their exclusion from public evangelical activities, and because of their identification with domestic, educational and health-related activities in North American culture, most women missionaries responded more strongly to the call to be civilizers, characterizing themselves as agents of change and emphasizing the "uplifting' nature of their activities" (Flemming 1989, 2–3). In fact, the "civilizing" or "modernizing" aspect of mission activities often drew more positive response from people they tried to convert than the strictly religious aspect did. In her analysis of American women missionaries in China, the historian Jane Hunter points out that what the Chinese wanted most was not a Western religion but modern knowledge and technology, and thus "the key to the impact of missionary women on Chinese women's history lies less in their religious program than in the secular message transmitted by their lives" (Hunter 1984, 26).

While women missionaries contributed to "modernizing" women in the mission field, there was a tension between evangelical goals and the modernizing forces at the time. Since missionaries viewed some modern characteristics to be anti-religious and culturally corrupt, their perception of true modern womanhood was not the same as what was prevailing in 1920s American society. Nonetheless, American women missionaries are often remembered by the people they served as pioneers in constructing modern womanhood largely because the most prominent accomplishments of women missionaries are found in their work in educational, medical, and social work-related areas.

Further Reading

Brouwer, R. (2002). *Modern women modernizing men: The changing missions of three professional women in Asia and Africa, 1902–69.* Vancouver: University of British Columbia Press.

Choi, H. (2009). *Gender and mission encounters: New women, old ways.* Berkeley: University of California Press.

Choi, H. & Jolly, M. (Eds.). (2014). *Divine domesticities: Christian paradoxes in Asia and the Pacific.* Canberra: ANU Press.

Flemming, L. (1989). *Women's work for women: Missionaries and social change in Asia.* Boulder: Westview.

Hill, P. (1985). *The world their household: The American woman's foreign mission movement and cultural transformation, 1870–1920.* Ann Arbor: University of Michigan Press.

Huber, T. & Lutkehaus, N. (1999). *Gendered missions: Women and men in missionary discourse and practice.* Ann Arbor: University of Michigan Press.

Hunter, J. (1984). *The gospel of gentility: American women missionaries in turn-of-the-century China.* New Haven: Yale University Press.

Kwok, P. (1992). *Chinese women and Christianity, 1860–1927.* Atlanta: Scholars Press.

Reeves-Ellington, B.; Sklar, K. K.; & Shemo, C. A. (Eds.). (2010). *Competing kingdoms: Women, mission, nation, and the American Protestant empire, 1812–1960.* Durham: Duke University Press.

Robert, D. (1996). *American women in mission: A social history of their thought and practice.* Macon, Georgia: Mercer University Press.

Ruether, R. R. & Keller, R. S. (Eds.). (1981). *Women and religion in America. Vol. 1: The nineteenth century.* San Francisco: Harper & Row Publishers.

Thomas, H. F. & Keller, R. S. (Eds.). (1981). *Women in New Worlds.* Nashville: Abingdon.

Thorne, S. (1999). *Congregational missions and the making of an imperial culture in nineteenth-century England.* Stanford: Stanford University Press.

Chanel, Coco

1883–1971—French fashion designer

Caryn E. NEUMANN
Miami University of Ohio

Although born into poverty, Coco Chanel rose to become an innovator and pioneer in women's fashion and perfumery. A savvy business leader, Chanel employed a brilliant sense of timing and leveraged her own sense of style and mystique into a brand and a look that forever changed the way that women wanted to dress.

A pioneer in women's fashion, Gabrielle "Coco" Chanel founded a business empire in the early twentieth century, leading women away from impractical clothing to designs that emphasized comfort and functionality as well as high style.

Born into poverty in the French town of Saumur in central France, Chanel learned to sew while attending a local convent school. In 1902, she took her first job as a dressmaker, becoming a milliner around 1908. Chanel's simply trimmed hats were a sharp contrast to the extravagant styles prevalent in the first years of the century. Fascinated by her unconventional approach to fashion, society women joined actresses and courtesans as customers of the rising designer. In 1910, Chanel opened her first shop, Chanel Modes, in Deauville, France. Her lease prevented her from competing with another dressmaking shop, but the women who bought Chanel hats admired the dresses worn by the milliner and requested copies. Sometime around 1910, Chanel also began selling clothing.

Rise of the House of Chanel

Although Chanel's artistry is indisputable, much of her success can be credited to timing. With the arrival in 1914 of World War I, conspicuous consumption suddenly seemed in extremely poor taste, and women pared down their attire. The many women who labored in support of the war effort sought versatile yet elegant clothing, and Chanel's designs satisfied these new dressing requirements by focusing on loose-fitting styles. She often favored masculine styles, elements of which were to survive even into her formal collections, in particular the small boater-shaped hats, neat collars, and shirt cuffs fastened with cuff links. Sleeves became a career-long obsession as the couturier constantly sought a design that would allow movement without distorting the line of the garment. By 1917, her loose sweater with a sailor collar and long, easy line had become a general fashion.

A shrewd marketer, Chanel anticipated the popularity of sportswear for outdoor living. During the war, she visited Biarritz, a fashionable resort in southwestern France that catered to the idle rich fleeing the ravages of war. Realizing that these moneyed refugees still wanted luxury in their lives, Chanel marketed her designs to them. War shortages in materials such as serge forced the couturier to use knitted jersey as a replacement, but she soon made it into a high-fashion item. Knitted jersey eventually became such a Chanel favorite (because of its comfort and shape) that the fashion magazine *Vogue* nicknamed her couture business "The Jersey House." Many of her later wool and cotton jersey fabrics were enhanced with silk to provide additional luster for added luxury.

Celebrity Marketing

By the 1920s, Chanel had become a celebrity with much-copied designs. While she never sold cheap goods, she did believe that her success depended in large part upon the dissemination of her styles. Her use of inexpensive textiles such as jersey and the minimal amounts of cloth that her styles required reduced the cost of duplication for the ready-to-wear market, while the loose shapes of her suits and dresses overcame sizing problems in manufacture.

To increase sales, Chanel exploited her personal celebrity status by using look-alike models in advertisements and cultivating an air of mystique. She also became the first designer to capitalize on her fame by marketing a perfume, Chanel No. 5, which launched in 1921 in a modernist bottle designed by Chanel herself. The simple name and bottle represented another break from tradition by moving away from the exotic titles and decorative flacons that had characterized perfume in the years before the war. To sell the perfume, Chanel sprayed samples in her fitting rooms, told her clients that only a small amount had been made up as gifts, and asked them if they thought it would sell. With a personal stake in the success of the perfume as a result of Chanel taking them into her confidence, these socialites helped promote Chanel's new luxury good and made it into an immediate success.

Fashion Innovations

An innovative leader, Chanel saw her business boom in the 1920s. In 1924, she branched into costume jewelry and became the first designer to gain social acceptance for these adornments. Pearls were a particular Chanel favorite, with her workshops producing masses of fake beads that defied nature in size and color. In 1926, Chanel introduced the "little black dress" that would eventually become a staple of women's wardrobes. Black had always been a popular choice for evening wear, but Chanel became the first to exploit the elegance and flattering qualities of the color with fabrics such as satin and silk velvet. She broke taboos by designing and wearing two-tone shoes and loose sailor-style trousers that ended above the ankle. The dramatic use of a combination of black and white in shoes as well as clothes became a Chanel trademark.

Chanel notoriously paid her workers little and gained a reputation as an irascible and autocratic leader. Her leadership as a couturier led Chanel into manufacturing. Many of the designers of this era endorsed products and designed textiles for manufacture as a means of gaining additional publicity and revenue. In 1928, Chanel opened her own factory, Tricots Chanel, in Asnières, northwest of Paris, to control production of her products better. The couturier would choose materials, explain her ideas to staff members, and then rely upon them to monitor production. She never drew designs but created them on a model, in the manner of a tailor. In 1930 she employed 2,400 workers in her factory and workrooms, with this number rising to 4,000 by the end of 1935.

Although Chanel had sold clothing during World War I, she closed her shop three weeks after the start of World War II in 1939 with the declaration that this was not a time for fashion. She continued to sell perfume and remained in Paris throughout the conflict. In 1953, Chanel reopened her business in an effort to help the sales of her perfume in a highly competitive marketplace. Her multicolored tweed suits in pastels as well as beige and white became favorites of society notables. On 10 January 1971, Chanel died in Paris.

A groundbreaking designer who combined elegance with ease of movement, Chanel changed the look of twentieth-century women's wear through shrewd marketing and an ability to capitalize on emerging needs.

Further Reading

Bailen, C. (1974). *Chanel solitaire*. New York: New York Times Books.

Baxter-Wright, E. (2013). *The little book of Chanel*. London: Carlton Books.

Charles-Roux, E. de. (1976). *Chanel*. London: Harvill Press.

De La Haye, A. & Tobin, S. (1994). *Chanel: The couturiere at work*. Woodstock, NY: Overlook Press.

Galante, P. (1973). *Mademoiselle Chanel*. Chicago: Henry Regnery.

Garelick, R. (2014). *Mademoiselle: Coco Chanel and the pulse of history*. New York: Random House.

Hess, M. (2015). *Coco Chanel: The illustrated world of a fashion icon*. London: Hardie Grant.

Madsen, A. (1990). *Chanel: A woman of her own*. New York: Henry Holt.

Wallach, J. (1998). *Chanel: Her style and her life*. New York: Nan A. Talese, Doubleday.

Alice Milliat and the Women's World Games

Allen GUTTMANN
Amherst College

Today's Olympic athletes may not realize the long road that brought women to compete in the summer games in 1928. Alice Milliat, a Frenchwoman, organized and oversaw four successive Women's World Games beginning in 1922 and worked tirelessly for the inclusion of women in the Olympic Games.

R alph Waldo Emerson asserted that every institution is the lengthened shadow of a great man. If one substitutes "woman" for "man," Emerson's hyperbole holds true for Alice Million Milliat (1884–1957) and the Fédération Sportive Féminine Internationale (FSFI), the organization that staged four successive Olympiques Féminins in the years 1922–1934.

The platform from which Milliat launched her remarkable career as a sports administrator was Fémina Sport, a Parisian club founded in 1911 to encourage sports among upper-class women. (Her own favorite sport was rowing.) In 1917, Fémina Sport joined a number of other clubs to form the Fédération des Sociétés Féminines Sportives de France (FSFSF). Although all of the clubs were led by men, Milliat was named the federation's treasurer. Early married, early widowed, and childless, Milliat had the time, the energy, and the material resources to dedicate herself wholeheartedly to women's sports. In 1918, she became the FSFSF secretary-general. A year later, she was elected president by a unanimous vote. A year after that, all the officers of the FSFSF were female.

After the FSFSF staged France's first track-and-field championships for women in 1917, Milliat worked hard to organize additional national championships in soccer, basketball, field hockey, and swimming. It is likely, although not certain, that it was also she who arranged, in 1918, for two Fémina Sport teams to play a game of soccer as a curtain-raiser to a match between the French and Belgian national teams. In 1920, a women's team formed from nine French sports clubs crossed the Channel to Lancashire to play a series of four matches against Dick, Kerr's Ladies, a soccer team formed by employees of the engineering firm Dick, Kerr & Co. The expedition was arranged by Alice Milliat.

It was, however, women's track-and-field sports, not soccer, that became the focus of Milliat's efforts. Although a number of historians have asserted that Milliat was the organizer of the Olympiade Féminine that was staged in Monte Carlo in the summer of 1921; that honor belonged to Camille Blanc, mayor of Beaulieu and president of the socially exclusive International Sporting Club of Monaco. On 31 October 1921, only five months after the games at Monte Carlo proved the viability of international competitions for women, Milliat was among the seven delegates who met in Paris to create the FSFI. By all rights, Milliat should have been named president of the organization, but Émile Antoine insisted that women lacked the aura of authority necessary to assume leadership of an international organization. A year later, it was obvious that Milliat had the necessary aura as well as a full measure of administrative talent. She became and remained president of the FSFI.

The success of the first Jeux Internationaux Féminins, otherwise known as the Jeux Olympiques Féminins or the Women's International Games, testified to Milliat's ability to lead. These games were held in Paris on 10 August 1922. Over 20,000 spectators crowded the Stade Pershing stadium to watch athletes from five nations compete in the eleven-event program, which included a 1,000-meter race, a distance then considered to be an enormous challenge for a young woman.

Opposition and Success on the Road to the Olympics

Although the French press was generally enthusiastic about these women's games, there was some adverse commentary from conservatives scandalized by the sight of young women running races in shorts and T-shirts. Milliat was not deterred. Responding to critics in *Le Miroir des Sports* (March 1925), she described female athletes as *une caste* that had to stand firm against opposition. While Milliat acknowledged the appeals of traditional femininity, she argued that a woman's strength, endurance, and speed were as socially desirable as charm, poise, and grace. Unlike more conventional advocates of women's sports, she seems to have had no qualms about muscular development. (As a fully committed feminist, she also fought for the right of women to vote.)

The most serious opposition to the Jeux Olympiques Féminins came from the International Olympic Committee (IOC) and the International Amateur Athletic Federation (IAAF). To appease the IOC, Milliat agreed to renounce all use of the word "Olympique." Although the Swedish president of the IAAF, Sigfrid Edström, was extremely unhappy about Milliat's challenge, he eventually opted for compromise and persuaded her, in 1926, and to accept IAAF rules and regulations (revised for women where necessary). The IAAF then persuaded the International Olympic Committee to include women's track and field in the program for the 1928 games in Amsterdam.

The Jeux Féminins Mondiaux, the second FSFI-sponsored games, took place in Göteborg, Sweden, in 1926. They were another resounding success. France's Marguerite Radieau ran 100 yards in 11.8 seconds, but the sensation of the games was nineteen-year-old Kinue Hitomi, the first Japanese woman to represent her country in an international sports competition. She won gold medals in the standing and the running long jump, a silver medal in the discus, and another for the 100-yard dash. (Göteborg was also the site for an international conference on women's sports, one of nine over which Milliat presided.)

The compromise with the IAAF left Milliat unsatisfied. At the Amsterdam games, women's track and field was limited to a mere five events: the 100-meter and 800-meter races, the high jump, the discus, and the 4 x 100-meter relay. The future of women's participation was endangered by the IOC's hysterical reaction to the sight of women who were exhausted by the 800-meter race. The panicky members voted in 1929 to eliminate women's track and field. As the Olympic Congress convened in Berlin in 1930, Milliat asked the IOC to reverse itself. Yet Count Henri de Baillet-Latour, the third president of the International Olympic Committee, wrote on August 31 1931, most likely to his predecessor, Pierre de Coubertin, founder of the committee: "I can only hope one thing: that the day may come soon that women liberate themselves completely from men's custody, that they organize the Women's World Games (Jeux Mondiaux Feminins), which would allow us to exclude them entirely from the Olympic Games" (Renson 2012). Thanks in part to assistance from Americans Avery Brundage and Gustavus T. Kirby, both major figures in the IAAF, Milliat did manage to persuade the IOC to change its collective mind and keep women's track and field on the program for the 1932 games in Los Angeles. The vote was seventeen to one.

The third Women's International Games took place in Prague in 1930. The program was expanded to include not only track-and-field contests but also four team-sport tournaments—in soccer, basketball, barette (similar to rugby), and hazena (similar to team handball). There were 214 athletes from seventeen countries gathered for the three-day event in Letna Stadium. The brightest star was Poland's Stanislava Walaciewitcz, subsequently known in the United States as Stella Walsh. She won three gold medals for races over 60, 100, and 200 meters.

The fourth Women's World Games took place in London in 1934. Nineteen teams competed, but the German women were so overwhelmingly superior that they garnered more points than the next three countries combined.

Joining the Olympics at Last

Meeting during the Berlin Olympics of 1936, the IAAF voted (fifteen to four with five abstentions) to sponsor rather than simply to recognize women's events, to accept the FSFI's records as official, and to recommend the expansion of women's Olympic track and field from six to nine events. These were among Milliat's goals, but the price she paid was the end of the FSFI as an independent organization. The last of the FSFI's quadrennial sports festivals, held in Vienna in 1938, was officially sponsored by the IAAF, but it was downgraded to the level of a European championship. Milliat, now over fifty, retired from the international stage and lived the rest of her life in undeserved obscurity. In a 1974 interview, Germaine Gagneux-Bisson, the secretary treasurer of the FSFI in 1936, admitted that Milliat was a willful person who sometimes antagonized her male colleagues—who were not accustomed to forceful women. Avery Brundage, who served with Milliat on many IAAF committees, was among those antagonized by her perseverance: "She was active for years and she demanded more and more. She made quite a nuisance of herself" (Guttmann 2003, 171). Another way to explain her achievements and to assess her personality and style of leadership is to say that she was canny enough to understand that nice girls finish last.

Further Reading

De Coubertin, P. (1979). *Olympic memoirs.* Lausanne, Switzerland: International Olympic Committee.

Drevon, A. (2005). *Alice Milliat, La Pasionaria du Sport feminine.* Paris: Vuibert.

Guttmann, A. (1984). *The games must go on: Avery Brundage and the Olympic movement.* New York: Columbia University Press.

Guttmann, A. (2003). *The Olympics* (2nd ed.). Urbana: University of Illinois Press.

MacAloon, J. J. (1981). *This great symbol: Pierre de Coubertin and the origins of the modern Olympic games.* Chicago: University of Chicago Press.

Morris, M. (Lord Killanin). (1983). *My Olympic years.* London: Seeker & Warburg.

Renson R. (2012). Stepping out of Coubertin's shadow: The count and the 1932 Winter Olympics. *Journal of Olympic History, 20*(3), 18–27.

Young. D. C. (1996). *The modern Olympics.* Baltimore: Johns Hopkins University Press.

Song Qingling

1893–1981—Political figure and philanthropist;
wife of Chinese leader Sun Yat-sen

Lijun HE and Caroline REEVES
*Pace University and Fairbank Center
for Chinese Studies, Harvard University*

One of the most prominent women in China in the early to mid-twentieth
century, Song Qingling was active in the political and the humanitarian
arenas over the course of her life. Known as the "the Mother of China,"
she was the second wife of Sun Yat-sen and re-defined the role of wives of
Chinese political leaders.

Wife and widow of the "Father of China" Sun Yat-sen (1866–1925), Song
Qingling is arguably one of the most influential women of the twentieth
century. Song Qingling was an inspirational figure in the creation of the
modern Chinese nation and in the development of the Communist regime, as important to the Chinese Communist Party (CCP) as her sister, Madame Chiang Kai-
shek was to the Nationalist party (the KMT). Both a political figure and a member
of the social elite, Song played a critical role safeguarding ideas of public social
welfare, particularly for women and children, throughout the establishment and
development of the People's Republic of China (PRC). Today one of China's best-
known philanthropists, Song Qingling is outstanding both as a woman leader and
as a compassionate public figure in a time of trauma and turmoil.

In the early years of the twentieth century, Song Qingling was an advocate for
the new Chinese nation in China and in the United States, where she was one of the
first Chinese women to study abroad. Although he was twenty-six years her senior
and a friend of her father, Sun Yat-sen and Song married in 1915, shortly after the
overthrow of the Qing Dynasty (1644–1911) and the founding of the Republic of
China, a revolution for which Sun is credited. As civil war divided her country, Song
championed her husband's Three Principles of the People—nationalism, democracy, and people's livelihood—and became the keeper of his vision and an outspoken representative of his ideals even after Sun's death in 1925. Song was wooed by
both the Nationalists and the Communists in their fight for control of Sun's legacy
and his Nationalist Party, but Song Qingling came down firmly on the side of the
Communists and China's vast peasant population, an allegiance she would not renounce even after her brother-in-law Chiang Kai-shek put a price on her head and
Red China became a pariah in the capitalist world of the 1950s.

An Overseas Education

Song Qingling was the second daughter of six children born into the wealthy, Christian family of Charlie Soong, a prominent Shanghai missionary, banker, and businessman. Born the same year as Mao Zedong (1893–1976), Song Qingling faced many of the same issues that Mao would grapple with: How to save China from the threat of Western (and also Japanese) domination, how to strengthen the Chinese people, how to improve the position of women and the poor, how to lead a life of action, rather than settling complacently into the social milieu into which they were born. In a time and place where women—in Mao's words—were often chained to men as little more than chattel, Song Qingling's challenge was, in many ways, exponentially more difficult than Mao's. Fortunately for her, however, the Song family was relatively progressive and extremely cosmopolitan. Her father chose to send her to school, first to the McTyeire School for Girls in Shanghai and then in 1908 to Wesleyan College in Macon, Georgia. In the United States, Song began her political life writing fiery essays about a future for China in which she saw students—male and female—returning from overseas as important catalysts for the improvement of the nation. Song also wrote about the injustice of arranged marriages, a tradition that she would personally contest, and global issues such as world peace.

Song graduated from Wesleyan in 1913, two years after her husband-to-be Sun Yat-sen led the revolution that overturned China's last imperial dynasty. When Song returned to China, she became reacquainted with Sun, who had been working with her father. As China erupted into chaos and warlordism, Sun left in exile for Japan. Song accompanied him there as his secretary, dedicated to their shared vision for China. Despite Sun's having been in an arranged marriage since he was nineteen, their relationship soon blossomed. Sun was forty-eight, with three children. Romantic love was still a novelty among the Chinese, and their affair was shocking: more because of Song's defiance of cultural mores regarding women's non-interference in their own marriage-choice and her Christian parents' objection to Sun's having to divorce than because of the age difference between the two lovers. When Song's parents opposed the marriage, Song, with the help of her maid, climbed out her window to join her husband-to-be. The two were even more celebrated as a married couple than Sun had been alone. Song Qingling became (as Madame Zhou Enlai, wife of CCP leader and future premier of China, called her at Song's funeral), "the image of a young woman revolutionary," embodying the pure ideals of the Chinese revolution. Within a decade, the marriage was cut short by Sun Yat-sen's death, but Song Qingling never remarried nor compromised her loyalty to her husband's principles. Song Qingling had become Madame Sun Yat-sen, "Mother of China."

Life with the Communist Party

From the late 1920s through her death, Song Qingling became an international political figure committed to Chinese communism. In 1923, she and Sun Yat-sen entered into a cooperative agreement with the Communist Party to unify a war-torn China. Many of Sun's core ideas about fighting imperialism and social reform resonated with the Russian revolutionary Vladimir Lenin, who praised Sun and sent military aid to help with the reunification attempt. During this period, Song

Qingling became a vital, active member of Sun's team, working closely with him and in significant roles with the CPC, whose hopes and vision for the future of China closely mirrored her own. After 1927, however, Sun's KMT (which he had founded in 1912) split into two violently opposed factions, left and right. Chiang Kai-shek, Song's new brother-in-law, set out on his own more conservative path, supported by another brother-in-law of Song, H.H. Kung, and her brother T.V. Soong, all of whom pressured her to bring her late husband's prestige and pedigree to bear on their political side. Song threw in her lot with the communists, however, making her point abundantly clear by going into self-imposed exile in Moscow in 1927.

In 1949, at the founding of the People's Republic of China (PRC), Song Qingling's importance to Communist China as a national figure was recognized, and she was named a vice chairman of the Central People's Government (one of six chairs, five of whom were men, and all of whom became historical luminaries). Song used her positions to help set the agenda for women's and children's rights and welfare in China. Song's earlier work advancing women's and children's health and well-being through the China Defense League (founded in 1938 in Hong Kong and first renamed the China Welfare Fund and later the China Welfare Institute) was also officially recognized in 1950, when Song was named chairman of the Chinese People's Relief Administration. This organization became the premiere vehicle for social welfare work for the new People's Republic. Song Qingling's symbolic importance to her nation was highlighted when she was appointed vice president of China in 1959 and finally, a week before her death in 1981, honorary president of the PRC, the only woman ever to serve in those roles.

Philanthropic Work

During WWII, Song put aside her ideological differences with the new KMT and raised funds and collected medicine and clothing for starving children in the war zones, capitalizing on her reputation in the international community to secure basic sustenance and rights for women and children. Active first in Hong Kong and later in Chongqing (where she was kept a virtual prisoner by her brother-in-law), Song founded and supported the China Defense League to accomplish her philanthropic goals. After the establishment of the PRC in 1949, Song further dedicated herself to public welfare, continuing her focus on children, women, and health. Song assumed important leadership roles in many non-governmental organizations, including serving as chairwoman of the All-China Democratic Women's Federation, the All-China Women's Federation, the China National Association for the Protection of Children and as a board member of the World Peace Council.

In 1951, Song received the Stalin Peace Award (the communist bloc equivalent of the Nobel Peace Prize) and donated her prize money to the China Welfare Institute. She later did the same with the royalties of her book *The Struggle for New China* (1953). Most of Song's work was carried out under the umbrella of this institute, including the establishment and funding of many hospitals, a penicillin research institute, and tuberculosis rehab centers. Through her work, Song clearly expressed her dedication to children, which she herself never had. Song also made tremendous contributions to gender equity in China and promoted women's rights around the world. In one of her speeches in Kobe, Japan in 1924, Song stated, "The position of women is the measure of the development of the nation…Today only a nation that understands this can become great." Song maintained this commitment to improving the lives of women and children throughout her life.

Similar to her near contemporary Eleanor Roosevelt (1884–1962) in the United States, Song Qingling redefined the role of "first lady" in China, both while her husband was alive and after his death. She stood out in her own right for her dignified elegance, her principled adherence to her own beliefs, and her advocacy for China's downtrodden, setting an agenda which philanthropists would follow over the next century. Coming of age in a time of social and political change in China, Song Qingling created her own path in her personal and public life, becoming a beacon of honorable loyalty and social action for her country, then and today.

Further Reading

Chang, J. & Halliday, J. (1986). *Madame Sun Yat-Sen: Soong Ching-Ling (Lives of Modern Women)*. Harmondsworth, Middlesex, England: Penguin Books.

China Welfare Institute. (2012). The roots and meaning of Song Chingling's childhood education. Retrieved May 26, 2016, from http://www.cwi.org.cn/zh/content.aspx?id=3347

China Welfare Institute. (2012). Great female leader. Retrieved May 26, 2016, from http://www.cwi.org.cn/zh/content.aspx?id=3343

Epstein, Israel. 1993. *Woman in world history: Soong Ching Ling*. Beijing: New World Press.

Mead, Margaret

1901–1978—US anthropologist

Frank A. SALAMONE
Iona College and University of Phoenix

The famous anthropologist Margaret Mead was the first person to study and write about human development from a cross-cultural perspective. As a teacher, writer, and speaker, she took a leadership role in addressing issues of women's rights, population control, nuclear proliferation, race relations, environmental pollution, and world hunger. She believed that the purpose of anthropology is to aid those who need help and to solve the problems of the world.

The most famous anthropologist of her time and perhaps even the most famous of all time, Margaret Mead pioneered the study of gender, anthropological feminism, the use of film in anthropological studies, the influence of culture on human development—especially adolescence—the generation gap, and numerous other topics of widespread interest and importance. The force of her personality and the pioneering nature of her work made her an outstanding leader. She took anthropology to the general public, demonstrating its usefulness in understanding problems of modern complex societies as well as those of technologically simpler ones.

Early Life and Education

Margaret Mead came from a line of strong-willed females and was educated at home, from time to time, by her grandmother. Both of her parents were social scientists, and she majored in sociology as an undergraduate and psychology for her master's degree before turning to anthropology. In 1919, she was a freshman at De Paul University and later transferred to Barnard College. At Columbia University, she came under the influence of US anthropologists Franz Boas (1858–1942) and Ruth Benedict (1887–1948).

She received her Ph.D. in 1929 for her work in Samoa, based mainly on her 1925 field trip there. That trip also resulted in the first of her twenty-three books, *Coming of Age in Samoa* ([1928] 1968). The book is still in print and sells well. It also demonstrates her use of observation to draw conclusions as well as her skill in using traditional societies to shed light on modern problems.

Her editors asked her to write a final chapter that looked at adolescence in the United States. It was that chapter that caught the attention of the general public. In the nature-versus-nurture controversy that was raging in the 1920s and continues into the present day, Mead was basically on the side of nurture or environment or, as it is sometimes termed, cultural determinism. She did not ignore biology, however, as Derek Freeman (1916–2001), a late-twentieth-century anthropologist, and others believed. She was simply interested in what culture does to shape or work on biology.

She wrote many other influential works over her career, including *Growing Up in New Guinea, Sex and Temperament in Three Primitive Societies, Balinese Character: A Photographic Analysis, Continuities in Cultural Evolution,* and *A Rap on Race* (1971, with James Baldwin). In addition to books, Mead wrote a regular column in *Redbook*, appeared on television numerous times, wrote popular articles for many magazines, testified at congressional hearings, gave numerous lectures, and taught from time to time.

She never held a permanent teaching position, although she was a brilliant teacher. She choose to work at the American Museum of Natural History in New York City because she did not want to get involved in the politics of academic life at a time when women were openly discriminated against in favor of less-qualified men. She saw how badly her former teacher and lifetime friend Ruth Benedict was treated at Columbia, where she was passed over for promotions in favor of less-qualified men. Mead felt that she could better use her energies to help other people if she did not have to waste time fighting for her own position. She did teach at an impressive number of schools, either as an adjunct or on temporary assignments, including Columbia University, Yale, Emory, and others. Later in her career, in 1968, she founded the Anthropology Department at Fordham University and chaired its Social Science Division until 1974.

The museum offered her a great deal of autonomy. She served there as assistant curator (1926–1942), associate curator (1942–1964), curator of ethnology (1964–1969), and curator emeritus (1969–1978). From that location she was able to carry on numerous field trips, stay in contact with colleagues all over the world, and promote causes important to her. She was also able to make numerous scientific contributions, staying close to the solid world that artifacts created.

Mead received numerous honors during her lifetime. She was president of the American Anthropological Association, the first president of the American Association for the Advancement of Science elected by its membership, president of the Anthropological Film Institute, president of the Scientists Institute for Public Information, president of the Society for Applied Anthropology, holder of twenty-eight honorary doctorates, and a posthumous recipient of the Presidential Medal of Freedom in 1979.

Contributions to Her Field and Beyond

Mead made numerous contributions to anthropology and to the promotion of causes in general. For her there was no distinction to be made between these two areas, for the purpose of anthropology is to aid those who need help. It is an applied science whose theory should aid parishioners, in her mind, to solve the problems of the world. In the battle between weak and strong, Mead stood firmly on the side of the underprivileged and was never afraid to speak her mind.

Her anthropological work, largely conducted among the peoples of Oceania, looked at the interrelationship between culture and psychological development. She was concerned with the cultural conditioning of sexual behavior, national character, and culture change. After World War II, she became intensely interested in culture change and how to ease its effects on a population.

Mead was the first, and aside from Napoleon Chagnon (b. 1938) and Clifford Geertz (1926–2006) about the only celebrity anthropologist. She was deeply concerned with the issues of women's rights, population control, childrearing, sexual morality, nuclear proliferation, race relations, drug abuse, environmental pollution, world hunger, poverty, human rights, and peace.

Mead's work in New Guinea with Reo Fortune (1903–1979), a brilliant anthropologist and her second husband, was set up to test yet another hypothesis. Her first work on Samoa tested the universality or the lack of the "storm and stress" nature of adolescence. The work on New Guinea tested the "childlike" nature of traditional peoples. Mead demonstrated that "primitive" people were no more childlike than any "modern" people, and that stages of human development had to be studied in specific cultural contexts. Each one of her works tested some basic concept. She was truly the first person to study human development from a cross-cultural perspective.

Mead looked at other issues from this perspective. She noted that gender roles differ from society to society. In Bali, with UK anthropologist Gregory Bateson (1904–1980), her third husband, she documented the connection between childrearing and adult behavior. They also explored the symbolic connection between childrearing, adult personality, and symbols.

On a more personal note, she and Bateson had a daughter, Mary Catherine Bateson (b. 1939), who, like her parents, was a significant anthropologist in her own right. Mead's pediatrician was Benjamin Spock (1903–1998), who has acknowledged his debt to "Maggie" for his approach to childrearing and development.

Much of Mead's ability to address so many issues came from her conviction, rooted in anthropology's holistic approach, that everything is interconnected. Ritual, for example, is related to food production. Thus, during World War II, Mead along with Ruth Benedict and others founded the Institute for Intercultural Studies, which led the way in applying anthropological techniques to the study of modern and technologically complex cultures.

After the war, Mead went back to Manus in 1953 to study the spectacular changes resulting from World War II and modernization. In *New Lives for Old* she argued that there are many possible futures. A society can choose the one best suited to it. Mead held that racism, warfare, and environmental exploitation are learned conditions. Traditions that condition these behaviors can be changed. New institutions can replace old ones.

Mead drew a great deal of criticism as well as praise. Her research methods were criticized as unscientific and accounts in her bestselling books on Samoa proved to be untrue. Some attacked her as being too radical because she argued for the legalization of marijuana and advocated trial marriages. She loved to stir up controversy. She did help shape the American family with her writing and teachings.

Although she said she was not a feminist but a woman who was feminine, Margaret Mead was named to the list of American's Leading Feminists two years after her death in 1978. Advocating issues that have come to be termed as feminist ones was but one of many of her outstanding contributions in which she took the lead. She promoted many causes, each of them trying to help the underdog achieve a better life in what her colleague and friend Ruth Benedict termed a synergistic way.

Further Reading

Freeman, Derek. (1983). *Margaret Mead and Samoa*. Cambridge, MA: Harvard University Press.

Howard, J. (1984). *Margaret Mead: A life*. New York: Simon and Schuster.

Kottak, C. P. (1997). *Anthropology: The exploration of human diversity*. New York: McGraw-Hill.

Mead, M. (1972). *Blackberry winter: My earlier years*. New York: Morrow.

Shankman, Paul. (2009). *The Trashing of Margaret Mead: Anatomy of an Anthropological Controversy*. University of Wisconsin Press.

Mother Teresa

1910–1997—Catholic nun and Nobel Peace
Prize winner

Carolyn M. YOUSSEF-MORGAN
Bellevue University

Mother Teresa founded her own congregation of nuns who ministered to
the poor, ill, and dying in Calcutta, India. She also instituted schooling for
destitute children and worked for the better treatment of AIDS patients in
the United States. Winner of the Nobel Peace Prize, she was a charismatic
leader who drew devoted followers from all walks of life and is remembered as one who led by example.

Mother Teresa was the recipient of the Nobel Peace Prize and the Popular
Prize for Peace in 1979, for her extensive, extraordinary service among the
poorest of the poor. She was the founder of the Missionaries of Charity,
which are now present in almost every country in the world. Her most remarkable
projects included care homes for the abandoned dying, which she called "Nirmal
Hriday" (home of the pure heart); a basic public education system that primarily
targeted children in slum areas with elementary lessons in hygiene, manners, matters of faith, math, and reading, which she called "Shishu Bhaven" (the children's
home in Calcutta for the Sisters of Charity); centers and mobile clinics that ministered to the needs of people with leprosy and AIDS; shelters for single mothers;
homes for handicapped children; soup kitchens for the homeless; visits and ministry to prisoners; and many others.

Early Years

Mother Teresa was born in 1910 in Skopje, Albania. Her father was a successful
businessman. He was poisoned in 1919 due to his high profile as a nationalist and
a councilman of the city government after Albania gained its independence from
the Turkish occupation in 1912. Her mother was a religious, loving housewife. She
worked as a dressmaker and weaver in order to provide for her family after her de-
ceased husband's business partner took over their business.

At the age of twelve, young Agnes Gonxha Bojaxhiu (Mother Teresa's original
name) started to have a strong desire to pursue a religious vocation, but she was
advised by the pastor of her church, the Parish Church of the Sacred Heart, to
wait, pray, and ask for light. Six years later, in one of her long, frequent meditation

visits to the nearby shrine of Our Lady of Letnice, she heard the divine call and consecrated herself forever to God and his service. She shared her heart with her mother who, in spite of her concerns about her daughter's departure and her weak health, fully supported her and encouraged her to take the necessary steps to put her decision into practice.

The Journey to India

In a long conversation with the pastor, Gonxha revealed her desire to serve the poor in India. The congregation that worked in India didn't have houses of formation in Albania, so she had to enroll in Ireland. In 1928, Gonxha went to Ireland, became part of the Sisters of Our Lady of Loreto, spent two months learning English, and was sent to Darjeeling, India, for two years of training and formation. In 1931, she made her first vows and chose the name Teresa, after Saint Thérèse of Lisieux. After one year, she made her final vows, and was assigned to a teaching position at Saint Mary's High School, which served the wealthy girls of Calcutta.

After witnessing the Gandhian struggle for independence in the mid-forties, Sister Teresa experienced a "vocational crisis," and felt that God was calling her toward something different, "to total self-surrender to the service of the poor . . . to a mission of charity" (Gonzalez-Balado 1997, 37). She left the Sisters of Loreto, where she had been content and happy for nearly twenty years, and pursued her calling. In order to best serve the poor, she went to Patna and studied at the school for nurses of the Medical Mission Sisters. Several months later, she returned to Calcutta, and lived with the Little Sisters of the Poor at Saint Joseph's Asylum for the Elderly. Each day she relentlessly worked in the slums among the abandoned. Meanwhile, she started looking for her own lodging, which was eventually furnished by the father of one of her former students. This humble place was the beginning of the Missionaries of Charity. In two years, the community grew to twenty-eight women, many of whom were Sister Teresa's former students, and all of whom adopted her modest lifestyle, distinguished by their blue-and-white saris. Eventually, the priests provided a larger place for Mother Teresa and her followers. This later became the headquarters of the Missionaries of Charity, a congregation now present in almost every country in the world, in some cases at the request of government leaders in countries where religious organizations were illegal, such as Cuba, the former Soviet Union, and Albania, Mother Teresa's home country.

Major Contributions in a Lifetime of Service

The first and most remarkable project that Mother Teresa embarked on was an attempt to assist the abandoned dying in the streets of Calcutta. By that time, Mother Teresa had received Indian citizenship. She met with the mayor and was granted a location to serve the dying homeless of all religions, which she called "Nirmal Hriday." There, the sisters tended to the dying (whom they usually collected from the streets), showing them that they were valued and respected. This place is now a popular tourist attraction, included in the city's official guidebooks. It also attracts many volunteers and medical student trainees.

Another field where Mother Teresa served the poor was teaching the children in the district of Motijhil, a slum near the high school where she used to teach. She taught basic lessons in hygiene, usually holding her classes outdoors, under a tree. Then, she gradually integrated instructions on manners, matters of faith, math, and reading. Later on, she used a donation that she received to rent a shack and purchase a blackboard. As the number of children grew, she acquired a building and surrounding acreage, which she called "Shishu Bhaven," through which she expanded her small system of public education. Today, such centers operate in many countries.

As the number of sisters grew to more than fifty, another group of the poor was added to their scope of services: people with leprosy. Mother Teresa started her "mobile clinics," which were basically a few sisters carrying small medicine kits and traveling by public transportation into the areas where people with leprosy dwelled. With time, Mother Teresa was able to establish centers that ministered to the specific needs of people with leprosy. The first center was constructed with the money collected from a public raffle of a limousine that was given to Mother Teresa by Pope Paul VI when he visited India in 1964, supposedly to facilitate her tough journeys. Later, Mother Teresa used the money from the Nobel Peace Prize she won in 1979 to construct a self-governing village in Titagarh, India, for the rehabilitation of people with leprosy.

In the mid-1980s, AIDS patients became another area of focus for Mother Teresa and her sisters. Mother Teresa began in New York City, asking the mayor for a local site where she and her sisters could serve AIDS patients, despite the severe opposition of local residents. A year later, she was asked, and supported by President Ronald Reagan, to open a home for AIDS patients in Washington, DC.

As time went by, Mother Teresa's service expanded into many diversified areas. Mother Teresa's congregation even gave birth in 1963 to a male congregation, the "Missionaries of Charity Brothers." Most of the first members were the biological brothers of some of the sisters. Mother Teresa started looking for a male leader who could handle the responsibilities of this new congregation, and found Father Ian Travers-Ball, a young Australian Jesuit priest, who left the Jesuits, and became the well-known preacher, Brother Andrew. Now, the Missionaries of Charity Brothers have spread all over the world.

Worldwide Reputation and Publicity

Mother Teresa's activities made her known worldwide and consequently opened doors for her ministry outside India. For example, in 1960, Mother Teresa gave her first presentation at the annual convention of the National Council of Catholic Women of the United States in Las Vegas. In addition to the large audience that attended this presentation, Mother Teresa made contacts during her visit and met with numerous well-known religious and political figures on her several stops in the United States. Many of these contacts proved important for her future work.

Around the same time, Mother Teresa was also publicly interviewed for the first time on a British Broadcasting Corporation radio program by the British journalist Malcolm Muggeridge, who proposed and facilitated the production of the first television documentary about Mother Teresa, and whose biography of Mother Teresa was translated into more than twenty languages. In 1982, Malcolm Muggeridge and his wife became Catholic.

Mother Teresa became more outspoken over the years, publicly advising politicians to spend more time on their knees in prayer in order to recognize the pain and injustice in their own systems, rebuking them when she felt that they made ungodly decisions, and speaking out against abortion as the greatest of crimes against children, women, and life. She even took part in marches and demonstrations against the legislation of abortion in Spain and Italy. She met and had conversations with many distinguished public figures, and was invited to address the world's political elite on important occasions. She always showed up in her modest white-and-blue sari and sandals, packing her travel necessities in cardboard boxes tied with string, and holding her cloth bag. Even when she was awarded the Nobel Prize, Mother Teresa requested the cost of the customary gala dinner celebration for hundreds of dignitaries from around the world to go to the poor. Fifteen thousand people enjoyed a special meal that day.

Due to her failing health, which was aggravated by her hectic lifestyle and malnourished diet, Mother Teresa resigned in 1996 as superior general of the Missionaries of Charity and died in 1997. She left an army of about four thousand missionaries, from all over the world, many of whom were college students or well-paid professionals, all of whom wore the white-and-blue sari, and refused any kind of salary or fixed income, preferring to be dependent on "divine providence."

Within two years of her death, the Church began proceedings to declare her a saint, with Pope John Paul II himself expediting the process. On 19 October 2003, she was beatified, meaning that for Catholics she was among "the blessed" and had lived a holy life. Her canonization as a saint occurred on 4 September 2016.

In the years before and after her death, critics have also come forth, including those who accused her of trying to convert Hindus under her care to Christianity. Others have decried the poor conditions of her treatment facilities, and questioned the standard of care she provided, her management of funds received, and ties to questionable political figures such as Haitian dictator Jean-Claude Duvalier. Even her nuns have come under attack for proselytizing and for reportedly baptizing the dying under their care.

Mother Teresa's Leadership

Driven by her mission, Mother Teresa devoted herself to the service of the poorest of the poor, which often meant being in a crisis-management situation. She always developed radical solutions to crises. She was expressive, self-determined, insightful, eloquent, and active. All of these qualities attracted even the mostly unlikely of followers to her congregation.

Many of Mother Teresa's first devotees were her former students from Saint Mary's High School, i.e., the wealthy girls of Calcutta, many from powerful families. Moreover, many affluent, successful people participated as coworkers in Mother Teresa's ministry on a part-time basis. Later, they formed an organization with its own official identity. So, what attracted, and still attracts, wealthy, well-educated people to Mother Teresa and her way of life? The answer is that most of those people did not only identify with Mother Teresa as a person, but also with her vision, her mission, and her goals. She was able to address a higher level of need inside them, beyond the initial attraction to a charismatic leader. Her humility, strong conviction, and worthwhile cause challenged them. She "conceive[d] and articulate[d] goals that lift[ed] people out of their petty occupations, carr[ied] them above the conflicts that tear a society apart, and unite[d] them in the pursuit of objectives worthy of their best efforts," as leadership scholar and political figure John Gardner described inspirational leaders (cited in Bass 1990, 207).

Due to her exemplary leadership style, Mother Teresa's followers perceived her as charismatic, even though she lacked the "glamour" that usually accompanies many charismatic leaders. In other words, her charisma was in the eyes of her beholders, and in her cause, rather than just in her own personal attractiveness. This made her followers attribute legitimacy to her, although she hardly had any legitimate power to use in accomplishing her goals. Mother Teresa had nothing to give or to promise her followers, except a tough life of poverty and hard work.

Reflecting on Mother Teresa's early years of life, one cannot fail to observe a very secure leader in the making, a characteristic which only strengthened with her faith and love for mankind. Does Mother Teresa's strong leadership style relate to her beginnings? Her biographers, as well as she herself, who said, "Spread love everywhere you go: First of all in your own house…" would testify that it did.

Further Reading

Bass, B. M. (1990). *Bass and Stodgill's handbook of leadership: Theory, research, and managerial applications* (3rd ed.). New York: Free Press.

Choi, Y. & Mai-Dalton, R. R. (1999). The model of followers' response to self-sacrificial leadership: An empirical test. *Leadership Quarterly, 10*, 397–422.

Conger, J. A. & Kanungo, R. A. (Eds.). (1988). *Charismatic leadership: The elusive factor in organizational effectiveness*. San Francisco: Jossey-Bass.

Gonzalez-Balado, J. L. (1997). *Mother Teresa: Her love, her work, her message*. Liguori, MO: Liguori Publications.

Le Joly, E. & Chaliha, J. (2002). *Mother Teresa's reaching out in love*. Lanham, MD: Barnes & Noble Books.

Muggeridge, M. (1971). *Something beautiful for God*. San Francisco: Harper Collins.

Popper, M.; Mayseless, O.; & Caternovo, O. (2000). Transformational leadership and attachment. *Leadership Quarterly, 11*, 267–290.

Saavedra, C. (1997). *Mother Teresa: In my own words: 1910–1997*. Westminster, MD: Random House Value Publishing, Inc.

Spink, K. (1998). *Mother Teresa: A complete authorized biography*. Scranton, PA: HarperCollins Publishers.

Weber, M. (1947). *The theory of social organizations* (T. Parsons, Trans.). New York: Free Press. (Original work published 1924).

Youssef-Morgan, C.M. (2016). The life and leadership of Mother Teresa. In Goethals & C. Hoyt (Eds.), *Women and leadership: History, concepts, and case studies*. Great Barrington, MA: Berkshire/Sage.

Yukl, G. (2001). *Leadership in organizations* (5th ed.). Englewood Cliffs, NJ: Prentice-Hall.

King, Billie Jean

b. 1943—US tennis champion and leader in the women's sport movement

Christine SHELTON
Smith College

Billie Jean King has led by example as she fought for greater equality for women tennis players and ushered the women's sport movement into the twentieth century. She continues to lead with energy and a sense of urgency to work for gender equity and for social change.

Born Billie Jean Moffitt, King began her tennis career at age eleven in the public parks of Long Beach, California, telling her mother, "I am going to be number one in the world." To help pay for her tennis equipment and excursions to tournaments, her mother went to work, and her father (a firefighter) took on a second job. Due to these circumstances, Billie Jean King has always resented the old-fashioned image of tennis as a pastime of the rich. In 1967, she spoke out against the United States Lawn Tennis Association's (USLTA) practice of "shamateurism"—paying top amateur players under the table so that they could afford the expenses of participating in USLTA-sponsored amateur tournaments. King felt the practice was corrupt and held tennis back by preventing the professionalization of the game. She led tennis into a more honest era in 1968 when promoters agreed to allow professionals and amateurs to compete against each other in tournaments.

Leadership Milestones

Throughout her career, King has been a strong and, some would say, natural leader—pushing the boundaries for social justice in sports.

The "Battle of the Sexes"

Billie Jean King was celebrated by women everywhere when she won the "battle of the sexes" match against Bobby Riggs in 1973. Riggs, a tennis champion in the late 1930s and 1940s, had been critical of the quality of women tennis players. He had tried many times to get King to compete against him, and she turned him down saying that she was devoting all of her time and energy to promoting the new

Virginia Slims Tour. Much to King's surprise, Margaret Court, the top-ranked women's player in the world, agreed to play Bobby Riggs in May 1973, and Riggs beat Court with ease. King then took Riggs up on his challenge to play a match, which turned out to be an event that created significant social change. The pre-match publicity was intensive, with Riggs sporting a "chauvinist pig" T-shirt in practice sessions and announcing, "If I am to be a chauvinist pig, I want to be the number one pig." On 20 September 1973, the match was held in the Houston Astrodome. King, then twenty-nine years old, ran the fifty-five-year-old Bobby Riggs ragged, winning the match, 6–4, 6–3, 6–3. The UK's *Sunday Times* called the match, "The drop shot and volley heard around the world." The match itself and King's victory over Bobby Riggs came to symbolize women's struggle for equality in the 1970s.

Creating Greater Opportunities for Women in Tennis

Due to decades of male domination in tennis circuits, King decided to put her energy and creativity into the establishment of a women's tennis tour. She led the boycott of tournaments where the ratio of prize money between men and women was 12 to 1, and in 1970 the Virginia Slims Women's Tennis tour was launched. In April 1973, the International Lawn Tennis Association (counterpart of the Men's Association of Tennis Professionals) declared that the women players must either submit to their national association or be banned from the Grand Slam tournaments (e.g., Wimbledon, the US Open) forever. The furor over this mandate forced the groups to compromise and merge under the USLTA. King was not satisfied with the merger and recognized a need for the women of professional tennis to form a group that would improve the conditions of their profession, speak out in the players' interest, and continue to carry the torch for women's tennis rights. In June of 1973, the Women's Tennis Association (WTA) was formed. Sixty-four of the top-ranked female players in the world voted Billie Jean King to be WTA president.

Expanding Opportunities for Coed Tennis

In 1974, King founded World Team Tennis (WTT) with husband Larry King. World Team Tennis has been an innovative coed tennis league designed to show young people that men and women can play together, cooperate on the court, and work together to win. King was the first woman to coach a coed team, the Philadelphia Freedoms. The popular 1975 Elton John song "Philadelphia Freedom" was inspired by the pop star's friendship with King, and the song has become the theme for the WTT franchise. Always creating new ways to promote tennis, King successfully led the negotiations to start a cable tennis channel that began in 2003.

Civil and Gay Rights Activism

In 1981, Billie Jean King's ten-year-long affair with hairdresser Marilyn Barnett, came to light in a palimony suit brought by Barnett. During the highly publicized case, King became the first American athlete to acknowledge a homosexual relationship.

Although Marilyn Barnett lost the suit, King estimated the episode cost her and her husband (they were later divorced) millions in endorsements. King went on to champion civil and gay rights causes in Chicago, where she lives, and in 1998 established the Billie Jean King Foundation to fund projects that reflect or promote equal opportunity for all, with a special emphasis on ensuring the rights of gay and lesbian youth.

Continuing Leadership and Legacy

During and after her career as a player (King retired from competitive tennis in 1984), Billie Jean King has been an author, commentator, promoter, coach, and activist. In 1974, she founded *WomenSports* magazine and started the Women's Sports Foundation, an organization dedicated to promoting and enhancing athletic opportunities for girls and women. King coached and captained the US Federation Cup in the late 1990s, and she coached the US Olympic tennis teams to gold medals in 1999 in Atlanta and in 2000 in Sydney.

In 2008, to commemorate the thirty-fifth anniversary of her match against Bobby Riggs, she published *Pressure is a Privilege: Lessons I've Learned from Life and the Battle of the Sexes*. She has been celebrated by *Life* magazine as one of the 100 most important Americans of the twentieth century, for her activism and astonishing athletic record. She has won twenty Wimbledon titles, seventy-one singles titles, and was the first woman athlete to win more than $100,000 in a single season in any sport. She is one of a very select few to have won a singles title in each of the four Grand Slam Tournaments.

King has also won many awards through the years for her leadership in sports and human rights causes, including the International Olympic Committee Women and Sport trophy in 2002 for her work as "an advocate for women's rights, within and outside sport." In 2009, King became the first female athlete to be awarded the Presidential Medal of Freedom, the highest civilian honor.

Expanding her influence further outside of sports, in 2014 King launched the Billie Jean King Leadership Initiative, in partnership with Teneo Strategies, to address equality and diversity in the workplace. With her energetic style on and off the court and tireless efforts on behalf of women in the sports world and in society, Billie Jean King has been a highly significant leader in the cause of women's tennis and in the fight for equality and social justice.

Further Reading:

Billie Jean King. (n.d.) Retrieved September 5, 2003, from http://www.wtt.com/about/billie.asp

Collins, B. (1975, May). Who's afraid of Virginia Slims? *WomenSports*, 29–31, 56–58.

Feinstein, J. (1991). *Hardcourts.* New York: Villard.

Gillespie, N. (1975, May). Love through the ages. *WomenSports*, 15–18.

King, B.J. with Starr, C. (1967). *We have come a long way: The story of women's pro tennis.* New York: McGraw-Hill.

Kort, M. (1988, February). Conversation. *Ms, 16*(8), 58–62.

Lane, B. K. (n.d.). *A champion of women's sports.* Retrieved September 5, 2003, from http://www.womens sportsfoundation.org/cgibin/iowa/athletes

Lichtenstein, G. (1974). *A long way baby: Behind the scenes in women's pro tennis.* New York: William Morrow.

Little, A. (1988). Suzanne Lenglen: Tennis idols of the twenties. Wimbledon, UK: Wimbledon Lawn Tennis Museum.

Lumpkin, A. (1981). *Women's tennis: A historical documentary of the players and their game.* Troy, NY: Whitson.

Parsons, J. (2001). *A Long Way Indeed.* Retrieved September 5, 2003, from http://www.wtatour.com/index.cfm?section=league&cont_id=90765

Schwartz, L. (2003, March 17). *Billie Jean won for all women.* Retrieved September 5, 2003, from http://espn.go.com/classic/biography/s/King_Billie_Jean.html

United States Lawn Tennis Association (USLTA). (1972). *USLTA official encyclopedia.* New York: Harper & Row.

Winfrey, Oprah

b. 1954—television producer and former US talk-show host

Jacob PARK

Known as the queen of the daytime talk show, Oprah Winfrey's widely popular show attracted millions of viewers around the world and influenced popular culture and even politics. A transformational and inspiring leader, she has led her peers in philanthropy and leadership development. Her current venture into TV programming, with her OWN network, could potentially impact an even greater audience.

Born to unwed parents in Kosciusko, Mississippi, in 1954, Oprah Winfrey was raised by her maternal grandmother, who taught her how to read and nourished her lifelong love of public speaking. She still lives by the philosophy she learned growing up in a small farming community in a house without electricity or running water: "You're good, but you could be better." As a *Biography* documentary on Winfrey noted, "Oprah's growing-up years were stormy, difficult, and marked by abuse. Yet she somehow managed not just to survive but to excel" ("Oprah Winfrey" 2002).

It is hard to overstate the importance of Oprah Winfrey as a business and cultural force over the past decades. Perhaps better than any other American, Oprah Winfrey symbolizes a brand celebrity whose opinions shape which authors make the best-seller list and which products come to be seen as "must buys" by the public. One magazine article stated that Winfrey has "more influence on the culture than any university president, politician, political, or religious leader except the pope" (*Vanity Fair*).

The fact that her talk show was watched by more than 22 million people every week, that she was the first African-American woman (the second person of African-American origin after Robert Johnson, the founder of Black Entertainment Television) to make it to the *Forbes* magazine's list of billionaires, and that *Time* magazine named her one of the hundred most influential people of the twentieth century overshadows the important impact of her multifaceted leadership style on the American private and public landscape. While no one disputes her as status as a former talk-show host or as an entertainment-business executive, it is arguably her leadership that will be the lens through which history books examine her life. She may be the only self-made billionaire who "happily admits that she cannot read a balance sheet" and has declined invitations to serve on the corporate boards of AT&T, Ralph Lauren, and Intel because she was not sure what she would be doing as a board member (Sellers 2002).

The Making of a Cultural and Business Icon

Oprah Winfrey began her broadcasting career in Nashville, Tennessee, while she was still in high school. At the age of nineteen, she became the youngest person and the first African-American woman to anchor television news in Nashville. As a host of television talk shows, Winfrey moved in 1976 to Baltimore and relocated to Chicago eight years later. By 1986, the Oprah Winfrey Show was launched as a nationally syndicated show with an annual revenue of $125 million and an initial viewing audience of 10 million people. The highest-rated talk show in television history, she was watched by an estimated 21 million viewers a week in the United States and was broadcast in more than one hundred countries. The power of her talk show is reflected not only in numbers like these, but also in the prestige of those who felt compelled to appear on her show. During the 2000 presidential elections, then-governor George W. Bush appeared on her program and planted a big, surprising kiss on her cheek.

Her impact has been felt far beyond the television medium. Her acting debut in 1985 as Sofia in Steven Spielberg's *The Color Purple* garnered her both Academy Award and Golden Globe nominations. The Oprah Book Club, which began in 1996, was an on-air reading club designed to get the country excited about reading books, mostly works of fiction. Each of the books selected, including the work of Toni Morrison, Joyce Carol Oates, Andre Dubus III, and others, became national bestsellers. Though she was an unrivaled star on television, Winfrey received the National Book Foundation's fiftieth anniversary Gold Medal for her contributions to reading and books. She is only the third American woman to own her own production company (her company name, Harpo, is Oprah spelled backward); she was preceded by the silent move star Mary Pickford (1892–1979) and the comedy queen Lucille Ball (1911–1989).

Winfrey had a unique ability to understand and connect with the tens of million people that made up her viewing public. She managed over the years to remain a deeply revered public figure amidst her struggles to lose weight, her admission of childhood abuse, and her entrance into the Marine Corps Marathon under the scrutiny of the often-unforgiving public. A 1998 article in *Time* magazine by a popular psychologist attempted to explain Winfrey's popularity by arguing that "women, especially, listen to Winfrey because they feel as if she's a friend. Girls' and women's friendships are often built on trading secrets. Winfrey's power is that she tells her own, divulging that she once ate a package of hot-dog buns drenched in maple syrup, that she smoked cocaine, even that she had been raped as a child. She turned the focus (of talk shows) from experts to ordinary people talking about personal issues."

The Leadership Mosaic: Principled, Reflective, and Transformative

Examining the importance of leadership is not new to Oprah Winfrey. She was appointed an adjunct professor of management and strategy at Northwestern University's Kellogg Graduate School of Management and co-taught a course called "The Dynamics of Leadership" in the fall semesters of 1999 and 2000. With the goal of positioning students "as leaders in charge of their own destinies, empowering them to more effectively lead others," the leadership course had a guest speaker list that would be the envy of any business course, including Amazon.com founder Jeff Bezos, ABC/Disney President Bob Iger, Henry Kissinger, and by satellite, Coretta Scott King (1927–2006).

While almost everyone would agree that Winfrey has remarkable insights into leadership, describing and analyzing her leadership style is a challenging task. Her leadership style can be best described as a mosaic, an overlapping blend of principled, reflective, and transforming leadership qualities. The first quality can be described as principled because Winfrey's leadership emphasizes the important impact individuals can make to improve the society at large. For example, Oprah's Angel Network (launched in 1997) has raised millions from viewer donations and many more millions from sponsors and celebrity contributions. Although many wealthy public figures establish charitable organizations, the focus of many of these groups tends to be on the disbursement of money. But Winfrey does much more than give money. She broadcasts the work of individuals who through their charitable organizations are actively working to improve the lives of the less fortunate. It is not a coincidence that one of her charitable programs under the Angel Network umbrella is called the "Use Your Life Awards" (rather than, say, win a million dollars for a good cause).

The second quality is the way Winfrey's expresses her leadership. While taking action is not discouraged, there is a premium placed on taking stock and reflecting on one's life before embarking on any plan of action. In this context, leadership is not necessarily about establishing or meeting goals, but rather about taking time to know who you are. Leadership is less about doing something out there and more about understanding who you are and your ability to grow as an individual. As author and expert in management development Kevin Cashman (1998) suggests in his book *Leadership from the Inside Out*: "…we will not analyze the external act of leadership into a formula of 'ten easy to follow' quick tips. Rather, we will take a reflective journey to foster the personal awakening needed to enhance our leadership effectiveness." In an interview with *Fortune* magazine (Sellers 2002), Winfrey underscored the importance of knowing oneself in the way she expresses her leadership when she noted that "…my message is, 'you are responsible for your own life.'" After all, it is difficult to lead or be expected be a leader when you are not sure who you are or want to be as a person.

The third leadership quality that can be seen in Winfrey is what historian and political scientist James MacGregor Burns calls "transforming." Transformative leadership differs from the more common transactional leadership, by emphasizing radical if not revolutionary change. Winfrey seems to have a visceral and instinctive way of predicting what actions are likely to lead to revolutionary positive change in society. The Oprah Winfrey Leadership Academy for Girls in South Africa, which she opened in the winter of 2002, has a radical goal, for example. With an initial investment of $10 million, the leadership academy aims to educate female students who are academically talented and exhibit leadership skills in their community, but whose families cannot support their educations.

Winfrey, who has donated at least 10 percent of her vast annual income to charity, goes beyond just exhorting people to become leaders and is herself willing to spend the necessary time, energy, and financial resources to invest in leadership in society at large. She does this most notably by focusing on the three causes she cares most deeply about: women, children, and education. As she herself put it in a 2002 article in *Fortune*: "'When you educate a woman, you set her free...Had I not had books and education in Mississippi, I would have believed that's all there was.'" She can obviously bring a lot of personal perspective to these issues since she spent her early years in a house in Mississippi without electricity or running water" (Sellers 2002).

Transforming Television Into a Personal Leadership Tool

Winfrey's rise from her humble beginnings in Mississippi to her current status as a global cultural and business icon can be seen as a powerful reminder of the rags-to-riches metaphor that remains so powerful in American society. What gets overlooked is her drive and determination to reawaken the latent personal leadership that exists in all of us to understand, to act, and perhaps most importantly, to help improve society. Television, her instrument of leadership instruction, had mainly been known as the source of several negative side effects including sedentary lifestyle and obesity in children. But when it is in the hands of a dynamic and charismatic magician like Winfrey, the medium becomes much more than an impersonal electronic box that invites passivity.

The true genius of Winfrey is recognizing television's true power: to blend the public and private toward personal empowerment. As noted in a *Time* magazine profile of Winfrey (Tannen 1998, 198): "While it links strangers and conveys information over public airwaves, TV is often viewed in the privacy of our homes. Grasping this paradox, Oprah exhorts viewers to improve their lives and the world. She makes people care because she cares. That is Winfrey's genius, and will be her legacy, as the changes she has wrought in the talk show continue to permeate our culture and shape our lives.

An example of this occurred on 1 January 2011 when she launched Oprah Winfrey Network (OWN), a joint venture of Harpo and Discovery Communications, after the farewell season of her talk show in 2010. While the network has struggled to attract an audience, news that Winfrey will be taking a more active role in its administration only bodes well for this new venture. Already it is the highest-rated network on cable television among African-American women, and among the top twenty for other women in the United States (*Wall Street Journal* 2016).

Further Reading

Brands, H. W. (1999). *Masters of enterprise: Giants of American business from John Jacob Astor and J.P. Morgan to Bill Gates and Oprah Winfrey*. New York: Free Press.

Burns, J. M. (2003). *Transforming leadership: The pursuit of happiness*. New York: Grove/Atlantic Inc.

Cashman, K. (1998). *Leadership from the inside out: Becoming a leader for life*. Provo, UT: Executive Excellence.

Goudreau, J. (2012, April 2). Oprah Winfrey admits her OWN regrets. *Forbes*. Retrieved July 11, 2016, from http://www.forbes.com/sites/jennagoudreau/2012/04/02/oprah-winfrey-admits-her-own-regrets/#65b8090f6018

How Oprah conquered the U.S. (2003, March 12). BBC Online News. Retrieved July 8, 2003, from http://news.bbc.co.uk/2/hi/uk_news/magazine/3042306.stm

Oprah Winfrey. (2002, November 26). Biography. A&E Television Networks.Niedzwiadek, N. (2016, March 20). Oprah Winfrey steers a turnaround at her OWN cable network. *Wall Street Journal*. Retrieved July 11, 2016, from http://www.wsj.com/articles/oprah-winfrey-steers-a-turnaround-at-her-own-cable-network-1458517015

Sellers, P. (2002, April 1). The business of being Oprah. *Fortune*.

Tannen, D. (1998, June 8). Oprah Winfrey. *Time*.

Epilogue: Further Reading and Resources

This book was designed as a guide to broad issues and to the historical development of women as leaders. We know, however, that readers will want to link the frameworks provided by our authors to current events, and to the challenges they face in their personal and professional lives. This section offers a few suggestions, and we encourage instructors to visit our website for updates and new resources on women and leadership worldwide.

There are many courses on women and leadership, but there has not been a general reader on the subject for over ten years. We are publishing *Women and Leadership: History, Concepts, and Case Studies* to fill this gap. Two key questions cut across all four sections of this book: "Are there real differences between women's and men's leadership?" and "What are the barriers to women's leadership?" There are a variety of ways to use these questions in teaching, and they are relevant whether the course is in political science, international relations, or executive leadership training.

Women and Leadership can also be used as a supplementary book for courses in women's and leadership studies, or for more traditional subjects such as world history and political science. Instructors who want to plan a course can find many examples of course syllabi online, and at our website we offer recommendations, along with links to our favorite lists of notable, famous, and influential women. A particularly useful and unique resource is the *Worldwide Guide to Women In Leadership* (www.guide2womenleaders.com) created by Martin Iversen Christensen, who has compiled lists of women who have ruled, anytime and anywhere, as well as listing women now holding political office.

Much writing and research on women and leadership—such as the otherwise excellent 2015 Pew Research Center survey—is focused on the United States only. Berkshire Publishing is known for global coverage, and *Women and Leadership*, which was written by scholars in different disciplines and from different countries, prominently features women leaders and important developments from around the world. Cross-cultural comparisons can also be a useful starting point for classroom discussion. Why did French courtesans and salonnières have such political influence? How does the Chinese woman warrior Mulan compare to Joan of Arc? How does media coverage of female political leaders vary in countries such as Germany, Taiwan, South Korea, or the United States?

In addition to making the book global, we have endeavored not to fall into either one of two common traps: underestimating the importance of women's leadership in human history (even during centuries when it was most often exercised in the background, or through men), or exaggerating and idealizing women's leadership. This book attempts to lay out important issues and debates for further discussion, and to illuminate the tremendous importance of past achievements that may seem obvious today, such as the right to own property and the right to control one's fertility.

Heroines are not automatically the same as leaders, but both real-life and fictional heroines can be role models for any woman seeking to become a leader. Biographies of influential women in history offer valuable insight into the historical challenges that have faced women in different times and parts of the world. Biographies can provide surprising information about how women evaded the restrictions of their times, and found ways to fulfill their dreams and destinies.

We can also learn about women and leadership from myriad fictional heroines, including those created by novelists like George Sand and George Eliot who wrote under male names, and male authors like Anthony Trollope who created remarkable female characters. From the Wife of Bath, Lady Murasaki, and Lady Macbeth to more recent characters like Sister Carrie, Nancy Drew, and Claire Underwood, the stories found in literature, popular fiction, and TV drama provide valuable material for classroom discussion, and are rich sources for anyone who wants to explore different perspectives on women and leadership.

The bibliographies at the end of each chapter provide a great avenue for further research, and on our website we recommend more general reading to those interested in deepening their understanding of women as leaders. Here are a few classic works that show both our connection with women who lived in times very different from our own, and how far women and men have come in the field of leadership:

- Mary Wollstonecraft, *A Vindication of the Rights of Woman: With Strictures on Political and Moral Subjects* (1792)
- Elizabeth Cady Stanton, "Declaration of Sentiments" (1848)
- Simone de Beauvoir, *The Second Sex* (1959)
- Betty Friedan, *The Feminine Mystique* (1963)

For additional resources and recommendations, visit www.berkshirepublishing .com/womenandleadership.

About the Editors

George R. GOETHALS holds the E. Claiborne Robins Distinguished Professorship in Leadership Studies at the University of Richmond. He is author of *Presidential Leadership and African Americans* (2015) and co-author of *Heroic Leadership: An Influence Taxonomy of 100 Exceptional Individuals* (2013) and *Heroes: What They Do & Why We Need Them* (2011). With Georgia Sorenson and James MacGregor Burns, he edited the *Encyclopedia of Leadership* (2004), developed by Berkshire Publishing for SAGE Publications. He was previously a member of the faculty at Williams College where he was founding chair of the Program in Leadership Studies.

Crystal L. HOYT is Professor of Leadership Studies and Psychology at the University of Richmond. Her research appears in journals such as *Psychological Science, Journal of Experimental and Social Psychology, Personality and Social Psychology Bulletin*, and *The Leadership Quarterly*. She has published over 50 journal articles and book chapters and she has co-edited two books. She received a PhD from the University of California, Santa Barbara in 2003 and a BA from Claremont McKenna College in 1997.

Karen CHRISTENSEN is an American entrepreneur, environmentalist, and author who cofounded Berkshire Publishing Group. Christensen began her publishing career in London, and became a speaker on women's issues for the UK Green Party (1990-1) and a founding member of the Women's Environmental Network (1989). She served on the board of the Software and Information Industry Association Content Division, and is a member of the National Committee on United States-China Relations and a trustee of the University of Pennsylvania Press.

Index

Bold entries and page numbers denote article entries.

Bold entries and page numbers denote article entries.

CPSIA information can be obtained
at www.ICGtesting.com
Printed in the USA
FFOW02n1136050218
44801272-44963FF

9 781614 720324